Lecture Notes of the Institute for Computer Sciences, Social Informatics and Telecommunications Engineering 163

More information about this series at http://www.springer.com/series/8197

Song Guo · Xiaofei Liao
Fangming Liu · Yanmin Zhu (Eds.)

Collaborative Computing: Networking, Applications, and Worksharing

11th International Conference, CollaborateCom 2015
Wuhan, November 10–11, 2015, China
Proceedings

Springer

Editors
Song Guo
School of Computer Science
and Engineering
The University of Aizu
Aizuwakamatsu
Japan

Xiaofei Liao
School of Computer Science
and Technology
Huazhong University of Science
and Technology
Wuhan
China

Fangming Liu
School of Computer Science
and Technology
Huazhong University of Science
and Technology
Wuhan
China

Yanmin Zhu
Department of Computer Science
and Engineering
Shanghai Jiao Tong University
Shanghai
China

ISSN 1867-8211 ISSN 1867-822X (electronic)
Lecture Notes of the Institute for Computer Sciences, Social Informatics and Telecommunications Engineering
ISBN 978-3-319-28909-0 ISBN 978-3-319-28910-6 (eBook)
DOI 10.1007/978-3-319-28910-6

Library of Congress Control Number: 2015959593

Printed on acid-free paper

This Springer imprint is published by SpringerNature
The registered company is Springer International Publishing AG Switzerland

Preface

On behalf of the Organizing Committee of the 11th EAI International Conference on Collaborative Computing: Networking, Applications and Worksharing, we are very pleased to present the proceedings in which researchers and contributors from the world share their research results and new ideas. The 11th EAI International Conference on Collaborative Computing: Networking, Applications and Worksharing serves as a premier international forum for discussion among academic and industrial researchers, practitioners, and students interested in collaborative networking, technology and systems, and applications.

We were also honored to have Prof. Jiannong Cao from Hong Kong Polytechnic University and Prof. Huadong Ma from Beijing University of Posts and Telecommunications as the keynote speakers. In addition, the technical program also included several jointly organized international workshops aiming to highlight the latest research developments in all aspects of collaborative computing.

We would like to thank the authors for submitting their research papers to the conference and contributing to the quality of the final program. We are also grateful to all Technical Program Committee members and the reviewers for their time, efforts, and comments in selecting high-quality papers for inclusion in our great technical program.

December 2015

Yanmin Zhu
Fangming Liu

Organization

Steering Committee

Imrich Chlamtac (Co-chair)	Create-Net, Italy
James Joshi (Co-chair)	University of Pittsburgh, USA
Calton Pu	Georgia Institute of Technology, USA
Elisa Bertino	Purdue University, USA
Arun Iyengar	IBM, USA
Tao Zhang	Cisco, USA
Dimitrios Gerogakopolous	CSIRO, Australia

Organizing Committee

General Co-chairs

Song Guo	University of Aizu, Japan
Xiaofei Liao	Huazhong University of Science and Technology, China

TPC Co-chairs

Fangming Liu	Huazhong University of Science and Technology, China
Yanmin Zhu	Shanghai Jiao Tong University, China

TPC Vice Chair

Deze Zeng	China University of Geosciences, China

Workshops Chair

Wenbin Jiang	Huazhong University of Science and Technology, China

Local Arrangements Chair

Hong Yao	China University of Geosciences, China

Publication Chair

Fei Xu	East China Normal University, China

Web Chair

Fei Xu	East China Normal University, China

Technical Program Committee

Shu-Ching Chen	Florida International University, USA
Maria Luisa Damiani	University of Milan, Italy
Schahram Dustdar	TU Wien, Austria
Federica Paci	University of Southampton, UK
Julian Jang-Jaccard	CSIRO ICT Centre, Australia
Ralf Klamma	RWTH Aachen University, Germany
Kun-Lung Wu	IBM T.J. Watson Research Center, USA
Ibrahim Korpeoglu	Bilkent University, Turkey
Dan Lin	Missouri University of Science and Technology, USA
Patrizio Pelliccione	Chalmers University of Technology and University of Gothenburg, Sweden
Agostino Poggi	University of Parma, Italy
Ravi Sandhu	University of Texas at San Antonio, USA
Shankar Banik	The Citadel, USA
Ting Wang	IBM Research, USA
Jinsong Han	Xi'an Jiaotong University, China
Chao Jing	Guilin University of Technology, China
Haiming Chen	Institute of Computing Technology, Chinese Academy of Sciences, China
Chunming Hu	Beihang University, China
Haibin Cai	East China Normal University
Tianyu Wo	Beihang University, China
Dong Li	Institute of Computing Technology, Chinese Academy of Sciences, China
Sabrina Leone	Università Politecnica delle Marche, Ancona, Italy
Fei Xu	East China Normal University

Contents

Collaborative Application

Sensor and Internet of Things

Security

Collaborative Cloud Computing

Adaptive Multi-keyword Ranked Search Over Encrypted Cloud Data

Daudi Mashauri[1], Ruixuan Li[1(✉)], Hongmu Han[1], Xiwu Gu[1], Zhiyong Xu[2], and Cheng-zhong Xu[3,4]

[1] School of Computer Science and Technology, Huazhong University of Science and Technology, Wuhan 430074, Hubei, China
daudimasha@live.com,
{rxli, hanhongmu, guxiwu}@hust.edu.cn

[2] Department of Mathematics and Computer Science, Suffolk University, Boston, MA 02114, USA
zxu@mcs.suffolk.edu

[3] Department of Electrical and Computer Engineering, Wayne State University, Detroit, MI 48202, USA
czxu@wayne.edu

[4] Shenzhen Institute of Advanced Technology, Chinese Academy of Science, Shenzhen 518055, Guangdong, China

Abstract. To preserve data privacy and integrity, sensitive data has to be encrypted before outsourcing to the cloud server. However, this makes keyword search based on plaintext queries obsolete. Therefore, supporting efficient keyword based ranked searches over encrypted data became an open challenge. In recent years, several multi-keyword ranked search schemes have been proposed in trying to solve the posed challenge. However, most recently proposed schemes don't address the issues regarding dynamics in the keyword dictionary. In this paper, we propose a novel scheme called A-MRSE that addresses and solves these issues. We introduce new algorithms to be used by data owners each time they make modifications that affects the size of the keyword dictionary. We conduct multiple experiments to demonstrate the effectiveness of our newly proposed scheme, and the results illustrates that the performance of A-MRSE scheme is much better that previously proposed schemes.

Keywords: Cloud computing · Searchable encryption · Multi-keyword query · Ranked search · Encrypted data

1 Introduction

Cloud computing is a model for enabling ubiquitous, convenient, on-demand network access to a shared pool of configurable computing resources, such as networks, servers, storage, applications and services, which can be rapidly provisioned and released with minimal management effort or service provider interaction [1]. Cloud computing provides affordable and convenient ways to store and manage huge amounts of data generated by data owners. However, even with all of its advantages, cloud computing still faces great challenges following a serious threat posed to data owners about

S. Guo et al. (Eds.): CollaborateCom 2015, LNICST 163, pp. 3–13, 2016.
DOI: 10.1007/978-3-319-28910-6_1

security and privacy, especially when it comes to sensitive data. Encryption of data before shipping to the cloud server offers a viable solution to data owners regarding data integrity and confidentiality. However, keyword searches based on plaintext queries became obsolete on encrypted data, and data owners have to download the entire database they own and start decrypting files one by one, looking for those of interest. It goes without saying that this is too much to bear, especially in today's pay-as-you use fashion.

Searchable encryption is the earliest scheme that utilizes keyword search over encrypted data [2, 3]. Solutions proposed by these schemes resolved the issues concerning security and privacy of data. However, they also introduced more obstacles as they encountered huge computation and communication overheads. These overheads resulted from the fact that the proposed solutions do not offer any ranking mechanism after performing a keyword search as they based on disjunctive searches. To resolve this issue, another era of ranked keyword search schemes over encrypted came to the rescue. Single keyword ranked search [4] was among the first published works providing a practical implementation. It fulfilled its designed goals as far as ranked searches are concerned. However, supporting only a single keyword search from thousands of encrypted files was not an efficient solution that data owners anticipated for a while.

Recently, a number of research works, such as [5, 6], have been done in order to facilitate multi-keyword queries over encrypted cloud data and they also support result ranking. MRSE [1] is one of the earlier works crowned in supporting multi-keyword ranked queries over encrypted data. It also provides a viable solution that works under practical implementation. Most of the recent works on multi-keyword ranked searches don't address the issues regarding any future modifications that will affect the size and content of the keyword dictionary. There is a large computation and communication overhead posed to data owners each time they modify their keyword dictionaries. As a privacy requirement, two query vectors resulting from similar set of keywords cannot be the same. Hence, the cloud server won't be able to determine if they come from the same set of keywords. However, the cloud server can still determine due to the fact that finally they will result into similar sets of ranked files, although they look different upon submission.

In this paper, we propose a new scheme called A-MRSE in order to resolve the resulting issues of modifications on keyword dictionaries. In our newly proposed scheme, we consider both real life scenarios where the data owners can either insert or remove certain keywords from the dictionary. We propose new algorithms that can be used each time the data owner makes these changes. They present minimum communication and computation overhead.

The contributions of this paper can be summarized as follows:

- We design a novel scheme that is adaptive and supports any modification made on the keyword dictionary, either inserting or removing keywords with minimum overhead.
- We improve security of the ranked results by sealing the cloud server from any form of statistical attacks.

The rest of this paper is organized as follows. Section 2 introduces our A-MRSE scheme, which is followed by results and a discussion in Sect. 3. Section 4 describes related works, and we conclude with future works in Sect. 5.

2 Adaptive Multi-keyword Ranked Search Over Encrypted Cloud Data

In this section, we will present our adaptive multi-keyword ranked search over encrypted cloud data (shorted as A-MRSE) scheme. In order to quantitatively evaluate the coordinate matching like in MRSE, we adopt "inner product similarity" in our work as well. Also like in MRSE [1], we define an index vector for each file based on the keywords it contains from the dictionary; two invertible matrices and a bit vector are also used for index vector encryption and trapdoor generation. However, our work solves the issue with MRSE in a sense that it allows more keywords to be added in the dictionary as well as some of them to be removed from it. The detailed design of A-MRSE scheme includes the following six aspects.

(1) *InitialSetup*: The data owner selects a set of $\boldsymbol{n}$ keywords from the sensitive plaintext dataset F, and $\boldsymbol{u}$ dummy keywords to be inserted in the indexing vector in order to strengthen security and maintain privacy. The index vector mandates any future modifications that can be made on the keyword dictionary. In MRSE, the index vector has three parts which are first $\boldsymbol{n}$ locations used to indicate presence or absence of real keywords, followed by $\boldsymbol{u}$ locations for dummy keywords, and terminated by the constant 1 at the last position as shown in Fig. 1.

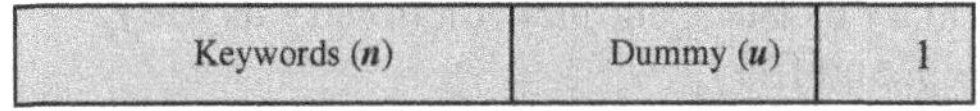

Fig. 1. MRSE index vector structure.

MRSE vector structure makes any modification on the keyword dictionary unworkable since positions of the keywords are fixed. However, in A-MRSE, we mirror the existing structure and derive a new vector structure having security locations (last constant dimension and dummy keywords locations) at the beginning, followed by $\boldsymbol{n}$ locations of real keywords as shown in Fig. 2.

Fig. 2. A-MRSE vector structure.

With this vector structure, A-MRSE supports any future modifications of the keyword dictionary size. For any file in the dataset, if it has real keyword W_j, then in the corresponding index vector $p[1 + u+j] = 1$, otherwise 0.

(2) *KeyReduce*: since A-MRSE supports keyword dynamics in the dictionary as compared to MRSE, the data owner calls this algorithm with number of keywords to be reduced as an input parameter to generate a new secret key **SK** $\boldsymbol{k_2}$ from the previously generated **SK** $\boldsymbol{k_1}$. Previously generated matrices M_1 and M_2 will then be resized into new matrices M'_1 and M'_2 each having **(*d-r*)** × **(*d-r*)** dimension. That is accomplished by removing the last ***r***-rows and ***r***-columns, which finally yields a ***d-r*** square matrix.

Modification of the splitting vector *S* demands special attention due the role played of each bit position in it. Basically, the dictionary size will change from ***n*** to **(*n-r*)** after removing ***r*** keywords. This algorithm inspects the new dictionary. If a keyword still exists in both dictionaries (the old and new sized), then that particular bit is copied into a new vector S' and omitted otherwise. The process continues for all ***n*** locations and finally gives a $(d - r)S'$ bit vector. Algorithm 1 shows how KeyReduce works.

Algorithm 1. KeyReduce(k_1, r)

Input: number of reduced keywords and original secret key.
Output: new secret key **SK** $\boldsymbol{k_2}$.
Method: the key reduce algorithm works as follows.

```
Receive the integer input parameter r;
Retrieve the original secret key SK k1 components;
Resize matrices M1, M2 to M'1, M'2 by applying dimension reduction;
Read the old dictionary as file f1 and new dictionary as file f2;
for each line in file f1 and file f2
    if (keyword in f1 exists in f2)
        copy the value of bit position for this keyword from S into S';
    else
        skip bit position;
    end if
end for
Give SK k2 with 3-tuple as {S', M'1, M'2};
```

---

(3) *KeyExtend*: after adding more files on the cloud server, the data owner will definitely need to include new keywords in the dictionary. In this case, MSRE cannot work any longer as it suffers huge computation overhead as well as bandwidth inefficiency. This is where A-MRSE comes into account as it allows easy expansion of the secret keys relative to the increase of keywords in the dictionary.

If z keywords are added, this algorithm generates two new $z \times z$ invertible matrices, M_{z1}, M_{z2}, and a new z bit vector S_z. These newly created matrices will be added to original matrices M_1 and M_2 and finally gives two modified matrices M_1' *and* M_2' having $(\boldsymbol{d} + z) \times (\boldsymbol{d} + z)$ dimension according to block diagonal matrix theorem [7].

On the other hand, splitting vectors S_z and S will be joined and make a new vector S' by copying all elements of vector S into S' then followed by appending elements of S_z. Algorithm 2 shows how KeyExtend works.

Algorithm 2. KeyExtend(k_1, z)

Input: original secret key and number of newly added keywords.
Output: new secret key **SK** $\boldsymbol{k_3}$.
Method: the key extend algorithm works as follows.

Receive the integer input z;
Retrieve original key SK k_1 components;
Generates two invertible matrices Mz_1, Mz_2 and a bit vector S_z;
Add Mz_1 to M_1, Mz_2 to M_2 by using diagonal block matrix operation and produces M'_1 and M'_2 having $(\boldsymbol{d}+z)\times(\boldsymbol{d}+z)$ dimensions;
for each bit position in vector S
    copy it into a new vector S';
end for
for each bit position in vector S_z
    copy and append it into new vector S';
end for
Give SK k_3 with 3-tuple as $\{S', M'_1, M'_2\}$;

---

(4) *BuildIndex*: this algorithm builds an encrypted searchable index for plaintext files in the original set F. Initially, the data owner applies similar procedures as in MRSE [1] before addition or reduction of keywords from the dictionary.

For each file, a bit vector pi is set. Then starting with security positions, $p[1]$ is set to 1, and values in dummy keyword positions between $p[1]$ and $p[2 + \boldsymbol{u}]$ are set to a random number ε. The remaining positions will be filled, indicating whether the file contains keywords from the dictionary. Therefore, $p[2 + \boldsymbol{u}]$ to $p[1 + \boldsymbol{u}+\boldsymbol{n}]$ will be set to 1 if the file contains a dictionary keyword and 0 otherwise. After setting all bit positions in vector pi, splitting procedures will then follow as in secure kNN computation [8] except that the index structure is reversed. This implies in A-MRSE, we start with security locations then followed by real keyword locations. The BuildIndex algorithm is shown in Algorithm 3.

Algorithm 3. BuildIndex(F, SK)

Input: the secret key SK, and the file set F.
Output: the encrypted searchable index.
Method: the build index algorithm works as follows.

Receive the file set F;
for each $F_i \in F$
    Generate a bit vector p_i;
    Set p[1] = 1, and $p[2] - p[1+u] =$ i;
    for $j = (u + 2)$ to $(1 + u + n)$
        if F_{idj} • W
            Set $p[j] = 1$;
        else set $p[j] = 0$;
        end if
    for $j = 1$ to $(1 + u + n)$
        if $S[j] = 1$
            $p_1[j] + p_2[j] := p[j]$;
        else $p_1[j] := p_2[j] := p[j]$;
Run $\tilde{p}_1 = M_1^T p_1, \tilde{p}_2 = M_2^T p_2$, and set $I_i = \{\tilde{p}_1, \tilde{p}_2\}$;
Upload encrypted files $\{F_i\}$ • C and $I = \{I_i\}$ to the cloud server;

(5) *TrapdoorGen*: Having a set of interested keywords, an authorized data consumer calls this algorithm to generate a secure trapdoor in order to search and retrieve a number of encrypted files from the cloud server. For a multi-keyword query q, a query vector is generated using the same strategy as in MRSE with $\boldsymbol{v}$ number of dummy locations set to 1 and all remaining locations set to 0.

A score is used to determine the location of the file in the matching result set. In MRSE, this score was calculated by using Eq. 1 for index file p_i.

$$p_i \cdot q = r\left(x_i + \sum \varepsilon^{(v)}\right) + t_i \tag{1}$$

Xu et al. [5] discovered the impact of values of the dummy keywords inserted in the final score, which causes "out-of-order" problem. This happens when a file with popular keywords obtaining lower score and finally will not be included in the returned list to the data consumer.

To ameliorate the in-order ranking result while maintaining privacy-preserving property, all locations containing real keywords are multiplied by random number $\boldsymbol{r}$, and all locations containing dummy keywords are multiplied by another random number $\boldsymbol{r_2}$ which is obtained by using Eq. 2. Finally, the score is calculated by using Eq. 3.

$$r2 = \frac{Random(0, r)}{(v * MAX((u - c), (u + c)))} \tag{2}$$

$$p_i \cdot q = I_i \cdot T = r \times x_i + r2 \times \sum \varepsilon^{(v)} + t_i \tag{3}$$

Finally, the trapdoor T will be generated as $\{M_1^{-1}q', M_2^{-1}q''\}$.

(6) *Query*: After receiving T from the data consumer, the cloud server calls this algorithm to calculate the score for each file in the encrypted index I. The data consumer also includes parameter K so that the cloud server will return a list of only top-K files after a ranked search over the encrypted index. The trapdoor generated from a similar set of keywords will be different each time. This prevents the cloud server from performing statistical attacks; however the cloud server can still determine the trapdoors came from the same keyword set since finally they all retrieve identical top-K files though with different scores.

To resolve this issue, in A-MRSE we designed a new way to obfuscate the cloud server from performing statistical attacks. We modify the total number of retrieved files by adding K' files randomly such that $K' < K$. The value of K' is obtained by using Eq. 4.

$$K' = \varepsilon \times K \tag{4}$$

The value of ε is used as a security parameter, and it grows from 0 % depending on the number of files to be retrieved from the cloud server. If it set to 0 %, the implication is that the data owner prefers efficiency over security. For instance, when K is less than 10, the value of ε can be set to 25 %, when K lies between 10–20 it can be set to 20 %, and when K reaches 50 % it can be 15 %. By doing so, the cloud server cannot determine whether two queries originated from the same keyword set.

3 Performance Evaluation

In this section we present the results obtained after performing multiple experiments with different settings. We selected a real life dataset, Enron Email Dataset [9], various numbers of emails were randomly selected from the dataset for each test. The workbench was a Dell Latitude E-5520 machine with an Intel CoreTM i7 CPU @ 2.20 GHz × 8 with 8 GB of RAM. The operating system is Linux Mint 15 (Olivia x64), simulation codes were implemented by using Java programming language and elements in invertible matrices were double, generated randomly by using a Jama-1.0.3.jar package [10]. For each test taken, we observed results for both A-MRSE and MRSE scheme and then we compared their performances.

(1) *Key Generation and Editing*: the total time in key generation includes the time to generate bit vector S, as well as the two invertible matrices which then followed by adding the time to transport and compute the inverse of these matrices. Figure 3 shows how A-MRSE outperforms MRSE during key generation starting from 1000 keywords dictionary size and keeps growing up to 8000. In this phase, the previously generated

1000 key size was used to create new expanding keys. For instance, for a 5000 key, A-MRSE uses 32.94 % of total time, and for a 6000 A-MRSE uses 37.85 % of total time as compared with MRSE.

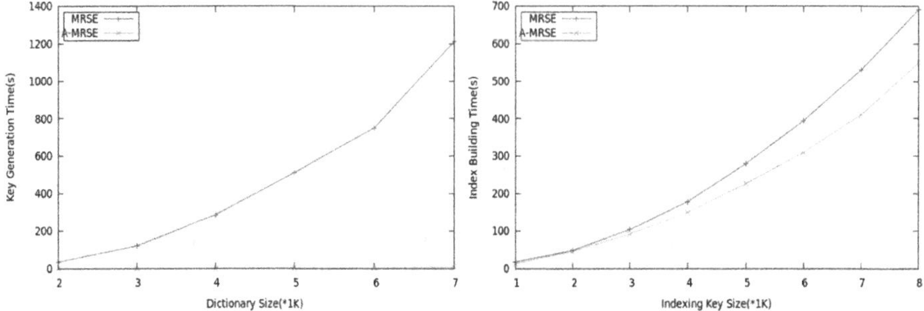

Fig. 3. Key reduction and generation

Fig. 4. Index building with different key sizes.

A remarkable gain is observed when the dictionary size is reduced. It took much less time to edit the key with A-MRSE than to regenerate with MRSE. As shown in Fig. 3, A-MRSE remains almost flat during key regeneration while MRSE raises as the keywords grow in the dictionary. For example, it took 0.33 % of the total time for A-MRSE to generate a 5000 key from an existing 6000 in case 1000 keywords are dropped from the dictionary where by MRSE took 298 times more than A-MRSE.

(2) *Index Building*: the time taken to build a searchable index I for all documents is the sum of the individual time taken to build indexes I for each document. This includes mapping of keywords extracted from file Fi to a data vector pi, followed by encrypting all the data vectors and finally builds a searchable index that will be uploaded to the cloud server. The cost of mapping or encrypting primarily depends on the dimension of the data vector which is tied up to the dictionary size. Also, the cost of building the whole searchable index I depends on the number of sub indexes which implies the total number of documents in the dataset.

Figure 4 shows a comparison of the time taken to build the searchable index for both MRSE and A-MRSE with different numbers of keywords in the dictionary where the documents in the dataset were fixed to 3000. A-MRSE outperforms MRSE, for instance building index with a 6000 key size, it took 44 % of the total time as compared with MRSE. Figure 5 shows comparison of the total time taken to build the searchable index between A-MRSE and MRSE for different numbers of files in the dataset ranging from 1 K to 8 K inclusive with the key size fixed to 2 K. Again, A-MRS saw off MRSE in terms of efficiency, for example it took 37.14 % of total time to build index for a 4000-files dataset.

As we can see, in all settings whether the key is fixed with increasing documents in the dataset or the other way round, A-MRSE still outperforms MRSE. This is because the keys in A-MRSE contain many zero-valued elements as a result of key expansion. This makes multiplications during index building to be much faster in A-MRSE than in MRSE.

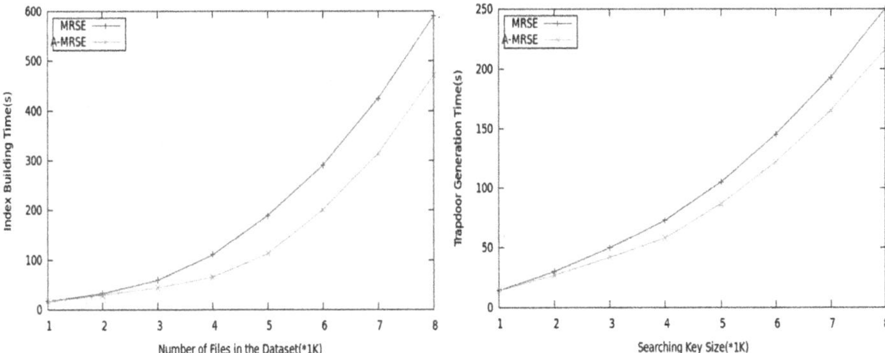

Fig. 5. Index building with different number of files in the dataset

Fig. 6. Trapdoor generation.

(3) *Trapdoor Generation*: trapdoor generation involves two multiplications of a matrix and a splitting query vector. Figure 6 shows the trapdoor generation cost for both A-MRSE and MRSE. Again, as seen from the graph, A-MRSE saw off MRSE as it takes less time to complete the whole process. For example, with 5000 keywords dictionary size, A-MRSE took 45.31 % of the total time as compared with MRSE scheme. As more keywords are added, more performance gain can be achieved with our A-MRSE. We are certain that this gain is highly contributed with many zero-values elements in A-MRSE matrices compared with the ones in MRSE.

(4) *Query:* the cloud server is responsible for performing query execution by using querying algorithm with which it computes and ranks the similarity scores for all documents in the dataset. We conducted several experiments for both A-MRSE and MRSE with fixed number of documents in the dataset while varying the dictionary size. The performances were almost comparable between A-MRSE and MRSE. The key point of our scheme is that, it enables data owners to make use of existing keys and generate new searching and indexing keys without the need of running key generation again from scratch. This is for both scenarios of increasing and decreasing number of keywords in the dictionary.

4 Related Works

Cloud computing is delivered as a product from both software and hardware evolutions as well as the Internet. It offers actual realization of the long waited utility computing service. However, with all its benefits, it still comes with a number of security challenges posed to both individual data owners as well as organizations which use cloud technology [11]. Enabling keyword search over encrypted data in cloud computing environment became an open question.

Song et al. [2] was among the earliest researchers to present a practical solution of keyword search over encrypted data. They offered a solution in which each word in the plaintext is encrypted with a two-layer encryption scheme that uses stream ciphers.

Boneh et al. [12] introduced a public keyword encryption scheme with keyword search. Similar works were also presented in [13] and [14] that put forward searchable encryption schemes. However, solutions based on public key encryption are usually very computation expensive. Furthermore, keyword privacy is not protected in public key setting since the server could encrypt any keyword with the known public key and then use the received trapdoor to evaluate its ciphertext.

Wang et al. [4] presented the earlier work that explores user's capability of ranked search over encrypted cloud data. Ranked search improves systems efficiency and usability by returning all matching files in a ranked order depending on predefined user rules, and for this case is its file length and document frequency. Other solutions are presented in [3] and [15], but all these works presented solutions based on single keyword search only. Singe keyword ranked search is computational inefficiency when the number of documents is quite large as the final result can include almost all documents in the set C as long as they contain a single searched keyword. Multi-keyword ranked searches came to puzzle out this issue, as initially presented by Cao et al. [1]. The scheme is semantically secure. However, it lacks actual implementation.

None of the above schemes addressed the challenges of varying keyword dictionary size following addition or reduction of files on cloud server. A-MRSE presents a novel scheme with new algorithms that address this issue and can support any dynamic in keyword dictionary size with minimum communication and computation overhead. A-MRSE achieves its desired goals and leaving no drawback as in [1].

5 Conclusion and Future Works

In this paper, we present a novel scheme that is adaptive and it supports multi-keyword ranked search over encrypted cloud data. We present a novel scheme, called A-MRSE, which uses new algorithms to solve the existing challenges on multi-keyword keyword searches over encrypted data. We also strengthen security and privacy by preventing the cloud server from performing statistical attacks based on the results to be returned to data consumers after performing a ranked search. A-MRSE can be easily deployed in many cloud scenarios, such as UniDrive, a synergizing multiple consumer cloud storage service [16]. We conducted multiple experiments under different settings and the results illustrates that our new A-MRSE scheme is much better than MRSE.

In the future, we are looking forward to building schemes that can work under stronger security threats especially when the cloud server is capable of colluding. We are working on building adaptive schemes that can work for fuzzy keyword searches.

Acknowledgments. This work is supported by National Natural Science Foundation of China under grants 61173170, 61300222, 61433006 and U1401258, Innovation Fund of Huazhong University of Science and Technology under grants 2015TS069 and 2015TS071, and Science and Technology Support Program of Hubei Province under grant 2014BCH270 and 2015AAA013, and Science and Technology Program of Guangdong Province under grant 2014B010111007.

References

1. Cao, N., Wang, C., Li, M., Ren, K., Lou, W.: Privacy-preserving multi-keyword ranked search over encrypted cloud data. In: Proceedings of INFOCOM, pp. 829–837. IEEE (2011)
2. Song D.X., Wanger, D., Perrig, A.: Practical techniques for searches on encrypted data. In: 2000 IEEE Symposium on Security and Privacy, pp. 44–55. IEEE (2000)
3. Kiltz, E., et al.: Searchable encryption revisited: consistency properties, relation to anonymous IBE, and extensions. In: Shoup, V. (ed.) CRYPTO 2005. LNCS, vol. 3621, pp. 205–222. Springer, Heidelberg (2005)
4. Wang, C., Cao, N., Li, J., Ren, K., Lou, W.: Secure ranked keyword search over encrypted cloud data. In: Proceedings of IEEE 30th International Conference in Distributed Computing Systems (ICDCS), pp. 253–262. IEEE (2010)
5. Xu, Z., Kang, W., Li, R., Yow, K., Xu, C.: Efficient multi-keyword ranked query on encrypted data in the cloud. In: The 18th International Conference on Parallel and Distributed Systems (ICPADS), pp. 244–251. IEEE (2012)
6. Jiad, Y., Lu, P., Zhu, Y., Xue, G., Li, M.: Towards secure multi-keyword top-k retrieval over encrypted data. IEEE Trans. Dependable Secure Comput. **10**(4), 239–250 (2013)
7. Feingold, D.G., Richard, S.V.: Block diagonally dominant matrices and generalizations of the Gerchgorin Circle theorem. Pacific J. Math. **12**(4), 1241–1250 (1962)
8. Wong, W.K., Cheung, D.W., Kao, B., Mamoulis, N.: Secure kNN computation on encrypted databases. In: Proceedings of the 2009 ACM SIGMOD International Conference on Management of Data, pp. 139–152. ACM (2009)
9. Cohen W.W.: Enron Email Dataset. http://www.cs.cmu.edu/~enron
10. Hicklin, J., Moler, C., Webb, P., Boisvert, R.F., Miller B., Pozo, R., Remington, K.: JAMA: Java Matrix Package. http://www.math.nist.gov/javanumerics/jama/
11. Mather, T., Kumaraswamy, S., Latif, S.: Cloud Security and Privacy: an Enterprise Perspective on Risks and Compliance. O'Reilly Media Inc., Sebastopol (2009)
12. Boneh, D., Di Crescenzo, G., Ostrovsky, R., Persiano, G.: Public key encryption with keyword search. In: Cachin, C., Camenisch, J.L. (eds.) EUROCRYPT 2004. LNCS, vol. 3027, pp. 506–522. Springer, Heidelberg (2004)
13. Mitzenmacher, M., Chang, Y.-C.: Privacy preserving keyword searches on remote encrypted data. In: Ioannidis, J., Keromytis, A.D., Yung, M. (eds.) ACNS 2005. LNCS, vol. 3531, pp. 442–455. Springer, Heidelberg (2005)
14. O'Neill, A., Bellare, M., Boldyreva, A.: Deterministic and efficiently searchable encryption. In: Menezes, A. (ed.) CRYPTO 2007. LNCS, vol. 4622, pp. 535–552. Springer, Heidelberg (2007)
15. Li, J., Wang, Q., Wang, C., Kao, N., Ren, K., Lou, W.: Fuzzy keyword search over encrypted data in cloud computing. In: Proceedings of INFOCOM, pp. 1–5. IEEE (2010)
16. Tang, H., Liu, F.M., Shen, G., Jin, Y., Guo, C.: UniDrive: synergize multiple consumer cloud storage services. In: ACM/USENIX/IFIP Middleware, Vancouver, Canada (2015)

A Collaborated IPv6-Packets Matching Mechanism Base on Flow Label in OpenFlow

Weifeng Sun, Huangping Wei, Zhenxing Ji,
Qingqing Zhang, and Chi Lin(✉)

School of Software, Dalian University of Technology, Dalian, Liaoning, China
{wfsun, c.lin}@dlut.edu.cn,
{1299856803, jasonjee1990, 1165331393}@qq.com

Abstract. Software Defined Networks (SDN), the separation of a network device's control and data planes, do not need to rely on the underlying network equipment (routers, switches, firewall).It is a new network which collaborated IP and a lot of relevant technical content. The control of SDN is completely open, the user can customize any rule strategy to achieve network routing and transmission, which is more flexible and intelligent. Internet Protocol version 6 (IPv6), with the 128-bit address, is the next generation Internet. In this paper, we present a Flow Table structure by using Flow Label and a matching approach which use Flow Label within IPv6 protocol to decrease the size of Flow Table with OpenFlow and the time of forwarding IPv6 packets in SDN based on OpenFlow. The simulations and analyses show that this flow table mechanism performs better.

Keywords: IPv6 · OpenFlow · Flow label · Compression of flow table

1 Introduction

The Software Define Networks (SDN) [1] is an approach or architecture to not only simplify computer networks but also to make it more reactive to the requirements of workloads and services placed in the network. Originally, the control planes and data planes are consolidated into network equipments such as the IP routers and the Ethernet switches. SDN collaborates a lot of network transmission protocols and functions. It allows for a centrally managed and distributed control, management, and data plane, which policy that dictates the forwarding rules is centralized, but the actual forwarding rule processing are distributed among multiple devices.

Internet Protocol version 6 (IPv6) [2] is the latest version of the Internet Protocol. It uses a 128 bit address, allowing 2128 times as many as IPv4, which uses 32 bit addresses. IPv6 is bringing many unique benefits when it is combined with emerging technologies such as Clouds Virtualization, Internet of Things, etc. These benefits include host automation, scalability in addressing, route aggregation, forwarding and traffic steering functions [3]. IPv6 enables the transformation that occurs at the networking infrastructure level which can make SDN and network easily easy to scale.

There is no doubt that most of the SDN solutions are based on the OpenFlow protocol [4], which was defined by Open Networking Foundation (ONF) [5]. OpenFlow was

S. Guo et al. (Eds.): CollaborateCom 2015, LNICST 163, pp. 14–25, 2016.
DOI: 10.1007/978-3-319-28910-6_2

originally imagined and implemented as part of network research at Stanford University. And Nick McKeown firstly descripts detail the concept OpenFlow [6]. However, as the IPv6 support in OpenFlow, It is a problem that how to reduce the size of the flow table faced with OpenFlow. According to the OpenFlow standard, the flow table can be achieved with TCAM, Ternary Content Addressable Memory that is based on the contents of the address to find. In the traditional network equipment, TCAM mainly for FIB, MAC, MPLS Label and ACL table because of the length of the match fields for each table vary, so it can be separately designed, and has the maximum capacity limits in order to achieve a minimum overhead. Although OpenFlow designed multi-flow table, in order to reduce the overhead stream table, forming a handle in the form of pipeline, reducing the total number of records in the flow table. With the increasing of the matching fields, the space of flow table will be limited. This problem will become more and more prominent with the increasing of hosts. The size of flow table and the matching processing of OpenFlow that be more complex restrict the IPv6 development in SDN.

In this paper, we propose the flow table structure by using Flow Label within IPv6 protocol, in order to decrease the bite of flow table and the time of forwarding IPv6 packets in SDN based on OpenFlow. OpenFlow is designed forwarding of L1-L4 layer forwarding entries. We use Flow Label of L3 layer to match, instead of the address of IPv6 and the port of TCP/UDP, the OpenFlow match fields of L3-L4 Layer.

The main contributions of this paper are:

(1) We propose the flow table structure by using Flow Label in IPv6 feature, instead of L3-L4 Layers elements of matching, in order to decrease the time of matching and the IPv6 flow table structure of OpenFlow.
(2) We analysis and compare the latency, the jitter and the size of flow table between flow table with flow label and flow table without flow label, and proved that the former can perform OpenFlow better in SDN.

2 Related Work

The first edition of OpenFlow focused on IPv4 and did not support IPv6 flow [7]. ONF started to consider how IPv6 flows could be accommodated. Then the ONF published their OpenFlow1.2 which is the first version that supports IPv6 packet matching [8]. The OpenFlow1.2 provides basic support for IPv6, OpenFlow1.2 compliant switch can match on IP protocol number (Ethernet type $0 \times 86dd$ = IPv6), IPv6 source/destination addresses, traffic class, flow label, and ICMPv6 types. This is a start at allowing IPv6 unicast and multicast traffics to match and OpenFlow flow table in a switch. When the ONF published the OpenFlow1.3 [9]. There is a few more IPv6 functions added in OpenFlow1.3 which expands the IPv6 Extension Header handling support and essential features including Hop-by-hop IPv6 extension header, Router IPv6 extension header, Router IPv6 extension header, access control, quality of service and tunneling support and had the same ability to match on IPv6 header fields such as source/destination addresses, protocol number (next header, extension header), hop-limit, traffic class, flow label, and ICMPv6 type as in Fig. 1. When the ONF release OpenFlow1.4 nothing changed regarding IPv6 support [10].

Ingress Port	Ethernet (L2)				IP (L3)			Tranport (L4)	
	Src MAC	Dst MAC	Type	VLAN ID	Src IP	Dst IP	Protocol	Src Port	Dst Port

Fig. 1. Ten-tuple for matching in OpenFlow

With the development of OpenFlow and IPv6, Chia-Wei Tseng combines the existing IPv6 protocol and the SDN (SDNv6) for future network, to provide the smarter and reliable network communication architecture. The SDNv6 [11] motivates a network architecture composed of reliable virtual entities, plug-and-play access with auto-configures and flexible service clouds over a physical network. Wenfeng Xia proposed a Software Defined Approach to Unified IPv6 Transition which unifies the variety of IPv6 transition mechanisms [12]. Xiaohan Liu proposes an IPv6 Virtual Network Architecture (VNET6) to support flexible services in IPv6 network. IPv6 is a critical protocol in VNET6 [13]. The VNET6 is adaptive to video service with high bandwidth and low tendency and improves quality of experiences to users. Batalle [14] proposes the IPv4 and IPv6 routing separation, and provides a different OpenFlow controllers conducted by the inter-domain routing OpenFlow network management method. Rodrigo, Fernandes and Rothenberg in Brazil and Hungary started to leverage these new features in OpenFlow1.3 [15]. Ivan Pepelnjak also uses the new features in IPv6 [16] to describe how OpenFlow can be used to help secure the IPv6 Neighbor Discovery Protocol (NDP) because it suffers from many of the same vulnerabilities as IPv4 ARP. William Stallings present about the various elements of an OpenFlow table [17] that includes the IPv6 header fields that can be matched. Araji and Gurkan present ESPM, Embedding Switch ID, Port number and MAC Address within IPv6 protocol and SDN technology, to decrease CAM table entries on the switch by forwarding the packets [18]. David R. Newman goes through the installation steps required to set up an OpenFlow protocol network using Mininet with OpenFlow1.3 support for IPv6, to evaluate IPv6 unicast and IPv6 multicast [19].

3 IPv6-Packets Flow Label Matching Mechanism

In this section, the matching approach by using Flow Label within IPv6 and the structure of flow table by using Flow Label within IPv6 is proposed and defined. Flow Label is a new field in the IPv6 protocol and it can be used for flow classification. And then, we shows the matching approach by using Flow Label in OpenFlow instead of L3-L4 Layer elements, the IPv6 source address, the IPv6 destination address, the protocol version, the TCP/UDP source port, the TCP/UDP destination port and Flow Label within IPv6 is introduced in Flow Table as the IPv6 required match fields to reduce the size of flow table. This paper considers the matching approach which flow label is used for match process and flow table can reduce the rate of IPv6 flow matching and the size of IPv6 Flow table, to provide the faster and more reliable network communication in OpenFlow.

3.1 Flow Label

Flow Label is a new field in the IPv6 protocol proposed and defined as the length of 20 bits. RFC defines the flow label which the source node can use the flow label of IPv6 header marked packets, and the source node request for specially treatment, such as, QoS services and other real-time transactions. Flow label can be resolved to meet the needs and rules by checking the flow label to determine which stream it belongs to. According to the forwarding rules, the routers and hosts which do not support the flow label need to flow label field to all zeros, and the receiving packets do not modified the value of flow label.

The traditional traffic classification process is as follows:

(1) Find a destination IP address;
(2) To compare the protocol number;
(3) Compare the destination port number (transport layer performed);
(4) Comparing the source IP address and filter address (here mainly is to determine whether the packet matches the filtering rules);
(5) Comparing the source port number.

However, a uniqueness flow must have the same attributes, including the source address, destination address, flow label. Therefore, we propose a matching method of using Flow label within the IPv6 protocol for OpenFlow which supports IPv6.

3.2 The Matching Approach by Using Flow Label Within IPv6 Based on OpenFlow

Flow is an important concept not only in the data flow communication network but also in OpenFlow. The Open Flow Switcher consists of one or more flow tables, which perform packet lookups and forwarding. The switcher communicates with the controller and the controller manages the switcher by the OpenFlow switch protocol. Using the OpenFlow protocol, the controller can add, update, and delete flow entries in flow tables. Each flow table in the switcher contains a set of flow entries; each flow entry consists of match fields, counters, and a set of instructions to apply to matching packets. A flow table entry consists of a set of L2/L3/L4 match conditions.

In the matching process of L3-L4 Layer which don't use the flow label, the OpenFlow agreement will check the packets which are the IPv4 packets or IPv6 packets, and compare the destination IP address. After the comparison of TCP/UDP source and destination port numbers, using multi-stream pipeline processing table can effectively enhance the flow table processing efficiency, especially in matching IP layer, IPv4 needed source IP address, destination IP address, and IPv6 IP address will be added to 128 bits, greatly increasing the flow table match delay. Before flow label field is introduced, the common matching process of L3/L4 layer is as follows:

(1) Compare the protocol number;
(2) Compare the source IP address and destination IP address which has 128 bits in IPv6;
(3) Compare the source port number and the destination port number (transport layer performed);

In the pipeline of multi-flow table, the matching process of flow table match is very complex as it is in Fig. 2, so that the delay of flow table match of OpenFlow Switcher will increases obviously, especially in the match of IPv6 address, which has 128 bits.

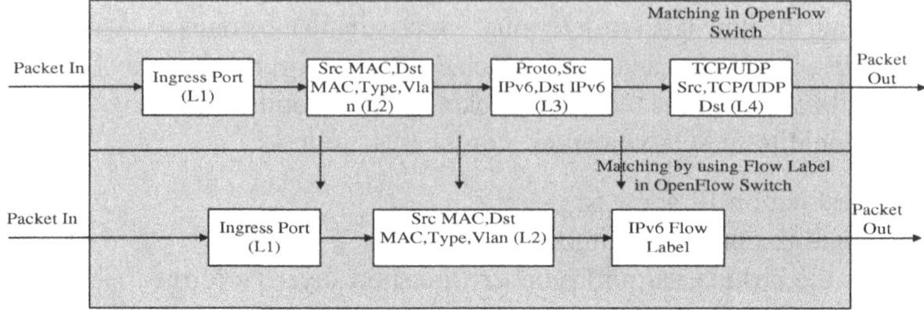

Fig. 2. IPv6 packets are matched against flow table in OpenFlow switcher

We propose a matching approach by using Flow Label within IPv6 feature in IPv6 based on OpenFlow instead of L3-L4 matching fields, such as IPv6 source address, IPv6 destination address, TCP/UDP source port, TCP/UDP destination port. In the IPv6 with flow label mechanism, we can use this field, flow label (20 bits), quintuple information will be combined to generate a random flow label serial number for each quintuple information, and generates the corresponding entries in the flow state, it can find the entry for traffic classification according to the value of each stream flow label. The different source node may randomly send the same flow label value, but the probability is very small (about 106 level), which can be considered that the source node will correspond the only flow label value in simple OpenFlow network. The possible Hash algorithm can be used in the matching of flow label. Thus, the process based on traffic classification IPv6 flow label can be simplified to a one-step process: Find the value of the stream flow state table based on the Flow Label. Obviously, in such a mechanism, matching process of match fields is simplified a lot when the IPv6 packets are matched against flow table.

3.3 Flow Table with Flow Label Within IPv6 Based on OpenFlow

Flow table is an important concept in OpenFlow, Flow Table are a pieces of the forwarding tables, as MAC table, IP table, ACL in tradition network. In OpenFlow agreement, each flow table composed by many Flow entries. Flow table entry is the smallest unit of flow table matched to each flow in network transmission. According to OpenFlow standard, A flow table consists of many flow entries, and each flow entry include: Match Fields which match packets, Priority matching precedence of flow entry, Counters which update when packets are matched, Instructions which can modify the action set or pipeline processing, timeouts that can maximum the amount of time or idle time before flow is expired by the switch, cookie of which the data value chosen by the controller. And a flow table can support L1-L4 matching, so the match fields can consists of L1-L4 matching element, such as L1 (Ingress port, physical port), L2 (VLAN ID, VLAN PCP, Ethernet source address. Ethernet destination address, Ethernet type), L3 (IP protocol number, IPv4 or IPv6 source address, IPv4 or IPv6 destination address, IP DSCP, IP ECN, Flow Label), L4 (TCP or UDP source port, TCP or UDP destination port), just as it is in Fig. 3.

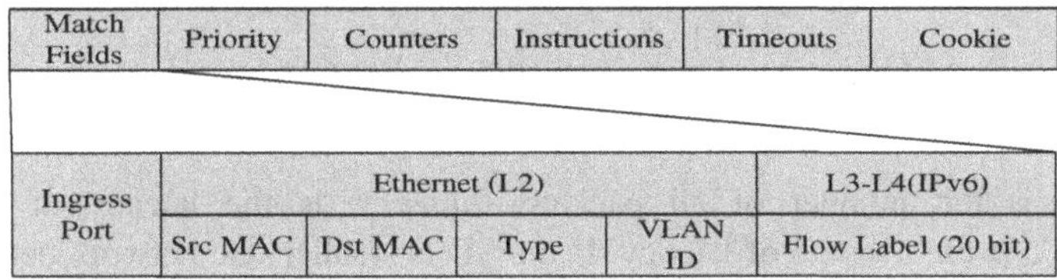

Fig. 3. Main components of a flow entry in a flow table with flow label

In this paper, we propose to use Flow Label fully within IPv6 protocol in place of the L3-4 match fields in IPv6 network match fields based on OpenFlow. For example, in IPv6 flow table based on OpenFlow, when a IPv6 host1 connect to a IPv6 host2, the Flow Labe will be assigned according to the Packet-in packet, not the match fields of L3-4 Layer, such as IPV6 source address, IPv6 destination address and TCP/UDP source port, TCP/UDP destination port. Especially in the match fields of IPv6 address, which has 128 bits, will increase the size of flow table obviously. Thus the controller automatically and naturally determines the flow label number of the flow based on its location in the IPv6 network.

3.4 The Analyses of Flow Label Matching Mechanism Based on OpenFlow

According to OpenFlow standard, OpenFlow defines the flow table entries of matching L1-L4 Layers match fields to lookup the match fields and forward packets. A flow table consists of flow table entries is designed to match against packets, which consists of the L1-L4 Layer metadata of matching flow table entry. When the packets are matched against multiple tables in the pipeline, the process of flow table match is very complex, the complexity of match is expressed:

$$T(n) = O(n! \times a(2^l)) \tag{1}$$

And n is the number of flow tables, a is the number of actions and l is the length of match fields. As the number of flow tables, the number of actions and the length of match fields is increasing, it will lead to the increasing of complexity in the pipeline process. So we analyze the flow label matching mechanism from theory and implementation in IPv6. The latency of packet forwarding is an important indicator of network performance. For the network performance of forwarding, we can use the arithmetic average to evaluate, and is shown in Eq. (2).

$$Average_{Latency} = \frac{1}{N}\sum_{i=1}^{n} \text{Latency}_i \tag{2}$$

For the fluctuation of delay, we use the standard deviation to evaluate, and it is shown in Eq. (3).

$$SD_{latency} = \sqrt{\frac{1}{N}\sum_{i=1}^{n} (Latency_i - Average_{Latency})^2} \tag{3}$$

And N is the number of all packets, $lantency_i$ is the latency of i packet. $Average_{latency}$ is the average of latency. If the SD is smaller, the network performance of fluctuation is better. The jitter of transmitting can react the stability of transmitting performance in network. The jitter of packet forwarding is shown in Eq. (4).

$$Jitter = \frac{1}{N}\sum_{i=1}^{n} (L_i - \bar{L})^2 \tag{4}$$

And N is the number of packets, L_i is the latency of the packet i. $\bar{L}$ is the average of the latency of n packets. According to OpenFlow1.3, OpenFlow defines the size of the match fields in IPv6 network based on OpenFlow, such as the size of IPv6 source address and IPv6 destination address are 128 bits, the size of IP Protocols is 8 bits and the size of TCP/UDP source port and TCP/UDP destination port are 16 bits, the size of IPv6 table Label is 20 bits. The size of flow table is shown in Eq. (5).

$$FL = Sum(match + prio + coun + inst + tout + cookie) \tag{5}$$

The compression of a flow table i of an OpenFlow switch at some moment is shown in Eq. (6).

$$Compression = (1 - \frac{FL'}{FL}) \times 100\% \tag{6}$$

And FL' is the size of flow table by using Flow Label, FL is the size of flow table by using IPv6 address and TCP/UDP port. In this paper, we mainly focus on the match fields in IPv6 based on OpenFlow, which uses flow label to replace the elements of L3-4 Layer, that uses IPv6 flow label (20 bits) instead of the IPv6 source address, IPv6 destination address, IP protocol number and TCP/UDP source port and TCP/UDP destination port. Therefore, The flow table i of the OpenFlow switcher at some moment is shown: $FL_i = match + otherelement$. The $match$ is the size of match fields of flow table i by using Flow Label or IPv6 address and the other element is the size of Priority, counters, instructions, timeouts and the cookie of flow table. The match fields of matching packets support the element of L1-4 Layer; the size of match fields of flow table i is $match = m_{l1} + m_{l2} + m_{l3} + m_{l4}$ and $m_{l1} - m_{l4}$ is the size of L1-4 Layer's match fields. The compression of a flow table i of an OpenFlow switcher is shown in Eq. (6),

$m_{l3} - m_{l4}$ is the size of L3-4 Layer's match fields of flow table i and e is the size of the L1-L2 Layer's match fields and others of flow table:

$$Comprsssion_i = (1 - \frac{m\prime_{l1-l2} + m\prime_{l3-l4} + otherele'}{m_{l1-l2} + m_{l3-l4} + otherele}) \times 100\% \quad (7)$$

For every table flow, m and e will be different. The compression of every flow table of an OpenFlow switcher at some moment is shown in Eq. (7), $Compression_i$ is the compress of a flow table i of an OpenFlow Switcher and n is the number of flow table of an OpenFlow switch: $Compression = \frac{1}{N}(\sum_{j=i}^{i+n} Compression_j)$. Analysis with Eq. (7), the gaps of m'_{l3-l4} and m_{l3-l4} is changeless to flow table because of L3-L4 Layer. So the sizes of m_{l1-l2} and e will be determined to the compress of flow table. In the common conditions of OpenFlow networks, the state of flow table accords with the complexity of Instruction. So there will be more space of flow table when there are more instructions in relative simple network, this mechanism of flow table which uses flow label will perform better.

4 Evaluation of IPv6-Packets Matching Approach

In this paper, we implement the evaluation to verify the feasibility and performance of our matching approach and Flow Table. We also implement the function of matching in Mininet 2.0. The controller is Ryu [20] which supports OpenFlow1.3 in Ubuntu 14.04. In the simulation, we used the 1-switch-2 hosts topology in Fig. 4. We did simulation with the matching approach by utilizing the Flow Label based on Openlow1.3 match fields in order to compare the difference performance between the flow table with IPv6 flow label and flow table including IPv6 addresses. The IPv6 matching approach implementation extends the OpenFlow1.3, we used OpenFlow1.3 because it is available at the time when the work was done, Through the evaluation metrics of the performance of network, The aim of the flow label matching approach obtained the best performance of the OpenFlow network system.

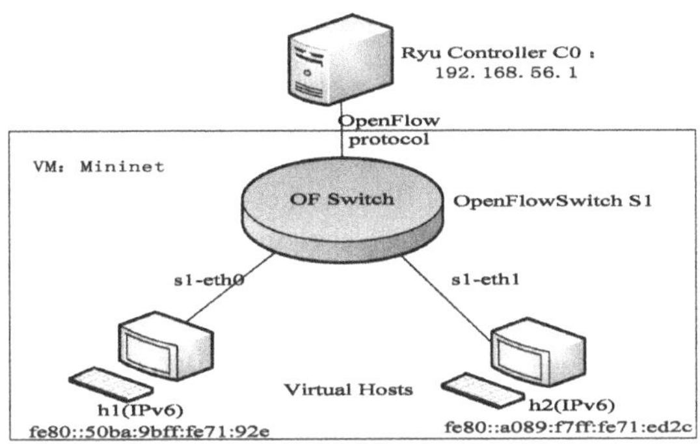

Fig. 4. Topology of 1-switch-n hosts simple network

We used three parameters, the latency of forwarding, the jitter of transmitting and the compression of flow tables, to evaluate the performance of network. We respectively added the flow table based on flow label and the flow table based on IPv6 address to the OpenSwitch in Mininet and we sent the 64 bytes packet per one second and send the 128 bytes UDP packets per one second in which the rate is 10 M. we compared the latency of 120 packets (2 min), the jitter of 30 s and the size of flow table in IPv6 based on the OpenFlow1.3 match fields and the matching by the model we proposed in Sects. 3.2 and 3.3. We assigned each one host an IPv6 address. Host 1 pings Host 2 and the IPv6 packet was analyzed by the Ryu, OpenFlow Protocol matched the flow table to make a decision on the forwarding of the flows. We got the statistical results of delay, jitter and flow table size of two matching mechanism during the simulation.

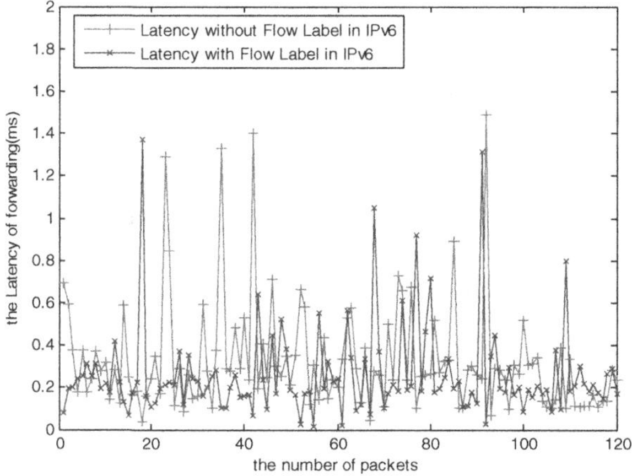

Fig. 5. The comparison of the latency between two different matching mechanisms

In Fig. 5, we use the arithmetic average and standard deviation of the delay to evaluate the performance of the network, according to the Eq. (2),

$$Average_{latency\,without\,flow\,label} = 0.3284\,\text{ms}$$

$$Average_{latency\,with\,flow\,label} = 0.2604\,\text{ms}$$

The average latency with IPv6 address is 0.3284 ms, but the average with flow label is 0.2604 ms in the forwarding of 120 IPv6 packets. From this value, we can see that the Latency of OpenFlow by using flow label in IPv6 network is smaller than the latency without flow label. And according to the Eq. (3),

$$SD_{latency\;without\,flow\,label\;in\;IPv6} = 0.0334\,\text{ms}$$

$$SD_{latency\;with\,flow\,label\,in\,IPv6} = 0.0167\,\text{ms}$$

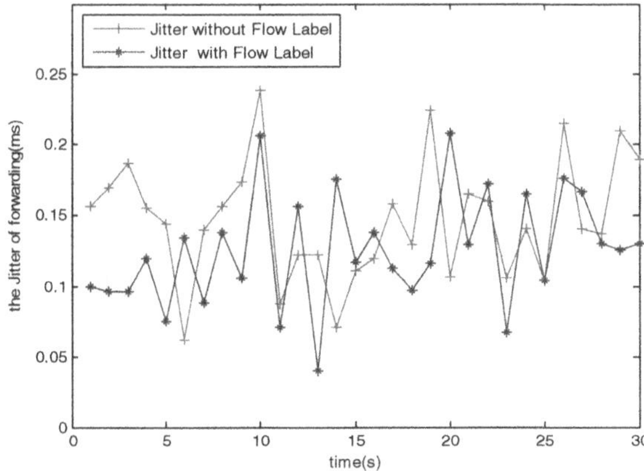

Fig. 6. The comparison of the jitter between two different matching mechanisms

From this value, we can see that the fluctuation of Latency by using flow label in IPv6 network is smaller than the fluctuation of latency without flow label. Thus, Fig. 5 shows that the latency without flow label is in general higher than the latency with flow label obviously.

And in Fig. 6, it shows that the jitter without flow label is higher than the jitter with flow label. The jitter time which is based on flow label is lower about 70 % than the matching mechanism without flow label in transmitting.

$$Average_{jitter\ without\ flow\ label} = 0.1469\,\text{ms}$$

$$Average_{jitter\ with\ flow\ label} = 0.1254\,\text{ms}$$

From these values, we can see that the fluctuation of Latency by using flow label in IPv6 network is litter smaller than the fluctuation of latency without flow label.

In Fig. 7, it shows the comparison of the size of flow table in two matching mechanism when host1 pings to h2 which send IPv6 packets in 1-switch-2 hosts topology. The size of flow table with flow label is less than the size of flow table without flow label obviously and the size of flow table with flow label is decreased about 20 % which compared with the size of flow table without flow label. So the flow table with flow label is better than the flow table without flow label in IPv6 based on OpenFlow1.3 in this scene.

For comparing the performance of different matching approach, which are between the flow table with flow label and the flow table without flow label, we recorded the latency of transmitting and the jitter between flow table with flow label and flow table without flow label when h1 pings to h2 which send IPv6 packets, in order to compare the performance of different matching approach in both network. In Figs. 5, 6, and 7, the performance of the latency, jitter and flow tables between flow table with flow label and flow table without flow label is obvious. From the result of simulation, we find that the network performance by using the Flow label could make OpenFlow perform better in 1-switch-2-IPv6 hosts topology.

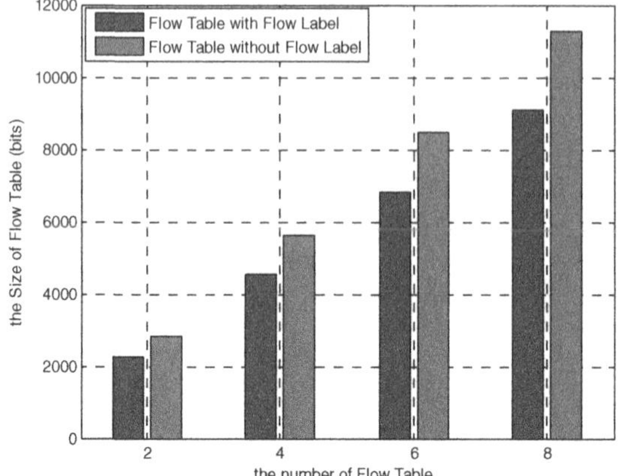

Fig. 7. The comparison of the size of flow table between flow table with flow label and flow table without flow label

5 Conclusion and Future Work

In this paper, we proposed a matching approach by using Flow Label within IPv6 protocol and a flow table structure by using Flow Label within IPv6 protocol in SDN based on OpenFlow, and compared the size of difference flow table between flow table with flow label and flow table without flow label in simple 1-switch-2-hosts topology based on OpenFlow1.3. Through the analysis and the simulation of the difference between the two flow tables in this paper, we concluded that the flow table by using Flow Label within IPv6 protocol can lead to the decrease of the latency of forwarding, the jitter of transmitting and the size of flow table space. The simulations compared the size of flow table between flow table with using flow label and flow table without using flow label and the result showed that the flow table by using Flow Label within IPv6 protocol can reduce the size of flow table effectively in simple network scenarios.

However, we will have a lot of work to do, we don't optimize the suitable flow label hash algorithm about IPv6 address and don't analyze the QoS and the security of OpenFlow which uses the flow label within IPv6 protocol. In addition, we experiment on simple network. We do not take these into consideration in this paper. In future work, we will talk about the analysis about the QoS and the security of OpenFlow which uses the flow label within IPv6 protocol, and our future work will involve more experiments and analyses of flow label scenarios.

Acknowledgement. This work is supported by the National Science Foundation, under grant No. 61471083 and grant No. 61300017. The Fundamental Research Funds for Central Universities (DUT15QY28, jg2015036).

References

1. Zhang, C.K., Cui, Y., Tang, H.Y., Wu, J.P.: State-of-the-art survey on software-defined networking (SDN). J. Softw. **26**(1), 62–81 (2015)
2. Deering, S.E.: Internet protocol, version 6 (IPv6) specification. RFC 2460. https://tools.ietf.org/html/rfc2460
3. Gu, D., Liu, X., Qin, G., et al.: VNET6: SOA based on IPv6 virtual network. In: Proceedings of the 2012 International Conference on Cloud and Service Computing, pp. 32–39. IEEE Computer Society (2012)
4. OpenFlow. http://www.OpenFlow.org/
5. Open Networking Foundation (2014). https://www.opennetworking.org
6. McKeown, N., Anderson, T., Balakrishnan, H., et al.: OpenFlow: enabling innovation in campus networks. J. ACM SIGCOMM Comput. Commun. Rev. **38**, 69–74 (2008)
7. Heller, B.: OpenFlow switch specification, version 1.0. 0 (2009)
8. O N F. OpenFlow switch specification version 1.2. 0 (2011)
9. OpenFlow Switch Specification 1.3.0. http://www.opennetworking.org
10. Specification-Version, OpenFlow Switch. "1.4. 0." http://www.opennetworking.org
11. Tseng, C.W., Yang, Y.T., Chou, L.D.: An IPv6-enabled software-defined networking architecture. In: 2013 15th Asia-Pacific Network Operations and Management Symposium (APNOMS), pp. 1–3. IEEE (2013)
12. Xia, W., Tsou, T., Lopez, D.: A software defined approach to unified IPv6 transition. In: 2013 International Conference Special Interest Group on Data Communication (SIGCOMM). Hong Kong (2013)
13. Liu, X., Qin, G., Yan, S., Luo, Z., Yan, B.: VNET6: SOA based on IPv6 virtual network. In: 2012 International Conference Cloud and Service Computing (CSC), pp.32–39 (2012)
14. Batalle, J: On the implementation of NFV over an OpenFlow infrastructure: routing function virtualization. In: Future Networks and Services (SDN4FNS), pp 1–6 (2013)
15. Denicol, R.R., Fernandes, E.L., Rothenberg, C.E., et al.: On IPv6 support in OpenFlow via flexible match structures. J. OFELIA/CHANGE Summer School (2011)
16. IPv6 First-Hop Security: Ideal OpenFlow Use Case. http://blog.ipspace.net/2012/10/ipv6-first-hop-security-ideal-OpenFlow.html
17. Stallings, W.: Software-defined networks and OpenFlow. Internet Protoc. J. **16**, 2–14 (2013)
18. Araji, B., Gurkan, D.: Embedding switch number, port number, and MAC address (ESPM) within the IPv6 address. In: 2014 Third GENI Research and Educational Experiment Workshop (GREE), pp. 69–70. IEEE (2014)
19. Newman, D.R.: Technology Validation Experiment: IPv6 and Multicast Support on OpenFlow (2014)
20. Ryu. http://osrg.github.com/ryu/

Traveller: A Novel Tourism Platform for Students Based on Cloud Data

Qi-Ying Hu[1], Chang-Dong Wang[1](✉), Jia-Xin Hong[1], Meng-Zhe Hua[1], and Di Huang[2]

[1] School of Mobile Information Engineering, Sun Yat-sen University, Zhuhai, China
changdongwang@hotmail.com
[2] SYSU-CMU Shunde International Joint Research Institute (JRI), Shunde, China

Abstract. Tourism is one of the top choices of contemporary university students for leisure on vacation. Desires that students want to travel extensively become increasingly stronger. However, few correct analysis on the tourism market of students in e-commerce results in its immature development, causing a difficulty in making a personalized travel plan to them. Concerning such a situation, it makes sense to provide students with more high-quality plans based on personalized analysis on their tourism preferences. Thus, it is necessary to design a safe, reliable, stable platform for students' travel, named *Traveller*. Cloud computing service is mainly designed for PC machines at present, but it is a trend of future development to combine the cloud computing and mobile application. From the viewpoint of technique, powerful computing capacity and storage capacity are sufficient to improve the user experience. From the viewpoint of mobile user, a sharp increase of users in recent years has become a driving force to push the advancement of mobile application. As a consequence, mobile computing will soon prove its prevalence. In this paper, tourist information will be collected by communicating through a mobile terminal to send requests to the server in the cloud, making full use of cloud server's features such as efficiency and convenience to update.

Keywords: Travel · Cloud-platform · Database · Application

1 Introduction

In step with the improvement of people's living standards, the tourism industry has become an indispensable part of people's life [1]. It is also universally popular among university students. As a special group, university students with independent economy, self-ability, relatively more spare time and adventurous spirit play an essential role in the whole tourism market. Moreover, the students are different from the other groups in many aspects. Students prefer group tourism and they also prefer natural attractions when choosing sites. Due to the limitation of school and the family, they generally lack travel experience, worry and hoping to get a more intuitive advice. At the same time, the young generation depends

S. Guo et al. (Eds.): CollaborateCom 2015, LNICST 163, pp. 26–35, 2016.
DOI: 10.1007/978-3-319-28910-6_3

more on the mobile phones, so the Apps for tourism find favor with them along with the gradual development of intelligent terminal technology.

Currently some Apps have been developed to meet this needs, like Qunar [2], Ctrip [3], Umetrip [4], etc. However, they have the following drawbacks [5]. Firstly, the pertinence of the Apps is not strong, making the App lack individuation and the features greatly reduced in practice. Secondly, Because the function of the App is complex and the target population is not explicit, it is obvious that only a few can find favor with people among the numerous Apps. Finally, for best reliability and performance, the traditional App should be constantly updated, which causes trouble for users to download installation package of the latest version over and over otherwise they cannot experience the benefits from the new features and functions.

Cloud computing is an emerging ICT framework and service model. It is an evaluation of distributed processing, parallel processing and network computing. It has advantages in high reliability, rapid deployment and on-demand service, which makes it extremely popular at present. Based on these merits, we intend to make use of cloud computing to develop a searching platform which can provide users with tourist information including student discount. That is why we want to design a mobile application on the basement of cloud platform.

Mobile cloud computing is a new computing paradigm to meet the urgent need not for applications and services of resource-constrained mobile devices. To overcome resource constraints on mobile devices, a general idea is to ship code and data to the cloud and back to prolong the battery life and speed up the application. Besides saving energy, cloud computing also enables enhanced mobile experiences by employing a client-server framework that consists of two parts, which run on the mobile device and the cloud, respectively. Overall, mobile cloud computing can solve the problem of energy consumption and bring convenience to the mobile users [6].

In summary, this project is aimed at developing a searching platform for students' traveling convenience based on mobile cloud computing. In addition to implementing some common functions in current applications, this cloud application can provide more personalized services. The main purpose of this application is to help students make a good choice. It can provide users with some useful information about traveling depending on their situations and preferences.

1.1 Related Work

Many mobile tourism applications have been released into the market in recent years, but most of them aim to bring users convenience to buy tickets or check schedules. Umetrip [4] is a mobile application released by Civil Aviation Administration of China to query flight information, then users' account can also save each flight they have taken or going to take, further more it can remind users of the latest flight they will take. Ctrip [3] can be defined as an online travel agency, providing ticket service, tourist information and gather strangers together to have a trip. Users can buy tickets online to get some discount, share their own travel experience and read some strategies posted by others. Airbnb [7] is aimed

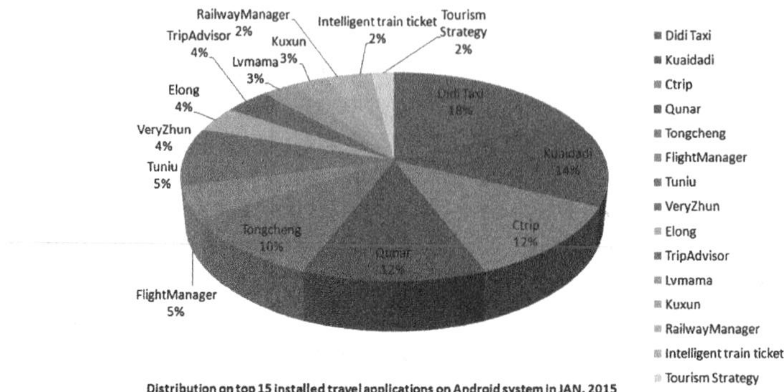

Fig. 1. Ranking of travel applications in China.

at making visitors feel like home at other places. Visitors can find local houses to stay for a short time to experience the local way of life. The living conditions are similar to those in hotels. Serving as private driver in more than 50 countries, Uber [8] provides different levels of car such as UberX and UberBlack for users. It makes users feel more comfortable and convenient to take this kind of car than a taxi. HHtravel helps users to have a top-level trip, such as Michelin restaurants and five-star hotels. The HHtravel [9] staffs can also organize a trip according to users' requirements. Lonely Planet Traveller [10] is transformed from a magazine with the same name. It introduces countries in a very detailed way by showing information about eating, playing, traffic, living, and even festival dates. Applications listed above are only a few of the whole travel application market. For more details we can see Fig. 1 about travel application download ranking in China in January 2015 [11].

In China, users prefer to use Ctrip [3], Qunar [2] and Tongcheng [12] (totally more than 30 %) which are defined as online travel agencies.

In conclusion, there are so many applications aimed at different travel aspects, such as tickets service, flight information, traffic, attraction information and so on, but few applications focus on university students who have gradually become main potential customers of tourism. Moreover, students have a vast number of requirements that cannot be satisfied by those applications. For example sometimes students want to check whether a specific scenery spot has student discount, yet unfortunately the information cannot be found easily. Also those most fascinating travel places are not actually what students are really interested in. They want to receive more recommendations from the same generation. In general there is no such an application that is personalized enough for university students. We expect to develop an application to provide convenience to students, giving them more opportunities to go out and see more. Meanwhile a students-friendly application can also save time for schedule with travel experience comments by those who have similar hobbies and preferences.

1.2 Our Work

To address the above issues, we develop a tourism platform for students based on the Aliyun [13], which sets up server in a virtual machine by using Apache and the remote database constructed in the server. Then the client can connect and call the database through the server program, as well as doing insertions, deletions, modifications and query to the database. In cloud server, we write Python code to make server receive requests from client, and obtain data from database according to the request. The cloud platform can run the code all the time to satisfy the need that the users get tourist information whenever they are. The configuration on it is easy to implement and the cost is relatively cheap.

Our idea is to develop a new application named *Traveller*, providing students with favourable tourist information. Students can log in the system and search for the destination they want to travel, get information of surroundings, and they can also grade the viewpoints where they have been to and make recommendations to others. The personalized recommendation is achieved on the server so that students can get more suitable and appropriate recommendations according to their own preferences. Even more, a student can make more like-minded friends by using this App and travel with them.

As to these functions, the framework of the application can be developed in two aspects: client and server. Eclipse is a good extensible development platform, which is open-source and able to support varied coding language. We can use Java to implement the function and this tool can help to construct the interactive interface of the application and implement the encapsulation of the data transmission via GET or POST request. For the server terminal, the cloud is used for its power in function and convenience in operation. All data will be stored in cloud and transmitted to the client in need.

Traveller is aimed at serving university students, so the objective is clear and functions are highly targeted. The current market lacks such App, so our application has strong market competitiveness. In addition, by keeping all the data in the cloud platform, it is easy to update all data and features, avoiding the need to constantly update the App to obtain the new properties.

The rest of the paper is organized as follows. In Sect. 2, the background knowledge of cloud computing is introduced. In Sect. 3, the proposed platform is described in detail. Section 4 reports the experimental results. We conclude our paper in Sect. 5.

2 Background

Based on the cloud platform, the main use in our application development is cloud computing. PaaS (Platform as a Service) [14] is referred to provide service for client. Utility computing is used to compute recommendation algorithms and also combine computing with storage. Socket is used as physical connection between the server and client which can transmit data.

Data transmits in different terminals by HTTP, which are a set of rules for computer communication through network [15]. Computer specialists designed

HTTP to satisfy the needs from client (such as mobile client), which requests information and service from Web server. All HTTP connections are formed with a set of requests and responses [16].

As a script, Python [17] deals with the requests coming from Android system while database system can utilize MySQL of the Ali virtual machine to aid this behaviour. What should be done first is to install MySQL and Python in the Ubuntu system. MySQL is useful to establish the database and it will be called in the Python script. This process needs the support of the library named MYSQLdB [18,19].

The server will get the requests send from the Android terminal, pick up the related datum, such as information about view, and return them as the format of string. Based on a subset of JavaScript, JSON [20] (JavaScript Object Notation) is a lightweight format to interchange data, it uses a text format which is completely independent to language, it also has similar habits like the C language family (including C, C++, Java, JavaScript, Python etc.). These properties make JSON ideal language to exchange data. It is not only easy to read and write, but also easy for machines to parse and generate.

3 The Proposed Platform

Based on the cloud server of Ali, we develop our platform in the Ubuntu system with SQL database [21]. Aliyun is a distributed application environment, providing developers an environment to develop server-side applications rapidly, and simplify the system maintenance work. For developers, it can be logically divided into two parts. One is management system which is responsible for providing management interfaces and storing data. The other is running system that is responsible for calculating, serving as a middle-ware to transmitting data between client and database, which promises the data security for different users.

- For the client-side, Android applications will send a request to get data from sever or send data to the server to update databases. Users can search for any tourist attractions or grade for those they have been to.
- For the server-side, when the server receiving a request, it will handle it by either getting data from databases or updating data to databases.

There is a highlight in our development. It is a double recommendation systems.

- The outer recommendation system is a global one. It can offer the most popular scenic spots to all users.
- The inner one is a personalized recommendation system. It will recommend scenic spots to users based on their preference.

3.1 Get Data

Users can log in the App by inputting username and password. The terminal will send a URL [22] of the username to the server to get the corresponding

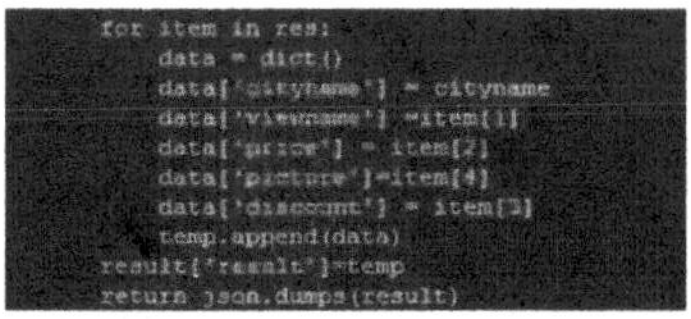

```
for item in res:
    data = dict()
    data['cityname'] = cityname
    data['viewname'] =item[1]
    data['price'] = item[2]
    data['picture']=item[4]
    data['discount'] = item[3]
    temp.append(data)
result['result']=temp
return json.dumps(result)
```

(a) The server returns the data in JSON format.

```
totalscore = viewscore*0.5 + foodscore*0.2 + servicescore*0.3
totalscore = str(totalscore)
con = Connect()
param = dict()
q1 = "lock table evaluate write"
r1 = Exec(con,q1,param)
para['totalscore'] = totalscore
query = "replace into evaluate values('%s','%s','%s',%f','%f','%f')
res = Exec(con,query,para)
q2 = "unlock tables"
r2 = Exec(con,q2,param)
```

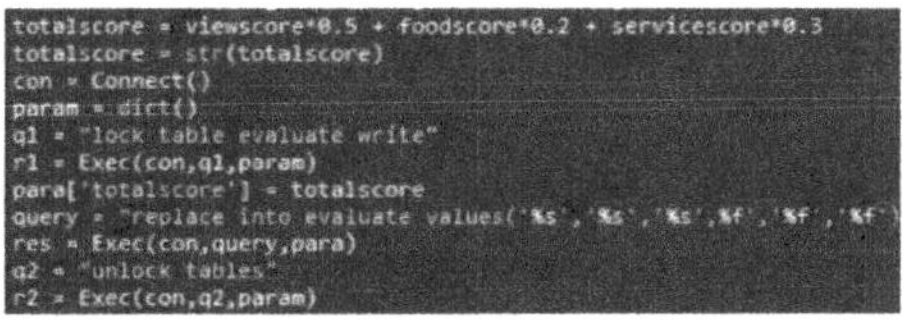

(b) The server returns the data in JSON format.

Fig. 2. Illustration of login.

password in the cloud and check whether the user can enter or not. After logging in successfully, the user will enter the searching interface. Using the name of city or attraction input by the user, the client packages URL and uploads it to the server, the server returns the result of all attractions searched in the database. Then the client receives data and parses the text information and pictures which will be displayed. Finally, in the list of results, user can click on appropriate spot, then it can jump to the details interface. The method of getting detailed information is the same as above.

The client is realized by JAVA language on Eclipse platform [18,23], it can get requests, set the connection timeout and read timeout settings, put the data on the URL and connect to the server. The server parses the URL string and extracts its data, through the JSON format statement it searches for the needed information and returns to the client as well as in JSON format [24,25], as is shown in Fig. 2(a).

3.2 Update Data

A function of this application is to grade a scenic spot if the user has already logged in and has been to this site. Score is divided into scenery score, food score and service score. After the user clicks the OK button, the client packages URL including the three scores, the name of view and username, and uploads it to the server. The server receives data and inserts it into the database by using the triggers [26] or update the data in the database if there exists the same item. Figure 2(b) illustrates the update of the score data.

3.3 Data Storage

The main function of our application is to search tourist information. Therefore one of the most significant components is data storage. Using cloud platform to store data is convenient and costless. A database with several tables satisfying different requests is created in our virtual machine by using MySQL. When there is a request to get view information, the database can be accessed easily [19].

3.4 Recommendation Algorithms

Our application development is based on the cloud platform from Ali and uses the Ubuntu System as server. In the server, we use MySQL to design database. To deal with HTTP request sent from Android client, we use Python as script language, which can also connect to database and retrieve data and then send back to client [27]. In our application, the key functions are two recommendation systems.

1. The first one is global recommendation system, which can be used before users log in the system. This option can provide all users scores of tourist attractions which are highly recommended by users who have been to them.
2. The second recommendation is particularly designed for certain users. When a user logs in his/her account and presses the menu button, the other hand-picked option will be presented to the user. For this option, we accomplished a personalized recommendation system to help users to find what they are really interested in.

Global Recommendation System. For a certain tourist attraction, we collect scores from users who have been to this place. The scores are divided into three parts, score for scenery, score for food and score for service. Three parts carry different weight in total scores. Scenery is the most importance, taking a percentage of 50, while food takes 20 percent and service takes 30 percent. We build the system based on all users' grading and take an average. After that we sort the average scores and pick out top five for all users. Global recommendation is not designed for a particular user so every one can reach the same view.

Personalized Recommendation System Based on Slope One. Slope one algorithm [28] is a kind of grading-based collaborative filtering algorithm. It is a simple algorithm in recommendation for it only needs a little bit of linear algebra without statistics involved. It is used to predict target users' grading for which are not done before according to any other users who have already graded. In slope one, what we need is a crowd of users, a group of views and some gradings by users who have been to the certain place. What we do is to recommend some places to a target client, which he may be interested in but has not graded yet. The algorithm consists of the following three steps [29]:

1. Calculate any two views' scores difference.
2. Input a user's ID, get his grading record and predict those not grading.
3. Sorted by grading and output top five views as what user is interested in.

4 Experiments

In this section, we will validate the proposed method. We test the performance of connection and data transmission between Android client and cloud server. For this purpose, we construct a database and make a simulation.

4.1 Data Description

We do some tests about the connection and data transmission between client and server. To this end, some data about tourism information are used in our experiments.

There are four tables in the database. The View table consists of information of all viewpoints. It contains 5 types of items including the name of city, the name of view, discounts for students, recommend score, and photo about the view. The student table contains information of all students including student ID and password after encrypting. Viewinfo, used to do recommendation, incorporates information of some viewpoints which have high recommend scores. The recommend score comes from the table Evaluate, which contains the scores of all students.

We test our schemes over these aspects:

1. whether the client can get the data from the server and send the data to the server successfully.
2. whether the data in the database has changed after being modified.
3. whether the slope-one algorithm works or not.

4.2 Results

Now the results of our experiments can be shown as follows:

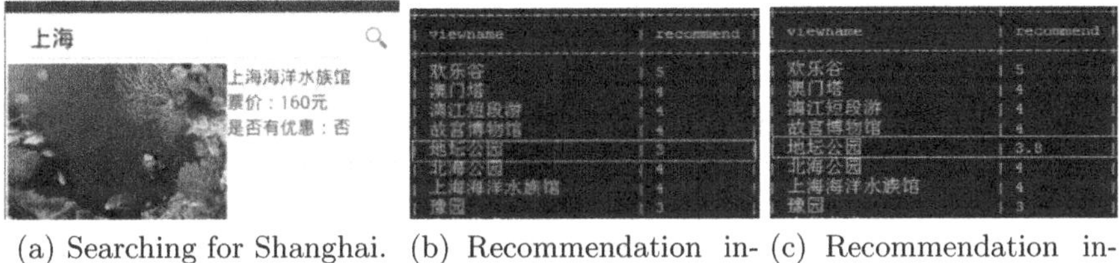

viewname	recommend
欢乐谷	5
澳门塔	4
漓江短段游	4
故宫博物馆	4
地坛公园	3
北海公园	4
上海海洋水族馆	4
豫园	3

viewname	recommend
欢乐谷	5
澳门塔	4
漓江短段游	4
故宫博物馆	4
地坛公园	3.8
北海公园	4
上海海洋水族馆	4
豫园	3

(a) Searching for Shanghai. (b) Recommendation index before scoring. (c) Recommendation index after scoring.

Fig. 3. Recommendation index when scoring.

Test of Login and Search. User can log in successfully when password is correct. From Fig. 3(a), we can get the sites given the name of the city. It proves that the method using in connection is correct.

Test of Grade and Recommendation. From Fig. 3(b), 3(c), it can be seen that in this test, after being graded, the score of this site has changed.

From Fig. 4(a), 4(b), the recommendations are different when the user has logged in, proving that the recommendation algorithm is useful.

(a) Recommendation before Login. (b) Recommendation after Login. (c) The password before modifying. (d) The password after modifying in database.

Fig. 4. Detail information.

Test of Modify the Password. It can be seen that in this test, the user can modify the password successfully. In Fig. 4(c) and 4(d), the password in the database will be changed if a user modifies the corresponding password.

From all results, the application can realize all the basic functions like connecting to the server, getting recommendations and modifying the database.

5 Conclusion

In this paper, we mainly introduce the development of our application based on cloud platform and implemented in Android client. We build database for our application in the cloud and it can be executed in the background; based on this database in cloud we can use an Android mobile-phone to run our application. Using the application, we can input the name of city or specific scenic sport we expect to visit and then get some information of tourist attractions. One novelty is that, our application is particularly designed for students particularly. As to the targeted users, a channel is built to check whether there is a discount for students. Moreover, each user will get some corresponding recommended attractions, which is implemented based on the slope one algorithm. Security is also guaranteed by verifying user's name and password.

In our future work, we want to implement more functions. Firstly it will have a function to provide a world map for users so they can mark where they have been to. Secondly, some information about our friends' wish list can be presented so that we can make a plan to travel with friends.

Acknowledgment. This work was supported by NSFC (61502543), CCF-Tencent Open Research Fund, and the PhD Start-up Fund of Natural Science Foundation of Guangdong Province, China (2014A030310180).

References

1. Zhang, Y.: Analyse the effective development of university students' tourist market. J. Inner Mongolia Agr. Univ. **4**(10), 105–106 (2008)
2. Qunar. http://app.qunar.com/
3. Ctrip. http://app.ctrip.com/
4. Umetrip. https://itunes.apple.com/cn/app/id480161784?mt=8
5. Zhang, L.: The survival and development prospect of China tourism internet, China Tourism Development, pp. 1–3 (2008)
6. Liu, F., Shu, P., Jin, H., Ding, L., Yu, J., Niu, D., Li, B.: Gearing resource-poor mobile devices with powerful clouds: architecture, challenges and applications. IEEE Wirel. Commun. **20**(3), 14–22 (2013)
7. Airbnb. https://itunes.apple.com/us/app/airbnb/id401626263?mt=8
8. Uber. https://itunes.apple.com/us/app/uber/id368677368?mt=8
9. HHtravel. http://www.hhtravel.com/
10. Lonely Planet Traveller. https://itunes.apple.com/us/app/lonely-planet-traveller/id563539341?mt=8
11. Ranking of the tourism Apps. http://www.ctcnn.com/html/2015-02-10/14628276.html
12. TongCheng. http://www.ly.com/
13. Aliyun. http://docs.aliyun.com/
14. Deng, R., Qin, C., Xie, X.: The application status of the mobile cloud computing and analysis of the existing problems. Chongqing Univ. Posts Telecommun. **6**(24), 716–723 (2012)
15. Zhang, W.: Scheme in transmission and storage security of user data on cloud computing, Beijing University of Posts and Telecommunications, pp. 4–71 (2011)
16. Kurose, J.F., Ross, K.W.: Computer Networking A Top-Down Approach, 4th edn. China Machine Press, Beijing (2014)
17. Hetland, M.L.: Beginning Python: From Novice to Professional, 2nd edn. The people's posts and telecommunications press, Beijing (2010)
18. Xu, Q., Wang, Z.: Application of cloud computing: the practice of developing (2012)
19. Wu, J., Ping, L., Ge, X., Wang, Y., Fu, J.: Cloud storage as the infrastructure of cloud computing. In: International Conference on Intelligent Computing and Cognitive Informatics (ICICCI), pp. 380–383 (2010)
20. JSON. http://www.json.org.cn/
21. SQL. http://www.w3school.com.cn/sql
22. Guo, H.: Android Application Development Comments. Electronic Industry Press, Beijing (2010)
23. Fengsheng, Y.: The reveal of Android application and development, pp. 130–200. Beijing: Mechanical Industry Press, Beijing (2010)
24. Smith, B.: Beginning JSON. Apress, New York (2015)
25. The Android use JSON format to transmit data. http://blog.csdn.net/lserein/article/details/6239460
26. Schwartz, B., Zaitsev, P., Tkachenko, V.: High Performance MySQL. Electronic Industry Press, Beijing (2013)
27. Fielding, R., Kaiser, G.: The Apache HTTP server project. IEEE Internet Comput. **1**(4), 88–90 (1997)
28. Wang, Y., Li'ang Yin, B.C., Yu, Y.: Learning to recommend based on slope one strategy. Web Technologies and Applications, pp. 537–544. Springer, Heidelberg (2012)
29. Lemire, D., Maclachlan, A.: Slope one predictors for online rating-based collaborative filtering. In: SDM, pp. 967–968 (2007)

Achieving Application-Level Utility Max-Min Fairness of Bandwidth Allocation in Datacenter Networks

Wangying Ye, Fei Xu(✉), and Wei Zhang

Shanghai Key Laboratory of Multidimensional Information Processing, Department of Computer Science and Technology, East China Normal University, Shanghai 200241, China
fxu@cs.ecnu.edu.cn

Abstract. Providing fair bandwidth allocation for applications is becoming increasingly compelling in cloud datacenters as different applications compete for shared datacenter network resources. Existing solutions mainly provide bandwidth guarantees for virtual machines (VMs) and achieve the fairness of VM bandwidth allocation. However, scant attention has been paid to application bandwidth guarantees for the *fairness of application performance*. In this paper, we introduce a rigorous definition of *application-level utility max-min fairness*, which guides us to develop a non-linear model to investigate the relationship between the fairness of application performance (utility) and the application bandwidth allocation. Based on Newton's method, we further design a simple yet effective algorithm to solve this problem, and evaluate its effectiveness with extensive experiments using OpenFlow in Mininet virtual network environment. Evaluation results show that our algorithm can achieve utility max-min fair share of bandwidth allocation for applications in datacenter networks, yet with an acceptable computational overhead.

Keywords: Bandwidth allocation · Max-min fairness · Application utility · Datacenter networking

1 Introduction

Cloud datacenters are increasingly hosting a variety of big data applications, *e.g.,* MapReduce, Spark, Dryad, transferring a large amount of data between servers [1]. Typically, such applications operate across dozens of servers and initiate a number of heavy network flows over the datacenter networks [2]. Meanwhile, network bandwidth oversubscription is not uncommon in modern datacenters, such as 40 : 1 in some Facebook datacenters [3], which inevitably leads to heavy contention for network resources of core switch bandwidth. Hence, providing fair bandwidth allocation for applications is becoming highly desirable, in order to guarantee the application performance in cloud datacenters [4].

S. Guo et al. (Eds.): CollaborateCom 2015, LNICST 163, pp. 36–46, 2016.
DOI: 10.1007/978-3-319-28910-6_4

However, the traditional TCP rate control mechanisms only provide the *flow-level* max-min fairness [5] or proportional fairness [6] in sharing network bandwidth for applications. Undoubtedly, a "selfish" big data application can request more bandwidth and break such *flow-level* fairness by arbitrarily initiating a number of TCP connections (*i.e.*, flows), thereby degrading the performance of other cloud applications. There have also been a number of works devoted to providing minimum bandwidth guarantees [7] for tenant virtual machines (VMs) and achieving the *VM-level* fairness [8] or *tenant-level* fairness [9]. Nevertheless, these solutions cannot provide the fairness of application performance (*e.g.*, completion time or throughput). Moreover, a number of existing bandwidth sharing solutions (*e.g.*, [8]) are based on the "ideal" *hose model*, where all VMs are connected to a non-blocking logical switch through dedicated network connections. As a result, there have been little attention paid to achieving the fairness of application performance and bandwidth allocation on *congested* switch links.

To solve the issues above, in this paper, we present a utility max-min fair bandwidth allocation algorithm for cloud applications in sharing datacenter network resources. Specifically, by presenting a rigorous definition of *application-level utility max-min fairness*, we develop a non-linear model to study the relationship between the fairness of application performance (utility) and bandwidth allocation of applications. Based on such analysis, we further develop a simple yet effective bandwidth allocation algorithm using Newton's method [10] and implement our algorithm in an OpenFlow [11] controller. Extensive experiment results demonstrate that our algorithm can reduce the variation of application performance (utility) by 5.8 % – 10.8 %, compared with the traditional TCP rate control mechanism and flow-level utility max-min fair allocation algorithm, thereby achieving utility max-min fairness of bandwidth allocation for applications in datacenter networks.

The rest of this paper is organized as follows. Section 2 presents a bandwidth allocation model to analyze the relationship between application bandwidth and the fairness of application utility (*i.e.*, performance), which enables the design of our application-level utility max-min fair bandwidth allocation algorithm. Section 3 evaluates the effectiveness and overhead of our algorithm. Section 4 discusses our contribution in the context of related work. Finally, we conclude this paper and discuss our future work in Sect. 5.

2 Achieving Application-Level Utility Max-Min Fairness of Bandwidth Allocation

In this section, we first present a model of *utility max-min fairness* of bandwidth allocation among cloud applications. Next, we devise a simple yet effective algorithm to achieve the application-level utility fairness of bandwidth allocation in datacenter networks.

2.1 Network Bandwidth Allocation Model for Applications

We consider the datacenter network with the representative tree topology, hosting a set of running applications, denoted by $\mathcal{N} = \{1, 2, \cdots, N\}$. Each application $i \in \mathcal{N}$ initiates a number of network flows, denoted by $\mathcal{F}_i = \{1, 2, \cdots, m_i\}$. Each flow is denoted by a two-tuple (i, f), representing that the flow is the f-ordered in $\mathcal{F}_i$. We use a binary variable $h^l_{i,f}$ to denote whether the flow (i, f) of an application i passes through the link l. We also use C_l and $\alpha_{i,f}$ to denote the bandwidth capacity of a network link l and the bandwidth allocated to a flow (i, f), respectively.

$$h^l_{i,f} = \begin{cases} 1, & \text{the flow } (i, f) \text{ passes through the link } l \\ 0, & \text{otherwise} \end{cases}$$

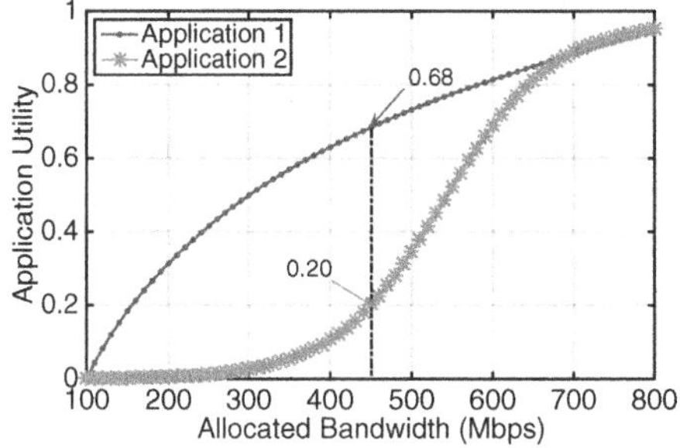

Fig. 1. Application utility: the application performance achieved by allocating different amount of network bandwidth.

Typically, the datacenter is hosting various types of workloads, ranging from CPU-intensive, data-intensive, to latency-sensitive applications. Different applications are able to achieve *different performance* when allocated the *same amount of network bandwidth*. As shown in Fig. 1, application 1 is able to achieve better application utility (*i.e.*, performance) than application 2, when allocated the same bandwidth of 450 Mbps. In this paper, we use *application utility* to measure the application performance according to the allocated network bandwidth. Specifically, with a particular focus on big data applications, we leverage the log function to formulate the application utility (*i.e.*, *utility function* [12] $f_i(\cdot)$ of an application i) as below,

$$f_i(\alpha_i) = \log_{r_i} \alpha_i, \tag{1}$$

where α_i denotes the network bandwidth allocated to the application i, and r_i denotes the bandwidth demand of the application i, which is limited by the bandwidth capacity C_l and the aggregated bandwidth demand $r_{i,f}$ of application flows. Accordingly, we have $r_i = \min(\sum_f r_{i,f}, C_l)$. Similarly, we formulate the *flow utility* [13] (utility function $f_{i,f}(\cdot)$ of an application flow (i, f)) as $f_{i,f}(\alpha_{i,f}) = \log_{r_{i,f}} \alpha_{i,f}$, where $r_{i,f}$ is the bandwidth demand of the flow (i, f).

Table 1. Key notations in our bandwidth allocation model.

Notation	Definition
$\mathcal{N}$	Set of applications in the datacenter
$\mathcal{N}_l$	Application set running on a link l
$\mathcal{F}_i$	Network flow set of an application i
$\mathcal{L}$	Set of links that host application flows in the network
r_i	Bandwidth demand of an application i
$r_{i,f}$	Bandwidth demand of a flow f of an application i
α_i	Bandwidth allocated to an application i
$\alpha_{i,f}$	Bandwidth allocated to a flow f of an application i
t_i	Bandwidth temporarily allocated to an application i
$t_{i,f}$	Bandwidth temporarily allocated to a flow f of an application i
C_l	Bandwidth capacity of a link l
$h^l_{i,f}$	Whether the flow f of an application i passes through the link l
$f_i(\cdot)$	Bandwidth utility function of an application i

Using the notations of application utility defined in Eq. (1), we proceed to define the *application-level utility max-min fairness* of the bandwidth allocation for different cloud applications running on a *congested* network link.

Definition 1. Application-level Utility Max-min Fairness: Given a feasible application bandwidth allocation vector $\mathbf{a} = (\alpha_1, \alpha_2, \cdots, \alpha_n)$, the utility-ordered application bandwidth allocation vector is $\overline{\mathbf{a}} = (\alpha_{r_1}, \alpha_{r_2}, \cdots, \alpha_{r_n})$, such that $f_{r_k}(\alpha_{r_k}) \leq f_{r_{k+1}}(\alpha_{r_{k+1}})$, $\forall k \in [1, n-1]$. An application-level utility max-min fair allocation vector is the largest feasible utility-ordered vector in the network bandwidth allocation space.

In particular, given two feasible utility-ordered vectors $\overline{\mathbf{a}_i} = (\alpha_{i_1}, \alpha_{i_2}, \cdots, \alpha_{i_n})$ and $\overline{\mathbf{a}_j} = (\alpha_{j_1}, \alpha_{j_2}, \cdots, \alpha_{j_n})$, we say $\overline{\mathbf{a}_i} > \overline{\mathbf{a}_j}$ if and only if there exists m such that $f_{i_k}(\alpha_{i_k}) = f_{j_k}(\alpha_{j_k})$, $\forall k \in [1, m)$, and $f_{i_l}(\alpha_{i_l}) > f_{j_l}(\alpha_{j_l})$, $\forall l \in [m, n]$. The important notations used in our model are summarized in Table 1.

Based on Definition 1, in order to achieve the application-level utility max-min fairness of bandwidth allocation on a *congested* link l (*i.e.*, the sum of application bandwidth demand exceeds the network link capacity), we formulate the application bandwidth allocation problem as below,

$$\begin{cases} f_i(\alpha_i) - f_j(\alpha_j) = 0, & \forall i, j \in \mathcal{N}_l \\ \sum_{i \in \mathcal{N}_l} \alpha_i - C_l = 0, & \end{cases} \tag{2}$$

In addition, we use a vector $\mathbf{a}$ to denote the bandwidth allocation set (α_i, $\forall i \in \mathcal{N}_l$), and $\mathbf{G}(\cdot)$ to denote the left parts of the equation arrays formulated above. As a result, the model we formulated in Eq. (2) can be simplified as

$$\mathbf{G}(\mathbf{a}) = \mathbf{0} \tag{3}$$

Remark 1. The bandwidth allocation problem formulated above is a *non-linear* model, which is difficult and time-consuming to solve. As our objective is to allocate network bandwidth for applications without bringing much computational overhead, we seek to design a heuristic algorithm that can be implemented in a real-world datacenter. In particular, if a network link l is not a *congested* link (*i.e.,* the sum of application bandwidth demand is less than the bandwidth capacity of the link l), the demands of application flows passing through this link can be satisfied directly.

2.2 Bandwidth Allocation Algorithm for Achieving Application-Level Utility Max-Min Fairness

As we have analyzed in Sect. 2.1, the bandwidth allocation problem formulated in Eq. (2) is hard to solve in polynomial time. To allocate the network bandwidth for applications in practice, we design a simple yet effective algorithm in Algorithm 1 to achieve application-level utility max-min fairness based on Newton's method [10]. The detailed procedure of our algorithm is elaborated as follows.

Consider a set of applications $\mathcal{N}$ with the bandwidth demand of network flows $r_{i,f}$ running on the datacenter links $\mathcal{L}$. For each *congested* network link l in the datacenter, Algorithm 1 first initializes several algorithm parameters, such as the iterator k. Using Newton iteration method [10], Algorithm 1 then calculates the temporary bandwidth allocation $t_{i,f}$ of network flows running on the link l. Specifically, for each iteration k, the temporary bandwidth allocation vector $\mathbf{t}^{(k)} = (t_1, t_2, \cdots, t_{N_l})$ for applications running on a link l is obtained by

$$\mathbf{t}^{(k)} = \mathbf{t}^{(k-1)} - \mathbf{A}_k \mathbf{G}(\mathbf{t}^{(k-1)}), \tag{4}$$

where $\mathbf{A}_k$ is a matrix used in Newton's method [10] that avoids the inverse calculation of the matrix $\mathbf{G}(\mathbf{t})$, and $\mathbf{G}'(\mathbf{t})$ is the Jacobian matrix of $\mathbf{G}(\mathbf{t})$. They can be calculated by Eqs. (5) and (7), respectively.

$$\mathbf{A}_k = 2\mathbf{A}_{k-1} - \mathbf{A}_{k-1}\mathbf{G}'(\mathbf{t}^{(k)})\mathbf{A}_{k-1}, \tag{5}$$

$$\mathbf{A}_0 = \mathbf{G}'(\mathbf{t}^{(0)})^{-1}, \tag{6}$$

$$\mathbf{G}'(\mathbf{t}) = \begin{pmatrix} \frac{\partial f_1}{\partial t_1} & \frac{\partial f_2}{\partial t_2} & 0 & \cdots & 0 \\ \frac{\partial f_1}{\partial t_1} & 0 & \frac{\partial f_3}{\partial t_3} & \cdots & 0 \\ \vdots & & & & \\ \frac{\partial f_1}{\partial t_1} & 0 & 0 & \cdots & \frac{\partial f_{N_l}}{\partial t_{N_l}} \\ 1 & 1 & 1 & \cdots & 1 \end{pmatrix}. \tag{7}$$

Algorithm 1. Achieving utility max-min fairness of bandwidth allocation among applications

Input: Application set $\mathcal{N}$, network link set $\mathcal{L}$, the relationship between flows and links $h_{i,f}^{l}$, the flow bandwidth demand $r_{i,f}$.
Output: Network bandwidth allocation for the application set $\mathcal{N}$.
while exists unallocated application flows ($\mathcal{N} \neq \varnothing$) **do**
  for all *congested* link $l \in \mathcal{L}$ **do**
    Initialize $k \leftarrow 0$, $\mathbf{t}^{(0)} \leftarrow$ the output of *binary search* algorithm, $\mathbf{A}_0 \leftarrow$ Eq. (6);
    Identify the application flows (i, f) on the link l (*i.e.*, $h_{i,f}^{l} \equiv 1$);
    while $k \leq T$ &&$\left\|\mathbf{t}^{(k)} - \mathbf{t}^{(k-1)}\right\|_1 > \delta$ **do**
      $\mathbf{t}^{(k)} \leftarrow$ Eq. (4); $\mathbf{A}_k \leftarrow$ Eq. (5); $k++$;
    end while
    $t_{i,f} \leftarrow$ Eq. (8);
  end for
  Identify the flow $(i, f)_{\min}$ with the minimum utility $f_{i,f}(t_{i,f})$;
  Allocate the minimum temporary bandwidth along the flow path $l \in \mathcal{L}$ to the flow $(i, f)_{\min}$, *i.e.*, $\alpha_{i,f} = \min(t_{i,f})$;
  if all the flows of an application i have been allocated bandwidth **then**
    Remove the application i from the application set $\mathcal{N}$;
  end if
end while
return the bandwidth $\alpha_{i,f}$ allocated to network flows of applications.

The iteration terminates in two conditions: (1) The iteration exceeds a maximum T. (2) The difference of iteration outputs $\mathbf{t}$ (*i.e.*, the first order norm of $\mathbf{t}^{(k)} - \mathbf{t}^{(k-1)}$) is less than a small value δ. In proportional to the bandwidth demand of network flows on the link l, the temporary bandwidth allocation $t_{i,f}$ is given by

$$t_{i,f} = t_i \cdot \frac{r_{i,f}}{\sum_{f \in \mathcal{F}_i} r_{i,f} h_{i,f}^{l}} \tag{8}$$

Finally, to achieve the application-level utility max-min fairness in Definition 1, Algorithm 1 identifies the flow $(i, f)_{\min}$ with the minimum flow utility and allocates the minimum temporary bandwidth $\min(t_{i,f})$ along the flow path to the flow $(i, f)_{\min}$. An application i requires to be removed from the set $\mathcal{N}$, if all its application flows have been allocated bandwidth. In particular, Algorithm 1 iteratively executes the procedure above until all the application flows are allocated network bandwidth.

Remark 2. First, Algorithm 1 can be periodically executed in the case that (1) new applications are running in the datacenter, and (2) the bandwidth demand of application flows has been changed. The algorithm execution period can be adjusted by the datacenter operator, ranging from several minutes to one hour. *Second,* given the detailed notations in Table 1, the complexity of Algorithm 1 is in the order of $\mathcal{O}(|\mathcal{N}| \cdot |\mathcal{L}|)$. In practice, the *congested* links are mainly restricted to the top-layered links in the tree topology [14], and accordingly, Algorithm 1 only requires running on the top-layered links to obtain the bandwidth allocation of application flows. *Third*, Algorithm 1 can be implemented in an OpenFlow controller, such as Ryu[1] and OpenDaylight[2]. After calculating the bandwidth allocation for application flows by Algorithm 1, the application bandwidth can be limited by setting the `meter table` in the OpenFlow v1.3 switches.

3 Experimental Evaluation

In this section, we evaluate the effectiveness and computational overhead of our bandwidth allocation algorithm in the context of application utility, algorithm running time and underutilized network bandwidth. We compare the evaluation results of our algorithm with that of the conventional TCP rate control mechanism and flow-level utility max-min fair allocation in large-scale simulations.

Experimental Setup. We set up a datacenter network with the representative tree topology in Mininet v2.1.0+[3] virtual network environment, by varying the network scale from 100 switches to 800 switches. We use the iPerf application[4] to generate the different network flows for 10 running applications. Each flow is randomly set in the range of [1, 100] Mbps. We implement our algorithm with Ryu v3.9 OpenFlow controller and OpenFlow 1.3 Software Switch[5].

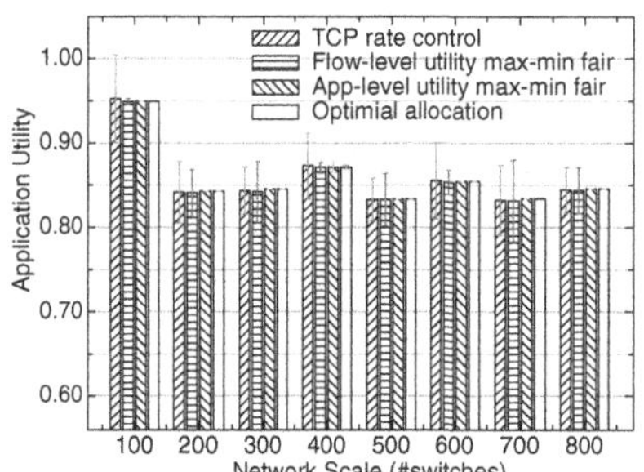

Fig. 2. Application utility achieved by different bandwidth allocation algorithms.

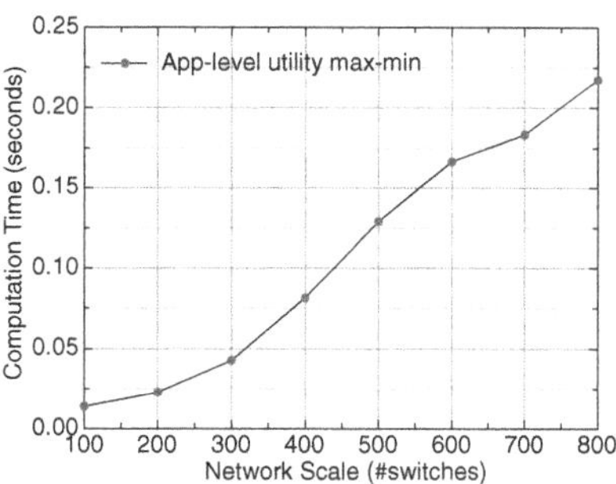

Fig. 3. Computation time of our bandwidth allocation algorithm.

Effectiveness and Computational Overhead. To examine the effectiveness of our bandwidth allocation algorithm, Fig. 2 compares the application utility achieved by three different algorithms. We observe that our application-level utility fair allocation algorithm significantly reduces the variation (*i.e.*, unfairness)

[1] http://osrg.github.io/ryu/.
[2] https://www.opendaylight.org.
[3] http://mininet.org.
[4] https://iperf.fr.
[5] http://cpqd.github.io/ofsoftswitch13/.

of application utility by 5.8 % – 10.8 %, compared with TCP rate control and flow-level utility max-min fair allocation algorithms, though the average application utility is comparable among different algorithms for each network scale. The rationale is that, our algorithm allocates the network bandwidth based on the aggregated flows of each application, and achieves utility max-min fairness for applications on congested links to circumvent the unfairness of application performance. Moreover, our algorithm achieves the application utility close to the optimal allocation, yet with a rough linear computational overhead of the number of network switches, as shown in Fig. 3. Such an overhead is consistent with the complexity analysis of our algorithm in Sect. 2.2. Specifically, the complexity of Algorithm 1 is reduced to $\mathcal{O}(|\mathcal{L}|)$ as the number of applications is a constant ($|\mathcal{N}| = 10$) in our experiment. In particular, the algorithm running time is within 0.25 s as the network scale increases to 800 switches.

We next examine the underutilized network bandwidth achieved by our bandwidth allocation algorithm. As shown in Table 2, the link bandwidth of datacenter networks is not efficiently utilized, *i.e.*, the total underutilized bandwidth of our algorithm is ranging from 132 to 938 Gbps as the number of network switches increases from 100 to 800. As a result, our algorithm achieves the application-level utility max-min fairness of bandwidth allocation *at the cost of* underutilizing the network resources. We illustrate this tradeoff by considering an example shown in Fig. 4, in which application A has two flows from A1 to A3 and A2 to A3, and application B has two flows from B1 to B3 and B2 to B3. Each flow has the same bandwidth demand 100 Mbps. All the links have the same bandwidth capacity 100 Mbps. Assume two applications have the same utility function. Our algorithm allocates 25 Mbps to the flows (A1, A3) and (A2, A3) and allocates 50 Mbps to the flow (B1, B3) on the congested link (S1, S2). The flow (B2, B3) is allocated 50 Mbps on the link (S1, S5). Hence, the underutilized bandwidth of network links between switches is summed up to 100 Mbps with our algorithm, which accounts for 25 % of switch bandwidth resources in the datacenter.

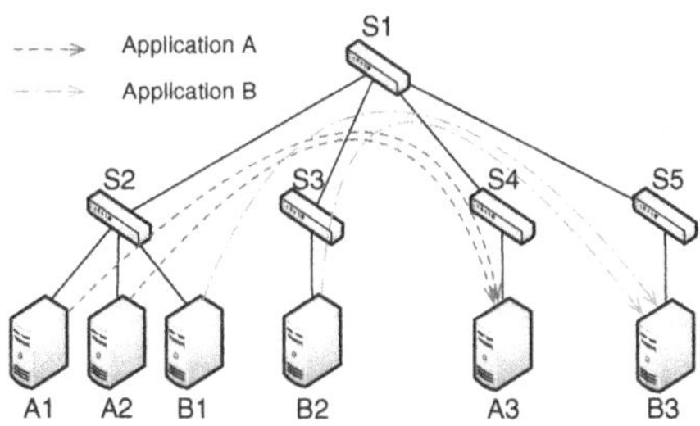

Fig. 4. Bandwidth allocation of two applications in an example tree topology.

Table 2. Underutilized network bandwidth achieved by our bandwidth allocation algorithm.

Scale (#switches)	Underutilized bandwidth
100	132 Gbps
200	214 Gpbs
300	331 Gbps
400	448 Gbps
500	692 Gbps
600	782 Gbps
700	808 Gbps
800	938 Gbps

4 Related Work

There have been a number of works on flow bandwidth allocation in traditional networks, with the aim of achieving max-min fairness [5], utility max-min fairness [13] and proportional fairness [6]. Several works have paid much attention to the *flow-level* utility. For example, Wang *et al.* [15] proposed an algorithm for guaranteeing the Quality of Service (QoS) of applications based on the flow-level utility. However, these works only provide the *flow-level* QoS and fairness, which is likely to impact the performance and fairness of applications with a number of network flows. Furthermore, the utility function of big data applications is quite different from that of the applications running in traditional networks.

With the evolution of datacenters, virtualization technique has been widely deployed to multiplex resources (*e.g.,* computing and bandwidth resources) and improve the utilization of servers. Recently, there have emerged a number of works that focus on providing bandwidth guarantees for tenant VMs in public clouds, such as deterministic guarantees [16], minimum guarantees [7], and proportional bandwidth share [9]. For example, Lam *et al.* [9] focused on achieving the tenant-level fairness of bandwidth allocation, while Shieh *et al.* [17] proposed a fair bandwidth share on the source VMs. Popa *et al.* [8] allocated bandwidth to achieve VM-pair level fairness. To cope with highly dynamic network traffic in datacenters, Guo *et al.* [18] proposed an efficient rate allocation algorithm to achieve both minimum guarantees and VM-pair level fairness. Different from these works, our work aims to achieve the *utility* max-min fairness among applications, in order to provide *performance guarantees* for cloud applications, while prior works provide bandwidth guarantees and achieve fairness at the tenant level or VM level. Moreover, prior works mainly implement the rate limiter on the Hypervisor [18], while our work makes an attempt to limit the bandwidth of network flows on the OpenFlow switches.

To provide application-level bandwidth guarantees, Kumar *et al.* [19] proposed to allocate bandwidth based on the communication patterns of big data applications, while Lee *et al.* [20] designed a VM placement algorithm to satisfy the bandwidth requirements of workloads. Chen *et al.* [21] presented a definition of performance-centric fairness and designed a bandwidth allocation strategy to achieve such fairness among applications. Different from prior works, our work defines the *application utility* to reflect the performance of various applications and achieves *utility max-min fairness* of bandwidth allocation, while [21] uses the reciprocal of the data transfer time to represent the application performance.

5 Conclusion and Future Work

To achieve the fairness of application performance, this paper proposes a rigorous definition of application-level utility max-min fairness, and design the utility fair bandwidth allocation algorithm that can be practically implemented in a real-world OpenFlow controller. Extensive experiment results using OpenFlow show that our bandwidth allocation algorithm can reduce the variation of application utility by 5.8 % – 10.8 % and achieve utility max-min fairness of bandwidth allocation for applications, in comparison to the conventional TCP rate control mechanism and flow-level utility max-min fair allocation algorithm.

As our future work, we plan to investigate the tradeoff between high utilization and utility max-min fairness of bandwidth allocation for applications. We also plan to deploy our bandwidth allocation algorithm in real OpenFlow switches and evaluate its effectiveness and running overhead.

Acknowledgments. The research was supported by a grant from the National Natural Science Foundation of China (NSFC) under grant No.61502172, and by a grant from the Science and Technology Commission of Shanghai Municipality under grant No.14DZ2260800. The corresponding author is Fei Xu.

References

1. Dean, J., Ghemawat, S.: MapReduce: simplified data processing on large clusters. ACM Commun. **51**(1), 107–113 (2008)
2. Yi, X., Liu, F., Liu, J., Jin, H.: Building a network highway for big data: architecture and challenges. IEEE Netw. Mag. **28**(4), 5–13 (2014)
3. Roy, A., Zeng, H., Bagga, J., Porter, G., Snoeren, A.C.: Inside the social network's (datacenter) network. In: Proceedings of SIGCOMM, pp. 123–137, August 2015
4. Xu, F., Liu, F., Jin, H., Vasilakos, A.V.: Managing performance overhead of virtual machines in cloud computing: a survey, state of art and future directions. Proc. IEEE **102**(1), 11–31 (2014)
5. Bertsekas, D.P., Gallager, R.G.: Data Network, 2nd edn. Prentice-Hall, London (1992)
6. Kelly, F.P., Maulloo, A.K., Tan, D.K.H.: Rate control for communication networks: shadow price, proportional fairness and stability. J. Oper. Res. Soc. **49**(3), 237–252 (1998)
7. Guo, J., Liu, F., Tang, H., Lian, Y., Jin, H., Lui, J.: Falloc: fair network bandwidth allocation in iaas datacenters via a bargaining game approach. In: Proceedings of ICNP, pp. 1–10, October 2013
8. Popa, L., Kumar, G., Chowdhury, M., Krishnamurthy, A., Ratnasamy, S., Stoica, I.: FairCloud: sharing the network in cloud computing. In: Proceedings of SIGCOMM, pp. 187–198, August 2012
9. Lam, T., Radhakrishnan, S., Vahdat, A., Varghese, G.: Netshare: Virtualizing Data Center Networks across Services. Technical Report CS2010-0957, Department of Computer Science and Engineering, University of California, San Diego (2010)
10. Wang, X.H., Han, D.F., Sun, F.Y.: Point estimates on deformation newton's iterations. Mathematica Numerica Sinica **1**(2), 145–156 (1990)
11. McKeown, N., Anderson, T., Balakrishnan, H., Parulkar, G., Peterson, L., Rexford, J., Shenker, S., Turner, J.: OpenFlow: enabling innovation in campus networks. ACM SIGCOMM Comput. Commun. Rev. **38**(2), 69–74 (2008)
12. Shenker, S.: Fundamental design issues for the future internet. IEEE J. Sel. Areas Commun. **13**(7), 1176–1187 (1995)
13. Cao, Z., Zegura, E.: Utility max-min: an application-oriented allocation scheme. In: Proceedings of Infocom, pp. 793–801, April 1999

14. Al-Fares, M., Loukissas, A., Vahdat, A.: A scalable, commodity data center network architecture. ACM SIGCOMM Comput. Commun. Rev. **38**(4), 63–74 (2008)
15. Wang, W., Palaniswami, M., Low, S.: Application-oriented flow control fundamentals algorithms and fairness. IEEE/ACM Trans. Netw. **14**(6), 1282–1291 (2006)
16. Ballani, H., Costa, P., Karagiannis, T., Rowstron, A.: Towards predictable datacenter networks. ACM SIGCOMM Comput. Commun. Rev. **41**(4), 242–253 (2011)
17. Shieh, A., Kandula, S., Greenberg, A., Kim, C., Saha, B.: Sharing the data center network. In: Proceedings of NSDI, pp. 309–322, March 2011
18. Guo, J., Liu, F., Huang, X., Lui, J., Hu, M., Gao, Q., Jin, H.: On efficient bandwidth allocation for traffic variability in datacenters. In: Proceedings of Infocom, pp. 1572–1580, April 2014
19. Kumar, G., Chowdhury, M., Ratnasamy, S., Stoica, I.: A case for performance-centric network allocation. In: Proceedings of HotCloud, pp. 9–9, June 2012
20. Lee, J., Turner, Y., Lee, M., Popa, L., Banerjee, S., Kang, J.M., Sharma, P.: Application-driven bandwidth guarantees in datacenters. In: Proceedings of SIGCOMM, pp. 467–478, August 2014
21. Chen, L., Feng, Y., Li, B., Li, B.: Towards performance-centric fairness in datacenter networks. In: Proceedings of Infocom, pp. 1599–1607, April 2014

Cost-Effective Service Provisioning for Hybrid Cloud Applications

Bin Luo, Yipei Niu, and Fangming Liu(✉)

Key Laboratory of Services Computing Technology and System,
School of Computer Science and Technology,
Huazhong University of Science and Technology, Wuhan, China
fmliu@hust.edu.cn

Abstract. A hybrid cloud, which combines a private cloud and a public cloud, has become more and more popular. For most corporations, they leverage one public cloud. However, with fierce competition among public cloud providers, public cloud services change frequently, which may lead to service unavailability and a less cost-effective hybrid cloud solution. As a result, leveraging multiple public clouds in the hybrid cloud is a potential solution. In this paper, we identify such a problem in current hybrid cloud and analyze the necessity of load balancing for hybrid cloud applications. Focusing on cost minimization and performance guarantee, we propose a Least Cost per Connection (LCC) algorithm so as to choose the most cost-effective clouds along with adapting changes among multiple public clouds. The simulation results show that our solution can significantly decrease the outsourcing cost as well as guarantee QoS of applications.

Keywords: Hybrid cloud · Multi-cloud · Cost-effective

1 Introduction

A hybrid cloud, which combines a private cloud and a public cloud, has become more and more popular. The state of the cloud report from RightScale points out that, among all the enterprise respondents, 55 % of them expect to use hybrid clouds [1].

However, for most corporations, they deploy their applications on single public cloud. First, cloud computing platforms sometime breakdown and update bug, which may influence their business. Second, cloud providers offer discount to attract users and occupy cloud computing market. For example, the price of AWS drops 12 times in 2013 while Google Compute Engine [2] made a cumulative reduction of 38 % in prices from January to October in 2014. When the price drops, deploying applications in single cloud makes it difficult to switch to other providers for lower price. Third, since more corporations join in the cloud

F. Liu—The research was supported by a grant from The National Natural Science Foundation of China (NSFC) under grant No. 61520106005.

S. Guo et al. (Eds.): CollaborateCom 2015, LNICST 163, pp. 47–56, 2016.
DOI: 10.1007/978-3-319-28910-6_5

market, cloud users are willing to avoid provider lock-in. As a result, deploying applications in multiple public clouds can contribute to obtaining a more cost-effective and stable hybrid cloud solution.

When leveraging multiple public clouds, we face the following challenges. First, since cloud users can leverage multiple clouds, it is challenging to distribute workloads among private and public clouds so as to obtain a cost-effective solution. Second, as cloud computing platforms sometime breakdown or update, it may lead to service unavailability or performance degradation. Such maintenance makes it more difficult to derive a cost-effective solution. Third, cloud computing price changes with time. Cloud users always want to use the most cost-effective cloud products. Deploying applications on unsuitable cloud products may cost more money and make applications inefficient.

To address these problems, we propose a cost-effective service for hybrid cloud applications, which selects the best public cloud for out-sourcing and adapts cloud price changes dynamically, along with provisioning global load balancing. The system uses a two-tier load balancing mechanism, provisioning virtual machine (VM) and cloud level load balancing. The system firstly chooses the best instance on each cloud for certain applications using CloudCmp [5] tools. Then the system uses the proposed Least Connection per Cost (LCC) algorithm to distribute job requests among public clouds. At last, the system scales up or down automatically according to the price and performance of each cloud.

The remainder of this paper is organized as follows. In Sect. 2, we introduce the system architecture and design objectives. Section 3 provides detailed description of implementation principles and proposes LCC job scheduling algorithm. Section 4 introduces a series of simulation experiments to test our system functions and performance. Section 5 provides an overview of related work. Finally, we conclude our paper and provide future works in Sect. 6.

2 Design Objectives

This system is designed to help the hybrid cloud users provision cost-effective services, especially for those who deploy multiple public clouds. Based on the fact that different types of applications require different computing resources, we classify all the applications into three representative types roughly:

* *CPU-intensive application.* In these applications, CPU resource is more eagerly needed than other computing resource. For example video processing, scientific computing and so on.
* *Memory-intensive application.* High IO throughput application such as large Map-Reduce tasks which depend on sufficient memory for data shuffling.
* *Disk-intensive application.* NoSQL database (e.g., Cassandra, MongoDB) or Distributed File System (e.g., HDFS) have high demand on storage.

Our design prefers processing workloads in the private cloud, and outsources excessive workloads to the public clouds. Since prices and performance of public clouds vary from cloud providers, we need to maintain high quality services as

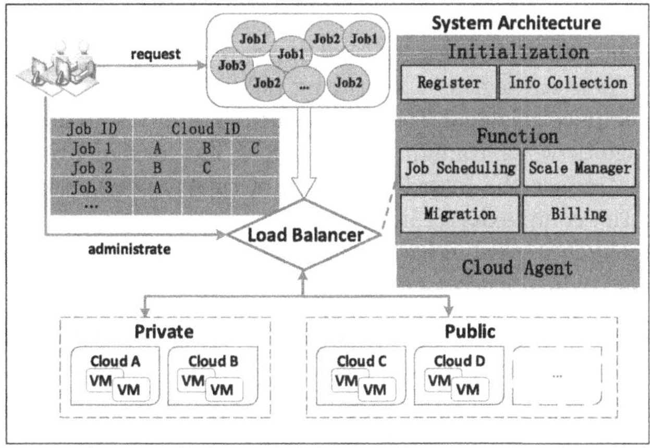

Fig. 1. Overview of load balance system design for a hybrid cloud.

well as save cost. Before the load balance system start working, we select the most suitable type of instances on each cloud in advance for the application. Since Li *et al.* [5] compare VMs of multiple cloud providers so as to find out which are the most suitable.

Figure 1 shows an overview of load balance system design for hybrid cloud applications. First, cloud users need to register their applications on the load balancer with a unique application id and provide detailed information of requested resource. Second, through administrating an application-cloud mapping table, the system selectively adds a private cloud and public clouds for certain applications.We deploy the application with cloud agent and generate a virtual machine template on the most suitable instance type. Cloud agent starts to collect and feedback the cloud load information to load balancer periodically.

The load balancer receives feedbacks and updates the priority of each cloud based on our load balance algorithm. Here the cycle length depends on the job requests arrival frequency. When the load balancer receives a batch of job requests, it checks the priority of each cloud and dispatches the job requests to the most cost-effective clouds.

Cost-Effective. Due to the unpredictable workloads, it's hard for a private cloud to predict an exact amount of hardware resources. As such, the private cloud is not capable of processing such immense workloads, and the public clouds can satisfy the requirements of high capacity and scalability. Considering the variety of cloud providers, users want to add or remove a cloud for their applications freely. When users deploy their applications on multiple clouds, how to choose the most cost-effective clouds becomes a critical problem.

In this paper, how much a job request costs is taken as the measurement of cost-effectiveness (CE ratio for short). For example, if the price of a VM of a cloud provider is P, and the VM can process N job requests per second, the CE ratio equals $\frac{P}{N}$. The number N is hard to figure out through calculation, so we use measurement tools of Cloudcmp to monitor it.

Flexibility. With rapid development of cloud computing market, services provisioned by public cloud providers change quite frequently. As such, cloud users need to change their strategies of leveraging public clouds.

In order to achieve this goal, the design of the system is guided by the asynchronous message-driven paradigm through RESTful design principle. We use RESTful API to reduce the interdependency of tightly coupled interfaces, generally lowering the complexity of integration.

Specifically, the System allows cloud users to choose on which clouds to deploy their applications, which leads to a many-to-many relationship.

Global Load Balance. Users' applications are deployed on multiple clouds. As such, we need to ensure global load balancing, so as to provision cost-effective services and make the best use of cloud resources we've bought.

Since load information collected from other clouds is transmitted via the Internet, the transmit latency must be low. We use short TCP connections for immediate reinforcement. To reduce the number of messages, we abstract a cloud as an unit to distribute workloads among clouds. For load balancing among VMs, each cloud can address it. The low-level quality of service is guaranteed by the service level agreement of cloud providers.

3 System Model

In this section we specifically describe how this system scheduling jobs and leveraging the auto scaling service for resource reallocation.

Job Scheduling and Resource Allocation Decoupling. Job scheduling and resource allocation are the two main tasks of load balancing. Job scheduling is highly required on bandwidth delay, while resource allocation is closely related to cost. Based on the characteristics of two different tasks, we discrete the job scheduling module and resource management module from logic view. Specifically, the job scheduling module only takes responsibility of receiving and dispatching job requests while resource allocation module takes charge of monitoring the cloud resource usage and decides on when to scale up or down.

Cloud-Level Load Balancing and VM-level Load Balancing Decoupling. In our system, we adopt a two-level hierarchical load balancing architecture, i.e., a cloud level and a VM level. On the cloud level, we take the cloud as an unit of scheduling object as shown in Fig. 1. On the VM level, we use cloud back-end load balancing services for job distribution among VMs. Almost all the public cloud providers provision load balancing services within their clouds. For example, Openstack [6] integrates LBaaS (Load-Balancing-as-a-Service) into Neutron component. LBaaS allows cloud users to scale their applications, detect unhealthy VM instances, balance loads across regions, route traffic to the closest VM and so on.

Centralized Management. Cloud agent is used to sent cloud information back to the load balancer. We add a heartbeat mechanism to report the cloud health status periodically.

3.1 Algorithm

Cloud Ability Measurement. Here we consider two sets of cloud resources, i.e., PUB and PRI. Let PUB be the set of public clouds, which is denoted as $\{u_1, u_2, ..., u_m\}$. Moreover, let PRI be the set of the private cloud, which is denoted as $\{r_1, r_2, ..., r_n\}$. Furthermore, we set the resource parameters{cpu, mem, disk, net}.

$$M_i(t) = \min\{\frac{\lambda_i^{CPU}(t)}{d_i^{CPU}}, \frac{\lambda_i^{MEM}(t)}{d_i^{MEM}}, \frac{\lambda_i^{DISK}(t)}{d_i^{DISK}}, \frac{\lambda_i^{NET}(t)}{d_i^{NET}}\} \tag{1}$$

Eq. (1) figures out the job request service rate of each VM in a cloud.

Job Scheduling. We denote the current number of connections on each cloud as $C_i(t)$. And the price of selected instance on each cloud is denoted by $P_i(t)$. Furthermore, the value of priority of each cloud is denoted as $\eta_i(t)$.

$$\eta_i(t) = \frac{M_i(t) - C_i(t)}{P_i(t)} \tag{2}$$

Algorithm 1. Least Connection-Cost Ratio Scheduling (LCC)

```
Denote (key,index) as cloud type and cloud ID
for each time slot t ∈ [0, 1, 2, ...] do
  key = 0
  for each cloud r_i ∈ PRI do
    if r_i is not alarmed then
      set key = 1
      calculate cloud priority η_i
    end if
  end for
  set index the private cloud ID with max priority
  for each cloud u_i ∈ PUB do
    if u_i is not alarmed then
      calculate cloud priority η_i
    end if
  end for
  set index the public cloud ID with max priority
  for each job J_i(t) ∈ [J_1(t), J_2(t), ... do
    if key Equals 0 then
      Dispatch the job J_i(t) to cloud u_index
    else
      Dispatch the job J_i(t) to cloud r_index
    end if
  end for
end for
```

We sort the priority obtained based on Eq. (2) of each cloud, and record the priority list in configuration files. When a job request arrives, the load balancer will select the cloud which has the maximum priority to server the request. If the heartbeat packet from the preferred cloud does not arrive in time, the preferred cloud will be the second one. The detailed algorithm is described as Algorithm 1.

Cloud Scaling. We set two thresholds for scaling up and down with a lower bound and an upper bound, denoted as σ_l and σ_u, respectively.

$$\sigma_i(t) = max\{\frac{\lambda_i^{CPU}(t) - \sum_{n=1}^{N(t)} d_{in}^{CPU}}{\lambda_i^{CPU}(t)}, \frac{\lambda_i^{NET}(t) - \sum_{n=1}^{N(t)} d_{in}^{NET}}{\lambda_i^{NET}(t)}, \frac{\lambda_i^{MEM}(t) - \sum_{n=1}^{N(t)} d_{in}^{MEM}}{\lambda_i^{MEM}(t)}, \frac{\lambda_i^{DISK}(t) - \sum_{n=1}^{N(t)} d_{in}^{DISK}}{\lambda_i^{DISK}(t)}\} \quad (3)$$

Algorithm 2. Cost-Effective Resource Allocation

```
set upscale = true, downscale = false
for each time slot t ∈ [0, 1, 2, ...] do
  for λ_i ∈ PUB do
    if σ_i(t) ≤ σ_u then
      upscale = false
    end if
    if σ_i(t) ≤ σ_l then
      downscale = true
    end if
  end for
end for
if upscale is true then
  send scale − up direction to the prior cloud
end if
if downscale is true then
  send scale − down direction to the worst cloud
end if
```

We use Eq. (2) to calculate the priorities of public clouds. Here, we use Eq. (3) to get the resource usage of the current cloud in simulation experiments. During each time slot, the load balancer checks whether each cloud needs to adjust its scale. In real world, cloud provider provisions API to get the states of cloud resources, which is much preciser. Algorithm 2 describes the resource allocation process.

4 Experiment

In this section, we conducted a series of simulation experiments from different perspectives. The results demonstrate that our load balance mechanism for hybrid cloud application could reach cost-effective, meanwhile it also provides information on the pros and cons.

4.1 Data Preparation

Requests: We first construct the realistic job requests according to the data traces obtained from Google data center, which include the job arrive/leave time and resource cost information. Then we simulate another three specific application requests which have high demand on CPU, memory, and disk respectively.

Clouds: As the requests vary in Google trace, request should be sent to the suitable cloud for handling. So using multiple public cloud is better than single public cloud. As an instance's startup need some delay, using multi-cloud can somehow reduce the delay. We use three public clouds and two private clouds to construct a hybrid cloud. The parameters of each instance on each cloud is set according to the typical instance types of Amazon EC2 and Google Computing Engine.

We list the public cloud parameters set in Table 1. We also list the resource demand of the three job requests used in experiment in Table 2.

Table 1. Parameters of public clouds

Cloud ID	CPU	MEM	DISK	Price
Cloud 1	8	8	20	0.628
Cloud 2	2	8	20	0.375
Cloud 3	2	3	80	0.453

Table 2. Requirement of resources

APP	CPU	MEM	DISK
CPU_APP	0.65	0.2	1.5
MEM_APP	0.2	0.68	2.5
DISK_APP	0.2	0.18	4.5

4.2 Experiment Results

Function Test. In this experiment, we show functions that the load balancer can reach. The system able to guarantee the private cloud resource use first, keep private cloud at a higher resource utilization. The system will choose most suitable cloud for out-sourcing according to the request type. Further more, it is responsible to the price changes keeps global load balanced.

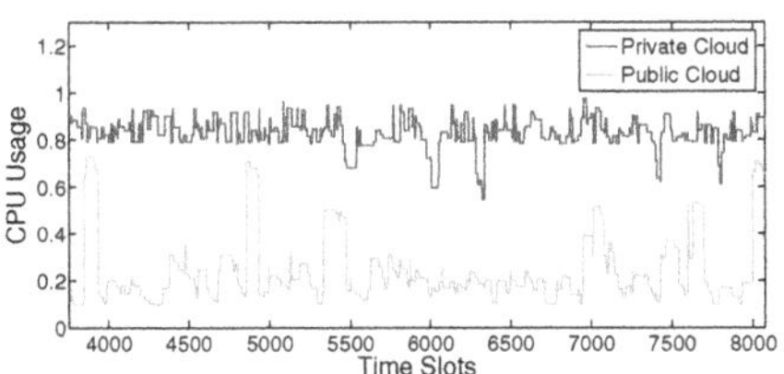

Fig. 2. CPU usage of the private and public clouds in a hybrid cloud.

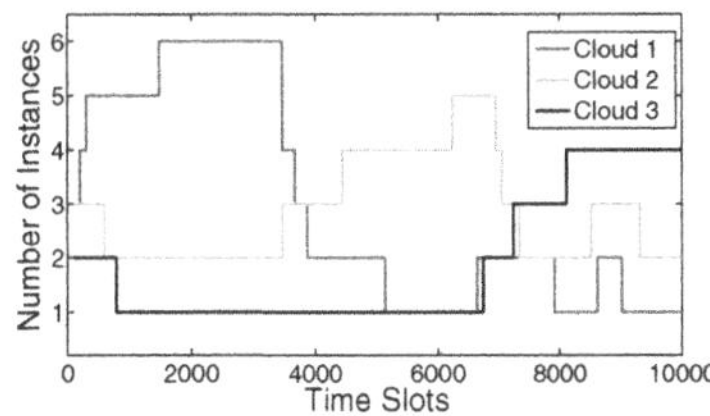

Fig. 3. Resource requirement trace of CPU-intensive, memory-intensive, and disk-intensive jobs.

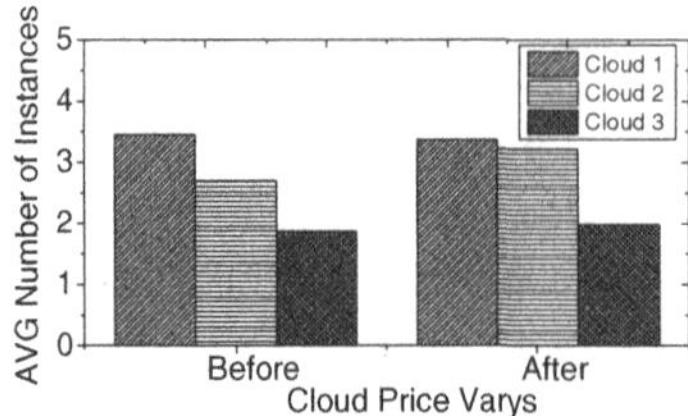

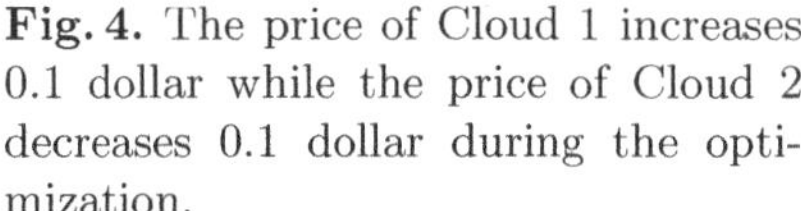
Fig. 4. The price of Cloud 1 increases 0.1 dollar while the price of Cloud 2 decreases 0.1 dollar during the optimization.

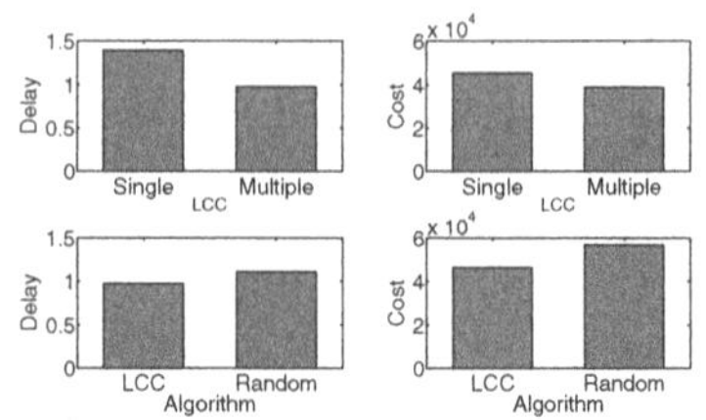

Fig. 5. Comparison test on different public clouds and comparison test between LCC and random algorithm.

Figure 2 demonstrates respective CPU usage of the private and public clouds in a hybrid cloud. As shown in Fig. 2, the average CPU usage of VMs in the private cloud stays above 0.8 in the whole process except five short time periods. Such a phenomenon indicates that our algorithm works based on our design concept. As mentioned in Sect. 3, to maintain the least cost, we use the private cloud as much as possible while outsource excessive workloads to the public cloud. Hence, we need to ensure the average CPU usage of VMs in the private cloud stays in a range stably. Meanwhile, the average usage of VMs in the public cloud fluctuates wildly, which is led by bursty workloads. Although the workloads is bursty, the CPU usage of private cloud is stable, which further demonstrates the effectiveness of our algorithm.

Figure 3 demonstrates the trends of the number of running VMs in three deployed clouds under different types of workloads. In the first time period, the workloads are CPU-intensive. The scale of Cloud 1 increases to the largest for it is good at processing CPU-intensive workloads. Then, when the type of workloads switch to the memory-intensive type, the scale of Cloud 1 goes down while the scale of Cloud 2 ramps up to the largest. Finally, the same trend can be observed in the third time period. As a result, our algorithm is sensitive about the changes in types of workloads and can adjust the scales of public clouds based on it.

Figure 4 shows the scales of public clouds when their prices change. In Fig. 4, the scale of Cloud 2 increases after its price goes down. Meanwhile, when the price of Cloud 1 increases, its scale decreases a little. The effects indicate that our algorithm can adapt the price volatility and choose the cost-effective clouds adaptively.

Performance Analysis. For comparisons, we use random algorithm which is most commonly used on load balance problems.

Figure 5 plots the effects brought by different strategies of deploying the public cloud. In Fig. 5, the average delay processed by single cloud is shorter than that processed by multiple clouds. Furthermore, the cost of deploying single cloud is less than that of deploying multiple clouds. Hence, by deploying multiple public

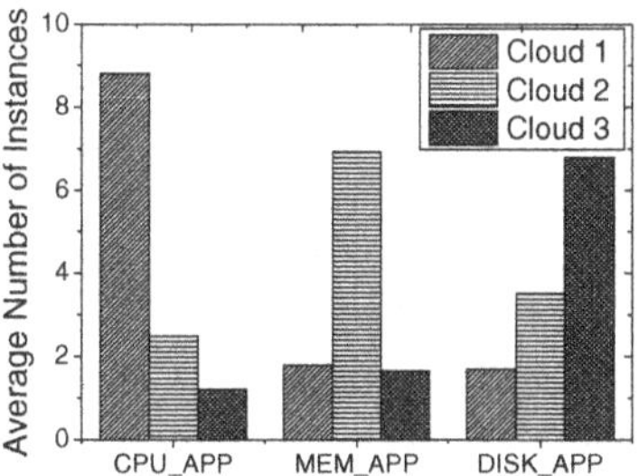

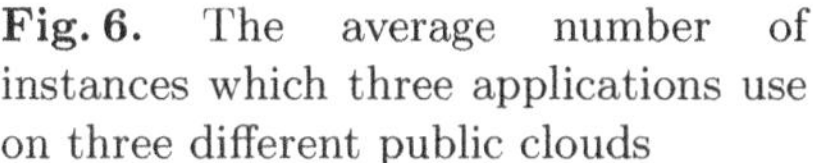
Fig. 6. The average number of instances which three applications use on three different public clouds

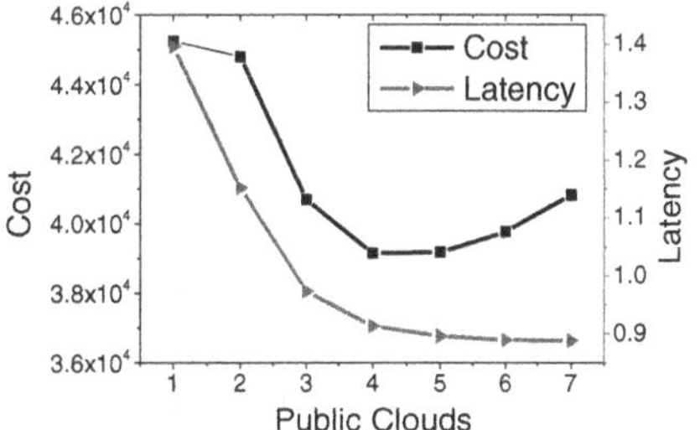

Fig. 7. Measurement on the global average cost and delay under the number of public clouds varying form 1 to 7.

clouds, we can provision high quality services as well as saving cost. Meanwhile, to show the effectiveness of LCC, we compare LCC to a random strategy. As plotted in Fig. 5, the delay of the random strategy is longer than LCC's while the cost is more than LCC's. As a result, our algorithm works well in the hybrid cloud environment.

Figure 6 shows different scales of public clouds in the hybrid cloud. As shown in Fig. 3, the average number of VMs in Cloud 1 is the largest when the workloads are CPU-intensive. Then, the number in Cloud 2 is the largest when the workloads are memory-intensive while the number in Cloud 3 is the largest when the workloads are disk-intensive. Such phenomenon indicates that our algorithm is aware of the types of workloads. Furthermore, our algorithm can adjust the scales of deployed clouds based on different types of workloads and make the best use of the public clouds.

Figure 7 plots the effects brought by different numbers of public clouds. As shown in Fig. 7, when the number of public clouds increases from 1 to 4, the values of latency and cost fall sharply. When deploying more clouds, our algorithm can adjust the respective scales as well as distribute workloads to provision cost-effective services. We have thought that the principle was "the more choices, the better", adding cloud provider only bring less cost or not, no higher. Because the load balancer can choose whether to use the cloud or not. However, when the number of public clouds increases from 4 to 7, the latency decreases slightly while the cost increases markedly. Since we need to maintain the least scale of each public cloud, deploying more clouds does not contribute to cost-saving. Furthermore, the capacity of hybrid cloud is too large to improve performance.

5 Related Work

With respect to studies on managing the performance overhead of VMs, part of the work in [10] summarizes it under diverse scenarios of the IaaS cloud. Li *et al.* in [5] focus on classifying and measuring the typical services which IaaS public clouds provide. Complementary to [10] and [5], we deal with performance issues of multiple public clouds in hybrid cloud scenarios. In terms of addressing network performance, Yi *et al.* take a close look at the unique challenges in building a network highway for big data in [9]. Complementary to [9], we consider network performance of web services when scheduling requests.

[8] gives out a hybrid cloud model which uses a workload factoring scheme to separate base workload and flash crowd workload. Furthermore, [11] models e-commerce web services and proposes an online algorithm to address the load balancing problem under flash crowds in hybrid cloud scenarios. Inspired by [11] yet different from it, we address the load balancing problem with considering multiple public clouds.

6 Conclusion

This paper proposes a Least Cost per Connection (LCC) load balancing algorithm for hybrid cloud applications, which can help provide cost-effective services. We design a system prototype for simulation experiment. The results show that our system can guarantee the private cloud usage as we expected and also achieves the goal of high performance with low cost. Compared with single cloud strategy, the cost and latency of our system decreases 30.2 and 10.1 % respectively. This system can be integrated into hybrid cloud manage platform (CMP) like CloudForms, ManageIQ and so on. Other works we are doing now are making this system a plug-in feature into ManageIQ [12].

References

1. State of the cloud report. Report, 2015 RightScale Inc, February 2015
2. Engine, G.C. https://cloud.google.com/compute/pricing
3. Cloud, R.H. http://www.rightscale.com/solutions/problems-we-solve/hybrid-cloud
4. Shaw, S., Singh, A.: A survey on scheduling and load balancing techniques in cloud computing environment. In: 2014 International Conference on Computer and Communication Technology (ICCCT), pp. 87–95, September 2014
5. Li, A., Yang, X., Kandula, S., Zhang, M., Cloudcmp: Comparing public cloud providers. In: Proceedings of IMC 2010, November 2010
6. OpenStack. http://www.openstack.org/
7. Scaling, A. http://aws.amazon.com/autoscaling/
8. Zhang, H., Jiang, G., Yoshihira, K., Chen, H.: Proactive workload management in hybrid cloud computing. IEEE Trans. Netw. Serv. Manage. **11**(1), 90–100 (2014)
9. Yi, X., Liu, F., Liu, J., Jin, H.: Building a network highway for big data: architecture and challenges. Network IEEE **28**(4), 5–13 (2014)
10. Xu, F., Liu, F., Jin, H., Vasilakos, A.V.: Managing performance overhead of virtual machines in cloud computing: a survey, state of the art, and future directions. Proc. IEEE **102**(1), 11–31 (2014)
11. Niu, Y., Luo, B., Liu, F., Liu, J., Li, B., When hybrid cloud meets flash crowd: towards cost-effective service provisioning. In: Proceedings of IEEE INFOCOM, April 2015
12. ManageIQ Open Source Project. http://manageiq.org/

Architecture and Evaluation

On Rule Placement for Multi-path Routing in Software-Defined Networks

Jie Zhang[1], Deze Zeng[1](✉), Lin Gu[2], Hong Yao[1], and Yuanyuan Fan[1]

[1] School of Computer Science, China University of Geosciences, Wuhan, Hubei, China
deze@cug.edu.cn

[2] School of Computer Science and Technology, Huazhong University of Science and Technology, Wuhan, Hubei, China

Abstract. Software Defined Network (SDN) is a newly emerging network architecture with the core concept of separating the control plane and the data plane. A centralized controller is introduced to manage and configure network equipments to realize flexible control of network traffic. SDN technology provides a good platform for application-oriented network innovations to improve network resource utilization, simplify network management, and reduce operating cost. With SDN devices (e.g., OpenFlow switches), routing becomes more flexible by simply changing the contents of flow tables. The flow table is usually implemented in expensive and power-hungry Ternary Content Addressable Memory (TCAM), which is thus capacity-limited. How to optimize the network performance with the consideration of limited TCAM capacity is therefore significant. For example, multi-path routing (MPR) has been widely regarded as a promising method to promote the network performance. However, MPR is at the expense of additional forwarding rule, imposing a heavy burden on the limited flow table. In this paper, we are motivated to investigate an MPR schedule problem with joint consideration of forwarding rule placement. An integer linear programming (ILP) model is formulated to describe this optimization problem. To address the computation complexity, we further design a three-phase heuristic algorithm. Its high efficiency is validated by the fact that it much approaches the optimal solution, according to our extensive simulation studies.

Keywords: Software defined network · Multi-path routing · Rule placement · Optimization

1 Introduction

In traditional network architecture, once the network is deployed, reconfiguration network equipments (e.g., routers, switches, firewall, etc.) to satisfy the changing communication demand is a very complicated task. Now, high stability and high performance of network is not enough to meet the business requirements any more, flexibility and agility are even more crucial. We urgently need a new network architecture innovation to catch up with the increasing demands. Software

S. Guo et al. (Eds.): CollaborateCom 2015, LNICST 163, pp. 59–71, 2016.
DOI: 10.1007/978-3-319-28910-6_6

defined networking (SDN) has emerged as a new paradigm that separates the data plane from the control plane. By such means, the whole network can be administered by centralized controllers using a uniform programming interface as it shields the differences from the underlying network devices. The network thus becomes more flexible and intelligent, making it quite easy to deploy new network protocols [1]. The control plane is completely open. Users can freely customize their network routing strategy according to the application requirements. SDN fills the gap between the application and the network. It is without-doubt the development trend of the future network.

To computer networks, routing is always a major concern and has attracted much attention from scientists and engineers. With the recent prosperousness of computer networks, pioneering researchers found that single-path routing fails to explore the increasing capacity of communication networks. Multi-path routing (MPR), which can find many available paths between communication pairs, was proposed as a promising solution [2]. It has already been proved that MPR is more efficient in improving the utilization of network bandwidth, reducing obstruction, and achieving load balancing. MPR therefore has attracted many interests in the literature [3–5].

It is therefore natural to introduce MPR into SDN for network performance promotion. However, some new challenges are also introduced. In SDN-enabled devices (e.g., OpenFlow switches [6]), the flow tables are made by expensive and power-hungry Ternary Content Aware Memory (TCAM), which is size-limited [3,7]. This limits the number of forwarding rules that can be placed in the flow table. Providing more paths for a network flow usually implies a higher performance, but it also requires more space in the flow table. Therefore, in SDN, MPR shall be carefully scheduled with the consideration of size-limited flow table. Actually, many efforts have been devoted to addressing the limited TCAM size. Most existing studies on forwarding rule optimization, e.g., forwarding rule placement, mainly focus on single-path routing. Taking MPR into consideration, how to jointly schedule the routing and forwarding rule placement is still under-investigated.

In this paper, we are motivated to study the MPR scheduling jointly with the forwarding rule placement in size-limited flow tables. Specially, we are interested in maximize the communication satisfaction with the consideration of communication demands. Our main contributions are as follows.

- To our best knowledge, we are the first to study MPR in SDNs with size-limited flow tables, for communication satisfaction maximization. We build an integer linear programming (ILP) model to describe the optimization problem, with joint consideration of MPR scheduling and forwarding rule placement.
- To address the computation complexity of solving ILP, we further propose a three-phase heuristic algorithm in polynomial time. Through extensive experiment results, the high efficiency of our proposed algorithm is validated.

The rest of this paper is structured as follows. We summarize related work in Sect. 2. We then formulate the problem into ILP in Sect. 3.2. A three-phase heuristic algorithm is presented in Sect. 4. Simulation results are shown in Sect. 5. Finally, we conclude our work in Sect. 6.

2 Related Work

2.1 Multi-path Routing in Traditional Networks

It is widely agreed that MPR has many advantages over single path routing on various aspects such as throughput, load balancing, reliability and so on. In this section, we briefly summarize some representative studies.

Ganjali et al. [8] first evaluate a load balancing problem in MPR. Wei et al. [9] investigate a throughput maximization problem with the goal of reducing bandwidth blocking and improving the average network throughput. They propose a dynamic multi-path provisioning algorithm, which tries to set up dynamic connections with single-path routing in a best-effort manner. Curtis et al. [10] design and evaluate a modification of the OpenFlow model load-balance data center traffic. In [11], it is demonstrated that the proposed flow management reducing overheads, which devolving decisions (as appropriate) to the switches. Al-Fares et al. [12] apply Equal Cost Multipath (ECMP) [2] to efficiently utilize the network resources while achieving network-wide load-balancing. Curtis et al. [13] present Mahout, a low-overhead yet effective traffic management system based on end-host elephant detection. Dasgupta et al. [3] make MPR scheduling based on reliability of the paths. Li et al. [14] study a utility maximization problem with joint consideration of MPR and MAC scheduling. The problem is solved using the primal-dual method. Xu et al. [15] present MPR-based anonymous routing protocol to improve the network effectiveness. Natarajan et al. [16] discuss a location prediction based routing (LPBR) protocol for mobile ad hoc networks (MANETs) and extend it for multicast and MPR.

2.2 Routing Optimization in SDN

Recently, many efforts have been contributed to the field of SDN. Guo et al. [17] consider the effects of large numbers of short flows and massive bursty traffic in data center networks, and design a distributed rate allocation algorithm based on the logistic model under the control-theoretic framework. In their later studies [18–20], they apply game-theoretic framework to the bandwidth allocation problem in data centers. Nemeth et al. [6] demonstrate a large-scale multi-path playground deployed on PlanetLab Europe, which can be used either by experimenters and researchers to test and verify their multipath-related ideas and also by early adopters to enhance their Internet connection [7]. It proves that the MPR is feasible in SDN. Giroire et al. [1] point out that the flow table in OpenFlow switch is implemented using expensive and power hungry TCAM and therefore a limited number of forwarding rules can be stored in SDN switches. Cohen et al. [21] conduct a thorough theoretical study of the bounded path-degree max-flow problem and present approximation algorithms for maximizing network utilization, with the consideration of size-limited flow table.

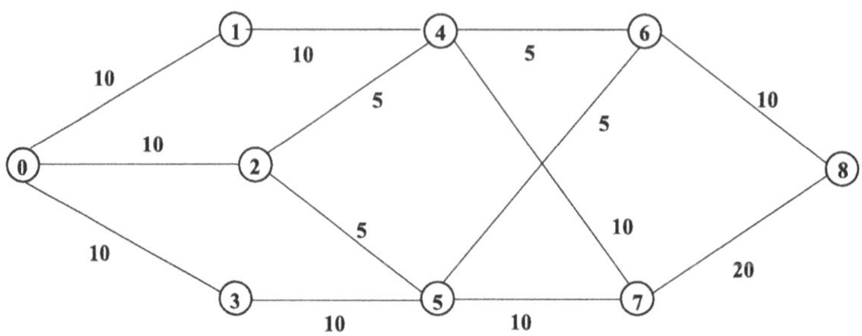

Fig. 1. A network example with 9 nodes and 11 links

3 Problem Formulation

3.1 System Model and Problem Statement

In this work, we consider a network that can be described as a graph $G = (V, E)$, where V is a set of nodes and E denotes the links between these nodes. Figure 1 gives an illustrative network example with 9 nodes and 13 links. Among these nodes, there is a set D of communication pairs. We denote a pair using its source and destination $(s, d) \in D$ where $s, d \in V, s \neq d$. Each pair (s, d) is associated with a traffic demand Π^{sd}. A traffic flow originating from s may go through many intermediate relay nodes (i.e., routers) until reaching destination d. We suppose all the relay nodes are SDN-enabled (e.g., OpenFlow switches). To customize the routing strategy, forwarding rules must be placed at corresponding routers according to the routing requirement. In MPR, the nodes on all forwarding paths for all sub-flows shall be placed with corresponding forwarding rules. Due to the capacity limitation of TCAM, the number of forwarding rules that can be placed on a node is limited. We denote the number of forwarding rules that can be placed on node $v \in V$ as S_v. Besides, the communication links are also capacity-limited. The capacity of link $(u, v) \in E$ is denoted as C_{uv}. For example, we have $C_{01} = 10$ in Fig. 1.

To the requirements of the communication pairs, we are interested in a max-min fairness scheduling which leads to high satisfaction. We define the satisfaction of a pair as the ratio between the achieved throughput and the desired demand. When the provisioned resources are not enough to satisfy the total communication demands, high satisfaction ensures high throughput with max-min fairness. On the other hand, when the achieved throughput is beyond the desired demand, high satisfaction indicates high residual capacity and hence high demand jitter tolerance. Therefore, it is significant to investigate how to maximize the minimum satisfaction of all communication pairs, with joint consideration of MPR and forwarding rule placement in size-limited flow tables.

3.2 Problem Formulation

Based on the system model as described above, we next present an integer linear programming (ILP) model to describe the problem studied in this paper.

Flow Conservation Constraints: As we have known, the traffic flow from node s may go across many different paths consisting of different links to its wanted destination d. We therefore define the flow of communication pair (s,d) on link (u,v) as f_{uv}^{sd}. According to the network flow theory, flow conservation must be reserved at all intermediate relay nodes, except the source and the destination nodes.

As a result, we shall have:

$$\sum_{(u,v)\in E} f_{uv}^{sd} = \sum_{(v,w)\in E} f_{vw}^{sd}, \forall (s,d) \in D, v \in V. \tag{1}$$

Note that the above flow conservation constraints can not be applied to the source and destination nodes, to which we have the following constrains:

$$\sum_{v\in V} f_{sv}^{sd} = F^{sd}, \forall (s,d) \in D, \tag{2}$$

and

$$\sum_{v\in V} f_{vd}^{sd} = F^{sd}, \forall (s,d) \in D, \tag{3}$$

respectively, where float variable F^{sd} indicates the throughput that can be achieved.

Link Capacity Constraints: A traffic flow may go through many different links. While, a link may have sub-flows of many different communication pairs. Nevertheless, the overall flow amount through a link shall not exceed its link capacity. That is,

$$\sum_{(s,d)\in D} f_{uv}^{sd} \le C_{uv}, \forall (u,v) \in E. \tag{4}$$

Flow Table Size Constraints: As we have known, besides link capacity constraints, SDN additionally introduces new constraints on the size of flow tables, indicating the number of forwarding rules that can be stored on the node. Whenever a flow or a sub-flow injects into an SDN node, a corresponding forwarding rule must be placed onto it. Note that no matter how many outgoing sub-flows are scheduled, we always need only one forwarding rule. Let binary variable x_v^{sd} denote whether a forwarding rule of pair $(s,d) \in D$ must be placed on node v. We shall have the following relationship

$$x_v^{sd} = \begin{cases} 1, \text{ if } \exists f_{uv}^{sd} > 0, u \in V, \\ 0, \text{ otherwise.} \end{cases} \forall (s,d) \in D, v \in V. \tag{5}$$

The above relationship can be translated into the following equivalent linear expression as

$$\frac{\sum_{(u,v)\in E} f_{uv}^{sd}}{A} \leq x_v^{sd} \leq \sum_{(u,v)\in E} f_{uv}^{sd} \cdot A, \forall (s,d) \in D, v \in V, \tag{6}$$

where A is an arbitrary large number.

For each node v, the total number of rules that can be placed onto it shall not exceed its flow table size S_v, i.e.,

$$\sum_{(s,d)\in D} x_v^{sd} \leq S_v, \forall v \in V. \tag{7}$$

ILP Formulation: Remember that our objective is to maximize the minimum satisfaction of all communication pairs. It is straightforward to define the satisfaction of a communication pair $(s,d) \in D$ as $\frac{F^{sd}}{\Pi^{sd}}$. Taking all the pairs into consideration, the objective can be described as

$$\max\min : \frac{F^{sd}}{\Pi^{sd}}, \forall (s,d) \in D. \tag{8}$$

In order to simplify the max-min objective into linear form, we define an auxiliary parameter Q with the following constraints

$$Q \leq \frac{F^{sd}}{\Pi^{sd}}, \forall (s,d) \in D. \tag{9}$$

Thus, by taking all the constraints discussed above, we obtain an ILP formulation of the max-min fairness problem as

$$\begin{aligned} &\max : Q \\ &\quad \text{s.t.}\ (1) - (4), (6), (7), (9). \end{aligned} \tag{10}$$

4 A Three-Phase Heuristic Algorithm

It is computationally prohibitive to obtain the optimal solution of the ILP problem formulated in last section for large-size SDNs. To tackle this issue, we propose a three-phase polynomial-time heuristic algorithm in this section. In the first phase, by excluding the TCAM size constraints, we first derive the MPR scheduling that can maximize the minimum satisfaction when the flow table is unlimited. We then further take the TCAM size constraints into consideration by checking whether all the nodes satisfy the capacity limitations. Only when no node in a path violates the flow table size constraint, it is feasible; otherwise, it is infeasible and needs to be rescheduled. To adjust these infeasible paths into

Algorithm 1. Find all potential paths

Require:
$G = (V, E)$, C_{uv}, $\forall(u, v) \in E$, D.
Ensure:
path set *Allpath* for every (s, d)
Initially, $Allpath = \emptyset$
Exclude constraints (6) and (7) to obtain a LP problem
Solve the LP to obtain $f_{uv}^{sd}, \forall(s, d) \in D, (u, v) \in E$
for all $(s, d) \in D$ **do**
  for all $(u, v) \in E$ **do**
    if $f_{uv}^{sd} > 0$ **then**
      save the f_{uv}^{sd} and link (u, v) to *Allpath* as a new path ;
      for each path in $Allpath[s, d]$ **do**
        sort all nodes in $Allpath[s, d]$;
      end for
    end if
  end for
end for

Algorithm 2. Test the feasibility of all paths

Require:
all paths *Allpath* for every (s, d) ;
flow f_{uv}^{sd}, $\forall(s, d) \in D, \forall(u, v) \in E$;
flow table size S_v, $\forall v \in V$;
Ensure:
dissatisfied paths *dispath* for every (s, d)
residual flow table capacity $Temps$
$Temp_S = S$
for all $(s, d) \in D$ **do**
  for all path p^{sd} in *Allpath* **do**
    if all nodes' rule capacity in this path > 0 **then**
      the path p^{sd} is feasible ;
      for each node $u \in p^{sd}$ **do**
        $Temp_S[u] = Temp_S[u] - 1$
      end for
    else
      the path p^{sd} is infeasible;
    end if
  end for
end for

feasible ones, we discard some sub-flows to make sure that no TCAM size limitation is violated. Further, some sub-flows are merged into the switches with residual flow table capacity to maximize the user satisfaction. The three phases are summarized in Algorithms 1, 2 and 3, respectively.

Phase 1 (Algorithm 1): We first exclude the flow table size constraints by excluding (6) and (7) in ILP. As the integers are only involved in (6) and (7).

Algorithm 3. Reschedule and update the throughput

Require:

all paths *Allpath* for every (s, d) ;
infeasible paths *dispath* for every (s, d) ;
flow $f_{uv}^{sd} \quad \forall(s,d) \in D, \forall(u,v) \in E$;
Residual flow table size $Temp_S$;

Ensure:

MPR scheduling and rule placement results

1: **for all** path $p^{sd} \in dispath$ **do**
2:   **if** there is a feasible path candidate p'^{sd} in *Allpath* **then**
3:     migrate the traffic of path p^{sd} to p'^{sd}
4:     update the throughput
5:   **else**
6:     remove the path p^{sd}
7:   **end if**
8: **end for**

A linear programming (LP) problem is thus obtained. By solving the LP problem, we obtain an MPR scheduling without flow table size constrains. By checking the values of $f_{uv}^{sd}, \forall(s,d) \in D, (u,v) \in E$, we can get whether a link, e.g., $(u,v) \in E$, is involved in the routing of flow, e.g., $(s,d) \in D$, or not. We save the links involved in the routing scheduling (lines 5 to 7). After that, we sort all node in corresponding path to get a full path from line 7 to 8.

Phase 2 (Algorithm 2): In this phase, we try to test whether the nodes in the path involved in MPR, according to the results of Algorithm 1, satisfies the flow table size constraint. As shown in Algorithm 2, we denote the residual flow table size as $Temp_S$, which is initialized with total flow table size S (line 1). By checking whether all the nodes involved in a path are with residual flow table size $Temp_S$ larger than 0, we can judge whether the path is feasible or not. If it is feasible, we subtract the residual flow table size of all the involved nodes by 1 to indicate that one forwarding rule is placed. Otherwise, the path is marked as infeasible and shall be rescheduled.

Phase 3 (Algorithm 3): In this phase, we reschedule all the infeasible paths found out in Phase 2, by migrating their forwarding task to another feasible path in the set found in Phase 1. Similarly, we check both the residual link capacity and flow table size constraints to verify the feasibility of the potential path candidates. If no constraint is violated, we consider the path as feasible (line 3) and migrate the traffic task to this feasible path (line 4). At the same time, the infeasible path is removed from the MPR scheduling (line 7). Otherwise, if no path candidate is found, we have to discard the infeasible path.

5 Performance Evaluation

To evaluated the performance of the proposed three phase rule placement method (“**Three-phase**”), we present the performance results compared to traditional

SPR algorithm ("**SPR**") and optimal solution ("**Optimal**"). In our experiments, we consider an SDN network consists of 200 nodes with the link-capacity of 1000 and TCAM size of 500 as default. The results proved that our three-phase algorithm significantly out-performances the traditional SPR schema and much approaches the optimal one. To solve our ILP problem and get the optimal results, commercial solver Gurobi[1] is used. We investigate how our algorithm performs and how various parameters affect the communication cost by varying the settings of TCAM Size, link capacity, network size and user demand in each experiment group, receptively.

5.1 On the Effect of TCAM Size

First, we show the max-min satisfaction ratio under different setting of TCAM size from 1 to 1000. Figures 2(a), (b) and (c) show the results with different link capacities of 500, 1000 and 2000, respectively. The experiment results show that the average max-min satisfaction ratio of the network first increases and finally converges with the increasing of TCAM size. This is because for an SDN network with certain user demand, when the TCAM size is small, e.g., from 1 to 100 in Fig. 2(a), the number of forwarding rules stored in flow table is small. Hence the number of flows that can go through a node is limited and the max-min satisfaction ratio is also low. With the increase of TCAM size, e.g., from 100 to 500 in Fig. 2(a), more rules can be stored in the flow table and therefore more flows can be handled at the same time, resulting in an increasing of satisfaction ratio. Finally, when the TCAM size becomes large enough, e.g., from 500 to 1000 in Fig. 2(a), the number of rules is already sufficient for all user demands. While, the link-capacity becomes the bottleneck as it limits the number of flows through a link. In this case, further increasing the TCAM size will not affect the throughput any more and thus all three algorithms converge. Nevertheless, we can always observe from Fig. 2 that our "Three-phase" significantly outperforms "SPR" and performs much close to "Optimal" under any TCAM sizes.

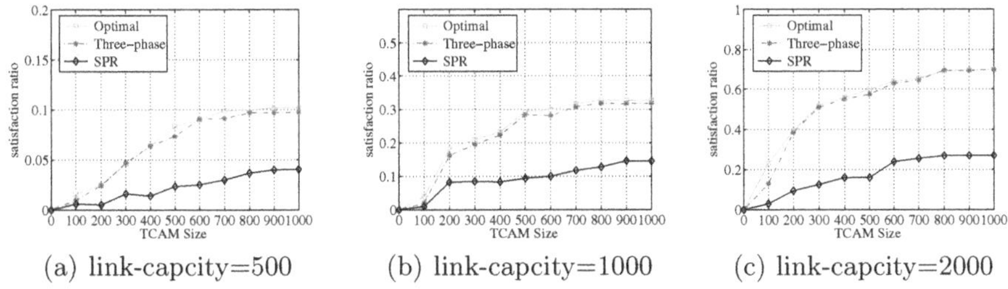

(a) link-capcity=500 (b) link-capcity=1000 (c) link-capcity=2000

Fig. 2. Satisfaction ratio under different TCAM sizes when $|N|$=200

[1] http://www.gurobi.com.

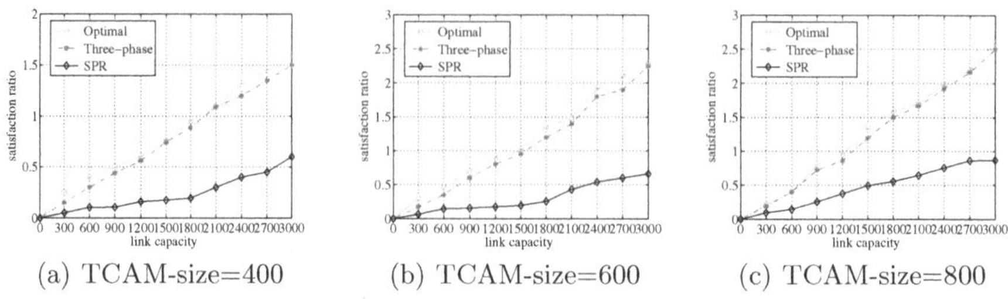

Fig. 3. Satisfaction ratio under different link capacities when $|N|$=500

5.2 On the Effect of Link-Capacity

Then, we investigate the impact of the link-capacity to satisfaction ratio by varying its values from 1 to 3000. Three different TCAM sizes, i.e., 400, 600 and 800, are considered and the results are shown in Fig. 3(a), (b) and (c), respectively. We first observe that the max-min satisfaction ratio of all three algorithms show as an increasing function of link-capacity, under any TCAM sizes. The reason behind such phenomenon is that as the link capacity increases, traffic on each path also increases. Without doubt that this shall lead to a larger max-min satisfaction ratio for a given TCAM size. Besides, the high efficiency of our algorithm is validated once again as we can see that our "Three-phase" algorithm gives a better performance than "SPR" from all three figures.

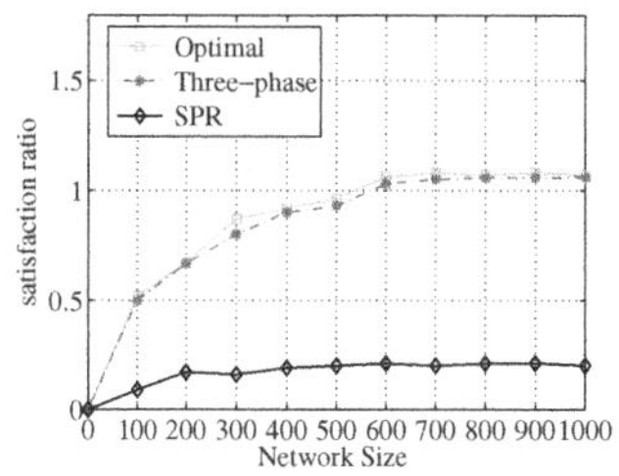

Fig. 4. Satisfaction ratio under different network sizes when TCAM size is 500

5.3 On the Effect of Network Size

Next, we change the network size from 1 to 1000 to investigate how it affects the max-min satisfaction ratio. From Fig. 4, we can see that the satisfaction ratio first increases fast and then converges with network size. The reason for this phenomenon is similar to Fig. 2. Increasing the network size potentially increases the number of TCAMs and the number of available network paths, hence providing more space for rules and more choices of routing paths. Therefore, satisfaction ratio increases with the increase of network size, e.g., from 1 to 750. After the network size is large enough, both the total TCAM size and available network path are already sufficient for current user demand. Under this circumstance, continuously increasing the network size does not take much benefit to the max-min satisfaction ratio. After reaching 750 in Fig. 2, both the link-capacity and TCAM size limit the performance, resulting in a slow increasing of the max-min satisfaction ratio.

5.4 On the Effect of Traffic Demand

Finally, we study the affects of the user traffic demand to the max-min satisfaction ratio. The performance evaluation results are reported in Fig. 5, from which we can see that the max-min satisfaction ratio shows as a decreasing function of the traffic demand. The reason is that, with fixed network topology, TCAM size and link-capacity, the maximum system throughput is also fixed. In this case, increasing the user demand leads to lower satisfaction ratios of all communication pairs, according to (7). Consequently, the max-min satisfaction ratio decreases. Nevertheless, our algorithm is always advantageous over "SPR" algorithm.

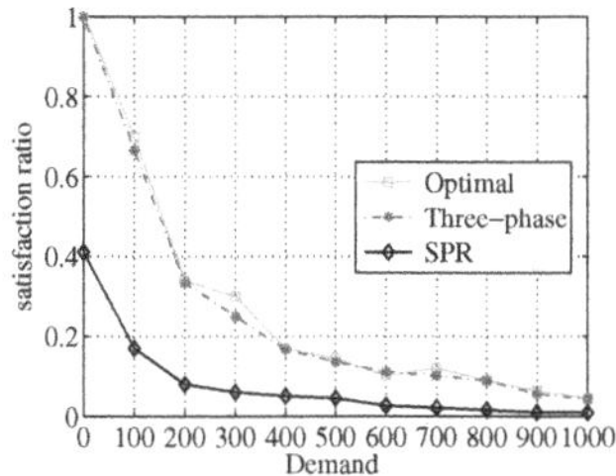

Fig. 5. Satisfaction ratio under different traffic demands

6 Conclusion

In this paper, we study an MPR scheduling problem to maximize the minimum satisfaction ratio of communication pairs in SDNs, with joint consideration of routing scheduling and forwarding rule placement. We first formally formulate the problem into an ILP problem. Then, to tackle the high computational complexity of solving this ILP problem, we propose a three-phase algorithm with polynomial time complexity. Through extensive experiments, we show that our algorithm exhibits substantial advantage over SPR algorithm, and much approaches the performance of the optimal solution.

Acknowledgements. This research was supported by the NSF of China (Grant No. 61402425, 61501412, 61272470, 61502439, 61305087, 61440060), the China Postdoctoral Science Foundation funded project (Grant No. 2014M562086), the Fundamental Research Funds for National University, China University of Geosciences, Wuhan (Grant No. CUG14065, CUGL150829), the Provincial Natural Science Foundation of Hubei (Grant No. 2015CFA065).

References

1. Giroire, F., Moulierac, J., Phan, T.K.: Optimizing rule placement in software-defined networks for energy-aware routing. In: Proceedings of GLOBECOM, pp. 2523–2529. IEEE (2014)
2. Hopps, C.E.: Analysis of an equal-cost multi-path algorithm (2000)
3. Dasgupta, M., Biswas, G.: Design of multi-path data routing algorithm based on network reliability. Comput. Electr. Eng. **38**, 1433–1443 (2012)
4. Cervera, G., Barbeau, M., Garcia-Alfaro, J., Kranakis, E.: A multipath routing strategy to prevent flooding disruption attacks in link state routing protocols for MANETs. J. Netw. Comput. Appl. **36**, 744–755 (2013)
5. Zheng, M., Liang, W., Yu, H., Xiao, Y., Han, J.: Energy-aware utility optimisation for joint multi-path routing and MAC layer retransmission control in TDMA-based wireless sensor networks. Int. J. Sens. Netw. **14**, 120–129 (2013)
6. Németh, F., Sonkoly, B., Csikor, L., Gulyás, A.: A large-scale multipath playground for experimenters and early adopters. In: Proceedings of SIGCOMM, pp. 481–482. ACM (2013)
7. Ford, A., Raiciu, C., Handley, M., Barre, S., Iyengar, J., et al.: Architectural guidelines for multipath TCP development. IETF, Informational RFC **6182**, 1721–2070 (2011)
8. Ganjali, Y., Keshavarzian, A.: Load balancing in ad hoc networks: single-path routing vs. multi-path routing. In: Proceedings of INFOCOM, pp. 1120–1125. IEEE (2004)
9. Lu, W., Zhou, X., Gong, L., Zhang, M., Zhu, Z.: Dynamic multi-path service provisioning under differential delay constraint in elastic optical networks. Commun. Lett. **17**, 158–161 (2013)
10. Curtis, A.R., Mogul, J.C., Tourrilhes, J., Yalagandula, P., Sharma, P., Banerjee, S.: DevoFlow: scaling flow management for high-performance networks. In: Proceedings of SIGCOMM, pp. 254–265. ACM (2011)
11. Mogul, J.C., Tourrilhes, J., Yalagandula, P., Sharma, P., Curtis, A.R., Banerjee, S.: Devoflow: cost-effective flow management for high performance enterprise networks. In: Proceedings of SIGCOMM, pp. 158–161. ACM (2010)
12. Al-Fares, M., Radhakrishnan, S., Raghavan, B., Huang, N., Vahdat, A.: Hedera: dynamic flow scheduling for data center networks. In: Proceedings of NSDI, p. 19 (2010)
13. Curtis, A.R., Kim, W., Yalagandula, P.: Mahout: low-overhead datacenter traffic management using end-host-based elephant detection. In: Proceedings of INFOCOM, pp. 1629–1637. IEEE (2011)
14. Li, Y., Zhou, L., Yang, Y., Chao, H.C.: Optimization architecture for joint multi-path routing and scheduling in wireless mesh networks. Math. Comput. Model. **53**, 458–470 (2011)
15. Xu, L., Zhao, W., Jiang, L., Jin, J., Gui, N.: Multi-path anonymous on demand routing protocol. In: Proceedings of IMCCC, pp. 858–863. IEEE (2013)
16. Meghanathan, N.: A location prediction based routing protocol and its extensions for multicast and multi-path routing in mobile ad hoc networks. Ad Hoc Netw. **9**, 1104–1126 (2011)
17. Guo, J., Liu, F., Huang, X., Lui, J., Hu, M., Gao, Q., Jin, H.: On efficient bandwidth allocation for traffic variability in datacenters. In: Proceedings of INFOCOM, pp. 1572–1580. IEEE (2014)

18. Guo, J., Liu, F., Tang, H., Lian, Y., Jin, H., Lui, J.: Falloc: fair network bandwidth allocation in iaas datacenters via a bargaining game approach. In: Proceedings of ICNP, pp. 1–10. IEEE (2013)
19. Guo, J., Liu, F., Zeng, D., Lui, J., Jin, H.: A cooperative game based allocation for sharing data center networks. In: Proceedings of INFOCOM, pp. 2139–2147. IEEE (2013)
20. Guo, J., Liu, F., Lui, J., Jin, H.J.: Fair network bandwidth allocation in iaas datacenters via a cooperative game approach. IEEE/ACM Trans. Netw. (2015)
21. Cohen, R., Lewin-Eytan, L., Naor, J.S., Raz, D.: On the effect of forwarding table size on SDN network utilization. In: Proceedings of INFOCOM, pp. 1734–1742. IEEE (2014)

Crowdstore: A Crowdsourcing Graph Database

Vitaliy Liptchinsky[1,2(✉)], Benjamin Satzger[2], Stefan Schulte[1], and Schahram Dustdar[1]

[1] Distributed Systems Group, TU Wien, Vienna, Austria
{liptchinsky,schulte,dustdar}@dsg.tuwien.ac.at
[2] Microsoft, Redmond, USA
benjamin.satzger@microsoft.com

Abstract. Existing crowdsourcing database systems fail to support complex, collaborative or responsive crowd work. These systems implement human computation as independent tasks published online, and subsequently chosen by individual workers. Such pull model does not support worker collaboration and its expertise matching relies on workers' subjective self-assessment. An extension to graph query languages combined with an enhanced database system components can express and facilitate social collaboration, sophisticated expert discovery and low-latency crowd work. In this paper we present such an extension, CRowdPQ, backed up by the database management system Crowdstore.

Keywords: Database theory · Graph query languages · Crowdsourcing

1 Introduction

Crowd-powered hybrid databases have gained momentum in recent years [8,16,17] due to their ability to combine human and machine computation. These database engines allow the specification of human-computable predicates that transform into Human Intelligence Tasks (HITs), which are posted online and are expected to be picked up by workers. In spite of being cumbersome for workers, as browsing HITs is time-consuming [10], such pull model has limitations for collaborative and expert work. The better-suited push model requires the crowd platform to support sophisticated worker discovery capabilities in order to assign or recommend tasks to workers.

Plethora of tasks require synchronous collaboration [9,10]. Successful collaboration can be largely influenced by social relations between human workers. Moreover, reusing teams that exhibited successful collaboration in the past can greatly increase chances of success for new assignments.

Realtime crowdsourcing is based on the concept of flash crowds [10]: groups of individuals who respond moments after a request and can work synchronously. The benefits of realtime crowdsourcing have been shown in [2,3]: paying workers a small wage to stay on call is enough to draw a crowd together within seconds.

In this paper we show how a graph query language can be extended to express synchronous collaboration, social formations (teams) of crowd workers, sophisticated worker discovery, as well as complex crowdsourcing patterns, such as

S. Guo et al. (Eds.): CollaborateCom 2015, LNICST 163, pp. 72–81, 2016.
DOI: 10.1007/978-3-319-28910-6_7

iterative computation, control groups, ranking, etc. Also, we show how classical database engine components, such as indexes, caches, and the buffer pool manager, can be extended to improve worker discovery, team formation, and flash crowds management.

2 Motivation

Consider following examples of crowdsourcing tasks:

1. Implement a web page, and create images for it. These two tasks require distinct skill sets. Also, to improve collaboration, workers assigned to the tasks should be socially related, or at least in close social vicinity.
2. You have a recorded melody fragment and want to know what song it belongs to. You want only those workers to work on it who like rock music.
3. You need a set of hand-drawn paintings. You ask crowd workers to draw and rate the paintings. To avoid biased ratings, workers rating the paintings should not be socially related to workers drawing the paintings.

Existing crowdsourcing query languages fall short of expressing complex relations between crowd workers working on related tasks, e.g., in the first example. Moreover, discovery of proper workers might be a crowdsourcing task itself, e.g., in the second example. Finally, even trivial crowdsourcing patterns, as in Example 3, are cumbersome to express in existing crowdsourcing query language adaptations.

In the next section we review existing query languages employed for crowdsourcing database scenarios.

3 Related Work

Table 1 provides an overview of existing hybrid human-machine databases. We analyze their ability to express complex crowdsourcing workflow patterns (such as control groups and ranking), social formations between workers, and sophisticated worker discovery. Also, we overview techniques they employ for query optimizations, i.e., to minimize the number of generated HITs under cooperative/collaborative scenarios, and approaches they utilize to enable realtime crowdsourcing.

Qurk [14,15] and hQuery [16] were among the first attempts on expressing crowdsourcing tasks as declarative queries. The SQL-based query language in Qurk [14] exploits user-defined scalar and table functions (called *TASK*) to retrieve, join, sort and filter data from the crowd. Qurk also extends SQL with a *POSSIBLY* clause to reduce the number of join candidates. Join optimizations in Qurk consider batching of items, thus minimizing the number of generated HITs. hQuery [16], a Datalog-like declarative model, features human-based and algorithm-based predicates. Authors focus on presence of uncertainty in

Table 1. Supported features in selected crowdsourcing databases

	Workflow	Query optimizations	Worker discovery	Social formations	Realtime crowdsourcing
Qurk [15]	+/-	+/-	-	-	-
hQuery [16]	+/-	+/-	-	-	-
CrowdDB [8]	+/-	-	-	-	-
CrowdSPARQL [1]	+/-	-	-	-	-
Deco [17]	+/-	-	-	-	-
CrowdSearcher [4]	+/-	-	-	+/-	-
Join optimizations [13,18,19]	N/A	+/-	-	-	-

the result set as well as optimization challenges, such as trade-offs between the number of certain answers, time allocated and monetary cost.

CrowdDB [8] introduces extensions to the SQL data definition language to define *CROWD*-enabled columns and tables, i.e., which should be fetched from an underlying crowdsourcing platform. Also, it introduces CROWDEQUAL and CROWDORDER extensions to the SQL data modification language.

CrowdSPARQL [1] introduces a hybrid query engine that allows executing SPARQL queries as a combination of machine- and human-driven functionality. Similar to *CROWD*-enabled columns and tables in CrowdDB, CrowdSPARQL defines crowdsourced *classes* and *properties* in VoID (Vocabulary of Interlinked Datasets). Also, CrowdSPARQL defines an *ORDER BY CROWD* operator.

The Deco [17] database semantics are defined based on the so-called *Fetch-Resolve-Join* sequence, i.e., data is fetched using *Fetch* rules, then data inconsistencies are resolved using *Resolution* rules and afterwards conceptual relations are produced by outer-joining the resolved tables.

CrowdSearcher [4] allows putting constraints on crowd workers via a mapping model, e.g., friends of a specific user, geo-localized people, workers on a selected work platform. However, it is not possible to specify either relations between workers, or social formations.

Neither of the query languages above allow specifying *CROWD*-enabled constraints on workers, nor relations between crowd workers themselves. Hence, these query languages cannot support examples provided in the previous section. Moreover, they lack capabilities to express complex workflows in a natural way.

Multiple papers discuss the problem of minimizing the number of HITs required to resolve JOIN operations. We have grouped those papers in the table under the "Join Optimizations" row. CrowdER [18] suggests using a hybrid human-machine approximation approach to filter out non-matching join pairs (with similarity ratio below certain threshold), aiming to minimize the number of HITs required to join entities. Wang et al. [19] discuss join optimization based on transitive relations. Contrary, in [13] authors discuss selectivity estimation performed by the crowd, which implies optimal join ordering. All these approaches focus on crowd-based and automatic join resolution, neglecting a query writer, who can have better insight into selectivity of the data queried and optimal join ordering.

While simple caching of results produced by HITs has been discussed (e.g., [15]), it has not been discussed how to cache successful workers and social formations (teams). Also, to the best of our knowledge, no papers have suggested application of classical database techniques and algorithms for realtime crowdsourcing.

4 Query Language

Efficient specification of social collaboration largely depends on the ability to specify complex social formations of crowd workers. Social formations can be intuitively represented as graph patterns [12], which makes graph query languages a natural choice for describing social collaboration. In this section we show how Conjunctive Regular Path Queries, a formalism behind many graph query languages [20], can be extended to overcome their shortcoming for incorporating free-text conditions and relations between data to be fetched and workers who fetch the data.

4.1 Preliminaries

A database is defined as a directed graph $K = (V, E)$ labeled over the finite alphabet Σ. If there is a path between node a and node b labeled with $p_1, p_2, ..., p_n$ we write $a \xrightarrow{p_1 p_2 ... p_n} b$. In the remainder of this section we give definitions of (conjunctive) regular path queries, similar to other works, like [6].

Definition 1 (Regular Path Queries). A regular path query (RPQ) $Q^R \leftarrow R$ is defined by a regular expression R over Σ. The answer $ans(Q^R, K)$ is the set connected by a path that conforms to the regular language $L(R)$ defined by R:

$$ans(Q^R, K) = \{(a, b) \in V \times V \mid a \xrightarrow{p} b \text{ for } p \in L(R)\}.$$

Conjunctive regular path queries allow to create queries consisting of a conjunction of RPQs, augmented with variables.

Definition 2 (Conjunctive Regular Path Queries). A conjunctive regular path query (CRPQ) has the form

$$Q^C(x_1, ..., x_n) \leftarrow y_1 R_1 y_2 \wedge ... \wedge y_{2m-1} R_m y_{2m},$$

where $x_1, \ldots, x_n, y_1, \ldots, y_m$ are node variables. The variables x_i are a subset of y_i (i.e., $\{x_1, \ldots, x_n\} \subseteq \{y_1, \ldots, y_m\}$), and they are called distinguished variables. The answer $ans(Q^C, K)$ for a CRPQ is the set of tuples $(v_1, ..., v_n)$ of nodes in K such that there is a total mapping σ to nodes, with $\sigma(x_i) = v_i$ for every distinguished variable, and $(\sigma(y_i), \sigma(y_{i+1})) \in ans(Q^R, K)$ for every RPQ Q^R defined by the term $y_i R_i y_{i+1}$.

4.2 CRowdPQ

CRowdPQ is derived from CRPQ by extending the notion of RPQ with DRPQ and RRPQ defined as follows.

Definition 3 (DRPQ). A descriptor regular path query (DRPQ) $Q^{DR} \leftarrow DR$ is a regular path query defined over the extended alphabet $\Sigma \bigcup \Gamma$, where Γ is a human-interpretable infinite alphabet of labels. Essentially, the *Descriptor* relations DR are free-text conditions that can be answered by human workers. Kleene star in descriptor regular path queries corresponds to iterative human computation.

Definition 4 (RRPQs). A resolver regular path query (RRPQ) $Q^{RR} \leftarrow RR$ is a regular path query over a predefined alphabet $P = produce \cup consume$, where the labels *produce* and *consume* correspond to dataflow producers and consumers respectively. The left operand of a *Resolver* relation RR always has to be a worker node supplied by an integrated crowdsourcing platform. Essentially, the *Resolver* relations are dataflow constructs between the data to be fetched and the workers working on the data. Note, Resolvers are not the only relations that can be specified between a worker and the task at hand, i.e., RPQs can be used to specify worker constraints. Kleene star and concatenation over the *produce* relation represent higher-order selection of workers, e.g., workers find workers who find workers who can fetch data.

4.3 Expressiveness

In this section we demonstrate the expressiveness of CRowdPQ by implementing the three use cases from the motivating scenario. For this purpose we employ a CRowdPQ-enhanced version of SPARQL 1.1: Descriptor (DRPQ) and Resolver (RRPQ) relations are denoted using triangle and square brackets respectively.

Synchronous Collaboration. Implement a web page, and create images for it. These two tasks require distinct skill sets. Also, to improve collaboration, workers assigned to the tasks should be socially related, or at least in close social vicinity (i.e., there exists a path between them of maximum length of 2).

```
SELECT ?webPage , ?pictures
WHERE
{
    ?webPage <``Design a web page''>.
    ?pictures <``Draw pictures for the web page''> ?webPage.
    ?webDesigner [produce] ?webPage.
    ?artist [produce] ?pictures.
    ?webDesigner friendOf[1, 2] ?artist.
    ?webDesigner [consume] ?pictures.
    ?artist [consume] ?webPage.
}
```

Worker Discovery. You have a recorded melody fragment and want to know what song it belongs to. You want only those workers to work on it who like rock music.

```
SELECT ?melodyName
WHERE
{
    ?melodyName <``Is similar to''> @file.
    ?melodyName <``Can you recognize the melody?''>.
    ?musicFan [produce] ?melodyName.
    ?musicFan <``Find a person passionate about rock music.''>.
    ?indexWorker [produce] ?musicFan.
}
```

Note, that the specification of workers with no constraints is optional, i.e., *?indexWorker* can be omitted.

Workflow and Social Relations. You need a set of hand-drawn pictures. You ask crowd workers to draw and rate the pictures. To avoid biased ratings, workers rating the pictures should not be socially related to workers drawing the pictures.

```
SELECT ?picture, ?ranking
WHERE
{
    ?picture <``Draw a funny sheep.''>.
    ?talentedPainter [produce] ?picture.
    ?mercilessCritic [consume] ?picture.
    ?mercilessCritic [produce] ?ranking.
    ?ranking <``How funny is this sheep?''> ?picture.
    FILTER NOT EXISTS { ?talentedPainter friendOf ?mercilessCritic }
}
```

Note, the example above can be easily changed to a control group (i.e., one worker creates a picture and another one filters it) by replacing the `?rank` variable with the `?filteredPicture` variable and adjusting descriptor relations appropriately.

5 Database Engine

In this section we show how classical database components can be extended to be able to cope with human workers as schemaless, volatile and context-dependent data sources.

5.1 Synchronous Collaboration: Social Formations and Caching

In Examples 1 and 3 of Sect. 4.3 we have shown the expressivity of our query language with respect to specifying social formations.

In traditional RDBMS, the purpose of query caching is to speed up query evaluation by reusing results from previous queries. While classical caching mechanisms of preserving query results are also applicable in Crowdstore, here we consider a different kind of caching. Instead of caching results, we cache workers and social formations of workers (teams) in case of synchronous collaboration. If a worker has been answering recently a similar query to the query at hand, she might be a good fit to the task. For example, if a worker has been searching recently through newspapers for information about charity events, she might be able to quickly answer a query of searching recent newspapers for road incidents.

The key element for efficiency of such caches is the ability to identify similarities between queries, which resorts to finding a similar subgraph in a list of cached query graphs (subgraph isomorphism). Matching descriptors can be achieved by finding similarity between texts (or extracting labels). Answering subgraph isomorphism is a NP-complete problem, so when using exact matching (isomorphism) the query cache will not scale. Moreover, for complex queries expressing dense social formations, like cliques, it might be difficult to find an exact match. To alleviate these two problems we can use approximate graph matching, which, however, might not return the most suitable workers. Depending on the importance of the relations between workers, we can choose either of the two heuristics: relax the input query graph by removing worker nodes or data nodes in order to focus on worker experience (i.e., who worked successfully on what) or maximize social similarity respectively (i.e., what teams were successful).

Such quality caches can be pre-built by running pre-labeled queries over gold standard data (e.g., [5,7,11]) and caching workers and teams that have shown good quality.

5.2 Crowd Indexes

In Example 2 of Sect. 4.3 we have shown how the discovery of crowd workers can be crowdsourced itself. We call index workers those workers that select and search for workers for a query at hand. The distinction to regular workers should be driven by different reward mechanisms applied to index workers, i.e., index workers should be rewarded depending on the work quality of the workers they choose. The Crowdstore design incorporates two techniques for worker indexes:

- Routing indexes. In the most trivial case the system can ask an index worker to simply enter a list of workers she thinks satisfy the descriptor relation(s), or a list of index workers who can route further. Routing indexes represent directed graphs, and Crowdstore needs to detect cycles.
- Zonemap indexes. If there are other relations in addition to descriptors that are adjacent to a worker node in a query graph, then Crowdstore can efficiently filter worker candidates. In such case, index workers can be presented with a list of workers they can select from. However, such lists might be immerse, so the system needs to group workers by available tags (e.g., by country, or age), presenting several hierarchical lists to index workers. This approach enables index workers to quickly filter the list of workers.

5.3 Query Optimization

One of the central aspects of query optimization is join ordering. Consider the following example: "Where was this picture taken? - this query should be answered by workers living in London". An extremely inefficient case of evaluating such query is sending the question to all the workers, and then filtering responses by workers living in London. When joining descriptor and regular relations the join order is predefined, as automated filtering is always more efficient than filtering done by a crowd. However, join ordering for two crowd-produced relations can be highly error-prone and inefficient as the cost of relations is not known beforehand. Contrarily to existing crowd-powered approaches, in Crowdstore we take a different approach by assuming that a query writer can have better insight into predicate selectivity than a crowd. CRowdPQ, as shown in Example 3 in Sect. 4.3, provides a query writer with the ability to specify join ordering by using *consume* relations. If no *consume* relations are specified, then existing joining techniques can be applied.

Another approach CRowdPQ provides is "denormalized" ("collaborative") joins: instead of asking crowd workers to work independently on two separate relations, Crowdstore can ask workers to collaborate and produce already matched and joined results. The benefit of "collaborative" join is that the worker produced data can be ambiguous and, without direct contact with the data producer, difficult to match. Moreover, creative tasks require collaboration, as shown in Example 1 in Sect. 4.3. If a single worker node in a query is connected with a *produce* relation to multiple nodes, then "denormalization" will result in sending a single HIT to a crowd worker asking to provide data for the whole query graph. When working on "collaborative" joins, crowd workers will need to use synchronous collaboration software.

Joining two crowd-produced relations without predefined join ordering allows two approaches. The first approach consists of two sets of workers producing data for relations independently and in parallel, and then a third set of workers joins the two produced relations. The second approach is inherent to relational DBMS, i.e., data is produced for one relation and then is used to filter in-place data for another relation.

5.4 Crowd Pool

In [2,3] the authors show that paying workers a small wage to stay on call is enough to draw a crowd together two to three seconds later. The problem here is which workers to keep on payroll based on variable query patterns, e.g., what subset of workers satisfy most queries given the budget constraints. If a worker becomes less active, it is better to replace the worker with another one. Basically, an efficient system needs to maintain a limited set of useful/active workers and efficiently replace ineffective workers with new ones. This scenario resembles problems addressed by the buffer pool manager in traditional RDBMs, i.e., limited working set, replacement of least recently used database pages. Henceforth, we draw here correspondence between crowd workers and database pages: similarly as how a crowd worker can generate/provide data, a database page can provide table records. The central part of the buffer pool manager in RDBMs is the clock algorithm, which evicts least-recently-used pages (LRU). The Crowd pool component in Crowdstore similarly evicts least-recently-active (LRA) workers. The Crowdstore adaptation of the clock algorithm, however, incorporates the following adjustments:

- Tracking slow-performing workers. The purpose of keeping a page in-memory in RDBMs is the ability to fetch results faster. Similarly, keeping a worker on payroll leads to the expectation of fast results. If a worker responds slower than other payroll (and non-payroll) workers, then Crowd pool can evict such worker.
- Delayed enrollment on payroll. In RDBMs when reading records from a database page it is necessary to fetch the page in memory (page-in). In Crowdstore, however, there is no such restriction, i.e., even if some query required workers with a skill set disjoint with skill sets in Crowd pool, such skill set might not be needed again. So, apart of counting how useful is a payroll worker, Crowd pool needs to count how useful a non-payroll worker is.

6 Future Work, Discussion and Conclusion

In this paper we present the hybrid human-machine database Crowdstore, powered by the graph query extension CRowdPQ. Contrarily to existing crowdsourcing query languages, CRowdPQ can express social collaborations between crowd workers, sophisticated worker discovery and complex crowdsourcing workflow patterns. Incorporation of dataflow constructs makes CRPQs slightly less declarative, since a query writer can directly influence execution plans. However, mispredictions in query evaluation performed by the crowd possess considerable cost overhead, rendering explicit join ordering critical. Crowdstore serves as a holistic design concept of a new generation crowdsourcing database, featuring extended indexes, caches and buffer pool manager. A more detailed description and evaluation of each of these components will be provided in our future work.

References

1. Acosta, M., Simperl, E., Flöck, F., Norton, B.: A sparql engine for crowdsourcing query processing using microtasks. Institute AIFB, KIT, Karlsruhe (2012)
2. Bernstein, M.S., Brandt, J., Miller, R.C., Karger, D.R.: Crowds in two seconds: Enabling realtime crowd-powered interfaces. In: Proceedings of the 24th Annual ACM Symposium on User Interface Software and Technology, UIST 2011, pp. 33–42, New York, NY, USA. ACM (2011)
3. Bernstein, M.S., Karger, D.R., Miller, R.C., Brandt, J.: Analytic methods for optimizing realtime crowdsourcing. Computing Research Repository (2012)
4. Bozzon, A., Brambilla, M., Ceri, S.: Answering search queries with crowdsearcher. In: Proceedings of the 21st International Conference on World Wide Web, WWW 2012, pp. 1009–1018, New York, NY, USA. ACM (2012)
5. C. Callison-Burch. Fast, cheap, and creative: Evaluating translation quality using amazon's mechanical turk. In Proceedings of the 2009 Conference on Empirical Methods in Natural Language Processing: Volume 1 - Volume 1, EMNLP 2009, pp. 286–295, Stroudsburg, PA, USA. Association for Computational Linguistics (2009)

6. Calvanese, D., Giacomo, G.D., Lenzerini, M., Vardi, M.Y.: Containment of conjunctive regular path queries with inverse. In: Proceedings of the 2000 International Conference on Knowledge Representation and Reasoning, KR 2000, pp. 176–185. Breckenridge, Colorado, USA (2000)
7. Downs, J.S., Holbrook, M.B., Sheng, S., Cranor, L.F., Are your participants gaming the system?: Screening mechanical turk workers. In: Proceedings of the SIGCHI Conference on Human Factors in Computing Systems, CHI 2010, pp. 2399–2402, New York, NY, USA. ACM (2010)
8. Franklin, M.J., Kossmann, D., Kraska, T., Ramesh, S., Xin, R., Crowddb: answering queries with crowdsourcing. In: Proceedings of the ACM SIGMOD International Conference on Management of Data, SIGMOD 2011, pp. 61–72, New York, NY, USA, 2011. ACM (2011)
9. Ishii, H., Kobayashi, M., Clearboard: a seamless medium for shared drawing and conversation with eye contact. In: Proceedings of the SIGCHI Conference on Human factors in computing systems, pp. 525–532. ACM (1992)
10. Kittur, A., Nickerson, J.V., Bernstein, M., Gerber, E., Shaw, A., Zimmerman, J., Lease, M., Horton, J.: The future of crowd work. In: Proceedings of the 2013 Conference on Computer Supported Cooperative Work, CSCW 2013, pp. 1301–1318, New York, NY, USA. ACM (2013)
11. Le, J., Edmonds, A., Hester, V., Biewald, L., Ensuring quality in crowdsourced search relevance evaluation: the effects of training question distribution. In: SIGIR Workshop on Crowdsourcing for Search Evaluation, pp. 21–26 (2010)
12. Liptchinsky, V., Satzger, B., Zabolotnyi, R., Dustdar, S.: Expressive languages for selecting groups from graph-structured data. In: Proceedings of the 22Nd International Conference on World Wide Web, WWW 2013, pp. 761–770, Republic and Canton of Geneva, Switzerland. International World Wide Web Conferences Steering Committee (2013)
13. Marcus, A., Karger, D., Madden, S., Miller, R., Oh, S.: Counting with the crowd. In: Proceedings of the 39th International Conference on Very Large Data Bases, PVLDB 2013, pp. 109–120. VLDB Endowment (2013)
14. Marcus, A., Wu, E., Karger, D., Madden, S., Miller, R.: Human-powered sorts and joins. Proc. VLDB Endow. **5**(1), 13–24 (2011)
15. Marcus, A., Wu, E., Karger, D.R., Madden, S., Miller, R.C., Crowdsourced databases: query processing with people. In: 5th Biennial Conference on Innovative Data Systems Research (2011)
16. Parameswaran, A., Polyzotis, N.: Answering queries using humans, algorithms and databases. In: Conference on Inovative Data Systems Research (CIDR 2011). Stanford InfoLab, January 2011
17. Parameswaran, A.G., Park, H., Garcia-Molina, H., Polyzotis, N., Widom, J., Deco: declarative crowdsourcing. In: Proceedings of the 21st ACM International Conference on Information and Knowledge Management, CIKM 2012, pp. 1203–1212, New York, NY, USA. ACM.(2012)
18. Wang, J., Kraska, T., Franklin, M.J., Feng, J.: Crowder: crowdsourcing entity resolution. Proc. VLDB Endow. **5**(11), 1483–1494 (2012)
19. Wang, J., Li, G., Kraska, T., Franklin, M. J., Feng, J.: Leveraging transitive relations for crowdsourced joins. In: Proceedings of the 2013 ACM SIGMOD International Conference on Management of Data, SIGMOD 2013, pp. 229–240, New York, NY, USA. ACM (2013)
20. Wood, P.T.: Query languages for graph databases. ACM SIGMOD Record **41**(1), 50–60 (2012)

An ARM-Based Hadoop Performance Evaluation Platform: Design and Implementation

Xiaohu Fan[1(✉)], Si Chen[1], Shipeng Qi[1], Xincheng Luo[1], Jing Zeng[1], Hao Huang[2], and Changsheng Xie[3]

[1] School of Computer Science and Technology, HUST, Wuhan, China
{fanxiaohu, M201272616, qishipeng, luoxc613, zengjing}@hust.edu.cn

[2] School of Software Engineering, HUST, Wuhan, China
thao@hust.edu.cn

[3] Wuhan National Laboratory for Optoelecgtronics, 1037 Luoyu Road, Wuhan, China
cs-xie@hust.edu.cn

Abstract. As the growth of cluster scale, huge power consumption will be a major bottleneck for future large-scale high performance cluster. However, most existing cloud-clusters are based on power-hungry X86-64 which merely aims to common enterprise applications. In this paper, we improve the cluster performance by leveraging ARM SoCs which feature energy-efficient. In our prototype, cluster with five Cubieboard4, we run HPL and achieve 9.025 GFLOPS which exhibits a great computational potential. Moreover, we build our measurement model and conduct extensive evaluation by comparing the performance of the cluster with WordCount, k-Means (etc.) running in Map-Reduce mode and Spark mode respectively. The experiment results demonstrate that our cluster can guarantee higher computational efficiency on compute-intensive utilities with the RDD feature of Spark. Finally, we propose a more suitable theoretical hybrid architecture of future cloud clusters with a stronger master and customized ARMv8 based TaskTrackers for data-intensive computing.

Keywords: HPC · ARM cluster · Cost-effective · Data-intensive

1 Introduction

As scale and dimension increase with the combination of Cloud Computing and Internet of Things in the Big Data era, massive data burden more pressure on compute and storage performance. Fortunately, Hadoop framework enables an alternative collaboration cluster implementation of High Performance Computing (HPC) and Data Center, which holds a strong market share. However, CTOs hesitated by the cost and security problems of an enterprise deployment. Besides, data-intensive applications require tremendous power. Cases [1, 2] show that total energy cost over a few years of operation exceeds the cost of the hardware. Along with the expansion of cluster scale, future HPC systems will be limited by power consumption.

S. Guo et al. (Eds.): CollaborateCom 2015, LNICST 163, pp. 82–94, 2016.
DOI: 10.1007/978-3-319-28910-6_8

Consequently, the weight of supercomputers ranking criterion gradually shifted from Top500 [3] to Green500 [4]. Most of the Top500 and Green500 leaders are x86 processor based system combined with GPU and other accelerate technologies. Analysis of current HPC shows that 40–60 % of the energy consumption is due to the compute nodes, 10 % to the interconnect and storage, and major remainder to infrastructure itself especially, cooling [1, 5]. Taking the performance and cost of power into account, the born nature of ARM chips is historically related to lower power consumption and cost efficient, which makes ARM a promising candidate in terms of future Data Centers. Nowadays, the 8 cores Cortex-A15 [6] processors provide satisfied performance in cost guaranteed A15 giant share of mobile field. The next generation ARMv8 instruction set, namely the A50 series [7] features a 64-bit address space, which makes ARM chips real alternate player for HPC and cloud computing.

Following this trend, we attempt to evaluate the performance of ARM based Hadoop cluster, considering network bandwidth, workload, performance and Total Own Cost of future enterprise Hadoop cluster. In this paper, we use A15 based Cubieboard4 to build a cluster with Hadoop and Spark. In order to verify whether ARM clusters is suitable for common data-intensive applications or not, we try to evaluate the performance and seek for constrains. With hardware environment limited and following common practice, we tried 3 different configuration settings to verify the optimized cluster performance with same workload on same application in weak scaling approach. Main contribution lies in: (1) Evaluate the feasibility of a Hadoop cluster based on the current leader chip in the mobile domain with common applications. (2) Present a simple method to estimate efficiency of cluster by abstracting the CPU execution time of a small cluster as prototype and learn experience. (3) Propose a customized hybrid architecture with stronger master node and ARMv8 TaskTrackers cluster. The experiments show that this architecture can achieve great performance under higher cluster bandwidth.

This paper is organized as follows. The Sect. 2 gives some background information of low power HPC. In Sect. 3, we propose our theory, measure method and model, bind the micro CPU time and macro execution time to evaluate the performance and the bottleneck of ARM based cluster. Experimental results, analysis and a case study of improvement is shown in Sect. 4 with a theoretical future architecture. Finally, Sect. 5 presents the conclusions.

2 Related Works

As great methods that Green500 leaders have taken. Google published its GFS [8], BigTable [9] and Map-Reduce [10] scheme during last decade, confirmed the distributed cluster is feasible in large-scale data applications. Supported by the Apache foundation, Hadoop collaborates the cluster performs satisfied and the rapid development is in continuous [11–13]. Besides, the emerging spark [14] using RDD to implement in-memory compute enhanced the performance of Hadoop clusters greatly.

However, vast majority Hadoop clusters are x86 based, barely ARM based trial except Raspberry Pi [15, 16] clusters of Cortex-A8 based with a 700 MHz processor and 512 MB RAM. Comparison of x86 and ARM architectures of data center has been discussed by [17]. In comparison of big data workload on wimpy nodes and traditional big nodes, the Cortex-A8 based AppleTV2 cluster [18, 19] running HPL in a cluster environment attempt to assess the low power solution, achieved 460.4 MFLOPS. For common utility, [16] establishing pi spark cluster, however, is constrained by A8's performance, 100 Mb network and I/O bandwidth. Barcelona Supercomputing Center used 96 cores of Cortex-A9 based Barcelona cluster [20] in 2013 and update the cores to Cortex-A15 as Tibidabo [2] to achieve a theoretical 1046MFLOPS/W, but it is a super-compute-oriented special customized cluster. The NUS researchers reach new levels of performance and cost-efficiency [21], and proved that ARM based cluster is not fit for I/O intensive workloads but good at databases query processing. Large data processing in the recent fiery geographic information [22–25] required larger amount of power-hungry clusters.

Generally, most existing work about improving the energy efficiency and performance of cluster focused on x86 based Hadoop clusters. As for wimpy node clusters, either attempt the simple application scenario or build super customized cluster. In this paper, we use 5 standard Cortex-A15 based Cubeborad4 to construct a small Hadoop cluster without other accelerate technique to establish analysis models and run several common algorithms to evaluate the performance and cluster efficiency. It carried out a comparative study of applications with same workload under different configuration and we tried to find out constraints and improvement via analysis. The results of comparison verify the feasibility and advantage of our scheme.

3 Measurements-Driven Modeling

Ideally, all nodes keep peak capability determines the performance upper bound of the cluster. Affected by network bandwidth, communication overhead, I/O and other latency, it is widely accepted that the total cluster performance gradually decrease with the nodes expansion. As for single node, performance of ARM CPU can be measured by the rate of CPU running time in the total program execution time to get the efficiency of single node. For the cluster, we focus on the parallel processing efficiency, and use throughput or parallel speedup ratio to indicate the efficiency. The whole roadmap of our experiments is described in Fig. 1.

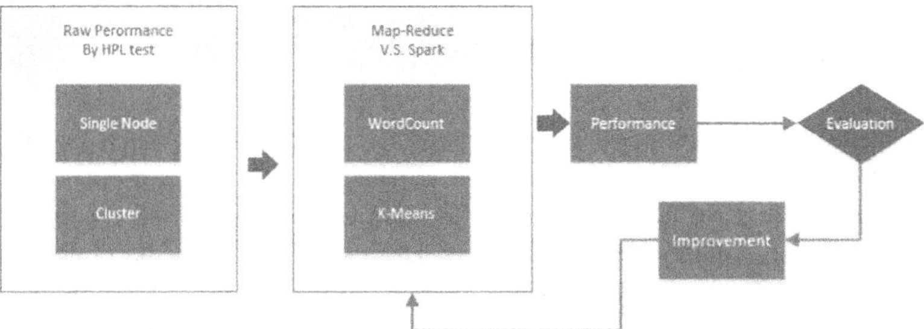

Fig. 1. Roadmap of experiments. Firstly, get peak performance. Then, analysis the performance according to the result, find the bottleneck to improve the efficiency of cluster and compare the result under different hardware settings

Firstly, we test the I/O and CPU performance of raw Cubieboard4 using simple command line and HPL with Ubuntu 14.04 on both single node and cluster to get actual results. Then, we evaluate the performance by running some applications in Hadoop and Spark. Finally, we improve the throughput according to our evaluation with bottleneck of Cubieboard4 cluster found.

We characterize data intensive execution on 1–5 small nodes by evaluating the performance of some well-known applications such as HPL, HDFS read/write, WordCount, k-Means, comparisons between Map-Reduce mode and Spark RDD. The analysis is based on the measurement of execution time, each actual throughput, CPU efficiency and power consumption.

Considering some negative effects: Cubieboard4, Linux OS, and Hadoop overhead themselves, communication offset of cores, attenuation of each node exist, we use the computation intensive HPL as a benchmark to determine whether the actual computing performance is suitable. Then, we use the performance of single node as the baseline of the cluster to evaluate the extension. According to [26] research, due to the overhead of CPU communication and offset of I/O the efficiency of large-scale clusters actually accounts for only a fraction of the running time. Thus, a Hadoop operation process is abstracted as Fig. 2 shown below, T is the total running time of the process, and T_{exe} is the CPU running time abstracted from the grey in the upper part of Fig. 2, $T_{cpu(i)}$ is the actual execution time of each CPU in the blue part. The red part in the T_{exe} is the communication synchronous overhead. Deviation does exist in this method, but simpler to measure and estimate with a viable accuracy.

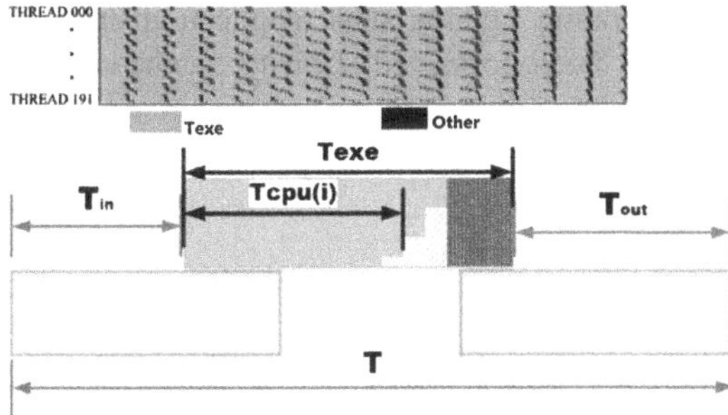

Fig. 2. Abstract CPU time in process of application on Hadoop (Color figure online)

As can be seen in Fig. 2, $T_{cpu(i)}$ is a micro measured value, T is a macro measured time. In order to facilitate the measurement we did not take a fixed large amount of the total task. For fairly comparison, each node is assigned the same sized task load, similar to a weak-scaling approach. According to Gustafson's law [27], communication overhead is a linear positive correlation with number of nodes in the cluster [28]. Thus, we are able to estimate the delay and overhead of cluster, and modeling the performance of cluster with deviation. We propose our estimate model as follow, n is the number of nodes, C is a constant for overhead, $C \times n$ is linear correlation with n.

$$Performance_{cluster} = \frac{Total\,Task}{Total\,Time} = \frac{n \times Task_{single-node}}{Time_{single-node} + C \times n} \quad (1)$$

In this method, once given the Task data and application, the workload is confirmed. With the results of the single node as a basic reference value, in addition with the results of the rest nodes, C value under the fixed workload could be calculated by fitting approach. The smaller constant C value is the greater performance of cluster achieves. Otherwise, similar type of application might not fit for ARM based cluster extension. In this model, execution time and total run time of the progress, CPU records are required for both single compute node and the whole cluster.

The cluster bandwidth depends on the minimal of network, board I/O interface, read/write of storage. Eff_{cpu} is a micro numerical calculation, while the Compute Ratio is a macro time accounting measurement, we can use results above to estimate the efficiency of the cluster, defined as $Eff_{cluster}$.

$$Eff_{cluster} = Eff_{cpu} \times Compute\ Ratio = \frac{\frac{\sum_{i=0}^{n} T_{cpu(i)}}{n}}{T_{exe}} \times \frac{T_{exe}}{T} = \frac{\sum_{i=0}^{n} T_{cpu(i)}}{n \times T} \quad (2)$$

4 Results and Analysis

We use 5 CubieBoard4 development boards to establish our cluster for evaluation via different hardware configuration running same application under same workload, in order to verify that whether the performance of cluster can be improved when hardware

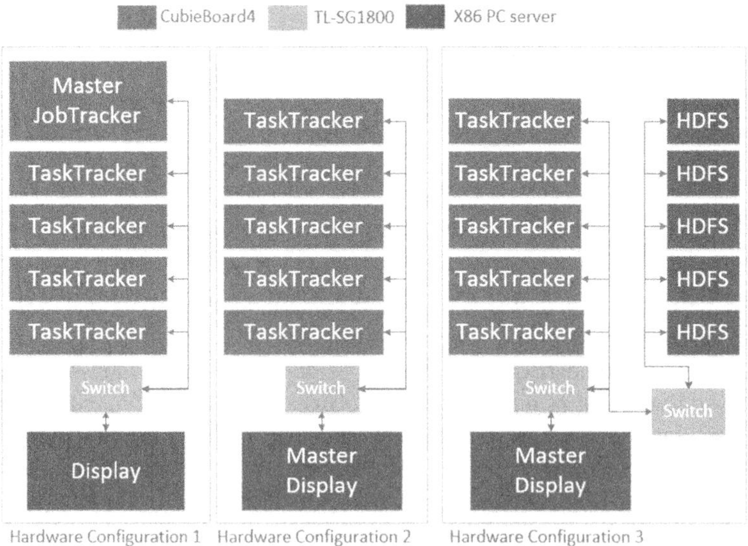

Fig. 3. Abstract architecture of 3 hardware configurations

limitation along with the factors changed. Following common practice, the bottleneck and constrains of the development board can be infer from the actual performance measurement. The architecture of hardware configurations is shown in Fig. 3.

Initially, we used 5 Cubieboard4 development boards to construct a pure ARM based cluster, as Configuration 1 shows. One x86 workstation is only used for console control and display by operators. The hardware parameters of experimental environment is shown in Table 1. Eight ports TP-LINK TL-SG1008 gigabit switch connected the cluster as a LAN,every ARM node and the x86 workstation are connected with CAT6 network cable.

Table 1. Hardware environment

Item	Intel	ARM	
CPU	Core i7	Cortex A15	Cortex A7
ISA	X86-64	ARMv71	
Cores	4	4	
Frequency	3.50 GHz	0.60–2.00 GHz	300–1.00 GHz
L1 Data cache	4x32 KB	32 KB	
L2 Cache	4x256 KB	2 MB	
Memory type	DDR3 2x8 GB	DDR3 2 GB	
USB	USB3.0	1xUSB3.0 OTG 4xUSB2.0	

4.1 Single Node Performance

We use Coremark, which is a platform-independent testing program developed by EEMBC, to evaluate the single node I/O performance of raw development board and x86 workstation before the Map-Reduce approach on the cluster. The testing results on single node comparison between ARM and x86 is shown in Table 2.

Table 2. Raw performance of single node

Performance		Intel	ARM	
		Core i7	A15 (big)	A7 (little)
CPU	CoreMark (iterations/MHz)	5.3	3.52	5.0
	Dhrystone (MIPS/MHz)	5.8	3.1	3.7
	Power Consumption (w/h)	50.6	15	11
Storage system	Write (MB/s)	165.0	24.5	21.7
	Read (MB/s)	173.0	31.6	26.5
Network	TCP bandwidth (Mbps)	944	421	411
	UDP bandwidth (Mbps)	810	405	399
	Ping delay (ms)	0.20	0.59	0.59

4.2 Performance of ARM Cluster

For the computational performance, we use HPL to test the computing ability of ARM cluster. Based on the single node performance, we record the results of 1 ~ 5 nodes and calculate the Eff_{cpu} and Speed-Up Ratio and actual performance of FLOPs and power, shown in Table 3.

Table 3. HPL performance results of raw cluster.

Nodes	Eff_{cpu}	Speed-up ratio	GFLOPS	PPW (MFLOPS/w)
1	100 %	Base	2.177	151.2
2	94.3 %	1.709	3.720	123.6
3	88.3 %	2.559	5.572	145.5
4	85.1 %	3.287	7.155	143.3
5	82.9 %	4.146	9.025	138.8

In order to verify our Hypothesis under fair environment, we perform a weak scalability test. We keep same feasible size per node as weak-scaling way to evaluate the speed-up ratio and performance. The actual measured data and model prediction comparison as follow.

Performance of WordCount. WordCount is a classic application which features on frequency read and write on HDFS in Map-Reduce way, while decreasing the read/write rate with RDD on Spark indicate better performance. Thus, we try to verify our idea with the actual results of both Map-Reduce and Spark on the cluster, and the results shown in conjunction with Fig. 5.

From the results of experiments we found that the performance of our original hardware configurations as a pure ARM based cluster is disappointing through the analysis of dashboard of master node. Constrained by CPU and memory capacity, the compile and delivery of task occupied too much time during the whole process, both in the Map-Reduce and Spark way. Making full use of x86 based workstation, larger memory, L2 cache and board bandwidth guarantee the better performance of master node for the scheduling and monitoring works. So we propose the hardware configuration 2 scheme: let x86 workstation be the master alone, and the rest ARM boards as the computational nodes. As presented in Fig. 4, the performance is greatly improved by the way of having a strong master node of configuration 2 than 1.

As can be seen from Fig. 4, a stronger master node indicated better performance of the cluster. However, WordCount is not a typically compute-intensive application, comparative low computational work with the size of task shows poor scalability. Besides, a decline shows in the speed up of the Map-Reduce mode at 5 nodes. The cluster efficiency is decreasing dramatically with node extension, the low throughput of HDFS I/O determines that this kind of application features frequently read or write on HDFS, is not fit for the ARM based cluster. The performance shrink ascribed to the mechanism of HDFS, which illustrated in Sect. 4.3.

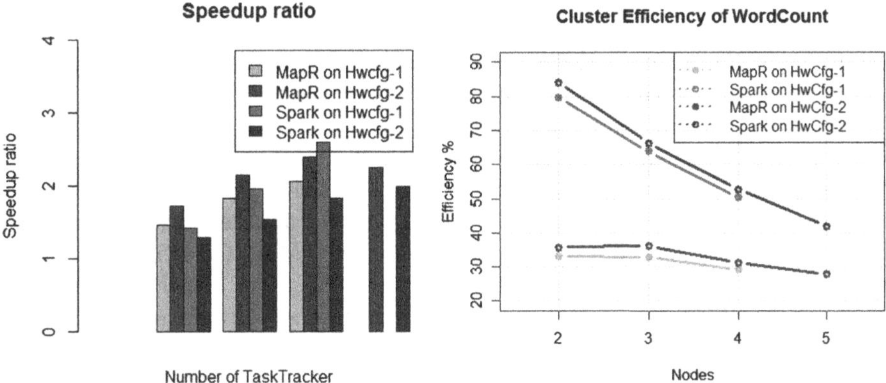

Fig. 4. Speed-up ratio and efficiency of cluster on WordCount.

Performance of k-Means. The nature of k-Means is the operation process of an iterative calculation. During this process, a lot of intermediate results and small data update will be put onto the HDFS in the Map-Reduce way, which indicates a great impact on Hadoop. Owing to the RDD of Spark approach, none write operation would be called until the result output, theoretically means great improvement in the performance of Spark. Thus, given 200 MB of workload, k = 8 and iteration for 6 times we calculate the results as shown in Fig. 5. 5, k-Means on Spark features CPU intensive with a relatively small amount of read/write tasks shows that I/O still is the main factor which restrict the performance of clusters.

Considering the number of nodes, running time, throughput and power, we can ascribe the inefficiency drawbacks on Map-Reduce model: mandated shuffle phrase and cumbersome reduce joins waste a large amount of computation on scheduling and synchronous, and communication overhead in HDFS. Map-Reduce model seems not fit for ARM based clusters, but RDD model on Spark with compute intensive application is feasible to ARM features.

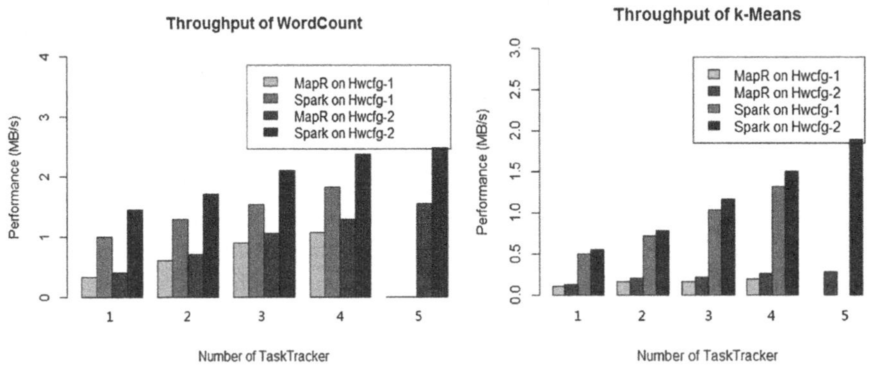

Fig. 5. Comparison of WordCount and K-Means by different configurations.

4.3 Case Study of Improvement on Different Setting

The results of CubieBoard4 is not satisfied enough due to the non-optimized development boards, as shown in Table 1, the inefficiencies due to the bottleneck of the I/O interface chips of USB. If the hardware performance of HDFS is improved, better performance would be achieved. So we try the hardware configuration 3 scheme: One x86 workstation as the master node, additional 5 × 86 workstation with sata3 HDD as HDFS, connect ARM cluster and x86 HDFS with gigabit networks. In this way, performance of HDD based HDFS is better than the 400 Mbps CubieBoard4 network capacity. Thus, the bottleneck is transferred from the USB to the network interface. So we use the TestDFSIO, which is the benchmark testing software to evaluate the throughput of HDFS on different hardware configuration, the results shown in Fig. 6.

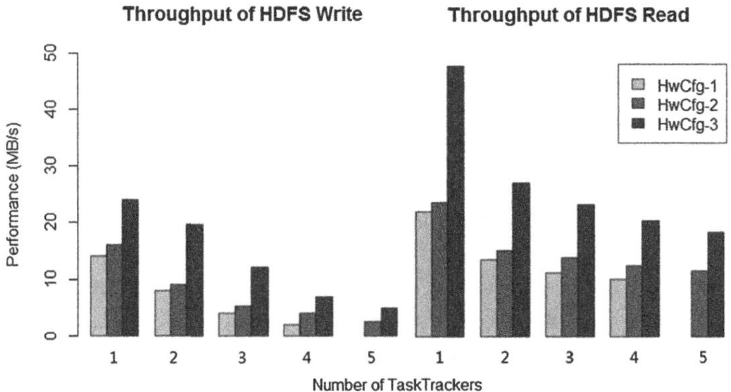

Fig. 6. Throughput of HDFS read and write operation.

As presented in Fig. 6, the throughput of HDFS decreased as nodes increased. Partly due to the hardware capability, as Configuration 3 performs better because higher I/O on HDD. Other factors of decrease lies in the scheduling and the 3-copies-redundance mechanism of HDFS itself. In hardware configuration 1, the performance of master node prolonged the total execution time. We replaced with a higher performance master node as configuration 2, the USB I/O interface inhibit the total performance. As we transfer the bottleneck to network capacity in configuration 3, the performance almost reach the hard limitation of the non-optimized development boards.

Then we recur our experiments of k-Means and WordCount on Spark under same workload by different hardware configurations to see the performance, plus a Map-Reduce results as basic reference value, shown in Fig. 7. Spark performs better than Map-Reduce model as the grey line compared with black line, and improved with higher hardware configurations. Compute-intensive application shows better improvement of performance. The cluster efficiency of each application is described in Table 4. Affected by HDFS, the efficiency of cluster decayed as the redundancy backup tripled the I/O loads.

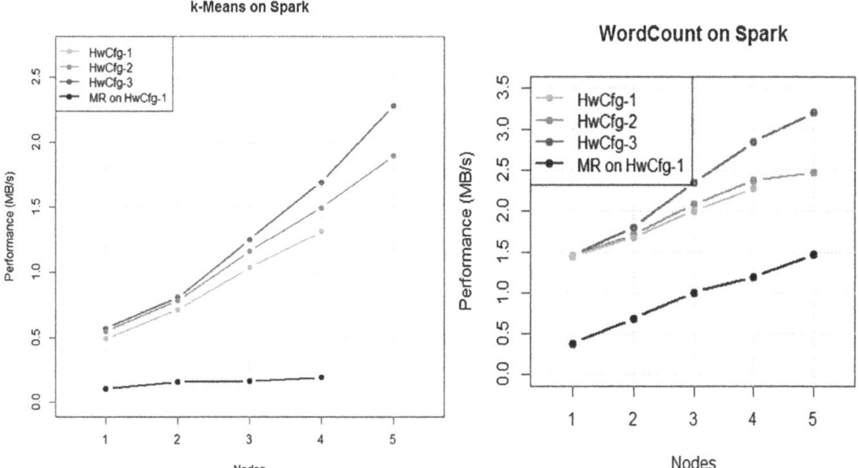

Fig. 7. Performance of K-Means and WordCount on 3 hardware configurations

Table 4. Cluster efficiency of spark

Application	k-Means			WordCount		
Hardware configuration	1	2	3	1	2	3
Nodes	Cluster efficiency					
2	85.88 %	88.38 %	90.8 %	79.7 %	81.4 %	85.8 %
3	71.56 %	75.98 %	82.78 %	63.79 %	66.23 %	74.5 %
4	58.41 %	64.7 %	74.97 %	50.43 %	52.68 %	62.99 %
5	N/A	51.5 %	68.89 %	N/A	41.96 %	54.47 %

The RDD mechanism reduced the HDFS read and write frequency, solved part of the I/O intensive operations inefficiency of ARM cluster. But compared with HPL result, the current performance of cluster is far from its limitation, which means abundant potential space for ARM cluster to improve. Besides, 2 GB memory constrains the performance of Spark, CPU utility is not high enough when the memory is full occupied, and insufficient to handle larger dataset. In order to get a fair compare, we use standard example programs without any optimized methods. Analysis under the current CubieBoard4 hardware configuration, to construct an ARM cluster only fit for compute intensive applications on Spark within a limited scale constrained by memory size.

ARMv8 with 64bit address bandwidth will solve the memory boundary, and customized hardware configuration that improve the I/O, network and board bandwidth to match the CPU performance are required in enterprise usage of ARM based cluster. Besides, there are lots of optimized methods at system and software level. Thus, one strong master node, which required by the Spark RDD mechanism, with customized ARM cluster, in addition with optimize methods is adequate to build an enterprise cluster under home-level temperature environment, which means a lower cost to build a

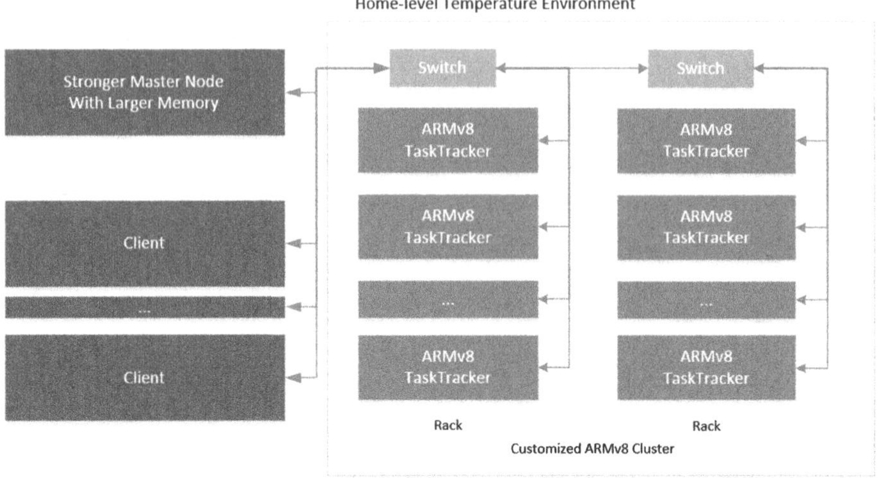

Fig. 8. Theoretical architecture of future ARMv8 cluster for enterprise application on spark

private Spark cluster. The theoretical architecture of the future ARM based clusters is shown in Fig. 8.

5 Conclusions

In this paper we present an ARM based Hadoop cluster with 5 CubieBoard4 development boards, which achieves 9.025 GFLOPS on HPL. We put forward our unique measurement modeling method to evaluate the cluster efficiency. Under 3 testing settings we systematically run the common applications to measure and evaluate the performance, efficiency of the cluster to verify the improvement. Through the experiments we assess the bottleneck of development boards and try to improve the performance, demonstrate that the RDD performance of spark on the ARM cluster is significantly better than the non-optimized Map-Reduce mode. The limitation of I/O interface chips of the pure development board constrained the performance since cluster bandwidth can not match the computational capacity. However, a customized setting is required for enterprise utility. Thus we present a heterogeneous architecture of a strong master node with customized I/O interfaces which may benefit the performance of the cluster.

One high performance JobTracker/Namenode with larger memory takes charge of scheduling, compiling and delivery the jobs is required by the Spark mechanism itself, TaskTrackers as the distributed compute nodes use a customized ARM cluster in Tibidabo way is competent to compute-intensive enterprise applications, such as regression, clustering, classification, collaborative Filtering recommendation and so on, in a lower cost way under home-level temperature environment. ARMv8's features may encouraging industrial attempt to accomplish the optimization of hardware and software, and ARM clusters are the alternate candidates in the near future.

References

1. GöDdeke, D., Komatitsch, D., Geveler, M., et al.: Energy efficiency vs. performance of the numerical solution of PDEs: an application study on a low-power ARM-based cluster. J. Comput. Phys. **237**, 132–150 (2013)
2. Rajovic, N., Rico, A., Puzovic, N., et al.: Tibidabo: making the case for an ARM-based HPC system. Future Gener. Comput. Syst. **36**, 322–334 (2014)
3. www.top500.rog
4. www.green500.org
5. Ebrahimi, K., Jones, G.F., Fleischer, A.S.: A review of data center cooling technology, operating conditions and the corresponding low-grade waste heat recovery opportunities. Renew. Sustain. Energy Rev. **31**, 622–638 (2014)
6. Turley, J.: Cortex-A15 "Eagle" flies the coop. Microprocess. Rep. **24**(11), 1–11 (2010)
7. ARM Ltd.: Cortex-A50 series. http://www.arm.com
8. Ghemawat, S., Gobioff, H., Leung, S.T.: The Google file system. ACM SIGOPS Oper. Syst. Rev. **37**(5), 29–43 (2003). ACM
9. Chang, F., Dean, J., Ghemawat, S., et al.: Bigtable: a distributed storage system for structured data. ACM Trans. Comput. Syst. (TOCS) **26**(2), 4 (2008)
10. Dean, J., Ghemawat, S.: MapReduce: simplified data processing on large clusters. Commun. ACM **51**(1), 107–113 (2008)
11. Leverich, J., Kozyrakis, C.: On the energy (in) efficiency of hadoop clusters. ACM SIGOPS Oper. Syst. Rev. **44**(1), 61–65 (2010)
12. Shvachko, K., Kuang, H., Radia, S., et al.: The hadoop distributed file system. In: 2010 IEEE 26th Symposium on Mass Storage Systems and Technologies (MSST), pp. 1-10. IEEE (2010)
13. Zaharia, M., Konwinski, A., Joseph, A.D., et al.: Improving MapReduce performance in heterogeneous environments. In: OSDI, 8(4), p. 7 (2008)
14. Zaharia, M., Chowdhury, M., Das, T., et al.: Resilient distributed datasets: a fault-tolerant abstraction for in-memory cluster computing. In: Proceedings of the 9th USENIX Conference on Networked Systems Design and Implementation, p. 2. USENIX Association (2012)
15. Fox, K., Mongan, W., Popyack, J.: Raspberry HadooPI: a low-cost, hands-on laboratory in big data and analytics. In: Proceedings of the 46th ACM Technical Symposium on Computer Science Education, p.687. ACM (2015)
16. Kaewkasi, C., Srisuruk, W.: A study of big data processing constraints on a low-power Hadoop cluster. In: 2014 International Computer Science and Engineering Conference (ICSEC), pp. 267–272. IEEE (2014)
17. Aroca, R.V., Gonçalves, L.M.G.: Towards green data centers: a comparison of x86 and ARM architectures power efficiency. J. Parallel Distrib. Comput. **72**(12), 1770–1780 (2012)
18. Klausecker, C., Kranzlmüller, D., Fürlinger, K.: Towards energy efficient parallel computing on consumer electronic devices. In: Kranzlmüller, D., Toja, A.M. (eds.) ICT-GLOW 2011. LNCS, vol. 6868, pp. 1–9. Springer, Heidelberg (2011)
19. Fürlinger, K., Klausecker, C., Kranzlmüller, D.: The AppleTV-cluster: towards energy efficient parallel computing on consumer electronic devices. Whitepaper, Ludwig-Maximilians-Universitat (2011)
20. Rajovic, N., Vilanova, L., Villavieja, C., et al.: The low power architecture approach towards exascale computing. J. Comput. Sci. **4**(6), 439–443 (2013)
21. Dumitrel Loghin, B.M.T., Zhang, H., Ooi, B.C., et al.: A performance study of big data on small nodes. Proc. VLDB Endow. **8**(7), 762–773 (2015)

22. Gu, L., Zeng, D., Guo, S., Yong, X., Hu, J.: A general communication cost optimization framework for big data stream processing in geo-distributed data center. IEEE Trans. Comput. (ToC) (2015)
23. Lin, G., Zeng, D., Li, P., Guo, S.: Cost minimization for big data processing in geo-distributed data centers. IEEE Trans. Emerg. Topics Comput. **2**(3), 314–323 (2014)
24. Hu, C., Zhao, J., Yan, X., Zeng, D., Guo, S.: A MapReduce based parallel niche genetic algorithm for contaminant source identification in water distribution network. Ad Hoc Netw. **35**, 116–126 (2015)
25. Gu, L., Zeng, D., Guo, S., Barnawi, A., Stojmenovic, I.: Optimal task placement with QoS constraints in geo-distributed data centers using DVFS. IEEE Trans. Comput. (ToC) **64**(7), 2049–2059 (2014)
26. Plugaru, V., Varrette, S., Pinel, F., et al.: Evaluating the HPC performance and energy-efficiency of Intel and ARM-based systems with synthetic and bioinformatics workloads. In: CSC (2014)
27. McCool, M., Reinders, J., Robison, A.: Structured Parallel Programming: Patterns For Efficient Computation. Elsevier, Waltham (2012)
28. Chou, C.-Y., Chang, Hsi-Ya., Wang, S.-T., Tcheng, S.-C.: Modeling message-passing overhead on NCHC formosa PC cluster. In: Chung, Y.-C., Moreira, J.E. (eds.) GPC 2006. LNCS, vol. 3947, pp. 299–307. Springer, Heidelberg (2006)

Research on Service Organization Based on Decorator Pattern

Jianxiao Liu[1(✉)], Zaiwen Feng[2], Zonglin Tian[1], Feng Liu[1], and Xiaoxia Li[1]

[1] College of Informatics, Huazhong Agricultural University, Wuhan 430070, China
liujianxiao321@163.com
[2] State Key Laboratory of Software Engineering, Wuhan University, Wuhan 430070, China

Abstract. With the development of web service applications, how to improve the efficiency of service discovery is an important research work in service computing era. Based on the service clusters which are formed through service clustering, this paper uses the Decorator Pattern ideology to organize the service clusters according to the collaborative relationships between them. The tree structure is used to express the organized service clusters with certain correlations, and it helps to realize service discovery efficiently. It also discusses how to add new services to the service cluster organization dynamically. The experiment results show the method can enhance the efficiency of services (atomic and composite services) discovery.

Keywords: Service clusters · Composite services · Service discovery · Decorator pattern · Service organization

1 Introduction

With the explosive growth of all kinds of services on the internet, how to discover the services that can meet user's diversified and individualized requirements quickly is an urgent problem to be solved in Service-oriented computing [1].

Services can be organized using some approaches, and this can help users discover the services efficiently and exactly. Service clustering methods cluster the services which realize similar function goal but have different *QoS* values into service clusters. In addition, some approaches are used to organize services, such as petri net-based [2], community-oriented [3], Multi-granularity [4], workflow method [5], FCA [6], VINCA [7], etc. These methods organize services from different views, like service execution constraint relationship, service behavior, etc. The problem is how to quickly discover the services which can realize service composition according to specific service request. In addition, in the fast-changing web environment, how to dynamically add new services to the proper position to realize service composition is another problem to be solved urgently. The existing service organization methods are lack of the consideration of these aspects.

S. Guo et al. (Eds.): CollaborateCom 2015, LNICST 163, pp. 95–105, 2016.
DOI: 10.1007/978-3-319-28910-6_9

This paper uses the Decorator Pattern ideology to organize service clusters according to the collaborative relationships between them. The decorated service clusters are selected firstly, then it uses tree structure to express concrete service organization construction and this can help to realize service discovery smoothly. Through this method, the composite services can be found more efficiently and services can be added to the service organization dynamically.

2 The Related Work

There exists some research work about the service organization. Wu et al. have used a logical petri net-based approach to compose service clusters in a virtual layer [2]. Services are clustered in [9] according to the service node, and services are organized from the aspect of business logic integration. Aznag et al. in [6] have used the Formal Concept Analysis (FCA) formalism to organize the constructed hierarchical clusters into concept lattices according to their topics. Sellami et al. have used community to organize and manage Web services [3]. The method in [5] mainly organizes services in the view of service execution process, and it can't deal with the situation of adding services to the service organization dynamically. The method in [7] supports business user programming and composition services are formed according to the business process. Zhou et al. have concentrated on the research of data providing services discovery [10]. They have not elaborated the detail process of how to organize service clusters. On the basis of Web service clustering, we have organized the service clusters from aspects of semantic interoperability [11] and users' requirement features (role, goal, process) [4].

Liu et al. in [12] have aggregated and organized services according to the users' personal requirements and only the atomic services can be discovered. A user-centric service composition method starts from users' needs and it realizes service organization in the exploratory manner [13]. Ye et al. have proposed a new concept, Autonomous Web Service (AWS), to search requirement autonomously [14]. The above three methods use different methods to organize services from users' requirements directly. But it does not organize services according to the users' requirements in real time and it can lay the foundation of on-demand service selection. The method in [15] mainly concentrates on the service interoperability but not the service clustering and organization. In the above approaches, the clustering method is not used and it can't deal with the services which realize similar function but have different *QoS* values. Therefore, the service discovery efficiency will be influenced.

3 Service Organization

3.1 Decorator Pattern

The class diagram of Decorator Pattern [8] is shown in Fig. 1.

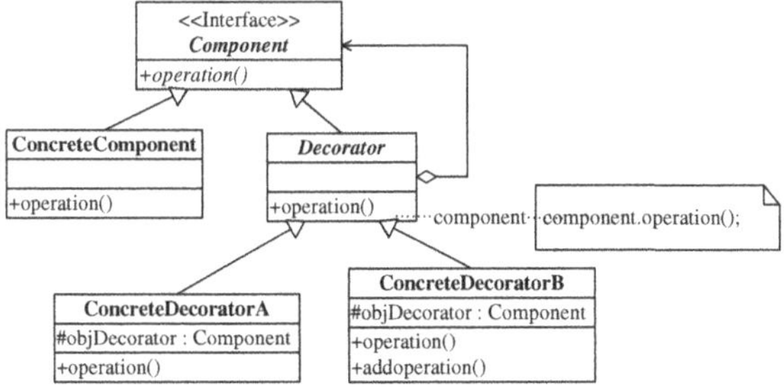

Fig. 1. The UML of Decorator Pattern.

3.2 The Rules of Organizing Service Clusters

The organization rules mainly include the following aspects.

(1) The collaborative relationships between service clusters are used to describe the "decorative" and "decorated" relationship.
(2) The role of Component interface is reflected in two aspects. On one hand, the collaborative relationships between service clusters are stored through the Component interface. On the other hand, the specific function that can be realized by service clusters collaboration can be manifested through it.
(3) When new services are added into the service group, the corresponding Decorator and Component Interface will be created.

3.3 Service Clusters Organization

Example 1. The following are some different service clusters: $WS = \{WS\_A, WS\_B, WS\_C, WS\_D, WS\_E, WS\_F, WS\_G\}$. The collaborative relationships among them are shown in Fig. 2.

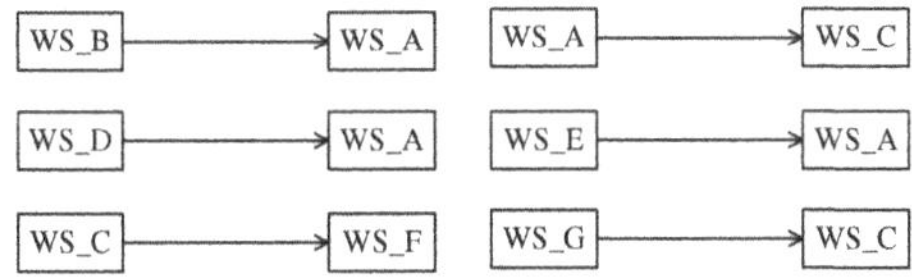

Fig. 2. The service clusters collaborative relationships.

Algorithm 1 is used to generate the tree structure of organizing services using Decorator Pattern ideology.

Algorithm 1.

```
Input: WS={ws_i, i=1,2...n}, Colla={<ws_i, ws_j>, i,j=1,2...n}
Output: Tree tree
1: CeCluster←∅, tree←∅
2: foreach <ws_i, ws_j>∈Colla
3:     CeCluster=ConGraph(<ws_i, ws_j>)
4: end for
5: foreach ws_i∈CeCluster
6:     construct ComponentNode_i, DecoratorNode_i of ws_i
7:     construct node_i of ws_i
8:     tree.add(<ComponentNode_i, DecoratorNode_i>)
9:     foreach ws_j∈WS
10:        if(<ws_i, ws_j>∈Colla || <ws_j, ws_i>∈Colla) then
11:            construct node_j of ws_j
12:            tree.add(<ComponentNode_i, node_i>)
13:            tree.add(<ComponentNode_i, node_j>)
14:        end if
15: end for
16: foreachws_i∈CeCluster
17:     foreach ws_j∈CeCluster
18:         if(<ws_i, ws_j>∈Colla) then
19:             if(node(ws_i).degree>node(ws_j).degree)
20:                 tree.add(<DecoratorNode_i, ComponentNode_j>)
21:             else
22:                 tree.add(<DecoratorNode_j, ComponentNode_i>)
23:         end if
24:     end for
25: end for
26: return tree
```

In the step 2–4 of the above algorithm, the constructing graph method is used to determine the degree of every service cluster. In step 5–15, the *ComponentNode*, *DecoratorNode* and *ServiceNode* of the corresponding ws_i in *CeCluster* are constructed firstly. Then the relationship between nodes is added into tree. The relations between nodes of *ws* are added into tree through step 16–25.

(1) Selection of decorated service clusters

We select the appropriate service clusters in *CeCluster* to play the role of *ConcreteComponent* in Fig. 1. These service clusters are called as the "decorated" service clusters. And we denote the "decorated" service clusters as central service clusters. It selects the central service clusters using the constructing graph method.

(1) The service clusters in *CeCluster* are denoted by nodes and the specific collaborative relationships between them are denoted by edges of graph. Through this method we can construct the graph of *CeCluster*. It is shown in Fig. 3.
(2) Then we calculate the degree for each node and the degree of node x can be denoted as C(x). We can get C(*WS_A*) = 4, C(*WS_C*) = 3, C(*WS_B*) = C (*WS_D*) = C(*WS_E*) = C(*WS_F*) = C(*WS_G*) = 1.
(3) The node whose degree is more than one will be selected to be the central service clusters. That means the node of "decorated" service clusters have at least two edges in the graph. *WS_A* and *WS_C* are selected as central service clusters and they are the "decorated" service clusters in Decorator Pattern.

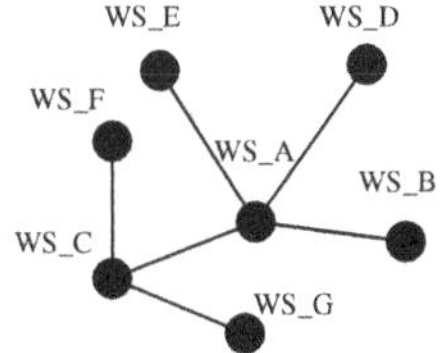

Fig. 3. The figure of graph.

(2) Service organization
The organization detail of service clusters is shown in Fig. 4.

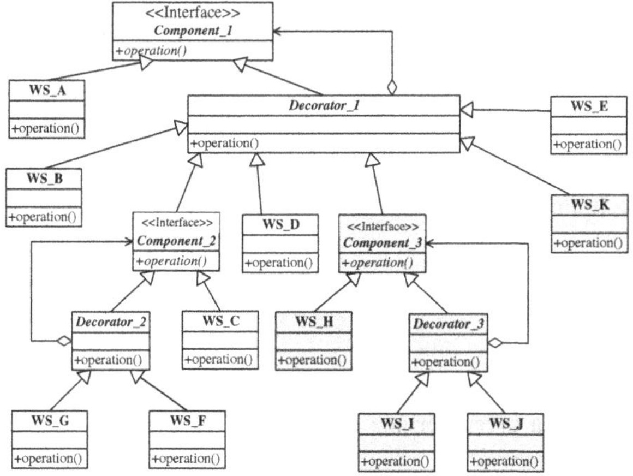

Fig. 4. The service clusters organization using Decorator Pattern.

In Fig. 4, we can conclude that *WS_A* is decorated by *WS_B*, *WS_C*, *WS_D* and *WS_E*. The corresponding Interface and Decorator are *Component_1* and *Decorator_1*. Both *WS_F* and *WS_G* decorate *WS_C*. There exist service clusters to decorate *WS_C*, the *Component_2* and *Decorator_2* are constructed.

In Algorithm 1, the tree structure is constructed to express service clusters organization using UML. The tree structure of Fig. 4 is shown in Fig. 5. In the figure, A represents *WS_A*, 1 represents *Component_1* and 1′ represents *Decorator_1*, etc.

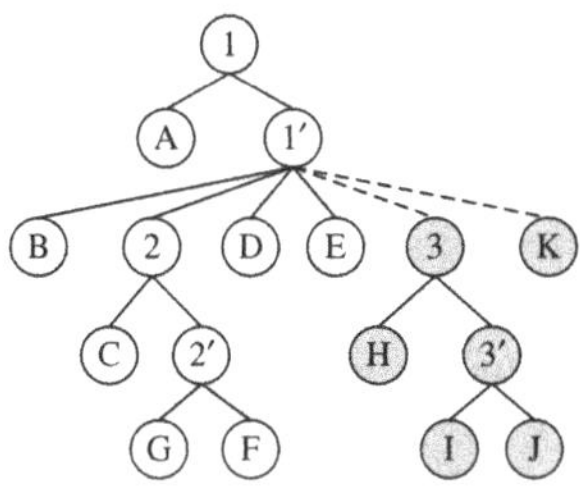

Fig. 5. The tree structure of service clusters organization.

3.4 Add Services Dynamically

We use the following method to add new service clusters to service cluster organization dynamically.

Example 2. There are some service clusters to be added: *WS_K*, *WS_H*, *WS_I*, *WS_J*. Their collaborative relationships are shown in the following: <*WS_K*, *WS_A*>, <*WS_H*, *WS_A*>, <*WS_H*, *WS_I*>, <*WS_H*, *WS_J*>.

(1) There exists collaborative relationship of Sequence between *WS_K* and *WS_A*. *WS_A* is a central service cluster as shown in Fig. 4. *WS_K* is added into the organization as a "decorative" service cluster of *WS_A*.
(2) We can discover that *WS_H* is a central service cluster among *WS_I*, *WS_J* and *WS_H*. As shown in the grey area of Fig. 4, *WS_H*, *WS_I* and *WS_J* are organized according to the relationships between them. *WS_H* is the "decorated" service cluster. *WS_I* and *WS_J* are the "decorative" service clusters. New components called *Component_3* and *Decorator_3* are constructed towards *WS_H*. The relationship between *WS_H* and *WS_A* is Sequence. We use *WS_H* to decorate *WS_A*. Then *WS_H*, *WS_I* and *WS_J* are dynamically added to the service cluster organization which already includes *WS_A*. They are shown in the gray area of Fig. 4.

4 Service Finding

Algorithm 2 is used to find the corresponding service clusters that include services to realize composition for a given service cluster.

```
Algorithm 2. GetCollaNode
Input: Tree tree, Node node
Output: Result={result_i, i=1,2...n}
i←1, result_i←∅
find the position of node in tree
if (node∈DecoratorNode.subnode) then
    result_i=result_i ∪ (node.root.root.leftnode→node)
end if
if (node∈Component.leftnode) then
    Result=Result ∪ (node.root.root.root.leftnode→node)
    Subnodes=node.root.rightnode.subnodes
    foreach subnode_i ∈ Subnodes
        if (subnode_i.type==cluster) then
            result_i=result_i ∪ (node→subnode_i)
            i++
        end if
        if(subnode_i.type==ComponentNode) then
            result_i=result_i ∪ (node→subnode_i.leftnode)
            i++
            node=subnode_i.leftnode, go to step 5
        end if
    end for
end if
```

For node D in Fig. 5, we can get service cluster composition of A→D through step 3–5 in Algorithm 1. For node C, we can get A→C through step 7. And we get C→G and C→F through step 9–13. Then we can get A→C→G and A→C→F.

Algorithm 3 is used to find services according to the users' specific requests.

Algorithm 3. *FindService*
Input: Tree *tree*, *WS*, *ws*={cluster[*i*], *i*=1,2,...n}, *request*
Output: rq_{ws}
1: rq_{ws}•∅, scp_{ws}•∅, c_{ws}•∅, *node*•∅, iws_{num}
2: foreach service $ws_i \in WS$
3:     if(*matchrequest*(*request*, ws_i)> β) then
4:         *node*=*tree*.find(ws_i)
5:         scp_{ws}=scp_{ws} ∪ *GetCollaNode*(*tree*, *node*)
6:     end if
7: end for
8: foreach path $p \in scp_{ws}$
9:     foreach $c_{ws} \in p$
10:         iws_{num}=service cluster number of c_{ws}
11:         *qws*=*QosFindService*(*request*, cluster[iws_{num}])
12:         rq_{ws}=rq_{ws} ∪ *qws*
13:     end for
14: end for
15: return rq_{ws}

In the step of 2–4, the corresponding tree node will be found firstly. Then it uses *GetCollaNode*() in Algorithm 2 to find the nodes which has relationship with the node using step 5. It uses step 8–14 to find the services with proper *QoS* values in the service clusters. The notation of β in step 3 is the threshold of similarity between service request and service provider.

5 Experiment and Evaluation

5.1 Experiment Environment

Software Environment: Windows XP, MyEclipse 6.0, Pellet reasoner, OWL-S API (http://www.mindswap.org/2004/owl-s/api/), xampp (http://www.apachefriends.org/en/xampp.html); Hardware Environment: CPU: double Intel (R) Core (TM)2 i5 CPU 760@ 2.80 GHz, Memory: 4G; Dataset: OWL-TC (http://projects.semwebcentral.org/projects/owls-tc/). We do the experiments in the education area.

5.2 Experiment and Analysis

We do the experiments in the education area within 300 services. The number of services that is included in every service cluster is shown in Table 1.

The Workflow [6] method uses the work-flow approach to organize the service clusters. And we denote the method that does not cluster and organize services as the Random method.

Table 1. The number of services in different service clusters.

Service clusters	1	2	3	4	5	6	7	8	9	10	11	12	13	14	15
Number of services	13	4	7	8	13	18	6	8	10	7	9	10	15	10	14
Service clusters	16	17	18	19	20	21	22	23	24	25	26	27	28	29	30
Number of services	6	7	8	12	5	10	12	12	8	9	7	14	10	12	8

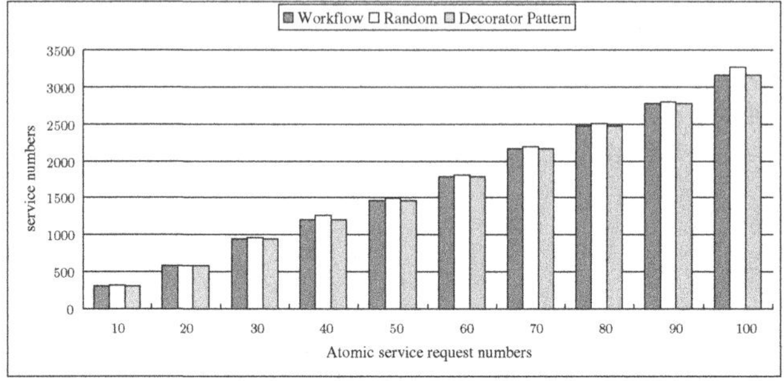

Fig. 6. Comparison of atomic service finding numbers.

Experiment 1. Comparison of atomic service finding efficiency and numbers.

In the case of using the Workflow, Random and Decorator Patten method to organize services, the experiment result is shown is Figs. 6 and 7.

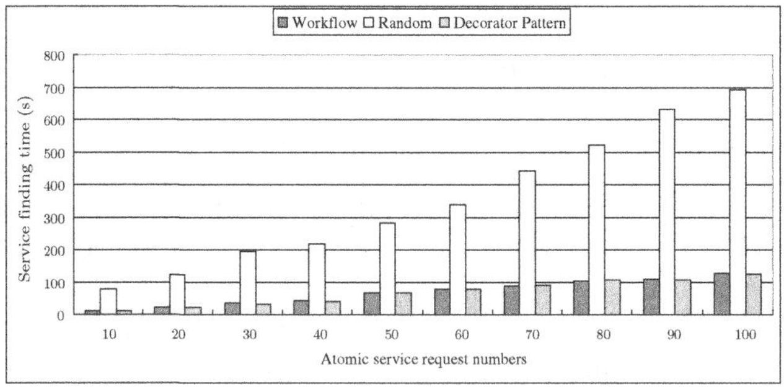

Fig. 7. Comparison of atomic service finding time.

We can conclude that the atomic service discovery recall rate of Random method is the best, but its efficiency is the lowest of all. The atomic service finding efficiency and recall rate of Workflow and Decorator Pattern method is about same.

Experiment 2. Comparison of composite service finding efficiency and recall rate.

The service finding time is shown in the following Fig. 8.

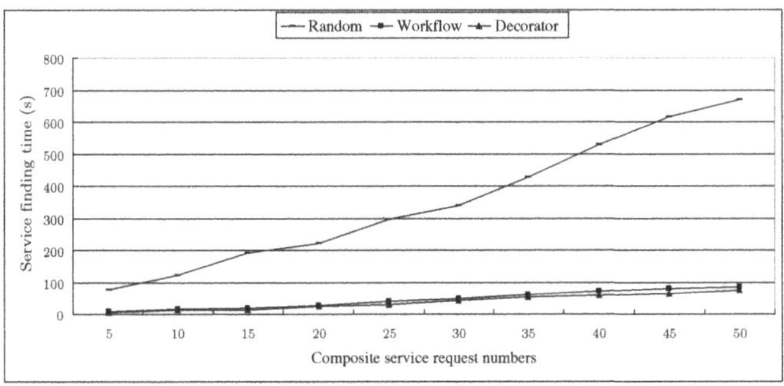

Fig. 8. Comparison of composite services finding time.

We can see the service finding time that uses Decorator Pattern and the Workflow methods to organize service clusters is significantly less than the time of the Random method. In Fig. 9, we can see the composite service finding recall rate is about same through the methods of Workflow, Random and Decorator Pattern. The recall rate of the Random method is about 100 %, and the rate of the other two methods is about 96 %.

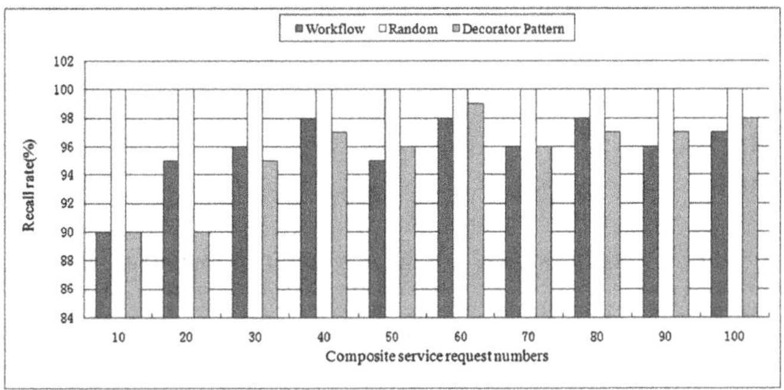

Fig. 9. Comparison of composite service finding recall rate.

5.3 Service Finding Complexity Analysis

Supposing the total number of services is N, the number of service clusters is m and the number of central service clusters is n. $N \gg m > n$. The average number of service clusters that have collaborative relationships with one central service cluster is $(m - n)/n$. The service finding complexity comparison is shown in Table 2.

We can conclude that the complexity of Random method is the largest of all apparently. Our Decorator Pattern method is lower than the Workflow method.

Table 2. Comparison of service finding complexity.

Different cases	Random	Workflow	Decorator pattern
The number of atomic service request is 1	$O(N)$	$O(m + N/m)$	$O(m + N/m)$
The number of composite service request is $r(r > 1)$	$O(rN)$	$O(m + N/m + (m - n)/n + N*n/(m - n) + 2*(r - 1)*N/m)$	$O(m + N/m + (r - 1)*((m - n)/n + N/m))$ or $O(m + N/m + (r - 1)*(n + N/m))$

6 Conclusion

In order to enhance service (including atomic and composite service) discovery efficiency, this paper uses the Decorator Pattern ideology to organize the service clusters. This approach not only realizes services to be added dynamically, but also enhances the efficiency of service discovery. The next research work is to set the threshold automatically according to the experiment result. The services will be organized from the semantic level to realize interoperable organization.

Acknowledgments. This research is supported by the National Basic Research Program of China under grant No. 2014CB340401, the National Training Programs of Innovation and Entrepreneurship for Undergraduates under grant No. 201410504064.

References

1. Papazoglou, M.P., Georgakopoulos, D.: Service-oriented computing. Commun. ACM **46** (10), 24–28 (2003)
2. Wu, H.Y., Du, Y.Y.: A logical petri net-based approach for web service cluster composition. Chin. J. Comput. **38**(1), 204–218 (2015)
3. Sellami, M., Bouchaala, O., Gaaloul, W., Tata, S.: Communities of web service registries: construction and management. J. Syst. Softw. **86**, 835–853 (2013)
4. Liu, J.X., Wang, J., He, K.Q., Liu, F., Li, X.X.: Service organization and recommendation using multi-granularity approach. Knowl. Based Syst. **73**, 181–198 (2015)
5. Hu, C.H., Wu, M., Liu, G.P.: An approach to constructing web service workflow based on business spanning graph. Chin. J. Softw. **18**(8), 1870–1882 (2007)
6. Aznag M., Quafafou M., Jarir Z.: Leveraging formal concept analysis with topic correlation for service clustering and discovery. In: IEEE International Conference on Web Services, pp. 153–160 (2014)
7. Zhao, Z.F., Han, Y.B., Yu, J.: A service virtualization mechanism for business user programming. Chin. J. Comput. Res. Dev. **41**(12), 2224–2230 (2004)
8. Farzin K.: Applications of decorator and observer design patterns in functional verification. In: International Conference of High Level Design Validation and Test Workshop, pp. 18–22 (2008)
9. Liu, S.L., Liu, Y.X., Zhang, F.: A dynamic web services selection algorithm with QoS global optimal in web services composition. Chin. J. Softw. **18**(3), 646–656 (2007)

10. Zhou, Z.B., Sellami, M., Gaaloul, W., Barhamgi, M., Defude, B.: Data providing services clustering and management for facilitating service discovery and replacement. IEEE Trans. Autom. Sci. Eng. **10**(4), 1131–1146 (2013)
11. Liu, J.X., He, K.Q., Ning, D.: Web service aggregation using semantic interoperability oriented method. J. Inf. Sci. Eng. **28**(3), 437–452 (2012)
12. Liu, X.Z., Huang, G., Mei, H.: Consumer-centric service aggregation: method and its supporting framework. Chin. J. Softw. **18**(8), 1883–1895 (2007)
13. Ding, W.L., Wang, J., Zhao, S.: A user-centric service composition method synthesizing multiple views. Chin. J. Comput. **34**(1), 131–142 (2011)
14. Ye, R.H., Jin, Z., Wang, P.W., Zhen, L.W., Yang, X.F.: Approach for autonomous web service aggregation driven by requirement. Chin. J. Softw. **21**(6), 1181–1195 (2010)
15. Wen, B., He, K.Q., Wang, J.: Building requirements semantics for networked software interoperability. J. Softw. Eng. Appl. **3**, 125–133 (2010)

Personalized QoS Prediction of Cloud Services via Learning Neighborhood-Based Model

Hao Wu[1(✉)], Jun He[2], Bo Li[1], and Yijian Pei[1]

[1] School of Information Science and Engineering, Yunnan University, Kunming 650091, China
{haowu,libo,pei3p}@ynu.edu.cn

[2] Nanjing University of Information Science and Technology, Nanjing 210044, China
hejun.zz@gmail.com

Abstract. This paper proposes neighborhood-based approach for QoS-prediction of cloud services by taking advantages of collaborative intelligence. Different from heuristic collaborative filtering and matrix-factorization, we set a formal neighborhood-based prediction framework which allows an efficient global optimization scheme, and then exploits different baseline estimate components to improve predictive performance. To validate our methods, a large-scale QoS-specific dataset which consists of invocation records from 339 service users on 5,825 web services on a world-scale distributed network is used. Experimental results show that the learned neighborhood-based models can overcome existing difficulties of heuristic collaborative filtering methods and achieve superior performance than state-of-the-art prediction methods.

Keywords: Cloud services · QoS prediction · Neighborhood model · Parameter learning

1 Introduction

The explosion of cloud services on the Internet brings new challenges in service discovery and selection [1]. As confronted with a number of functionally similar cloud services, a user may feel hard to judge what is the extent of candidates in line with the individual needs. A further comparison of the non-functionality of candidates (generally the properties of QoS) is needed in order to make the best choice. However, due to constraints on time, costs and other factors [2], service providers cannot dispose a large number of software sensors in cloud environments to monitor QoS information for every service. Also, it is not realistic for users to carry out large-scale testings to experience the individual differences of QoS. Consequently, how to obtain personalized QoS of cloud services and assist users selecting appropriate services become one urgent issue.

Recently, researchers begin to pursuit solution for this problem by drawing lessons from recommender systems [2–12]. The main idea of their works is to

S. Guo et al. (Eds.): CollaborateCom 2015, LNICST 163, pp. 106–117, 2016.
DOI: 10.1007/978-3-319-28910-6_10

analyze the QoS usage data of users in service-oriented systems, further exploit collaborative intelligence to prediction unknown QoS values. With distinguishable quality values of candidate services, users can take a decision on choosing appropriate services. In such a manner, it can avoid direct QoS measurement [13], and thereby save time and economic costs for both service providers and users.

As for the collaborative QoS-prediction, neighborhood-based collaborative filtering (NbCF) [3–7] and matrix-factorization (MF) [2,8–12] are commonly used methods. NbCF is simplicity, justifiability and efficiency [14]. However, the model is not justified by a formal model. Moreover, heterogenous similarity metrics and sparsity-sensitive problem make these models not robust and scalable enough. In contrast, MF approaches comprise an alternative way to CF with the more holistic goal to uncover latent features from user-service usage data, and thus can mitigate the problem of sensitivity to sparse data. Since MF can be presented as a formal optimization problem and solved by machine learning methods, thus it provides attractive accuracy and scalability for QoS prediction. However, MF is always uncertain, resulting in difficulty as explain the predictions for users. It is an important issue as users of cloud services certainly hope to get reasonable explanations for the QoS predictions provided by a service recommendation system. Inspired by this, we propose learning neighborhood-based models for personalized QoS-prediction of cloud services, to have the best of both worlds (NbCF and MF). We define formal neighborhood models which permit an efficient global optimization scheme and exploit different baseline estimate components to improve prediction performance. Experimental results demonstrate that learning neighborhood model can overcome existing difficulties, and perform superior to the-state-of-art prediction methods.

The remainder of the paper is structured as follows. We review some existing works that are most relevant to ours in Sect. 2. We provide details of the proposed neighborhood-based prediction approaches in Sect. 3. We measure the effectiveness of the proposed methods via a set of experiments on real QoS data in Sect. 4 and conclude in Sect. 5.

2 Related Works

2.1 QoS Prediction Based on Neighborhood Model

Shao et al. [3] at first proposed the use of NbCF based on the user. Firstly, pearson correlation coefficient (PCC) measurement is utilized to calculate pairwise-similarity among all users on the user-service matrix of QoS data. Secondly, historical quality values of target service provided by the top-k similar users of active user are fused to achieve prediction result. Follow-up research works basically follow this idea but concentrate on improving the similarity metrics to accurately quantify the correlations of users or services. Zheng et al. [4] proposed a mixed model that integrated user-based and item-based approaches linearly by confidence weights and proved the mixed model is better than a single one. Sun et al. considered the distribution characteristics of QoS data to calculate the similarity [5]. Wu et al. [6] and Chen et al. [7] proposed location-aware similarity metrics to find neighbors of users and services. These methods have not been exploited machine learning technology, hence can be seen as heuristic-based prediction ways. NbCF became very popular because they are relatively simple to implement and provide intuitive explanations for the prediction results. However, some concerns about NbCF always exist. Most notably, these methods are not justified by a formal model. The selection of heterogenous similarity metric clearly affects the accuracy of QoS-prediction, thus make these models not robust. When the QoS data are sparse, the predictive power can be significantly reduced, resulting in the sparsity-sensitive problem. This motivates us to develop more accurate neighborhood models to resolve existing difficulties.

2.2 QoS Prediction Based on Matrix Factorization

MF can partially alleviate the sparity-sensitive problem of collaborative filtering, and thus improves the accuracy of QoS prediction. In recent years, numerous efforts have been made on improving MF-based models. The works are focused on utilizing additional information, such as spatial and temporal information associated with users or services. Zhang et al. [9] use collective matrix factorization that simultaneously factor the user-service quality matrix, service category and location context matrices. Yin et al. [10] develop a location-based regularization framework for PMF prediction model. Lo et al. [12] exploit PMF with a localtion-based pre-filtering stage on QoS matrix. He et al. [11] develop location-based hierarchical matrix factorization. Yu et al. [8] experience trace-norm regularized MF. MF is still uncertain, resulting in difficulty as explain the predictions for users. Also, data sparsity has a negative effect on these methods, as data becomes extremely sparse, the prediction performance will be not optimistic.

3 Learning Neighborhood-Based Model for QoS Prediction

We reserve special indexing letters for distinguishing users from services: for users u, v, and for services i, j. A QoS r_{ui} indicates the observed quality of user u on service i. We distinguish predicted quality from known ones, by using the notation $\hat{r}_{ui}$ for the predicted value of r_{ui}. The (u,i) pairs for which r_{ui} is known are stored in the set $\mathbf{E} = \{(u,i)|r_{ui} \quad is \quad known\}$.

3.1 Neighborhood-Based Models(NbModels)

In cloud computing, the context with users is more complicated and dynamic than that of services. Prediction leveraged by similar users other than services is more reasonable. Thus, our focus is on user-oriented approaches, but parallel techniques can be developed in a service-oriented fashion, by switching the roles of users and services. We borrow ideas from collaborative filtering research [15], which allows an efficient global optimization scheme and offers improved accuracy. To facilitate global optimization, we abandon user-specific weights in favor of global weights independent of a specific user. The weight from user v to user u is denoted by w_{uv} are able to be learned from the data through optimization. By this, we can overcome the weaknesses with existing neighborhood-based models. An initial sketch of the model describes each quality score r_{ui} by (1):

$$\hat{r}_{ui} = b_{ui} + \sum_{v \in \mathcal{N}_u} (r_{vi} - b_{vi}) w_{uv}, \tag{1}$$

where $\mathcal{N}_u$ is the neighbor set of user u, b_{ui} is the basic estimate that we will gradually construct considering different factors.

With respect to the interpretation of weights, usually they represent interpolation coefficients relating unknown quality scores to the existing ones in a traditional neighborhood model. Here, we adopt them in a different viewpoint that weights represent offsets to basic estimates and residual, $r_{vi} - b_{vi}$, are viewed as the coefficients multiplying those offsets. For two similar users u and v, w_{uv} is always expected to get high, and verse visa. So, our estimate will not deviate much from the basic estimate by a user v that accessed i just as expected ($r_{vi} - b_{vi}$ is around zero), or by a user v that is not known to be predictive on u (w_{uv} is close to zero).

Generally, we can take all users in $\mathcal{N}_u$ other than u, however, this would increase the number of weights to be estimated. In order to reduce complexity of the model, we suggest pruning parameters corresponding to unlikely user-user relations. Let $\mathcal{N}_u^k$ be the set of k users most similar u, as determined by a similarity measure (e.g. PCC). Further, we let $\mathcal{N}_{(i;u)}^k \triangleq \mathcal{N}_i \cap \mathcal{N}_u^k$, where $\mathcal{N}_i$ is the set of users have used the service i. Now, when predicting r_{ui} according to Formula (1), it is expected that the most influential weights will be associated with users similar to u. Hence, we replace (1) with:

$$\hat{r}_{ui} = b_{ui} + |\mathcal{N}_{(i;u)}^k|^{-\frac{1}{2}} \sum_{v \in \mathcal{N}_{(i;u)}^k} (r_{vi} - b_{vi}) w_{uv} \tag{2}$$

When $k = \infty$, rule (2) coincides with (1). When $k = 0$, $\hat{r}_{ui} = b_{ui}$. However, for other values of k, it offers the potential to significantly reduce the number of variables involved. This final prediction rule permits fast online prediction, since more computational works, such as similarity calculation and parameter estimation, have been made in the pre-processing stage. Recall that unlike matrix-factorization, neighborhood models allow an intuitive explanation of their predictions, and do not require re-training the model for handling new services.

3.2 Components for Estimating b_{ui}

Baseline estimate. Typical QoS data exhibit large user and service effects-i.e., systematic tendencies for some users to achieve better QoS than others, and for some services to receive better QoS than others. It is customary to adjust the QoS data by accounting for these effects, which we encapsulate within the baseline estimates. Denote by μ the average QoS value observed in the entire dataset. A baseline estimate for an unknown QoS r_{ui} is denoted by b_{ui} and accounts for the user and service effects:

$$b_{ui} = \mu + b_u + b_i \tag{3}$$

The parameters b_u and b_i respectively indicate the observed deviations of user u and service i from the average. Suppose we want to estimate the response-time of Google-Search service by Tom. Now, leave the average response time, μ=2ms. Further, since Google-search is recognized better than an average search service, we can suppose it is faster 0.5ms than the average. In addition, Tom's network condition is not a good, which tends to be 1ms delay than the average. Thus, the baseline estimate for Google-Search's response-time by Tom would be 2.5ms by calculating: 2-0.5+1. Substituting (3) into (2), we will obtain NbModel1. To estimate b_u, b_i and w_{uv} one can solve the least squares problem:

$$\begin{aligned}\min_{w*,b*} \sum_{(u,i)\in\mathbf{E}} [r_{ui} - b_{ui} - |\mathcal{N}^k_{(i;u)}|^{-\frac{1}{2}} \sum_{v\in\mathcal{N}^k_{(i;u)}} (r_{vi} - b_{vi})w_{uv}]^2 \\ + \lambda_1 \sum_{v\in\mathcal{N}^k_{(i;u)}} w^2_{uv} + \lambda_2(b^2_u + b^2_i)\end{aligned} \tag{4}$$

Here, the first term $\sum_{(u,i)\in\mathbf{E}}(.)^2$ strives to find b_u's, b_i's and w_{uv}'s that fit the given usage data. The second part and the third part both are the regularizing terms, employed to avoid overfitting by penalizing the magnitudes of the parameters. λ_1 and λ_2 are the specific regularization parameters [15].

Weighted features. The baseline estimate just considers the mean effect of user and item in an intuitive manner. However, more bias information (such as user features, item features, time bias) can be used to enhance the prediction model. We may consider an unknown quality value r_{ui} as a linear combination of the features of user and item. Here, the user-specific QoS mean and the service-specific QoS mean are taken as the two key features, because they strongly reflect the bias effect of users and services, and the expect prediction of QoS can be found in a value domain determined by them. Denote by μ_u the average QoS value observed by user u and μ_i the average QoS value observed by service i. A feature-weighted estimate for r_{ui} is denoted by b_{ui} as followings:

$$b_{ui} = w_u\mu_u + w_i\mu_i \tag{5}$$

The parameters w_u and w_i indicate the feature importance of user u and item i, respectively. Substituting (5) into (2), we will obtain NbModel2. To estimate w_u, w_i, we need to solve the following least squares problem:

$$\begin{aligned}\min_{w*} \sum_{(u,i)\in\mathbf{E}} [r_{ui} - b_{ui} - |\mathcal{N}^k_{(i;u)}|^{-\frac{1}{2}} \sum_{v\in\mathcal{N}^k_{(i;u)}} (r_{vi} - b_{vi})w_{uv}]^2 \\ + \lambda_1 \sum_{v\in\mathcal{N}^k_{(i;u)}} w^2_{uv} + \lambda_3(w^2_u + w^2_i)\end{aligned} \tag{6}$$

Here, regularizing term, $\lambda_3(w_u^2 + w_i^2)$, avoid overfitting by penalizing the magnitudes of the parameters w_u's and w_i's.

Hybrid approach. Beyond estimating b_{ui} based on either the baseline estimate or the weighted features, we may combine them together to have the best of both worlds. This leads to a new prediction rule for b_{ui}:

$$b_{ui} = \mu + b_u + b_i + w_u \mu_u + w_i \mu_i \tag{7}$$

Substituting (7) into (2), we will obtain the combined model-NbModel3. To estimate w_u, w_i, b_u, b_i, we need to solve the regularized least squares problem as followings:

$$\begin{aligned} \min_{w*,b*} & \sum_{(u,i)\in \mathbf{E}} [r_{ui} - b_{ui} - |\mathcal{N}^k_{(i;u)}|^{-\frac{1}{2}} \sum_{v\in \mathcal{N}^k_{(i;u)}} (r_{vi} - b_{vi}) w_{uv}]^2 \\ & + \lambda_1 \sum_{v\in \mathcal{N}^k_{(i;u)}} w_{uv}^2 + \lambda_2 (b_u^2 + b_i^2) + \lambda_3 (w_u^2 + w_i^2) \end{aligned} \tag{8}$$

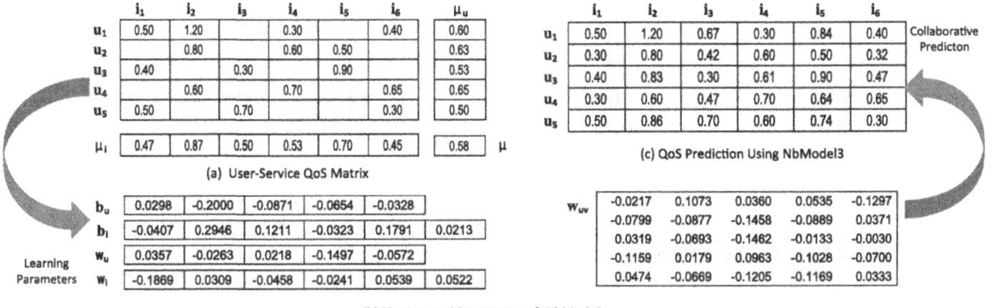

Fig. 1. An example on QoS prediction with learning NbModel3.

3.3 Models Learning

In a sense, our neighborhood models provide two-tier models for personalized QoS prediction. The first tier, b_{ui}, describes general properties of the service and the user, without accounting for any involved interactions. The second tie-"Neighborhood tier" contributes fine grained adjustments that are hard to profile. Model parameters are determined by minimizing the associated regularized squared error function through gradient descent. Recall that $e_{ui} \triangleq r_{ui} - \hat{r}_{ui}$. We loop over all known scores in $\mathbb{E}$. For a given training case r_{ui}, we modify the parameters by moving in the opposite direction of the gradient, yielding:

- $b_u \leftarrow b_u + \gamma_1(e_{ui} - \lambda_2 b_u)$
- $b_i \leftarrow b_i + \gamma_1(e_{ui} - \lambda_2 b_i)$

- $w_u \leftarrow w_u + \gamma_1(e_{ui}\mu_u - \lambda_3 w_u)$
- $w_i \leftarrow w_i + \gamma_1(e_{ui}\mu_i - \lambda_3 w_i)$
- $\forall v \in \mathcal{N}^k_{(i;u)}$: $w_{uv} \leftarrow w_{uv} + \gamma_2 \left(|\mathcal{N}^k_{(i;u)}|^{-\frac{1}{2}} e_{ui}(r_{vi} - b_{vi}) - \lambda_1 w_{uv} \right)$

Note that, update rules set forth can fit all of the least squares problems in Formulas (4), (6) and (8). When assessing the method on a given dataset, we took advantage of following values for the meta parameters: $\lambda_1 = \lambda_2 = \lambda_3 = 0.001$, $\gamma_1 = \gamma_2 = 0.001$. It is beneficial to decreasing step sizes (the γ's) by a factor of 0.9 after each iteration. For another parameter k, our experiments demonstrate that increasing k always benefits the RMSE. Hence, the choice of k should reflect a tradeoff between prediction accuracy and computational cost. A toy-example on Qos prediction using NbModel3 is given in Fig. 1, where we let $k = 5$.

4 Experiments

4.1 Datasets

To evaluate the QoS prediction performance, we use a large-scale dataset collected by Zheng et al. [2]. The dataset consists of a total of 1, 974, 675 real-world web service invocation results are collected from 339 users on 5, 825 real-world web services [2]. This dataset can be considered as a set of usage data for real-world cloud services from distributed locations. In our experiments, we only think the response time (the range scale is 0-20s). However, the proposed approach can be applied to additional QoS properties easily.

4.2 Evaluation Metrics

Mean absolute error (MAE) and root mean squared error (RMSE) metrics, two basic statistical accuracy metrics [16], have been extensively used in performance evaluation of rating predictions [15], are used to measure the QoS-prediction performance of selected methods. MAE and RMSE are defined in (9), where r_{ui} is the observed QoS value, $\hat{r}_{ui}$ is the predicted one, N is the number of test cases. The MAE measures the average magnitude of the errors in a set of forecasts, without considering their direction [16]. The RMSE is a quadratic scoring rule which measures the average magnitude of the error.

$$MAE = \sum_{u,i} |r_{ui} - \hat{r}_{ui}|/N \quad RMSE = \sqrt{\sum_{u,i} (r_{ui} - \hat{r}_{ui})^2/N} \tag{9}$$

4.3 Comparison

To show the prediction accuracy of our neighborhood-based approaches, we compare our methods with the three kinds of popular approaches:

1. *Statistical approaches. GMEAN* takes the average QoS value of the whole dataset as the predictive QoS value of user u to service i, i.e. $\hat{r}_{ui} = \mu$; *UMEAN* takes the average QoS value known by u as the predictive QoS value of u to i , i.e., $\hat{r}_{ui} = \mu_u$; *IMEAN* takes the average QoS value observed from i as the predictive QoS value of u to i, i.e. $\hat{r}_{ui} = \mu_i$;
2. *Heurstic-based CF. UPCC* is user-based collaborative prediction model. Top-k neighbors of users are found using PCC-based similarity [3]; *IPCC* is item-based collaborative prediction model. Top-k neighbors of items (services) are found using PCC-based similarity [4]; *UIPCC* combines the user-based and item-based collaborative prediction approaches and employs both the similar users and similar services for the QoS value prediction [4].
3. *MF-based approaches. PMF* uses probabilistic matrix factorization [17] to factorize user-service QoS matrix for the prediction [2]; *NMF* uses non-negative matrix factorization [18] to factorize the QoS matrix into two matrices p and q, with the property that all three matrices have no negative elements; *BiasedMF* exploits a combination of baseline estimate (same to (3)) and matrix factorization prediction rule for collaborative filtering [15]. We adopt it for the QoS prediction.

Table 1. Performance comparisons of QoS prediction models using different matrix density, where 'a' and 'b' indicate 1st-class and 2nd-class, respectively.

Methods	MD=0.5 %		MD=1 %		MD=5 %		MD=10 %	
	MAE	RMSE	MAE	RMSE	MAE	RMSE	MAE	RMSE
GMEAN	0.9721	1.9735	0.9915	1.9726	0.9860	1.9740	0.9920	1.9725
UMEAN	0.8873	1.8914	0.8899	1.8705	0.8746	1.8600	0.8744	1.8575
IMEAN	0.8317	1.9326	0.7870	1.8136	0.7002	1.5746	0.6890	1.5410
UPCC	0.9709	1.9727	0.9468	1.9457	0.6173	1.3925^b	0.5446	1.3119
IPCC	0.9721	1.9735	0.9888	1.9716	0.6675	1.4272	0.6430	1.3798
UIPCC	0.9708	1.9725	0.9453	1.9430	0.6162	1.3900^b	0.5439	1.3102
PMF	0.8317	2.0624	0.8195	2.0010	0.6354	1.5071	0.5541	1.3393
NMF	0.7656^a	1.8480	0.7092^a	1.7650	0.6516	1.5145	0.6461	1.4527
BiasedMF	0.8052	1.7643	0.7832	1.7128	0.6376	1.4361	0.5518	1.3088
NbModel1	0.7986	1.6989^a	0.7471	1.6163^a	0.6106	1.5333	0.5336	1.3563
NbModel2	0.7678^a	1.7942	0.7196^b	1.6436^b	0.5817^b	1.3943^b	0.5156^b	1.2832^b
NbModel3	0.7838^b	1.7847^b	0.7428	1.6582	0.5793^a	1.3795^a	0.5138^a	1.2739^a

For the CF-based methods, we choose the neighborhood size of users at $k = 10$ and services at $k = 50$. For the MF-based methods, the regularization parameters for user and service are set at $\lambda_u = \lambda_v = 0.001$, and the dimensionality of latent factors is fixed at 10. For all selected methods, we use their implementations in LibRec (http://www.librec.net/index.html). Note that, for a fair comparison of selected methods, all of them exploit only the information supplied by the user-service QoS matrix, and no additional information (e.g., geo-locations of users) is allowed. To examine the impact of data sparsity in experiments, we randomly remove entries from the user-item matrix with different density, specially, we take 0.5 % – 1 % for the case of sparse data and 5 % – 10 % for the case of dense data. For instance, MD (Matrix Density)=0.5 % means that we randomly select 0.5 % of the QoS entries to predict the remaining 99.5 % of QoS entries. The original QoS values of the removed entries are used as the expected values to study the prediction accuracy. All selected methods and neighorhood-based variants, NbModel1, NbModel2 and NbModel3, are used to forecast the QoS values of the removed entries. The experimental results are shown in Table 1.

Depending on Table 1, NbModel3 and NbModel2 respectively rank the first class and the second class on both MAE and RMSE in the case of dense data. Both models obtain smaller MAE and RMSE values consistently for response-time with MD=5 % and MD=10 %. MAE and RMSE values of neighborhood models become smaller, since denser matrix provides more information for the missing value prediction. In the case of sparse data, NMF achieve best performance in term of MAE followed by three neighborhood models. However, our methods perform much better than all other counterparts on RMSE. Among all the prediction models, our methods achieve better performance on both MAE and RMSE, telling that learning neighborhood model can achieve higher prediction accuracy. Also, neighborhood-based models preserve the explainability of memory-based CF, and enable to give users a reason for their predictions.

4.4 Impact of Top-K

To examine the influence of top-k neighbors selection on our prediction models, we distinguish from two cases: sparse data and dense data. With sparse data, we found that increasing k value cannot lead to significant performance improvements and sometimes we may experience decreased performance. There are two reasons for this. One is that sparser matrix cannot offer the "neighborhood tier" more information to contribute fine-grained adjustments. The other is that the leaned component b_{ui} (sees (2)) has given ideal predictions. Nevertheless, "neighborhood ties" can be invoked as a regularization component to

Table 2. Performance of neighbordhood-based models in case of sparse data.

Methods	k	MD=0.5 %		MD=1 %	
		MAE	RMSE	MAE	RMSE
NbModel1	0	0.7987	1.6990	0.7411	1.5770
	80	0.7986	1.6989	0.7471	1.6163
NbModel2	0	0.7678	1.7942	0.7428	1.6567
	80	0.7678	1.7942	0.7196	1.6436
NbModel3	0	0.7840	1.7848	0.7409	1.6474
	80	0.7838	1.7847	0.7428	1.6582

avoid the overfitting of baseline predictor even if the usage data are sparse. The experimental results are shown in Table 2, where $\hat{r}_{ui} = b_{ui}$ if $k = 0$.

In the case of condensed data, we conduct experiments to see the impact of top-K similar users based on NbModel3. The experimental results are shown in Fig. 2. From Fig. 2, we find that the RMSE consistently decreases as increasing the value of k with different matrix density (range from 5 % to 15 %). While the value distribution of MAE presents U-shaped curve, and the best configuration for our dataset is about $k = 80$. In addition, more gains can be noted when the matrix becomes denser as for neighborhood-based models. For the neighborhood models, since the computational cost always increases with the increment of K, the choice of k should reflect a tradeoff between prediction accuracy and computational cost.

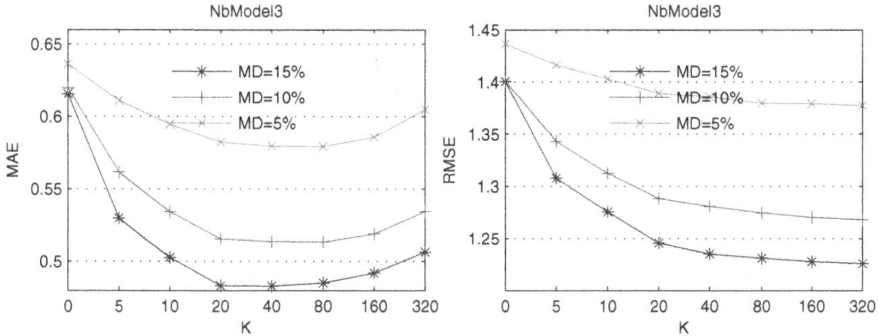

Fig. 2. Performance of NbModel3 with different k and matrix density.

5 Conclusion and Future Works

Founded on the principles of collaborative filtering and machine learning, we propose a neighborhood-based framework for making personalized QoS-prediction of cloud services. It provides an efficient global optimization scheme, thus offers robust and accurate prediction results. Also, it preserves explainability for QoS-prediction tasks which would be helpful for users make more definite selections. The extensive experimental analysis indicates the effectiveness of our approach.

Since neighborhood-based models are distinctly of MF, we would want to integrate them together to have both of worlds in the future. We currently conduct experimental studies only on response-time, thus expect to adapt the proposed methods to the prediction tasks of other cloud service QoS properties, such as reliability, throughput and scalability. In addition, extra information, such geo-information of users and items, temporal use of service invocation, can enter into this framework to offer more accurate prediction results.

Acknowledgements. This work is supported by the Special Funds for Middle-aged and Young Core Instructor Training Program of Yunnan University, the Applied Basic Research Project of Yunnan Province (2013FB009,2014FA023), the Program for Innovative Research Team in Yunnan University (XT412011), and the National Natural Science Foundation of China (61562090,61562092,61472345).

References

1. Sun, L., Dong, H., Hussain, F.K., Hussain, O.K., Chang, E.: Cloud service selection: state-of-the-art and future research directions. J. Netw. Comput. Appl. **45**, 134–150 (2014)
2. Zheng, Z., Ma, H., Lyu, M.R., King, I.: Collaborative web service QoS prediction via neighborhood integrated matrix factorization. IEEE T. Serv. Comput. **6**(3), 289–299 (2013)
3. Shao, L., Zhang, J., Wei, Y., Zhao, J., Xie, B., Mei, H.: Personalized QoS prediction for Web services via collaborative filtering. In: 2007 IEEE International Conferenceon Web Services, ICWS 2007, pp. 439–446. IEEE Press, New York (2007)
4. Zheng, Z., Ma, H., Lyu, M.R., King, I.: QoS-aware Web service recommendation by collaborative filtering. IEEE T. Serv. Comput. **4**(2), 140–152 (2011)
5. Sun, H., Zheng, Z., Chen, J., Lyu, M.R.: Personalized Web service recommendation via normal recovery collaborative filtering. IEEE T. Serv. Comput. **6**(4), 573–579 (2013)
6. Wu, J., Chen, L., Feng, Y., Zheng, Z., Zhou, M., Wu, Z.: Predicting quality of service for selection by neighborhood-based collaborative filtering. IEEE Trans. Syst. Man Cybern.: Syst. **43**(2), 428–439 (2013)
7. Chen, X., Zheng, Z., Yu, Q., Lyu, M.R.: Web service recommendation via exploiting location and QoS information. IEEE Trans. Parallel Distrib. Syst. **25**(7), 1913–1924 (2014)
8. Yu, Q., Zheng, Z., Wang, H.: Trace norm regularized matrix factorization for service recommendation. In: 2013 IEEE 20th International Conference on WebServices, ICWS 2013, pp. 34–41. IEEE Press, New York (2013)
9. Zhang, R., Li, C., Sun, H., Wang, Y., Huai, J.: Quality of web service predictionby collective matrix factorization. In: 2014 IEEE 11th International Conferenceon Services Computing, SCC 2014, pp. 432–439. IEEE Press, New York (2014)
10. Yin, J., Lo, W., Deng, S., Li, Y., Wu, Z., Xiong, N.: Colbar: a collaborative location-based regularization framework for QoS prediction. Inf. Sci. **265**, 68–84 (2014)
11. He, P., Zhu, J., Zheng, Z., Xu, J., Lyu, M.R.: Location-based hierarchical matrix factorization for Web service recommendation. In: 2014 IEEE International Conference on Web Services, ICWS 2014, pp. 297–304. IEEE Press, New York (2014)
12. Lo, W., Yin, J., Li, Y., Wu, Z.: Efficient Web service QoS prediction using local neighborhood matrix factorization. Eng. Appl. AI **38**, 14–23 (2015)
13. Tsai, W., Zhou, X., Chen, Y., Bai, X.: On testing and evaluating service-oriented software. IEEE Comput. **41**(8), 40–46 (2008)
14. Desrosiers, C., Karypis, G.: A comprehensive survey of neighborhood-based recommendation methods. In: Ricci, F., Rokach, L., Shapira, B., Kantor, P.B. (eds.) Recommender Systems Handbook, pp. 107–144. Springer, US (2011)
15. Koren, Y.: Factor in the neighbors: scalable and accurate collaborative filtering. ACM Trans. Knowl. Discov. Data **4**(1), 1 (2010)
16. Hyndman, R.J., Koehler, A.B.: Another look at measures of forecast accuracy. Int. J. Forecast. **22**(4), 679–688 (2006)

17. Salakhutdinov, R., Mnih, A.: Probabilistic Matrix Factorization. In: Advances in Neural Information Processing Systems 20, NIPS 2007, pp. 1257–1264. Curran Associates, Inc. (2008)
18. Lee, D.D., Seung, H.S.: Algorithms for non-negative matrix factorization. In: Advances in Neural Information Processing Systems 13, NIPS 2000, pp. 556–562. MIT Press (2000)

Collaborative Application

Multi-core Accelerated Operational Transformation for Collaborative Editing

Weiwei Cai, Fazhi He(✉), and Xiao Lv

School of Computer, Wuhan University, Wuhan, China
fzhe@whu.edu.cn

Abstract. This article proposes a parallel operational transformation (OT) algorithm for collaborative editing. OT maintains the eventual consistency of replicated data in optimistic way, allowing users to manipulate the shared document simultaneously. It has been the first choice for most collaborative applications. However, existing approaches must keep the number of operations generated in a session small so that it can provide a decent responsive time. The multi-core/many-core architectures are becoming pervasive in recent years. Unfortunately, there is no prior work which has explored accelerating operational transformation algorithms with available computation power. We present a lock-free operation history which are accessed by a batch of remote operations at the same time. Moreover, a data parallel computation model is constructed to accelerate the integration of local operations. To the best of our knowledge, this is the first parallel OT algorithm. Experimental results show our proposed algorithm outperforms the stat-of-art algorithms for collaborative editing.

Keywords: Collaborative computing · Collaborative editing · Operational transformation · Parallel computing

1 Introduction

Collaborative editing systems constitute a class of collaborative computing systems where users modify the shared data separately and achieve a consistent result. To satisfy the requirement of high responsiveness and availability, these systems are based on data replication. Each user can freely edit any part of local copy and changes are immediately reflected on user interface. The generated updates are propagated to other users. The different execution order of these operations may lead to a divergence. Operational transformation (OT) maintains the consistency of replicas by changing the execution form of received operations. The technique has been applied in supporting various collaborative applications, such as Google Docs, Microsoft CoWord and CoPowerPoint [1], CoRED [2], SyncLD [3], and CoCAD [4].

OT transforms received operations with executed operations before executing them. Concurrent operations are commutative by transformations. As an example, consider the scenario where user1 inserts 'a' at position 1 and concurrently user2 deletes element at 2. Here, a document is represented as a string

S. Guo et al. (Eds.): CollaborateCom 2015, LNICST 163, pp. 121–128, 2016.
DOI: 10.1007/978-3-319-28910-6_11

of characters, "abc". When receiving remote operations, the deletion is transformed to operation at position 3 because user1 has inserted a character before its effect operation and the insertion does not change itself after transformation. As a result, both of the user1 and user2 obtain the consistent result "aab". All executed operations are recorded in history. The state of the art OT has a time complexity of $O(n)$ [5], where n is the number of editing operation in the history. Therefore, it is important to keep the operation history small for high responsiveness. With the widespread use of multi-core/many-core processors, the parallel computing power can efficiently address this limitation.

In this paper, we design a lock-free queue storing executed operations which allow several threads to process transformations in parallel. When there is an actual conflict between operations, some of them need to retry but never be blocked. Local operations are integrated individually but can still benefit from the parallel loop.

2 Related Work

The transformation function changes the operation form so that a pair of operations can execute out of order. It should satisfy the transformation properties (TP1 and TP2) [6]. TTF (tombstone transformation function) constructs a two-tier model with an extra layer which retains the deleted objects. It is correct based on the fact transformed operations do not consider the effect of delete operations. Imine et al. [7] contribute a set of correct transformation functions for the modified insertions. From another perspective, ABT [8] requires all insert operations must be located before delete operation in history. In terms of the basic theory, they are equivalent. Recently, Imine et al. [7] contribute a set of correct transformation functions for the modified insertions. The added attribute records the number of deletions which have been executed before the effect position.

The relationship between operations is traditionally determined by the state vector [9]. Based on this technique, algorithms perform poorly on separating concurrent operations from history [10]. WOOT algorithm [11] defined that a newly inserted element semantically depends on the previous and next element. It maintains the data model like TTF. The improved version WOOTH has a time complexity $O(n)$, where n is the number of inserted elements. As the asynchronous version of ABT, ABST [5] provides the transformation of long operation sequences and improved the time complexity to $O(H)$, where $|H|$ is the size of history.

3 Parallel Implementation

Operation history is both modified by local and remote threads. Therefore, they should be executed in mutual exclusive manner. In the following, we discuss the integration of local and remote operations respectively.

3.1 Data Model

Two tier data model is constructed as Fig. 1, where the logical view corresponds to the user view and the physical view retains the deleted objects. Both of them are modeled as a linear collection of elements. In logical view, the element can be various data type, such as characters, XML nodes. In physical view, each slot records the identifiers of operations which have inserted them, the number of visible element before it and the visible flag. Because an operation can uniquely be identified with the site identifier and local sequence number, it is easy to find its effect element.

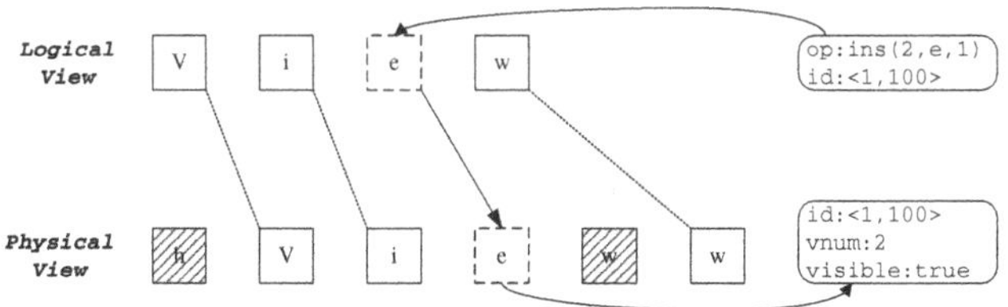

Fig. 1. Data model.

3.2 Operation Dependency Relation

The traditional dependency relations are based on the happened-before theory defined by Lamport [12]. If o_1 is executed before o_2, it is widely accepted that the precedence order should be preserved at all sites. As a matter of fact, there exist extensive cases where a pair of $o_1 \rightarrow o_2$ is able to execute out of order. For instance, assume that $o_1 \rightarrow o_2$ and $o_1 = ins(1, a)$, $o_2 = ins(3, b)$, then $[ins(1, a)\ ins(3, b)] = [ins(2, b)\ ins(1, a)]$. If two adjacent operations in history are not transformation-based commutative, the latter one is semantically dependent on the former one [13]. In other words, the boundary of causal and concurrent operation is naturally the dependent one.

However, this relation is determined by checking all operations executed before the target operation one by one, which is not easily parallelized. From the perspective of object positions relation, the operation of an element is only semantically dependent on operations which have manipulated its directly adjacent elements.

3.3 Integration of Local Operations

When users issue an operation, it is instantly executed and reflected on user interface. Then, the algorithm computes its corresponding position in physical view and sends the update to other users. Suppose the user executes an insertion $ins(p, e)$, the conversion has to find the $(p-1)$-th visible element in physical view. This procedure is generally implemented with a while-loop. However, it is not efficient to execute while loop in parallel due to the uncertain stop condition. To make it easier, each element records the number of visible elements before it. Now, the computation of position is a parallel for loop with the definite lower and upper bounds. After that, the dependency information becomes clear. As discussed above, the operation depends on the one which has inserted the previous or next object, or does not depend on any operation. The procedure of integrating insert operations is described in Algorithm 1. The same idea applies when integrating a delete operation.

Algorithm 1. The integration of insert operations

```
pos_l = op.pos;
if op.type = ins then
    #parallel for
    for i = 0;i < |P|;i + + do
        if P[i].vnum == pos_l − 1 then
            pos_p = i;
        else if P[i].vnum >= pos_l then
            P[i].vnum + +;
        end if
    end for
    P.insert(pos_p, newEle);
end if
```

3.4 Integration of Remote Operations

We integrate a sequence of remote operations in parallel. Based on the fact that transforming o_1 against o_2 does not change o_2, each remote operation can safely be transformed with the operation history. Received operations are stored in a lock-free queue, denoted as *RQueue*, which can be processed by parallel thread. This concurrent containers can be found in some implementations, such as Intel's Threading building blocks[1] and open source library libcds[2]. Therefore, a batch of operations can be processed simultaneously in non-blocking way. If a pending operation satisfies the dependency relation, it is dequeued from *RQueue* and transformed with the operation history. Otherwise, it is appended to the *RQueue*. The operation history is also stored in a lock-free queue, denoted as *HQueue*, which only has the enqueue function. Because no operation node should be released, ABA problem does not exist [14].

Since the transformed operations are appended to the end of *HQueue*, only the *tail* node may be modified by simultaneous thread. Therefore, the observed operation history can be transformed with remote operations safely. Only when the thread reads *tail* node without interference, it enqueues the target operation. It needs the help of synchronized primitive *CAS* which is supported

[1] https://www.threadingbuildingblocks.org/.
[2] http://libcds.sourceforge.net/doc/cds-api/index.html.

Algorithm 2. Integrate of remote operations

```
op = RQueue.dequeue();
cur = RQ.head, end = RQ.tail, newNode = newNode(op.pos, op.id);
if op.dep = null then
    LTransform(op, cur, end), newNode.pos = op.pos;
    while !CAS(RQ.tail, end, newNode) do
        end = RQ.tail;
        LTransform(op, cur, end); newNode.pos = op.pos;
    end while
else
    while cur! = end.next do
        if cur.id = op.id then
            while !CAS(RQ.tail, end, newNode) do
                end = RQ.tail;
                LTransform(op, cur, end), newNode.pos = op.pos;
            end while
            break;
        end if
        cur = cur.next
    end while
    RQ.enqueue(op);
end if
```

by most multiprocessor architectures. $CAS(reg, oldValue, newValue)$ compares the contents of a memory location (reg) to a given old value, only if they are the same, successfully modifies the contents of that memory location to a given new value. Algorithm 2 describes the integration of remote operations. $LTransform(op, cur, end)$ transforms op against operations from the current node to the end node, and finally cur and end point to the same location. If the $tail$ node is modified during this period, the target operation continues to be transformed until the current node reach the end and then check the $tail$ node again. After all remote operations is completed, they will sequentially update the physical view without extra computation.

4 Evaluation

We evaluate the time consuming of local and remote operation with parallel OT algorithm (POT), and compare it with representative algorithms, WOOTH [15], and ABST [5]. All the algorithms were implemented in C++ and compiled with the same flags. Because ABST only maintains the operation history and WOOTH maintains the two tier data model like Fig. 1 but no need of the history, we simulate collaborative workloads on a non-empty document (with 10,0000 characters) and empty document. By convention [15–17], we construct the operation history with 10,0000 operations, where 80 % are insertions and positions are uniform distribution. Then we calculate the total time of integrating 100

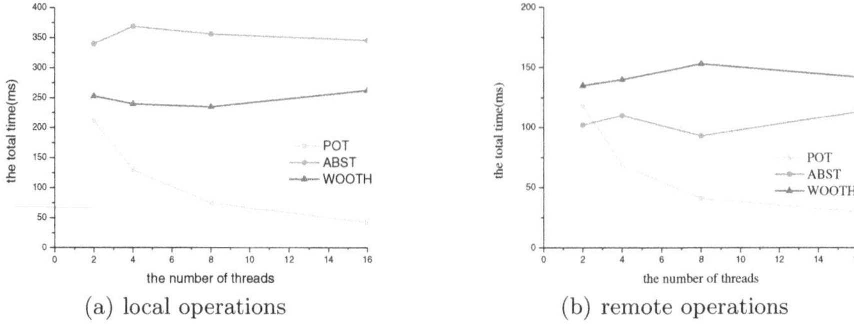

(a) local operations (b) remote operations

Fig. 2. Empty document scenario.

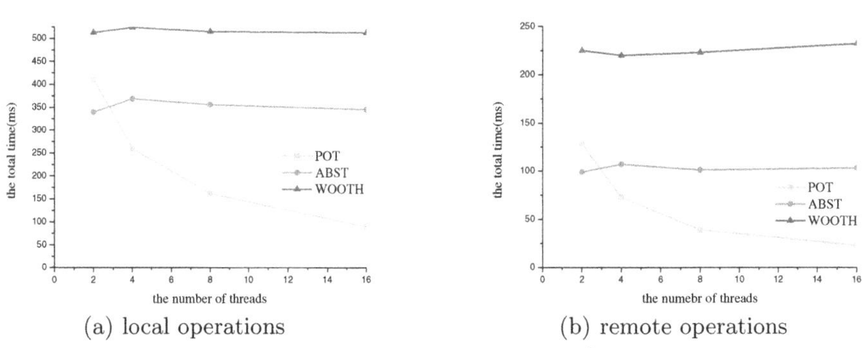

(a) local operations (b) remote operations

Fig. 3. Non empty document scenario.

local and remote operations, respectively. The experiments were performed on a platform of two 4-core Intel i7-4770 with HyperThreading, 16 GB DDR3 RAM.

According to Fig. 2, ABST algorithm consumes more time in integrating local operations for the reason that it orders the history according to the effect position relation. However, when processing remote operations, ABST outperforms WOOTH and POT (with 2 threads). In Fig. 3, the number of elements in physical view is the double of that in the empty-document scenario, causing that the performance of WOOTH and POT both degrade, but it has little influence on ABST. When integrating remote operations, comparing with the empty-document scenario, only WOOTH slightly increases the time cost. POT acquires great improvement with more parallel thread in both scenarios. As a whole, POT outperforms the WOOTH and ABST.

5 Conclusion

In this paper, we contribute a parallel OT algorithm (POT) for collaborative editing. The proposed method accelerates the integration of local and remote operations with the support of multi-core architecture. We construct a two tier data model which helps compute the position in physical view and dependency relation of local operations in parallel. To remote updates, a lock-free queue storing executed operations can be accessed by simultaneous threads. It greatly improves the throughput in transforming a batch of operations. The comparative experimental results showed that POT outperforms the other well-known algorithms in a large collaborative workload. In future work, we try to extend our multi-core accelerated idea to other collaborative applications, such as CAD&Graphics systems [18–26].

Acknowledgment. This paper is supported by the National Science Foundation of China (Grant No. 61472289) and Hubei Province Science Foundation (Grant No. 2015CFB254).

References

1. Sun, C., Xia, S., Sun, D., Chen, D., Shen, H., Cai, W.: Transparent adaptation of single-user applications for multi-user real-time collaboration. ACM Trans. Comput. Hum. Interact. **13**(4), 531–582 (2006)
2. Lautamäki, J., Nieminen, A., Koskinen, J., Aho, T., Mikkonen, T., Englund, M.: Cored: browser-based collaborative real-time editor for java web applications. In: Proceedings of the ACM Conference on Computer Supported Cooperative Work, pp. 1307–1316. ACM (2012)
3. Nicolaescu, P., Derntl, M., Klamma, R.: Browser-based collaborative modeling in near real-time. In: The 9th International Conference on Collaborative Computing: Networking, Applications and Worksharing, pp. 335–344 (2013)
4. Liu, H., He, F., Zhu, F., Zhu, Q.: Consistency maintenance in collaborative cad systems. Chin. J. Electron. **22**(1), 15–20 (2013)
5. Shao, B., Li, D., Gu, N.: A sequence transformation algorithm for supporting cooperative work on mobile devices. In: Proceedings of the 2010 ACM Conference on Computer Supported Cooperative Work, pp. 159–168. ACM (2010)
6. Ressel, M., Nitsche-Ruhland, D., Gunzenhäuser, R.: An integrating, transformation-oriented approach to concurrency control and undo in group editors. In: Proceedings of the 1996 ACM Conference on Computer Supported Cooperative Work, pp. 288–297. ACM (1996)
7. Randolph, A., Boucheneb, H., Imine, A., Quintero, A.: On synthesizing a consistent operational transformation approach. IEEE Trans. Comput. **64**(4), 1074–1089 (2015)
8. Li, D., Li, R.: An admissibility-based operational transformation framework for collaborative editing systems. Comput. Support. Coop. Work **19**(1), 1–43 (2010)
9. Ellis, C.A., Gibbs, S.J.: Concurrency control in groupware systems. In: ACM SIGMOD Record, vol. 18, pp. 399–407. ACM (1989)
10. Suleiman, M., Cart, M., Ferrié, J.: Serialization of concurrent operations in a distributed collaborative environment. In: Proceedings of the ACM Conference on Supporting Group Work: The Integration Challenge, pp. 435–445. ACM (1997)
11. Oster, G., Urso, P., Molli, P., Imine, A.: Data consistency for p2p collaborative editing. In: Proceedings of the 2006 20th Anniversary Conference on Computer Supported Cooperative Work, pp. 259–268. ACM (2006)

12. Lamport, L.: Time, clocks, and the ordering of events in a distributed system. Commun. ACM **21**(7), 558–565 (1978)
13. Imine, A.: Flexible concurrency control for real-time collaborative editors. In: The 28th International Conference on Distributed Computing Systems Workshops, pp. 423–428. IEEE (2008)
14. Michael, M.M.: Hazard pointers: safe memory reclamation for lock-free objects. IEEE Trans. Parallel Distrib. Syst. **15**(6), 491–504 (2004)
15. Ahmed-Nacer, M., Ignat, C.-L., Oster, G., Roh, H.-G., Urso, P.: Evaluating crdts for real-time document editing. In: Proceedings of the 11th ACM Symposium on Document Engineering, pp. 103–112. ACM (2011)
16. Li, D., Li, R.: An operational transformation algorithm and performance evaluation. Comput. Support. Coop. Work **17**(5–6), 469–508 (2008)
17. Shao, B., Li, D., Gu, N.: A fast operational transformation algorithm for mobile and asynchronous collaboration. IEEE Trans. Parallel Distrib. Syst. **21**(12), 1707–1720 (2010)
18. He, F., Han, S.: A method and tool for human-human interaction and instant collaboration in cscw-based cad. Comput. Ind. **57**(8), 740–751 (2006)
19. Jing, S.-X., He, F., Han, S.-H., Cai, X.-T., Liu, H.-J.: A method for topological entity correspondence in a replicated collaborative cad system. Comput. Ind. **60**(7), 467–475 (2009)
20. Huang, Z., He, F., Cai, X., Zou, Z., Liu, J., Liang, M., Chen, X.: Efficient random saliency map detection. Sci. China Inf. Sci. **54**(6), 1207–1217 (2011)
21. Liu, H., He, F., Cai, X., Chen, X., Chen, Z.: Performance-based control interfaces using mixture of factor analyzers. Vis. Comput. **27**(6), 595–603 (2011)
22. Li, X., He, F., Cai, X., Zhang, D.: Cad data exchange based on the recovery of feature modelling procedure. Int. J. Comput. Integr. Manuf. **25**(10), 874–887 (2012)
23. Li, X., He, F., Cai, X., Zhang, D., Chen, Y.: A method for topological entity matching in the integration of heterogeneous cad systems. Integr. Comput. Aided Eng. **20**(1), 15–30 (2013)
24. Cheng, Y., He, F., Cai, X., Zhang, D.: A group undo/redo method in 3d collaborative modeling systems with performance evaluation. J. Netw. Comput. Appl. **36**(6), 1512–1522 (2013)
25. Cai, X.T., He, F.Z., Li, W.D., Li, X.X., Wu, Y.Q.: Encryption based partial sharing of cad models. Integr. Comput. Aided Eng. **22**(3), 243–260 (2015)
26. Zhang, D.J., He, F.Z., Han, S.H., Li, X.X.: Quantitative optimization of interoperability during feature-based data exchange. Integr. Comput. Aided Eng., 1–20 (2015, preprint)

NFV: Near Field Vibration Based Group Device Pairing

Zhiping Jiang(✉), Jinsong Han, Wei Xi, and Jizhong Zhao

Xi'an Jiaotong University, Xi'an, China
jiangzp.cs@gmail.com

Abstract. In this paper, we propose a group device pairing system called NFV to enable group communication using mobile device equipped with motion sensors. A group of people put their mobile devices on the table and wait for a secure connection. We propose a vibration-propagation based key delivery scheme to transmit a secure connection key among a group of trusted mobile devices. Based on this key, group users establish a confidential communication channel between their devices. NFV achieves group devices pairing without the complex operations needed in prior works. We implemented NFV using off-the-shelf Android smartphones. The experimental results shows the efficiency and security of our system.

Keywords: Vibration channel · Accelerometer · Pulse-width modulation · Ad hoc group pairing

1 Introduction

Mobile device has infiltrated into our daily lives, and it has enabled multiple new applications, such as photo sharing, mobile collaborative gaming [1], or mobile clouding [2,3], which require neighboring devices engaging in spontaneous interaction without prior configuration [4,5]. Numerous application scenarios based on *Human-to-Human* interaction could be observed or foreseen in the near future. For instance, conference attendees exchange notes and contact informations, or family members share files and photos.

Such promising desire requires neighboring devices to be aware of the intent and established a trustful connection. For example, most of existing solutions requires a prior wireless communication channel, such as WiFi or Bluetooth, to communication with target device, and the procedure is troublesome for most of the circumstances (scanning for neighboring devices and select particular target from a list [4]). Some other techniques even transmit a priori [6] or do synchronization action [7] in advance to make potential target devices aware of the purpose. Due to the energy constraint, mobile devices cannot provide continuous channel monitoring in the background to discover nearby devices, so that manual initiation is necessary for both transmission device and target devices.

S. Guo et al. (Eds.): CollaborateCom 2015, LNICST 163, pp. 129–140, 2016.
DOI: 10.1007/978-3-319-28910-6_12

Point & Connect (P&C) [5] initiates a connection with target device through a simple pointing gesture. Spartacus [4] has introduced a spatially-aware neighboring device interaction technique without configuration beforehand. By using a continuous audio-based low power listening, this system utilizes acoustic technique based on Doppler effect to enable devices to establish connection with particular target accurately. These two systems only achieve *One-to-One* device pairing, which is inconvenient to deploy in multiple devices' scenario for continuous connecting because it's time consuming.

In this paper, we seek to further abandon such inconvenience by accomplishing an ambient-aware context-based device *Group Pairing* strategy. We propose NFV, a mobile group file sharing and exchanging protocol, which enables users to interact with a nearby group of target devices without prior configuration. The proposed solution of NFV works as follows. A group of people put their mobile devices on the table for certain sharing purpose, and wait for a ad hoc connection. We assume all the devices on the table are legitimate users. We propose a vibration-propagation based key delivery scheme to establish a secure connection among a group of trusted mobile devices. An initiator on the table starts the connection by self-vibration, which could be broadcasted through the surface of the table as a secure channel and sensed silently by the surrounding devices on the same table. The self-vibration is programmable, so that the target devices capture the vibration through motion sensors, and extract information for generating connection key. Meanwhile, the initiator broadcasts encrypted information through high frequency acoustic signal, and receivers will decrypt the information through the information propagated through vibration. Although eavesdroppers could also record the encrypted information through public channel, they still cannot decrypt the original information. When original information is retrieved as shared key, all the target devices on the table will establish a secure connection through Wi-Fi Direct.

The main purpose of such design contains three folds. First of all, the key generation is convenient and secure, and the key distribution is much faster than traditional naive solutions, such as input key individually. Second, the protocol could defend Men-In-The-Middle attack. Even if the attacker could capture the encrypted information broadcast in the public channel, it still cannot retrieve the shared key for the connection. Then, we use zero-cost Wi-Fi Direct to replace the need for routers for connection, and it also consumes less power compared to Bluetooth.

The fundamental challenge here is how to capture such intention of patterned vibration on the table, and extract common information for generating shared key. That is, when placing on the surface of table, different material or structure of table may weaken the vibration intensity. Meanwhile, such intensity would be influenced by the distance between the target device and the tapping location, or even overwhelmed by the internal noise of motion sensor if the vibration is mild. It is a non-trivial problem to detect the sharing intention among devices robustly. Another equal challenge comes from the common key delivery strategy to establish secure communication channel.

Compared with other existing works, the main contribution of this paper is as follows:

1. We propose a novel and secure ambient-aware devices group pairing protocol initiated by simple self-vibration.
2. We develop a pulse-width modulation (PWM) based key delivery scheme based on the tiny vibration broadcast through the surface of the table, and establish a secure group communication channel without prior connection.
3. We implement NFV on Android smartphones and tablets, and evaluate the system using various device models under different interaction scenarios. And the evaluation indicates that the protocol is reliable and secure.

2 System Overview

NFV offers a group device sharing solution in close proximity, and works with state-of-the-art mobile devices with standard hardware settings. It does not rely on any additional devices or OS modification to establish a group device pairing.

2.1 Application Scenarios

The main purpose of this application is to simplify information sharing, file synchronising, and message exchanging. The typical setting for a NFV application scenario is that a group of mobile devices (*e.g.*, smartphones, tablets) are located within a short range, and intent to establish a connection. The Fig. 1 illustrates showcase of scenario in a conference room, where users intends to pair their devices on the table to synchronize their meeting notes. The system do not require extra equipments for establishing both public and secure channels to exchange information, and both the initiator and the target devices extract secret key from the exchange channel to establish a connection.

Fig. 1. Motivation scenario

NFV operates when the participated devices are stationarily located on the same surface, such as table. It makes use of the desk as a broadcast medium, and transmit secret information through the surface. NFV targets a group pair of devices that initiate interaction at with short delay, and all the devices on the same surface extract the same key to establish instantaneous connection automatically, such as WiFi direct.

2.2 Design Guidelines

NFV explore an ambient-aware pairing initiation design without taking any assisted actions. A group of users will prepare the interaction by putting their devices on the desk. An initiator will broadcast secret information through vibration according to certain pattern, and transmit coded information through acoustic signal. The software and the motion sensors in modern smart mobile devices will work together to overcome the limitation of devices.

Although we assume the devices on the same desk are all trustful, we still provide a verification function to validate the target devices in case of eavesdroppers nearby. For example, attackers can easily capture the acoustic signal or hear slight vibration noise through microphone. The main purpose of the verification function is guarantee the pure audio information cannot retrieve the secret key for connection.

NFV also has to seek the robustness of the system when initiating interaction, and the design complexity. The design of NFV should be robust under a variety of imperfect opening environment, especially when it comes to the desk with different materials and thickness, or covered with tablecloth. It should also functions well facing unpredicted environment noises.

2.3 Design Challenges

Our protocol typically contains three stages, connection attempt detection, secure common key delivery, and group communication channel establishment.

- Due to the internal mechanism of motion sensors, the measurement noise and ambient-variance may influence the sensory data, which may hinder the device to detect the pairing attempt at the first place. Especially the devices are placed on the table freely and randomly, and sometimes the distance between the devices and the knocking location is large.
- In order to establish a secure group communication channel, a shared secure key is needed. However, improper prior communication for key exchange in public channel is insecure, generate shared key through the vibration broadcast from simply knocking is difficult.
- Despite the variance of sensory data, the pattern of general vibration, especially the Simple harmonic vibration is similar. If the key delivery strategy is designed based on such coarse-grained pattern, attackers are more likely to launch collision attack, and eventually break the secure communication. Therefore, the shared key should not depend on coarse-grained knocking vibration.

3 System Design

NFV delivery the secret session password via two distinct channel, the secret vibration channel, and an arbitrary public channel. Given a session password pw_s to be shared with legitimate users, we delivery the encrypted version of pw_s, *i.e.* $enc(pw_s, k)$ via public channel, and the short key k via vibration channel. Upon receiving these two pieces of information, the receiver decrypts $enc(pw_s, k)$ with k, and use pw_s to establish the ad-hoc network.

3.1 Vibration Channel Analysis

Since NFV requires all the devices in the group communicate through both acoustic channel and vibration channel. Therefore, in this section, we will mainly discuss our preliminary analysis on both vibration channel detection and propose the system architecture based on our analysis.

Current mobile devices customize vibrator to provide a vibration intensity, frequency or duration in certain pattern to deliver tactile notification to users [8]. However, the vibration provided by the phones are subtle and private [9], and it only have binary settings (on or off), which limits the communication capability. Haptics researches suggest using vibrotactile patterns to deliver ambient information on mobile phones [10]. Motivated by such works, we explore the capacity of vibration communication on both transmission and receiving. Ideally, there would be a specific vibration pattern broadcasted from the initiator, and all the receivers on the same desk receive the vibrotactile message through motion sensors (*e.g.* accelerometer and gyroscope). However, generating various distinguishable vibrotactile could be difficult on commodity mobile devices, although the API for Android support user-defined durations for which to turn on or off the vibrator in milliseconds. Therefore, one technique issue has to be conquered is how to retrieve the initial cue from the sensory data (Fig. 2).

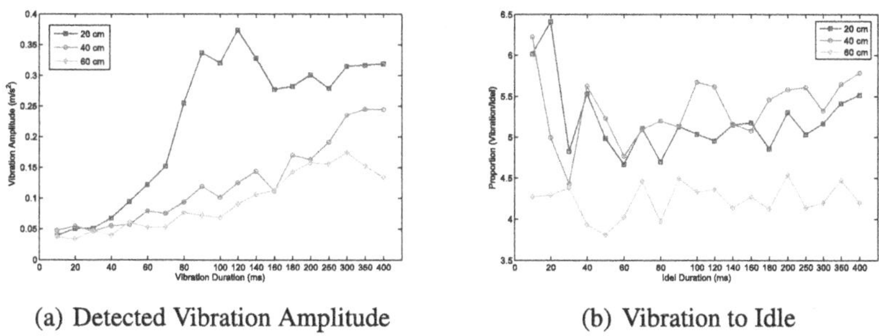

(a) Detected Vibration Amplitude (b) Vibration to Idle

Fig. 2. Vibration analysis.

PeopleTones [11] adjusts the duty cycle of the vibrotactile actuator to generate vibration in various levels. However the amplitude of the vibration cannot be detected precisely because of the various distance between the initiator and the receiver. The vibration generates mechanical wave, which spreads on the surface of the desk, and the target device on the same surface could record the vibration through motion sensors. Empirically, the amplitude of the sensed vibration is affected by three main factors: the distance between the vibrator and the receiver, the material of the surface where the devices are put, and the vibration frequency and duration. We conducts a comprehensive experiments on detecting the vibration broadcast from the initiator device.

The Android provides API to operate the vibrator on the devices, and the vibration pattern is determined by the input array of ints that are the duration for which to turn on and off the vibrator in milliseconds. Generally, due to the internal noise of motion sensor, the first issue is distinguishing the vibration from continuous sensory data. In this experiment, we deploy two Nexus 5 smartphones on the table with 20 cm to 60 cm apart. We take two set of experiments to handle how long should the vibrator work to be detected, and how long should the vibrator to rest to distinguish two continuous vibration. We set one phone to vibrate from 10 ms to 400 ms with 500 ms idle between two successive vibrations, and plot the result in Fig. 3(b). In this figure, we learn two facts: with the vibration duration increases, the sensed vibration from accelerometer increase as well; and shorter distance between sender and receiver, the more sensitive the receivers' motion sensor.

Figure 3(a) illustrates the proportion of vibration to idle in acceleration under the circumstance that the sender vibrator 500 ms and rest from 10 ms to 400 ms until next vibration. It is obvious that when the idle time period is only 10 ms, the proportion is relatively high, especially when the distance between the two devices is close. During this experiment, the receiver cannot distinguish each vibration clearly, the receiver only consider this as a continuous vibration. When the interval increases, the device could distinguish the two successive vibration from the sensory data, because of the obvious vibration amplitude difference. We thought the accelerometer only capture measurement noise when idle, which turned to be wrong eventually. The device vibrating on the table generates mechanical wave, which broadcasts through the table surface. And such vibration transferred into simple harmonic vibration for each particle on the face of the table. According to Hooke's Law, the particle on the table will continuous vibrating even if the source stops vibrating. In this case, the accelerometer captures both simple harmonic vibration and measurement noise during idle period, and longer idle period indicates more noise. Therefore, the proportion increase when the idle duration grows.

3.2 PWM-Based Vibration Channel

In this part, we have to design the encoding pattern to fulfill two goals: increasing the transmission bit rate, and guaranteeing the correctness of decoding from vibration. In the previous section, we notice that both the duration of vibration and idle should last longer than 80 ms to be identified by the target devices. Pursuing a balanced protocol, we propose an pulse-width modulation (PWM) based vibration channel. Pulse-width modulation uses a rectangular pulse wave whose pulse width is modulated resulting in the variation of the length of the vibration. To balance the transmission rate and the error rate, the pulse idle is set as 80 ms to achieve a distinguishable gap between pulses. Each pulse has 4 candidate length representing a 2-bit code. The pulse lengths are 80/100/120/140 ms. In this way the average transmission rate is about 10 bit/s, *i.e.* it only takes 4 s to transmit the key. That is acceptable in practical scenarios.

3.3 Demodulation

NFV communicate via the vibration propagation through the table medium. Ideally, when the transmitter stops vibration, the medium should stop soon. However, in real table medium, the vibration still remains long after the transmitter stops. It brings big challenge to the receiver side. The oscillation of table medium will introduce inter-symbol interference and vague timming at the received signal, which makes it hard to distinguish the "0" and "1" of modulated PWM signal. To help precisely determine the timing at the receiver side, the transmitter plays short beeps every 20 ms, which is synchronized with the timing of vibration channel PWM. These short beeps allow the receivers to synchronize the demodulator with PWM signal and eventually decode the secret key.

3.4 Acoustic Channel and Group Pairing

NFV demands another communication channel to broadcast the encrypted session key and necessary protocol signals. This channel could be an insecure or secure channel. Pursuing the robustness and efficiency, we choose acoustic channel. Each device randomly chooses a 200 Hz bandwidth between 17 kHz to 19 kHz and then claims its possession to the channel with a random delay. If channel collision is detect, the latter one will try another channel. We adopt the simple 4-FSK modulation due to its robustness and asynchronous property. According to our real world, over 150 bit/s transmission rate can be achieved, which is acceptable in our prototype.

Once the session key is successfully decrypted. All devices will initiate Wi-Fi Direct connections with the identical session key. In this way, a group pairing is established.

4 Prototyping and Evaluation

4.1 Prototype Implementation

We implement NFV on Android platform. Our test devices include 2×Nexus 4, 3×Nexus 5, and 2× Samsung Galaxy S4. The accelerometer sampling rate is 100 Hz for all devices.

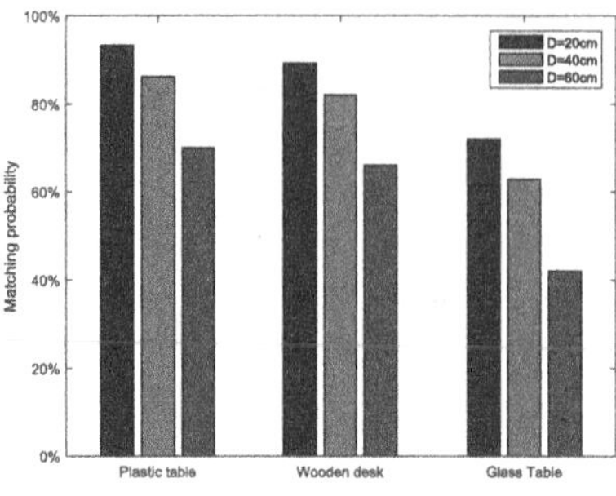

(a) Transmission Success Rate on Different Material

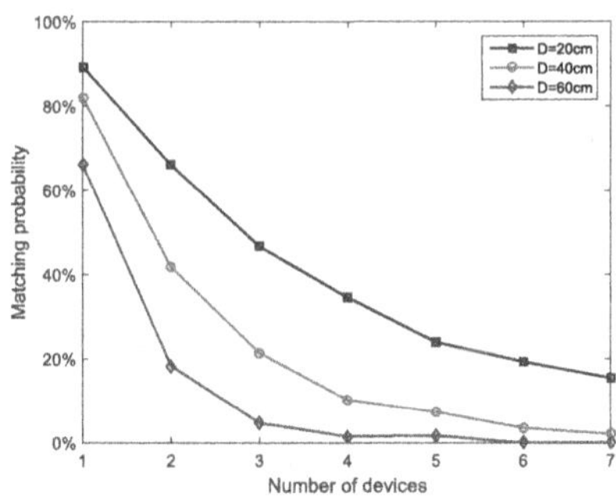

(b) Devices Pairing Success Rate

Fig. 3. (a) Transmission success rate on different material. (b) Group pairing success rate in different distance.

4.2 Prototype Performance Evaluation

Performance of Vibration Channel. We first evaluate the transmission success rate of 32-bit key over vibration channel. We conduct 20 times transmission on different table material and the distance varies from 20 cm to 60 cm. The test table material are plastic table, wooden desk, and glass table. They are usually seen in practical scenario.

Figure 3(a) shows the result. We see that the success rate drops along with the table material. The stronger the table material, the lower success rate. This is because, the stronger material is related to higher density, which requires higher energy to vibrate the table. The success rate also drops with the mutual distance. This is because the longer the distance, the smaller the vibration energy is at the receiver. Based on the test, we recommend the suitable distance between devices is within 40 cm.

Capacity of NFV. Due to the transmission error found in the vibration channel, the success rate of establishing a NFV channel decreases along with the number of devices. We conduct experiments to evaluate its performance.

Figure 3(b) shows the result. We see clearly from the figure that, as the distance among devices grows the success rate drops rapidly. When within 20 cm, the average success rate is more than 70 % for 5 devices. The success rate drops even faster when the distance goes to 60 cm. In this case, it can only support 2 devices pairing.

4.3 Security Evaluation

Acoustic Leakage. The security of NFV is based on an assumption that, the eavesdroppers seated at another desk cannot recover the key extracted from local desk vibration. We use mutual information to evaluate the similarity of acoustic signal and vibration signal. The acoustic signal is low-passed to 0–100 Hz, and we then use the same protocol to extract the initial key from the acoustic signal.

Table 1 shows the correlation between vibration signal and the acoustic under different environmental noise level. The result shows that when in quiet environment the vibrator's noise can be captured with some success rate regardless of table material. While in relatively noisy and very noisy environment, the correlation drops rapidly, indicating that the attacker's very low probability to guess the key.

Table 1. Acoustic leakage evaluation

	-80 db	-60 db	-40 db
Plastic table	0.43	0.321	0.11
Wooden desk	0.37	0.22	0.05
Glass table	0.49	0.32	0.08

5 Related Work

NFV leverages built-in vibrator and motion sensors on commodity mobile devices for both initiating connection and intention detection. It also utilizes microphones and speakers on the devices to transmit and listen interaction information. In this section, we review previous works about device interacting and acoustic sensing.

5.1 Device Pairing and Interaction

Interacting with nearby devices usually requires candidate devices to be identified by name so as to be retrieved during the scanning process. When connecting, users have to choose the target manually which heshe thinks is right. SyncTap [12] requires both users to press and release the button on the devices simultaneously to achieve pairing. Amigo [13] uses shared radio environment to prove their location proximity for pairing devices, but still use traditional synchronous action to accomplish pairing.

Interacting with neighboring mobile devices requires each devices being capable of both selecting the right target and interacting. [14] indicates that touching, scanning, and pointing are the most basic three stages for mobile device interacting with smart objective. Point & Connect (P&C) [5] utilizes time difference of arrivals of acoustic signals to initiate interactions in close proximity by pointing phone towards the intended target. However, this system requires users to open the broadcast channel manually so as to allow others to discover, which is troublesome. Spartacus [4] is quite similar to [5], which utilizes Doppler effect to initiate a connection with neighboring devices. The largest difference is that it runs as a system service to detect potential interaction intentions periodically and uses duty-cycled audio listening mechanism to save energy consumption. SoundWave [15] also uses Doppler effect to detect user gestures for human-computer interaction in close range. The detection of frequency shift achieved with high accuracy in this system since the computer plays both the transmitter and the receiver to double the frequency shift. Shake Well Before Use [16] capture sensory data from synchronous action, which could be used to detect the right pairing devices.

Existing works of detecting neighboring devices and interaction requests usually require additional equipments. PANDAA [17] relies on ambient sound to achieve centimeter-level device locating accuracy in indoor environment without using extra infrastructures, and none human-intrusive. Polaris [18] provides an orientation-dependent indoor device interaction techniques without additional devices.

5.2 Acoustic Sensing

Acoustic sensing on mobile devices has been used in several purposes. SurroundSense [19] utilizes audio data with sensory information to infer logical location. CenceMe [20] analyzes human social activities based on human conversations. SoundSense [21] employs signal processing pipeline for audio sensing, and distinguish music from noise. Similarity, Auditeur [22] detects acoustic events in real-time based on mobile-cloud platform [2,3,23]. There are some other applications which handles different types of sounds. For example, Nericell [24] detects horn of vehicles, iSleep [25] monitors people's sleep state using acoustic sensing, Ear-phone [26] is used to monitor noise pollution in urban environment. SwordFight [1] continuously outputs accurate distance between two smartphones using time different of acoustic signal's arrival.

6 Conclusion

This paper introduce a secure and efficient group device association method based on shared table vibration. We introduce a two-step process to establish such a secure ad hoc association. The robust Golay coding is first adopted to extract a session initialization vector from the raw accelerometer readings. This session initialization vector is passed to an secure group key exchange process to generate a high entropy session key. We prototype our system on off-the-shelf smartphone. Extensive evaluations have proved the security, efficiency, and convenience of our system.

References

1. Zhang, Z., Chu, D., Chen, X., Moscibroda, T.: Swordfight: enabling a new class of phone-to-phone action games on commodity phones. In: ACM MobiSys 2012 (2012)

2. Liu, F., Shu, P., Jin, H., Ding, L., Yu, J., Niu, D., Li, B.: Gearing resource-poor mobile devices with powerful clouds: architectures, challenges, and applications. IEEE Wirel. Commun. **20**(3), 14–22 (2013)
3. Liu, F., Shu, P., Lui, J.: Appatp: an energy conserving adaptive mobile-cloud transmission protocol (2015)
4. Sun, Z., Purohit, A., Bose, R., Zhang, P.: ACM MobiSys 2013 (2013)
5. Peng, C., Shen, G., Zhang, Y., Lu, S.: Point & connect: intention-based device pairing for mobile phone users. In: ACM MobiSys 2009 (2009)
6. Goodrich, M.T., Sirivianos, M., Solis, J., Tsudik, G., Uzun, E.: Loud and clear: human-verifiable authentication based on audio. In: IEEE ICDCS 2006 (2006)
7. Hinckley, K.: Synchronous gestures for multiple persons and computers. In: ACM UIST 2003 (2003)
8. Barton, S.: Programmable notifications for a mobile device. US Patent App. 11/116,860, 28 April 2005
9. Hansson, R., Ljungstrand, P., Redström, J.: Subtle and public notification cues for mobile devices. In: Abowd, G.D., Brumitt, B., Shafer, S. (eds.) Ubicomp 2001. LNCS, vol. 2201, pp. 240–246. Springer, Heidelberg (2001)
10. Poupyrev, I., Maruyama, S., Rekimoto, J.: Ambient touch: designing tactile interfaces for handheld devices. In: ACM UIST 2002 (2002)
11. Li, K.A., Sohn, T.Y., Huang, S., Griswold, W.G.: Peopletones: a system for the detection and notification of buddy proximity on mobile phones. In: ACM MobiSys 2008 (2008)
12. Rekimoto, J., Ayatsuka, Y., Kohno, M.: SyncTap: an interaction technique for mobile networking. In: Chittaro, L. (ed.) Mobile HCI 2003. LNCS, vol. 2795, pp. 104–115. Springer, Heidelberg (2003)
13. Varshavsky, A., Scannell, A., LaMarca, A., de Lara, E.: Amigo: proximity-based authentication of mobile devices. In: Krumm, J., Abowd, G.D., Seneviratne, A., Strang, T. (eds.) UbiComp 2007. LNCS, vol. 4717, pp. 253–270. Springer, Heidelberg (2007)
14. Rukzio, E., Leichtenstern, K., Callaghan, V., Holleis, P., Schmidt, A., Chin, J.: An experimental comparison of physical mobile interaction techniques: touching, pointing and scanning. In: Dourish, P., Friday, A. (eds.) UbiComp 2006. LNCS, vol. 4206, pp. 87–104. Springer, Heidelberg (2006)
15. Gupta, S., Morris, D., Patel, S., Tan, D.: Soundwave: using the doppler effect to sense gestures. In: ACM CHI 2012 (2012)
16. Mayrhofer, R., Gellersen, H.-W.: Shake well before use: authentication based on accelerometer data. In: LaMarca, A., Langheinrich, M., Truong, K.N. (eds.) Pervasive 2007. LNCS, vol. 4480, pp. 144–161. Springer, Heidelberg (2007)
17. Sun, Z., Purohit, A., Chen, K., Pan, S., et al.: Pandaa: physical arrangement detection of networked devices through ambient-sound awareness. In: ACM Ubicomp 2011 (2011)
18. Sun, Z., Purohit, A., Pan, S., Mokaya, F., et al.: Polaris: getting accurate indoor orientations for mobile devices using ubiquitous visual patterns on ceilings. In: ACM MCSA 2012 (2012)
19. Azizyan, M., Constandache, I., Roy Choudhury, R.: Surroundsense: mobile phone localization via ambience fingerprinting. In: ACM MobiCom 2009 (2009)
20. Miluzzo, E., Lane, N.D., Fodor, K., et al.: Sensing meets mobile social networks: the design, implementation and evaluation of the cenceme application. In: ACM SenSys 2008 (2008)

21. Lu, H., Pan, W., Lane, N.D., Choudhury, T., Campbell, A.T.: Soundsense: scalable sound sensing for people-centric applications on mobile phones. In: ACM MobiSys 2009 (2009)
22. Nirjon, S., Dickerson, R.F., Asare, P., Li, Q., Hong, D., et al.: Auditeur: a mobile-cloud service platform for acoustic event detection on smartphones. In: ACM MobiSys 2013 (2013)
23. Shu, P., Liu, F., Jin, H., Chen, M., Wen, F., Qu, Y.: etime: energy-efficient transmission between cloud and mobile devices. In: Proceedings IEEE on INFOCOM 2013, pp. 195–199. IEEE (2013)
24. Mohan, P., Padmanabhan, V.N., Ramjee, R.: Nericell: rich monitoring of road and traffic conditions using mobile smartphones. In: ACM SenSys 2008 (2008)
25. Hao, T., Xing, G., Zhou, G.: iSleep: unobtrusive sleep quality monitoring using smartphones. In: ACM SenSys 2008 (2008)
26. Rana, R.K., Chou, C.T., Kanhere, S.S., Bulusu, N., Hu, W.: Ear-phone: an end-to-end participatory urban noise mapping system. In: ACM IPSN 2010 (2010)

A Novel Method for Chinese Named Entity Recognition Based on Character Vector

Jing Lu[1,2,3](✉), Mao Ye[2], Zhi Tang[1,2], Xiao-Jun Huang[2], and Jia-Le Ma[2]

[1] Institute of Computer Science and Technology, Peking University, Beijing, China
10548887@pku.edu.cn
[2] State Key Laboratory of Digital Publishing Technology, Peking University Founder Group Co., Ltd., Beijing, China
{jing.lu,yemao.apb}@founder.com.cn
[3] Postdoctoral Workstation of the Zhongguancun Haidian Science Park, Beijing, China

Abstract. In this paper, a novel method using for Chinese named entity recognition is proposed. For each class, A posteriori probability model is acquired by combing probabilistic model and character vector, which are acquired from each class by using training data. After segment Chinese sentence into words, the posteriori probability of every words in each class can be calculated by using model we proposed, and thus the type of word could be determined according to maximum posteriori probability.

Keywords: Named entity recognition · Word vector · Character vector

1 Introduction

The research of Named entity recognition (NER) is a basic work in nature language process (NLP). First, NER is an important technology not only in parsing but also in information retrieval and automatic answering system. Second, the result of recognition Named entity could affect subsequent work.

Usually, the dictionary can be acquired and map the word to appropriate type. But most named entities were not logged in dictionary and new words turn up every day in the network age. So it is necessary to recognize them correctly without excessive reliance on the dictionary and Make sure the subsequent work process would not be effect.

Generally speaking, the purpose of Chinese NER is to categorize the words in the text into appropriate classes (type), which including seven broad classes (1. person name, 2. institution name, 3. toponymy, 4. time, 5. date, 6. current and 7. percentage) [1, 3, 5, 6].

For obviously pattern makes it easier to recognize the classes of time, date, current and percentage, the NER often refer to recognize person name, toponymy, and institution name, which is also the main part of this article.

S. Guo et al. (Eds.): CollaborateCom 2015, LNICST 163, pp. 141–150, 2016.
DOI: 10.1007/978-3-319-28910-6_13

The research of NER has a history of 10 more years, the popular method being used nowadays is to recognize extracting features of specified entities, for instance, the family names or the words ahead of "县" (county), "市" (city) are the special features of names or area names, respectively. Then statistics model such as CRF [8, 11] or SVM [1] was trained by using training data and use for recognizing entities. Another method being used is analyze the latent semantics in Named Entity and use semantics to recognition Named Entity [4].

Although the above method could achieve good effect, there were obviously drawbacks. Firstly, it is difficult to acquire adequate training data. Secondly, the adapt ability of this method is low, which rely on training data and domain knowledge. Thirdly, it is unavoidable to extract feature by labor who usually is the expert in respective field and this makes inconvenience for subsequent research. Finally, the poor performance in test data leads to the difficult in generalization.

The method which called distributed representation map the atomic semantic unit to higher vector space. Atomic semantic units are mapped into points in vector space and the distance between points represent the distance in semantic means. In English, the word is the atomic semantic unit in a sentence. In Named Entity, the word is consisted atomic semantic, and there are many Named Entity Recognition research based on atomic semantic [2]. However, the definition of the atomic semantic unit is not unchangeable. For instance, the root could be considered as the atomic semantic unit in a English word. Unlike English, the word in Chinese is formed by characters and each character indicates a semantic means (type). So the Chinese character can be considered as atomic semantic unit. For instance, the means of "省长" (governor of a province) is consisted of "省" (province) and "长" (governor). The character "省" (province) refer to a scope and the character "长" (governor) means the social status in this scope. So when we see a word "市长" (governor of a city), we can classify "市长" (governor of a city) and "省长" (governor of a province) to a same class because the only one different character is the range of scope, and the semantic meaning of "省" (province) and "市" (city) is close.

Take a person's name "张小明" (Zhang Xiao Ming) for example, "张" (Zhang) is close to "赵" (Zhao) and "王" (Wang), so "王小明" (Wang Xiao Ming), "赵小明" (Zhao Xiao Ming) can be attribute to a person's name according the class "张小明" (Zhang Xiao Ming) belongs to.

Summing up, in Chinese named entity recognition, it is important to grasp the semantic meaning in the character and distances of meanings.

Based on the meaning and the performance of vector of character, this paper proposes the Chinese named entity recognize model based on character vector.

2 Our Approach

Figure 1 shows the Flow chart of algorithm in this paper:

Firstly, it is need to prepare training data for each named entity classes, then the initial statistical model and character vector of each class are obtained respectively by using training data. Then the recognition models of each class are acquired by combing character vector and initial statistical model. When input a string, the recognition model

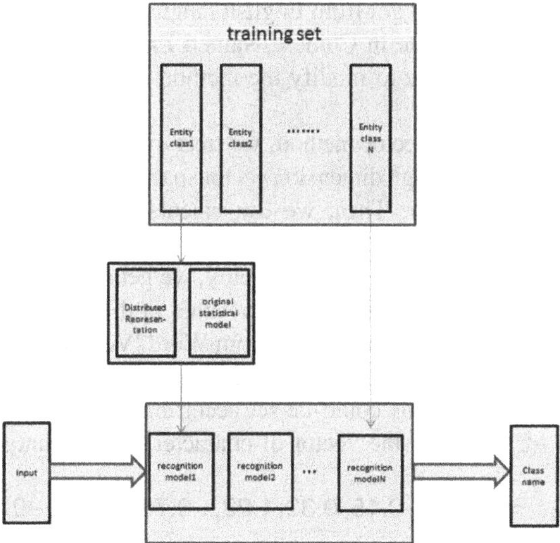

Fig. 1. The flow chart of paper

can output the posterior probability of corresponding class. Finally, the class of input string will be determined according maximum posterior probability.

In above steps, we could find out recognition models will be obtain independently. So, for easier presentation, the rest part of Sect. 2 would only discuss the class toponymy as an example of all other classes.

In Sect. 2.1, we will discuss the significance of character vector and the method to acquire them. In Sect. 2.2, the statistical model of named Entity will be proposed. In Sect. 2.3, the recognition models will be obtained by combining the character vector (Sect. 2.1) and statistical model (Sect. 2.2), and the recognition models will be applied in NER.

2.1 Training Character Vector

In Sect. 2, we discuss the importance of the semantic of character in Chinese NER. But Conventional methods treat more than 3000 common used Chinese characters as independent type, thus the semantic distance between characters is ignored. But in a same entity class, characters in close semantic distance can be replaced by each other in most conditions. Furthermore, through the replacement of characters, many Named Entities will be categorized, so it is urgent to calculate semantic distances of characters.

The Distributed representation is proposed in recent years. The basic idea of Distributed representation is mapping the word unit which is basic unit of sentence into high dimension vector space [8, 9]. The result of this method also be called word vector.

In vector space, the distances between word vectors refer their semantic distance. It is more likely they have same semantic meaning if they get close enough to each other.

The idea of word vector was got from English language which the word is the basic semantic unit in sentence. While in Chinese Named Entity, the character is the basic semantic unit. So it is necessary to modify the method of word vector and apply it in NER.

Take the idea of the word vector method, we treat every Chinese character as basic semantic unit and map them to high dimension vector space by the same way. The mapped result is called character vector. Then, we can calculate the distance between these character vectors and close distance usually means semantic similarity and replaceable.

Given that some Chinese character is polysemy, we get character vector by classes. The same character usually has different vector value in different class.

In this paper, character vector is obtained from Word2Vec offered by Google. After training, every character of entity string can be represented as vector with 8 dimensions. The number of dimensions could be set according to actual demand.

Take toponym for example, the vector of character “县” (county) and “市” (city) were:

$$V_{toponymy,\text{"县"}} = [0.23, -0.15, 0.33, 1.23, -0.78, -0.28, -0.28, 0.2]$$

$$V_{toponymy,\text{"市"}} = [0.27, 0.07, 0.0, 0.27, -0.42, 0.03, -0.04, 0]$$

The character vector of toponym are showed in 2-Dimension coordinate in Fig. 2. It is obviously that characters “县” (county), “市” (city), “省” (province) are closer, and apart from above three words, characters “东” (east), “南” (south), “西” (west), “北” (north) are close to each other. This fact indicates the substitutability of characters. The closer distance they have, the chance of they replace each other is higher. Furthermore, mapping the word to vector will strongly promote the generalization ability of the model.

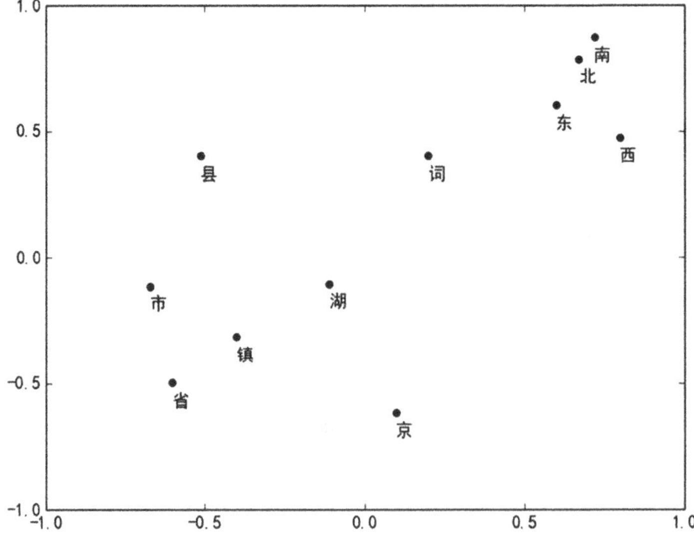

Fig. 2. The character in 2-Dimensions

2.2 Probabilistic Model

In above section, we discuss the importance of the semantic of character in Chinese NER. But Conventional methods treat more than 3000 common used Chinese characters as independent type, thus the semantic distance between characters is ignored. But in a same entity class, characters in close semantic distance can be replaced by each other in most conditions. Furthermore, through the replacement of characters, many Named Entities will be categorized, so it is urgent to calculate semantic distances of characters.

In this paper, the character is divided into three categories according to their location in the word, which is the First Character,the Inner Character and the End Character, respectively. These three types of models plus one-order Markov Process makes one kind of class named entity can be represented into four sub-models.

Still take toponymy for example. For string str = "上海市" (Shang Hai City), we define the probability of the model generate it shows as follow:

$$\begin{aligned}
&P'(\text{"上海市"} \mid class = Toponymy) \approx P'_B(\text{"上"} \mid class = Toponymy) \\
&\prod_{i=2}^{end-1} P'_M(str(i) \mid class = Toponymy) \\
&P'_E(\text{"市"} \mid class = Toponymy) \\
&\prod_{i=1}^{end-1} P'_{Markov}(str(i) \mid str(i-1), class = Toponymy)
\end{aligned} \tag{1}$$

The $str(i)$ represent the i-th character in str.

$$\prod_{i=2}^{end-1} P'_M(str(i) \mid class = Toponymy) = \prod_{i=2}^{end-1} P'_M(海 \mid class = Toponymy)$$

$$\prod_{i=1}^{end-1} P'_{Markov}(str(i) \mid str(i-1), class = Toponymy) =$$

$$P'_{Markov}(\text{"海"} \mid \text{"上"}, class = Toponymy) P'_{Markov}(\text{"市"} \mid \text{"海"}, class = Toponymy)$$

Every sub-model will be calculated by using training data, the formulas shows as follow:

$$\begin{aligned}
P'_B(cc|class = AreaName) &= \frac{1}{N}\sum_{n=1}^{N} f_B(cc, data_n) \\
f_B(cc, str) &= \begin{cases} 1 & str(1) = cc \\ 0 & Otherwise \end{cases}
\end{aligned} \tag{2}$$

$$
\begin{aligned}
P'_M(cc|class = AreaName) &= \frac{1}{N}\sum_{n=1}^{N} f_B(cc,\ data_n) \\
f_M(cc, str) &= \begin{cases} 1 & str(i) = cc \\ 0 & Otherwise \end{cases}
\end{aligned} \tag{3}
$$

$$
\begin{aligned}
P'_E(cc|class = AreaName) &= \frac{1}{N}\sum_{n=1}^{N} f_B(cc, data_n) \\
f_E(cc, str) &= \begin{cases} 1 & str(end) = cc \\ 0 & Otherwise \end{cases}
\end{aligned} \tag{4}
$$

$$
\begin{aligned}
P'_{Markov}(cc|class = AreaName, cc_{pre}) &= \frac{1}{N}\sum_{n=1}^{N} f_{Markov}(cc|cc_{pre}, data_n) \\
f_{Markov}(cc|cc_{pre}, str) &= \begin{cases} 1 & str(i+1) = cc\ \&\&\ str(i) = cc_{pre} \\ 0 & Otherwise \end{cases}
\end{aligned} \tag{5}
$$

N is the size of training data in toponymy. cc_{pre} means the one character ahead of character cc.

2.3 Probabilistic Model Based on Character Vector

Using training data, we acquire the four sub-models of toponymy. To further improve the generalization ability of the probability model, the character vector is applied. The application of character in probabilistic model shows as follows:

$$
P_B(cc|class = toponymy) = \frac{1}{Z_B}\sum_{cc' \in Set} P'_B(cc'|class = toponymy)dis(cc, cc') \tag{6}
$$

$$
P_M(cc|class = toponymy) = \frac{1}{Z_M}\sum_{cc' \in Set} P'_M(cc'|class = toponymy)dis(cc, cc') \tag{7}
$$

$$
P_E(cc|class = toponymy) = \frac{1}{Z_E}\sum_{cc' \in Set} P'_E(cc'|class = toponymy)dis(cc, cc') \tag{8}
$$

$$
P_{Markov}(cc|class = toponymy, cc_{pre}) = \frac{1}{Z_{Markov}}\sum_{cc' \in Set} P'_{Markov}(cc'|class = toponymy, c_{pre})dis(cc, cc') \tag{9}
$$

Where Z_B, Z_M, Z_E, Z_{Markov} is the normalized coefficient, function $dis(cc, cc')$ is using to calculate distance between character cc and cc'

$$dis(cc, cc') = \frac{V_{toponymy,cc} V^T_{toponymy,cc'}}{\left|V_{toponymy,cc}\right| \left|V_{toponymy,cc'}\right|} \tag{10}$$

Where $V_{toponymy,cc}$ is the vector of character CC in toponymy.

So we can acquire the posterior probabilistic model of the toponymy type based on character vector, the formula shows as follow:

$$\begin{aligned} L(class = toponymy|str) &= Log(P(str|class = Toponymy)) + Log(P(class = Toponymy)) - Log(P(str)) \\ &\propto Log(P(str|class = Toponymy)) \propto \\ &= coefficient_{B,toponymy} Log(P_B(str(1)|class = toponymy)) \\ &+ coefficient_{M,toponymy} \sum_{i=2}^{end-1} Log(P_M(str(i)|class = toponymy)) \\ &+ coefficient_{E,toponymy} Log(P_E(str(end)|class = toponymy)) \\ &+ coefficient_{Markov,toponymy} \sum_{i=1}^{end-1} Log(P_{Markov}(str(i)|class = toponymy)) \end{aligned} \tag{11}$$

In the above formulas, each sub-models is weighted with coefficients and finally get the posterior probabilistic. The coefficients are calculate as follows:

$$coefficient_{B,toponymy} = \frac{1}{sum} \frac{1}{|entropy(B, toponymy)|} \tag{12}$$

$$coefficient_{M,toponymy} = \frac{1}{sum} \frac{1}{|entropy(M, toponymy)|} \tag{13}$$

$$coefficient_{E,toponymy} = \frac{1}{sum} \frac{1}{|entropy(E, toponymy)|} \tag{14}$$

$$coefficient_{Markov,toponymy} = \frac{1}{sum} \frac{1}{|entropy(Markov, toponymy)|} \tag{15}$$

where sum is the normalized coefficient, $entropy(B, toponymy)$ is the entropy of sub-model:

$$entropy(B, toponymy) = \sum_{cc \in Set} P_B(cc|class = toponymy) \log P_B(cc|class = toponymy) \tag{16}$$

Each posterior probabilistic $L(classname|str)$ can be acquired according to above method. We can judge the class string "str"s by using the follow formula:

$$class^* = \underset{class \in EntityNames}{Arg\max} \left(L(class|str)\right) \tag{17}$$

3 Experimental Results

In practical application, some words, such as "如果" (if), "其它" (otherwise), "但是" (but), which do not belong to any classes of named entity, need to be rejected. These words constitute of reject class, and the model of reject class will be acquired by using the same method.

In this paper, words randomly selected consist of reject class. Although they could be the named entity, the dispersion and rare characteristic makes they rarely affect the result. By using ICTCLAS offer by Chinese Academy of Sciences, we segmented sentences into words and randomly selected 20000 words as reject words for model training.

We compare our method with the method which called Chinese Named Entity Recognition via Joint Identification and Categorization (JIC) [13].

We train the Model by choosing People's Daily In February to April 1998 data as pattern,and still use data in People's Daily January 1998 as test data, the result was shown in Table 1.

Table 1. Our method vs. JIC (People's Daily offer training data)

	Our method			The result based on JIC
	Right rate	Recall rate	F-Measure	F-Measure
Person name	93.1 %	90.2 %	91.6 %	91.3 %
Toponym	90.2 %	91.1 %	90.64 %	89.7 %
Organization name	91.1 %	86.2 %	88.58 %	87.4 %

The result shows that the method proposed in this paper could recognize the Chinese Named Entity with higher right rate than JIC.

Second, in order to test the effectiveness of this method applying in other data set, the data set is acquired from Apabi Company and words are classified to 1. person name, 2. toponymy, 3. organization name or 4. official position. The number of each class in the training data was shows in Table 2:

Table 2. The number of pattern from Apabi Company

Entity class	Train pattern	Test pattern
Person name	20000	200
Toponym	20000	200
Offical position	20000	200
Organization name	20000	200
Reject	20000	200

The result in test data was showed in Table 3.

Table 3. The Right and Recall rate on data of Apabi Company

Entity class	Right rate	Recall rate
Person name	97.2 %	67.2 %
Toponym	98.1 %	70.1 %
Official position	99.5 %	72.1 %
Organization name	95.3 %	69.3 %

It could be finding that the right rate could also reach a higher level.

Compared with the conventional method, the method we proposed could not only recognize 3 big classes, but also other type entity, such as official Position, literary works, without extracting feature based on Specialized processing.

4 Conclusion and Prospect

In this paper, we introduce a new method character vector into the Named Entity Recognition. The result of experiment from this paper shows that this new method could achieve good effectiveness in Chinese Entity Character recognition and the most advantage of this method is to recognize Named Entity without type limit.

The method mentioned in this paper has obtained ideal recognition rate. The reasons are as follows. First, we described Chinese named entity in the form of probability by using markov process, and parameters of the probability model were obtained from training data. Second, the semantic distance of Chinese characters is proposed to be represented by the space distance of character vectors in this paper. This idea liberated the human labor from manually identifying the similarity distance and also removed the man-made interference during the process. Third, in order to improve the generalization ability of the model, we incorporate the character vectors with markov model. This incorporated model could achieve higher recognition rate. In summary, the method proposed in this paper theoretically could be used widely in most type of named entities for it removing human interfere during the process.

There were still some unsatisfied aspects need to be improve. First, a number of each type of entity should be prepared for training the model before used. Second, the effectiveness would be weakening if the training data and test data has big differences. Third, it lack of proper rejection mechanism to reject class which do not included in any class and that could lead to the misjudgment to the reject string. So the follow work could process with this three points and further improve this method.

References

1. Qi, Z., Zhao, J., Yang, F.: A new method for open named entity recognition of Chinese (2009)
2. Iwakur, T.: A named entity recognition method based on decomposition and concatenation of word chunks. ACM Trans. Asian Lang. Inf. Process. (TALIP) **12** (2013)

3. Pan, S.J.: Transfer joint embedding for cross-domain named entity recognition. ACM Trans. Inf. Syst. **31**(2), 7:1–7:27 (2013)
4. Konkol, M., Brychcín, T., Konopík, M.: Latent semantics in Named Entity Recognition. Expert Syst. Appl. **42**(7), 3470–3479 (2015)
5. Zhang, H., Liu, Q.: Automatic recognition of Chinese personal name based on role tagging. Chin. J. Comput. **27**(1), 85–91 (2004)
6. Yu, H.: Recognition of Chinese organization name based on role tagging. In: Advances in Computation of Oriental Languages, pp. 79–87 (2003)
7. Wang, N., Ge, R.: Company name identification in Chinese financial domain. J. Chin. Inf. Process. **16**(2), 1–6 (2002)
8. Zeng, G.: CRFs-based Chinese named entity recognition with improved tag set. Master degree theses of master of Being University of Posts and Telecommunications (2009)
9. Collobert, R., Weston, J., Bottou, L., Karlen, M., Kavukcuoglu, K., Kuksa, P.: Natural language processing (almost) from scratch. J. Mach. Learn. Res. (JMLR) **12**, 2493–2537 (2011)
10. Tomáš, M.: Statistical language models based on neural networks. PhD thesis, Brno University of Technology (2012)
11. Yao, J.: Study on CRF-based Chinese named entity recognition. Master degree theses of master of Suzhou University (2010)
12. Yu, H.: Chinese named entity identification using cascaded hidden Markov model. J. Commun. **27**(2), 87–94 (2006)
13. Zhou, J.: Chinese named entity recognition via joint identification and categorization. Chin. J. Electron. **22**(2), 225–230 (2013)

Android Apps Security Evaluation System in the Cloud

Hao Wang[1], Tao Li[1,2(✉)], Tong Zhang[1], and Jie Wang[1]

[1] School of Computer Science and Technology,
Wuhan University of Science and Technology, Wuhan 430065, Hubei, China
{1593487967, zt1996816, 909901326}@qq.com,
litaowust@163.com

[2] Hubei Province Key Laboratory of Intelligent Information Processing and Real-Time Industrial System, Wuhan 430065, Hubei, China

Abstract. It is an uncertain problem that evaluating the security of Android Apps. We can't be sure of the danger with sensitive permissions in an individual of Apps. Permissions are an important factor in security decisions of Apps. For the Apps security evaluation, the paper proceed from the Android permission mechanism, proposes a classified dynamic security evaluation method. Apps security evaluation system include the large-scale permissions capturing and classification risk evaluation algorithm. The system could find the minimum permissions which are the common features of Apps. The minimum permissions can be dynamically changed according to different classified Apps. We adopt Euclidean distance-based similarity calculation algorithm to evaluate risk. The difference value determines the APP's malicious risk. Experiments prove that the system has reference value to the APP security assessment.

Keywords: Android · App security · Evaluation system · Similarity calculation

1 Introduction

At the first part of 2014, the new malware on the Internet is more than 367 k. 99 % of them are on the Android system [1]. The permissions on android system is the key factor of the Apps security. Because of the different permissions and features, Apps security is an uncertain problem. It can increase the difficult of Apps security evaluation. So we can know that the permissions of one App aren't able to solve the security problem. For example, both of WeChat and flashlight read the contacts. WeChat is a kind of sociality Apps, so we think it is normal. Flashlight is a kind of tools, we think it is dangerous to have the permission. According to the example, we can't judge whether App is dangerous by one kind of permission.

Currently, there are two ways to evaluate the android malware. One is the static analysis method, the other one is dynamic detection. Dynamic detection [2] is monitoring the system calls. It can identify the malicious software by clustering analysis. Static analysis [3] uses the static analysis tools to find out the method called and get the goal by classification algorithm. The two ways have good accuracy. There is in low

S. Guo et al. (Eds.): CollaborateCom 2015, LNICST 163, pp. 151–160, 2016.
DOI: 10.1007/978-3-319-28910-6_14

efficiency when the number of Apps are large. We must use the features of the Android system to deal with. Yue Zhang [4] chose two parts which are the permissions feature selection and permissions feature weighting. It is hard to assess the security of App by the individual.

The paper presents a set of Security Classification Evaluation System. The dynamic system is based on Android App permissions correlation. We put similar Apps analog to a population, and find the set of the minimum permissions in the population with the idea of big data, the other hands the system determine the difference between each individual and the minimum permissions by Euclidean distance-based similarity calculation algorithm.

2 Overview

2.1 Evaluation System

Mobile Android platform provide privacy protection mechanism to prevent the user privacy to leakage. The permission is an important factor in App security. It is difficult to discuss malicious tendencies for App individuals. We put similar Apps likened to a population from the perspective of Big Data. We assume that population has individual which is in line with the minimum security permissions rules. In our opinion, Apps security risk classification evaluation standard should be adjusted dynamically with the Apps updated. Then we identify differences in each App and analyze malicious tendency of App by Euclidean distance algorithm.

2.1.1 Structure

Security Classification Evaluation System includes capture tools and App security classification and evaluation algorithms. Figure 1 is a system configuration diagram.

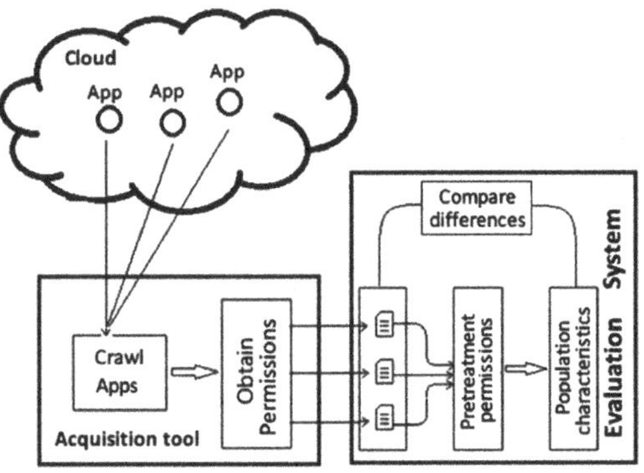

Fig. 1. System structure

2.1.2 Capture Tool

Capture tools should deal with the following key issues.

1. Crawl App automatically to improve response time.
2. Module should be efficient, stable and no-repeated. And it can install quickly and large-scale.
3. Capture for permissions is efficient.

To deal with them, we produce a crawler tool that focus on key words with Scrapy and crawl automatically. Then Apps are installed into testing machine by ADB-tools. Android offers PackageManger class for developers. We get and store all information.

2.1.3 Pretreatment Permissions

All information capture tools to obtain are discrete. And matrix structure we chose makes data storage for analysis. Android official website lists 146 kinds of the permissions for API 19 (Android 4.3 System) [5]. Permissions categories are divided into Normal, Dangerous, Signature and Signature System. We set risk values for all involved permissions. Risk value range: *0 <= Risk value <=100*. And the more dangerous permission is, the higher value is. For example, risk values in the dangerous are greater than in the normal. When i-th App has j-th permissions, i-th App set risk value for permission j.

2.1.4 Safety Evaluation

We find the minimum permissions set of App with the minimum set of permissions search algorithm. The minimum set is a common feature of the App within the population. It is the smallest of privileges for Apps. We identify differences in each App and analyze malicious tendency of App by Similarity Computing algorithm. The minimum set of permissions is determined by population evolution of Apps. So evaluation standard are automatically adjusted. The system can handle out changing App Store.

2.2 Case

We choose flashlight class that features is more specific in tools class. 725 kinds of flashlight App were crawled by capture tool. Then we searched the minimum set of permissions by algorithm. According to the result of experiments, we found out 725 flashlight Apps involved 95 permissions, which contain internet, contact and call. Then total of 578 Apps called network permissions and total of 14 Apps called contacts permission. Similarity calculation algorithm calculated differences from each flashlight and minimum permission set. However, we compared results with downloads in top 10, and found they totally do not coincide. So stores need our evaluation system.

3 The Model of Apps Security Classification and Evaluation System

App has different types and different functions, calls different permission. App individuals themselves permission to discuss the risk judgment malicious tendencies is very difficult, which is also an important factor in App security. Danger of App and its function showed great correlation. For example, video software and malware contains network access, but video software is less dangerous than malware. It is difficult to evaluate for the individual. We assume that population has individual which is in line with the minimum security permissions rules. Then we analyze malicious tendencies by searching the minimum set of permissions and comparing difference.

3.1 The Minimum Set of Permissions

The minimum set of permissions is determined by population evolution of App. We define the concept of permissions and populations before defining the concept of the minimum set of permissions.

3.1.1 Definition

Permissions of App: $Permission_{app} = \{pi \mid pi \in permissions\ of\ Android\}$. It indicates that it Indicates that the set of permissions is subset all of privileges of Android. Permissions storage structure: $PermissionMartix = \{p_{ij} \mid i = 1,2,\ldots,m;\ j = 1,2,\ldots,n;\}$; In PermissionMatrix, if App_i has a permission j, $p_{ij} = 1$; if not, $p_{ij} = 0$;

The minimum set of permissions: $MinPermission = Permission_1 \cap Permission_2 \cap \ldots \cap Permission_i$. It means the minimum set of permissions is the intersection all of set of App in population. Non-essential set of permissions: $nPermission = Permission_{app} - MinPermission$. It represents individual differences.

Population: $P = (Class, Permissions, MinPermission)$. Class is the name of population, Permissions stores all information of each App permissions, and MinPermission is the minimum set of permissions in this class. MinPermission is also called population characteristics. Population operation: $\exists P' = (A_0, A_1, A_2)$, $P = (B_0, B_1, B_2)$, if $A_0 = B_0$, $P' + P = (A_0, A_1 + A_2, A_2 \cap B_2)$. The operation shows how population is operated.

3.1.2 The Minimum Set of Permissions Search Algorithm

Input: Capture tool provides a class of permission information with each App;
Output: The minimum set of privileges such App;

1. Define the minimum set of permissions:
   `MinPermission = Android's Permissions;`
2. Traverse all App:
   `foreach Appi in Permissions.`
3. Calculate the intersection of MinPermission and App_i:
   `MinPermission = MinPermission ∩ Appi;`
4. `Return MinPermission;`

According to the definition of the minimum set of permissions, the minimum set of permissions is the intersection all of set of App in population. The minimum set of permissions search algorithm traverse all Apps permissions in the current population information. And calculates the intersection of App permission, which is the minimum set of permissions. The time complexity is *O (n)* because of the intersection of operation.

3.1.3 Dynamic Evolution of the Minimum Set of Permissions

App security risk classification evaluation standard should be adjusted dynamically with the App updated. We presented updated minimum set of permissions algorithm based on population calculation.

Population characteristics update algorithm:

Input: Capture tool to capture new population P', the current system all populations P;

1. Traverse current population P:
   `foreach Pi in P:`
2. Analyze the new population P' whether existed within current system:
   `if Pi.Class == P'.Class`
3. Update population:
   `Pi.Permissions = Pi.Permissions + P'.Permissions;`
   `Pi.MinPermission = Pi.MinPermission + P'.MinPermission;`
4. `Return Pi;`
5. The system adds new population P ':
   `P.Add(P');`

Since the App of the App Store constantly updated iteration, the evaluation criteria for App is updated dynamically. Algorithms developed App evaluation standard dynamic update rules. It is mainly to detect whether a certain group of newly captured App is an existing population. If the population doesn't exist in system, we should develop a standard for it. Of course, if existing, we should update the minimum set of permissions. The main operation of the algorithm is to determine whether the newly captured populations already exist in the system. So the time complexity is $O_{(1)}$ in best case, and the time complexity is $O_{(n)}$ in the worst case.

3.2 Evaluation of Similarity Calculation

3.2.1 Individual Differences in Similar App

Population mutation is uncertain. We identified the differences App and population characteristic by Euclidean distance-based similarity calculation algorithm [6, 7]. The larger the difference is, the greater malicious tendency is, and the more dangerous App is. There is are eigenvector $(I_0, I_1, \ldots, I_n)$ and discrete distribution point $(A_0, A_1, \ldots, A_n)$ in traditional Euclidean distance similarity calculation algorithm. So the similarity distance d is calculated as:

$$d = \sqrt{(A_0 - I_0)^2 + (A_1 - I_1)^2 + \ldots + (A_n - I_n)^2} \quad (1)$$

We propose the improved algorithm based on Euclidean distance to calculate the similarity. We have developed the following rules.

$\exists$ *population P = (Class,Permission,MinPermission), and Permission = {P_i | P_i is a set of permissions in each App in the same class}*; *$nPermission_i$* is non-essential set of permissions for each App. And *$nPermission_i$ = {p | p∈$Permission_i$ − MinPermission, 0 < i < n}*. So every value of similar distance can be calculated.

$$\mathrm{di} = \sqrt{nPermission_i} = \sqrt{p_0^2 + p_1^2 + \ldots p_k^2}, \ (\mathrm{p_0, p_1, \cdots, p_k} \in \mathrm{nPermissioni}); \quad (2)$$

d_i determines the difference App and population characteristic. The higher d_i is, the lower similarity is and the higher malicious tendency is. And App is more dangerous. The minimum set of permissions is the basis of similarity calculation. This paper selects the similarity analysis of the Euclidean distance algorithm is due to the algorithm can effectively distinguish the similarity of App. The main function of the algorithm is the difference between the performance of each App behavior and the minimum set of permissions. And a lot of similarity algorithms are based on distance such as K-means and K- center algorithm.

4 Experimental Evaluation

Based on the system-designing, we did three experiments to evaluate the system. We crawled 725 flashlight Apps and stored on local computer from 360 market with Scrapy framework. On Android 4.1.2, we installed all Apps by ADB-tools and got their permission. According to the result of experiments, we found out 725 flashlight Apps involved 95 privileges.

Experiment 1: With the help of statistical methods, we calculate that how many Apps called permission.

1. Traversing permissions information matrix.
2. Calculating the number of permission to be called.

Figure 2 displays case sensitive permission to call.

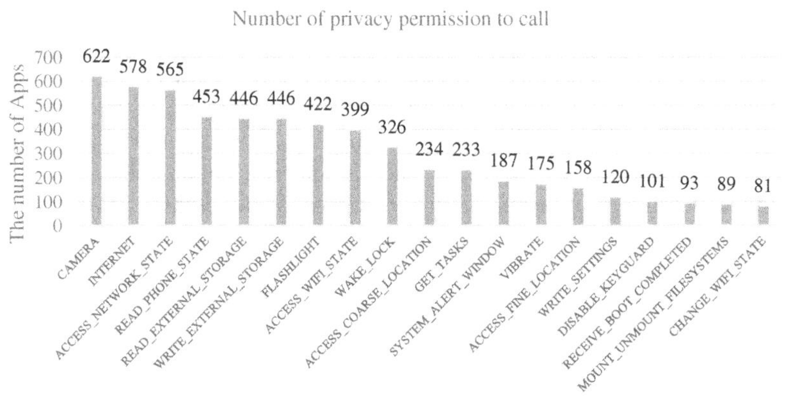

Fig. 2. Number of privacy permission to call

The majority of the 725 flashlight Apps contain some sensitive permission such as CAMERA, INTERNET, ACCESS_NETWORK_STATE, ACCESS_PHONE_STATE. Those permissions couldn't match with the features of flashlight. There is conclusion that the minimum set of permissions is empty. This means flashlight could run with no privilege. So these permissions increased malicious tendency of Apps.

Experiment 2: Calculate similar distance and analyze relations similar distance values with permissions.

1. Traverse permissions martix after pretreatment;
2. Calculate the value of similar distance of the App with minimum permissions in the improved Euclidean distance algorithm.

Figure 3 shows Similar Distance values in descending order.

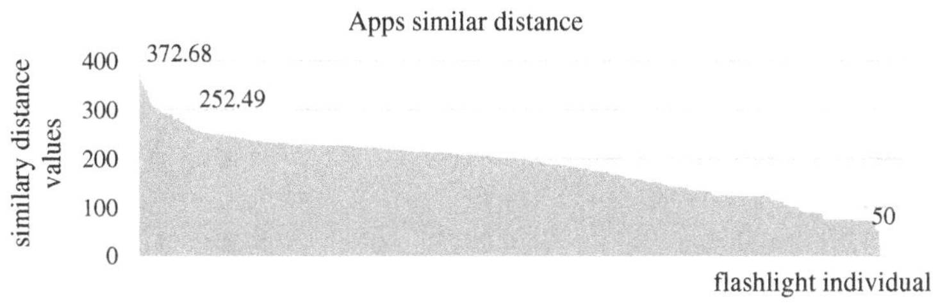

Fig. 3. Apps similar distance

Excerpt of data shows (the value of similar distance of com.sskj.flashlight is 372.68, the value of similar distance of com.mika.flashlight is 252.49 and the value of similar distance of com.htc.flashlight is 50). The larger the value of similar distance, the greater the tendency malicious Apps. We could get more information on Fig. 3. The minimum of the value of similar distance is zero, the Maximum is 372.68 (the result is concerned about permission dangerous scores). It is a clear difference between each App. Euclidean distance algorithm could effectively differentiate the malicious tendencies. We can conclude App risk evaluation system classification is workable and practical.

Figure 4 shows the relations similar distance values with permissions of the App.

It is a non-linear relationship between the number of App permission to call and similar distance values. The same number of permission is not necessarily the same distance. The higher the risk of sensitive permissions, the greater the impact on similar distance (the result is concerned about permission dangerous scores).

Experiment 3: Calculate permissions for each App owned by mathematical methods.

1. Traverse permissions martix after pretreatment;
2. Calculate permissions for each App owned.

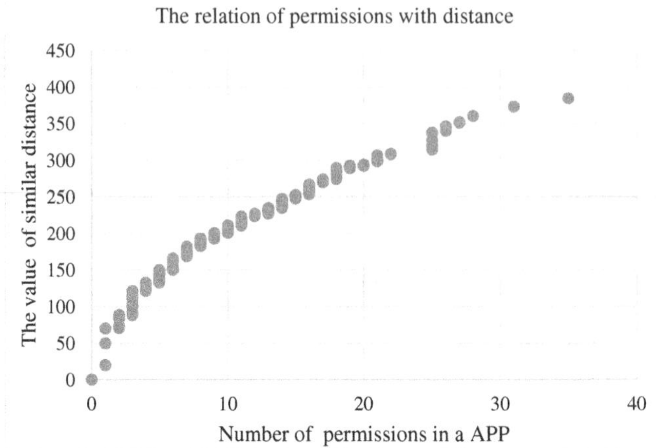

Fig. 4. The relation of permissions with distance

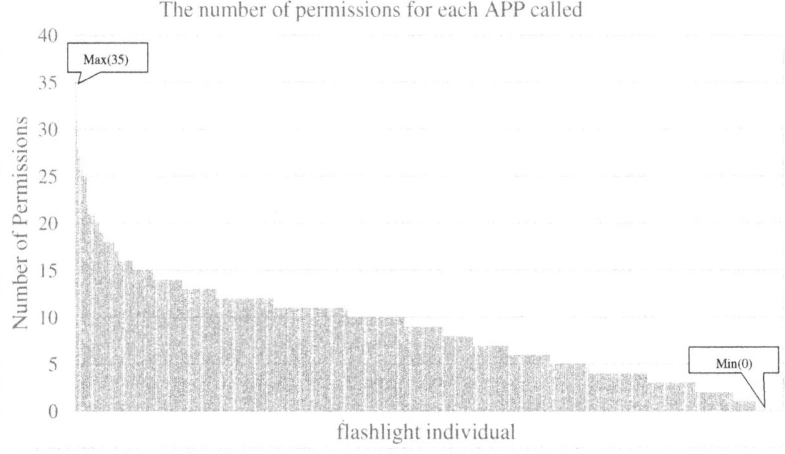

Fig. 5. The number of permissions for each App

Figure 6 could display that the number of Apps within the range of same permissions number.

In Fig. 7, we counted the number of permission that Apps called from 7 to 14.

We could conclude an App can call 35 kinds of permissions and a safe App should have no privilege in flashlight class from Figs. 5, 6 and 7. There are malicious tendency in rare of Apps. These permissions such as READ_EXTERNAL_STORAGER and WRITE_EXTERNAL_STORAGE would be called frequently in the majority of Apps.

From the above chart, we have a comprehensive understanding of the flashlight-type Apps. These Apps are also dependent on a number of other permissions in addition to the basic. Most of the flashlight-type Apps call these permissions purpose

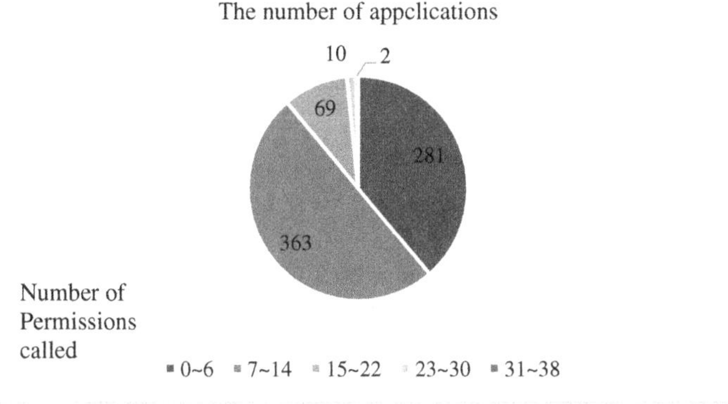

Fig. 6. The number of Apps (Color figure online)

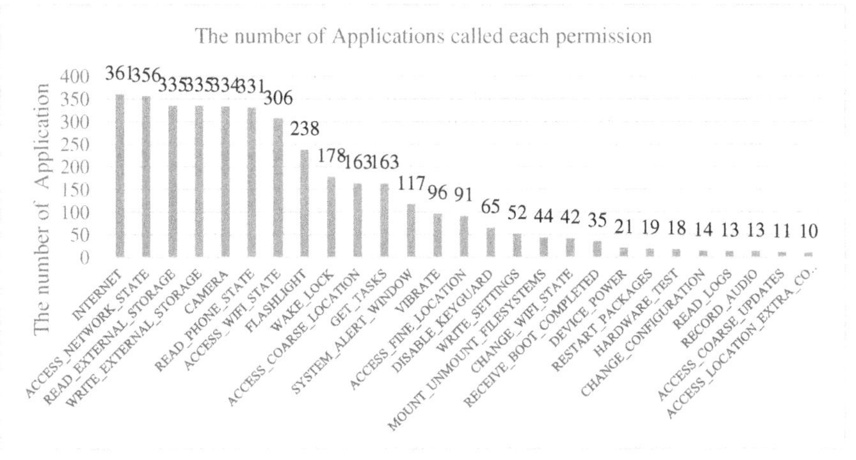

Fig. 7. The number of Apps called permissions

to advertise and market. However, the existence of a very small number of malicious App to read user contacts (Similar distance largest App). This sample may indicate that the Euclidean distance algorithm is effective and App security risk classification evaluation can be applied for evaluating App security.

5 Conclusion

Experimental results show that the Euclidean distance algorithm operability and practicability of App hazard classification. But there are still insufficient. For example, capture tools crawl App certain failure rate, whether the Euclidean distance algorithm is the most Appropriate. So there are to be further optimization in the evaluation model.

Acknowledgement. Authors are partially supported by Colleges and Universities in Hubei Provincial College Students' Innovative Entrepreneurial Training Program (No.201510488006), National Natural Science Foundation of China (No.61273225), Humanities and Social Sciences Foundation of Education Ministry of Hubei Province (No.2012D111).

References

1. Internet environmental remediation report at 2014 first half[R/OL] 10 September 2014
2. Burguera, I., Zurutuza, U., Nadjm–Tehrani, S.: Crowdroid: behavior-based malware detection system for Android. In: Proceedings of the 1st ACM Workshop on Sercurity and Privacy in Smartphones and Mobile Devices, pp. 15–26. ACM, New York (2011)
3. Schmidt, A.D., Bye, R., Schmidt, H.G., et al.: Static analysis of executable for collaborative malware detection on Android. In: Proceedings of the 2009 IEEE International Conference on Communications, pp. 631–635. IEEE Press, Piscataway (2009)
4. Zhang, Y., Yang, J.: Android malware detection based on permissions. Comput. Appl. **34**(5), 1322–1325 (2014)
5. Google.Mainfest.permission[EB/OL], 01 November 2013. http://developer.android.com/reference/android/Manifest.permission.html
6. Song, Y., Zhang, Y.,, Meng, H.: Research Euclidean distance clustering method based on weighted. Computer Engineering and Applications (2007)
7. Liu, R.: Weighted Euclidean distance and its application. Mathematical Statistics and Management (2002)

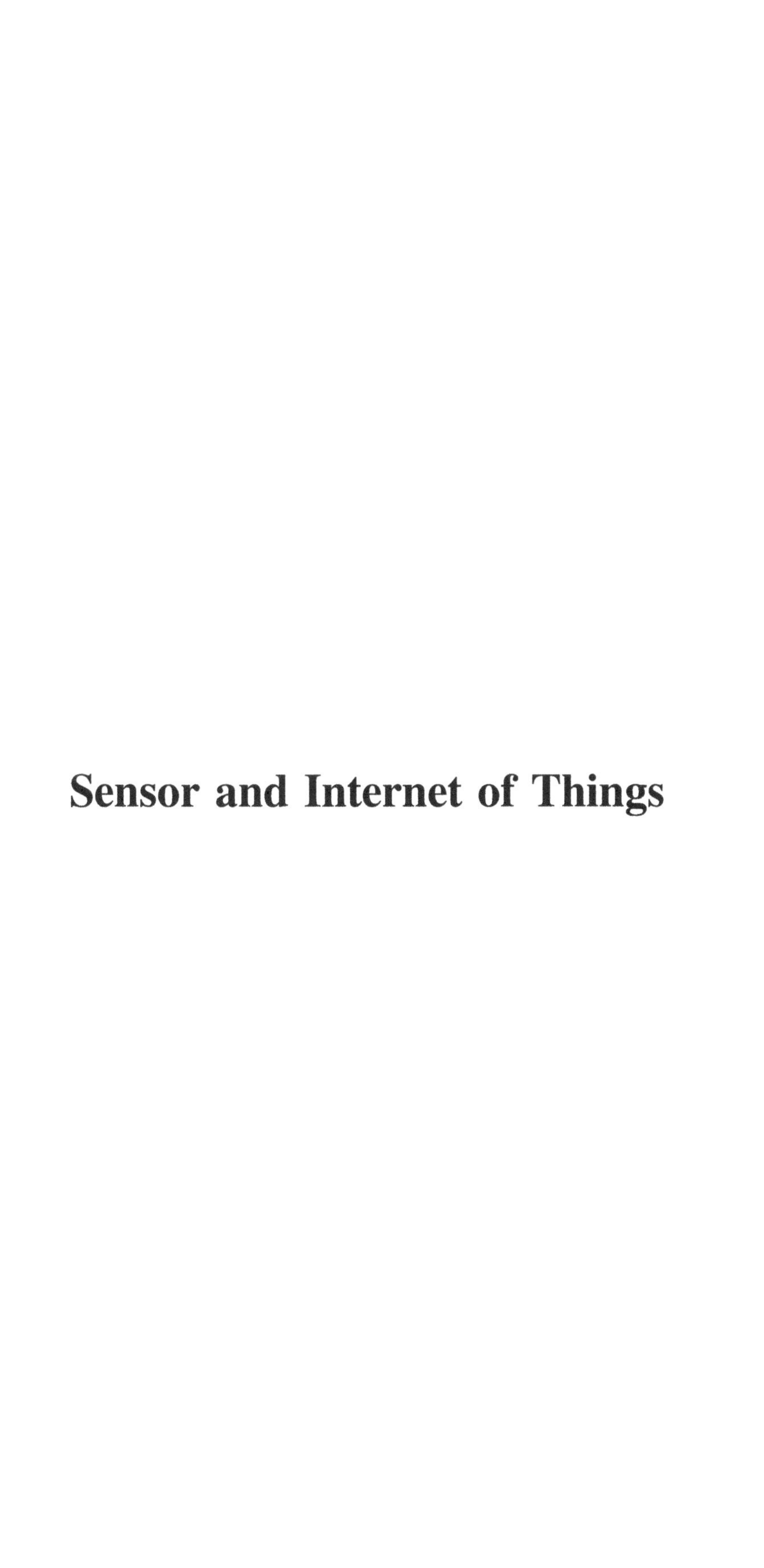

Sensor and Internet of Things

Protecting Privacy for Big Data in Body Sensor Networks: A Differential Privacy Approach

Chi Lin[1,2], Zihao Song[1,2], Qing Liu[1,2], Weifeng Sun[1,2(✉)], and Guowei Wu[1,2]

[1] School of Software, Dalian University of Technology, Dalian, China
{c.lin,wfsun}@dlut.edu.cn
[2] Key Laboratory for Ubiquitous Network and Service Software of Liaoning Province, Dalian, China

Abstract. As a special kind of application of wireless sensor networks, Body Sensor Networks (BSNs) have broad perspectives especially in clinical caring and medical monitoring. Big data acquired from BSNs usually contain sensitive information, which are compulsory to be appropriately protected. However, previous methods overlooked the privacy protection issue, leading to privacy violation. In this paper, a differential privacy protection scheme for big data in body sensor network is proposed. We introduce the concept of dynamic noise thresholds which makes our scheme more suitable for processing big data. It can ensure privacy during the whole life cycle of the data, which makes privacy protection for big data in BSNs promising. Extensive experiments are conducted to outline the merits of our scheme. Experimental results reveal that our scheme has higher level of privacy protection. Even in the case where the attacker has full background knowledge, it still provides sufficient ambiguity, which ensures being unable to match people based on the ECG data characteristic so as to preserve the privacy.

Keywords: Body sensor networks · Big data · Differential privacy

1 Introduction

As a special application system tailored for body health caring, the widespread use of Body Sensor Networks (BSNs) make it possible for realizing real-time monitoring [1–4]. In BSNs, big data which directly or indirectly reveal a person's physical condition are collected, aggregated and transmitted. For example, continuous ECG data are used in diseases tracking [13] and physiological condition monitoring [14].

Data transferred throughout BSNs usually share two critical features that should be paid attention to: sensitivity and vulnerability. Sensitivity means that data can reflect the status of the body, location or other sensitive information, which are needed to be appropriately preserved. Vulnerability indicates that data are forwarded in an open environment, therefore, data contents are easily to be trapped by the enemies or attackers. Once the data in BSNs are not well preserved, the privacy will be destroyed, leading the unexpected exposure of

S. Guo et al. (Eds.): CollaborateCom 2015, LNICST 163, pp. 163–172, 2016.
DOI: 10.1007/978-3-319-28910-6_15

physical information. Hence, preserving the privacy of sensitive data in BSNs is necessary and urgent.

In recent years, great efforts have been made for Big Data Privacy Protection (BDPP) in BSNs. In general, previous approaches fall into three kinds: (1) data collection protection [5–7], (2) data releasing protection [8–10] and (3) data analysis protection [11,12]. These approaches indeed provided effective methods for strengthening the privacy protection level in BDPP. However, they still suffer from some limitations:

- With respect to data accuracy, traditional methods added noise and implemented anonymous scheme, which sacrificed the accuracy of the data. Data transmitted under such conditions will be no longer accurate, which thus directly influences the data availability.
- With respect to data privacy protection, in traditional methods, such as k-anonymity, l-diversity or m-invariance etc., the values of k, l or m are required, which are not easy to be quantified or determined.
- With respect to data analysis [15], for example, in data water marking technology, only the static data set are well preserved, which are not feasible to be used for protecting dynamic and massive data. Therefore, such technology is not suitable for protecting data privacy in BSNs.

Researching the BDPP mechanisms in BSNs has significant contributions to our human life. Once big sensitive data are not properly preserved, users' privacy will be greatly damaged. Our motivation is to develop a method for solving the privacy protection problem based on differential privacy techniques. In our scheme, we proposed a protection model which covers the entire life cycle of data based on differential privacy technique.

The contributions of this paper can be summarized as follows:

1. To the best knowledge of the authors, this is the first time that differential privacy scheme is applied in protecting sensitive big data in BSNs. We propose a differential privacy protection model, which significantly reduces the risk of privacy exposure while ensuring data availability and accuracy.
2. To ensure the feasibility of the ECG big data, we introduce the concept of dynamic noise thresholds. It is used to interpret the relationships between noise size and data set size, which makes our scheme more suitable for big data.
3. To verify the advantages of our scheme, extensive experiments are conducted. Experimental results demonstrate that our scheme has a better performance in privacy protection. Even when the attacker grasps full background knowledge, our scheme still provides enough interference, making it unable to target a certain person by eavesdropping sensitive big data.

The remainder of this paper is structured as follows. Section 2 gives a brief overview on the preliminaries of this paper. Section 3 presents our scheme in detail. In Sect. 4, extensive experiments are conducted to show the advantages of our scheme. Finally, we conclude this paper and point out the future work in Sect. 5.

2 Preliminary

In this section, related preliminaries are introduced for comprehending our idea.

2.1 Problem Description

Traditional BDPP methods (as shown in Fig. 1) focused on data releasing and data mining issues. Once adversaries successfully eavesdrop sensitive data, data will be completely exposed, even worse, totally lose their effects. Simple encryption mechanisms cannot cover the entire life of data protection including data generating, data collecting, data transmitting and data publishing and so on. An effective alternative is to encrypt data during the transmission progress. However, in that case, data will be exposed to the public, which are prone to attacks. Once data are hacked, the real identity of the owner will be recognized, leading to privacy leakage. Although obfuscation scheme is widespread regarded as a useful method in privacy protection, the availability and accuracy are compromised.

Therefore, we develop a privacy protection scheme based on differential privacy, which appropriately solves the above concerns.

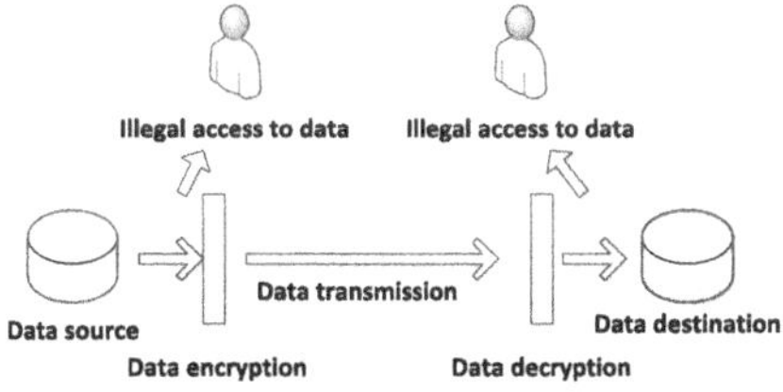

Fig. 1. Traditional privacy protections for BSNs

2.2 Identification and Data Characteristics of Electrocardiogram

Identification technology of ECG (electrocardiogram, ECG) has two main directions: one is extracting identification based on ECG feature points, the other is analyzing ECG waveform. As shown in Fig. 2, for a typical ECG, a cardiac cycle is made up of a P-wave, QRS wave, T wave and U waves. Usually, U waves are relatively small and inconspicuous.

In extracting identification, ECG feature points, such as P-wave width, QRS wave width, the period of PQ and QT, the R-wave peak and T-wave peak are regarded as important sources of information.

3 Our Scheme

In this section, we develop a secure way to minimize the cost to hide the ECG data. Here, we introduce the idea of differential privacy into privacy protection for big sensitive data in BSNs.

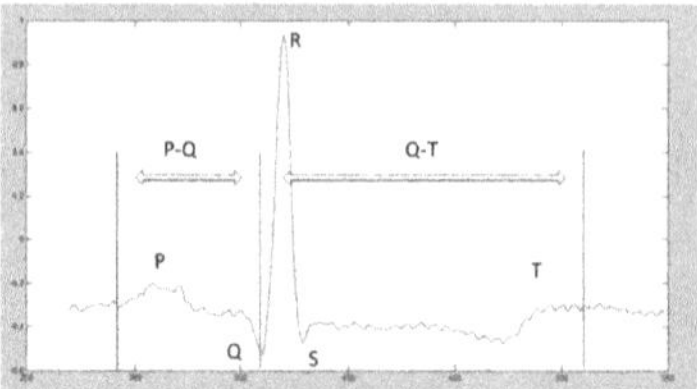

Fig. 2. Identification technology for ECG

A strict privacy protection model, defined by the differential privacy, will be considered as a standard of this program. To the best knowledge of the authors, this is a new direction that applies differential privacy technique into periodic stream data for safeguarding against malicious attacks. In our work, we choose the peak and valley data as characteristics points and put forward a simple example to clarify our method.

At first, we need to pre-process ECG data. We assign weights to each characteristic based on its importance for identification, for example, assuming that the identification significance of the peak value is greater than the valley value, thereby, peak value's weight will be bigger. Then bigger weights will be set to the parent nodes to construct the feature classification tree. This classifying method ensures that, ECG data can be divided into different equivalence classes. Suppose that the number of eigenvalue in ECG is n, then the final number of equivalence class in ECG features will be 2^n. Data that are divided into the same equivalence class will share approximate characteristic.

According to the concept of differential privacy, we introduce Eq. (1) as a strict standard.

$$\Pr[K(D1) \in S] \leq \exp(\varepsilon) * \Pr[K(D2) \in S] \tag{1}$$

Here, $D1$, $D2$ are two adjacent data sets, K is privacy protection algorithm for our design, $Pr[]$ is denoted as the risk of privacy exposure.

Taking big data identification into considerations, in our work, data are processed sequentially. There is no doubt to use the counting query with the sensitivity of count 1. We choose to take the variance reflecting data fluctuations as Pr. Assuming that the overall variance is influenced heavily, then apparently this set of data is clearly unexpected to this group of data. We thereby choose the variance of the data as a reflection of private exposure risk, which is intuitive and convenient.

$$\Pr[x]_n = s^2 = \frac{\sum\limits_{i=1}^{n} (x_i - \bar{x})^2}{n-1} \tag{2}$$

So far, we have already illustrated the basis for achieving protection based on differential privacy. We believe that an ideal noise generation must be able to change as the data changes. For example, when the number of data is $2n$, the number of noise data, in fact, must be associated with the existing $2n$ data.

When the amount of data is n, the minimum value of the intensity available noise will be determined, which fluctuates with the change of existed data. We take peak values of characteristics as examples, the calculation method of dynamic characteristics of interference threshold is computed by Eq. (3).

$$H(x) = \left| \frac{\sum_{i=1}^{n-1} x_{n-1}}{n-1} - x_n \right| \times \ell \tag{3}$$

Here, $H(x)$ stands for the interference threshold when the nth data arrive. x is denoted as the data in the data set, ℓ is the interference correction value of this characteristic, which depends on specific features. Its purpose is to enable the real-time updates of data and provides a standard for dealing with the next arrival data.

Under the premise of a great amount of data, we can avoid duplicating the operations of the aforementioned data to increase the viability of ECG protection scheme. Based on the above definition of thresholds and limitations of differential ideas, we can find a sufficiently large enough one to (1) prevent the loss of privacy, and (2) carry out a devastating impact on data availability. Meanwhile, we add values at the point in feature noise, which is normally distributed with a typical value of $H(x)$ and the variance of 1.

Due to the limits of the private difference protection model, only a small amount of noise will be generated. As for the data in the same equivalence class, order processing cannot be carried out with the regular order, we choose the data from the beginning of the n data. Since we need the frontal $n-1$ data to initialize the feature interaction threshold value. Therefore, the processing order is shown in Fig. 3.

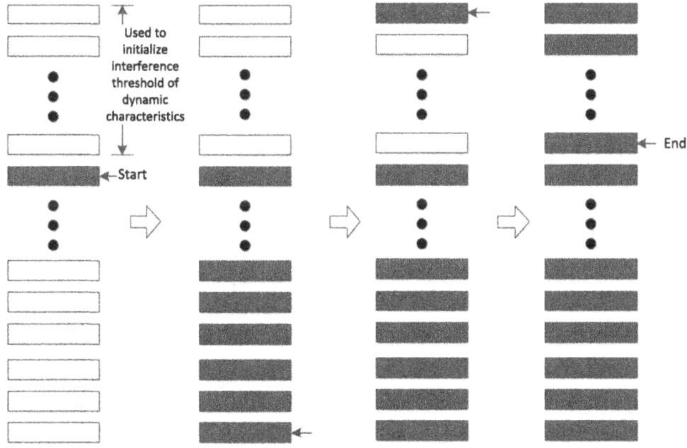

Fig. 3. Data processing order

In summary, our ECG privacy algorithm proceeds as Fig. 4. The first step is to scan ECG data set and extracting feature vectors. Then, characteristics classification tree is constructed and we divide ECG features to equivalence classes according to a feature vector. After that, we partition equivalence into classes and initialize feature interference thresholds. Next, we process the data one by one and add noise according to the important features. As the purpose of differential privacy is to maintain the available data as much as possible. In case of failure in adding noise, we additionally put new violence in the data. After completing categorizing data into an equivalence class, our algorithm is completed and the privacy of data is protected.

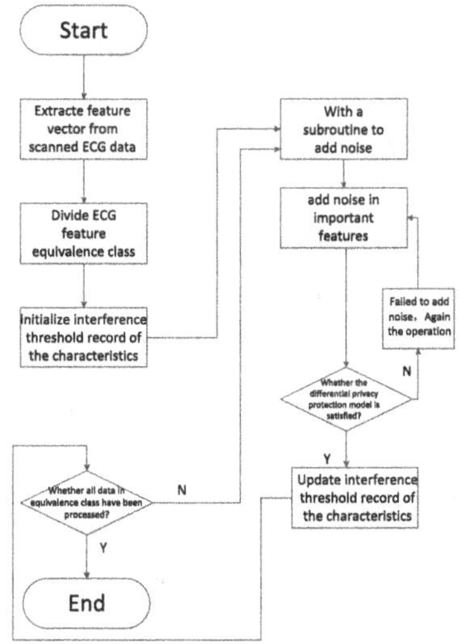

Fig. 4. ECG privacy algorithm process

4 Experimental Results

4.1 Experimental Setup

We collected experimental data using Shimmer [16] as shown in Fig. 5.

In our experiment, we collect 30 sets of ECG data by using Shimmer. The average size of each data is 4.3 MB, the size of the post-processing data is 2.2 MB. Each data contains sufficient cardiac cycles for determining characteristic point values. Two features, peaks and valleys, are selected and the requirement of privacy budget is set 0.6. The result of equivalence class partitioning is shown in Table 1.

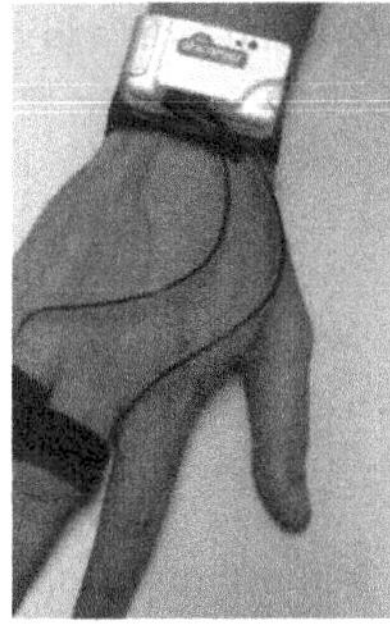

Fig. 5. Collecting data by Shimmer [16]

Table 1. Equivalence class partitioning

Equivalence class	Data bulk
Equivalence class I	6
Equivalence class II	8
Equivalence class III	11
Equivalence class IV	5

4.2 Privacy Protection Experiments

In this section, several experiments are conducted to show the performance of our scheme.

As shown in Fig. 6, it is obvious that the difference between data before and after processing is big. After applying our differential privacy protection scheme, such differences are migrated. Figure 7 shows the comparison of data 6 before and after treatment, which indicates that our scheme produces enough interferences. This ensures that feature points generated by our scheme will not reveal the real identity of a certain user so as to achieve privacy protection.

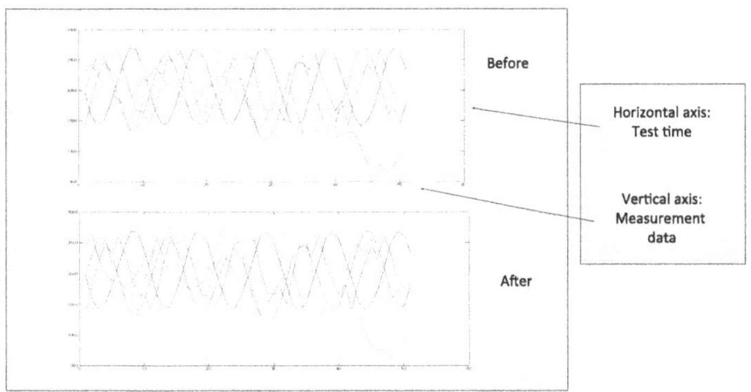

Fig. 6. Contrast before and after processing

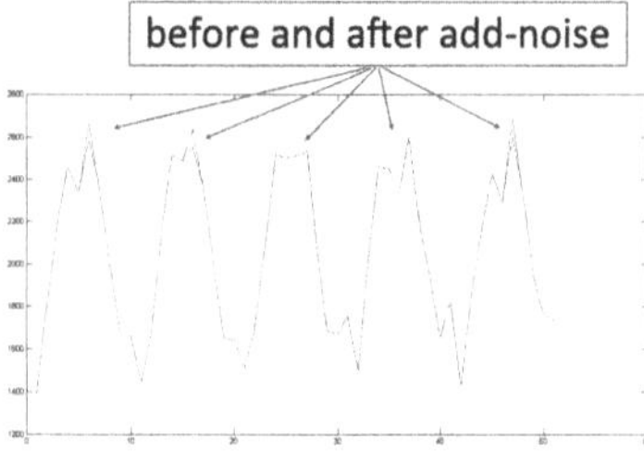

Fig. 7. Contrast before and after adding noises

To illustrate the effectiveness of our privacy scheme, we model and introduce an attacking model. We intend to demonstrate that our scheme is capable of defending an attack. In the attack, the attacker grasps full background knowledge such as the feature points of the ECG of a certain target user. He seeks for finding out a target user based on the data generated by our scheme. In our experiment, the attacker aims at linking the person's data from his background knowledge so as to find out the physical condition of the target victim. The attack is taken by two steps: (1) determine whether the personal data of the target user are contained in the current data set, and (2) mount an identity linking attack.

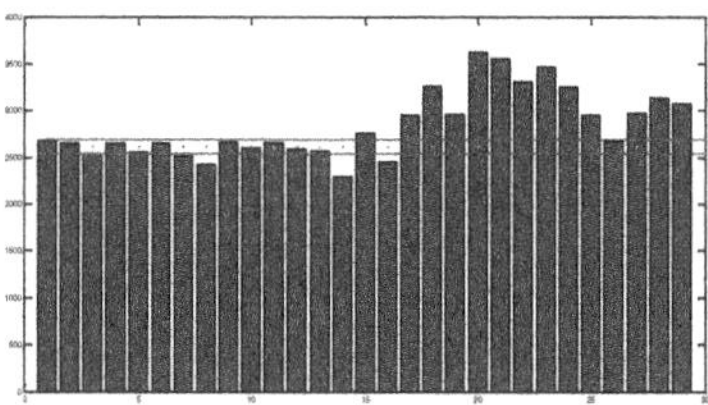

Fig. 8. Probability of exposure to privacy

As shown in Fig. 8, during the 24 experiments, when only one feature value is chosen, the probability of exposure of data privacy is $1/5$. We assume that the actual amount of data is $30 \times n$. Therefore, for a single feature, the risk of exposure to privacy is $1/(5n)$. When we choose m feature values for preserving privacy. The probability of privacy exposure will be calculated as:

$$\frac{m}{5n} \leq p' \leq \left(\frac{1}{5n}\right)^{m} \tag{4}$$

Consider that the data itself are vague, therefore, eventual, the probability p of privacy exposure is:

$$\frac{m}{5n} \leq p < \left(\frac{1}{5n}\right)^{m} \tag{5}$$

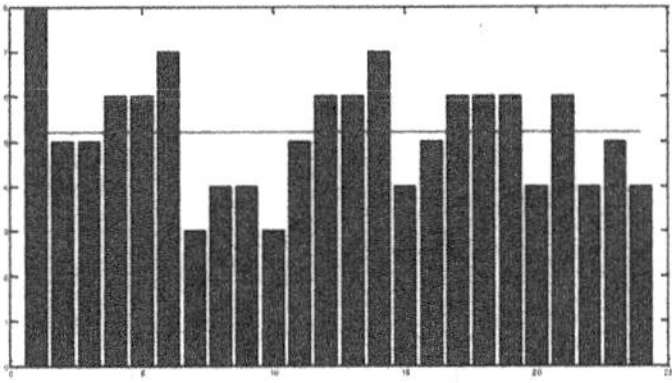

Fig. 9. Privacy level obtained by the user

As shown in Fig. 9, the value of m must be a single-digit, because the number of the feature points is not big. When the magnitude of data is higher, our algorithm will provide a reliable privacy protection for them. We note that, in our work, tricky data will provide better protections. Moreover, more data are input, better protection will be obtained.

In conclusion, our experimental results show that the ECG privacy protection programs achieve desired privacy requirements.

5 Conclusions and Future Works

In this paper, we proposed a differential privacy protection model, which significantly reduces the risk of privacy exposure and greatly ensures the availability of data. We introduce the concept of dynamic noise thresholds to lift the direct relationship between the added noise and data set size, making our scheme more suitable to process big data. At last, several experiments are conducted to show the performance of our scheme. Experimental results reveal that our scheme can provide ideal protection effect. Even in the case that the attacker has full background knowledge, our scheme still can produce enough interference, and the attacker is unable to match the objective person from the ECG data.

As part of our future works, we will put forward theoretical analysis on how to apply differential privacy scheme for big sensitive data in BSNs.

Acknowledgements. This research is sponsored in part by the National Natural Science Foundation of China (No. 61173179, No. 61402078) and Program for New Century Excellent Talents in University (NCET-13-0083). This research is also sponsored in part supported by the Fundamental Research Funds for the Central Universities (No. DUT14RC(3)090).

References

1. Zheng, Z., Zhu, J., Lyu, M.R.: Service-generated big data and big data-as-a-service: an overview. In: IEEE International Congress on Big Data, pp. 403–410 (2013)
2. Huang, Z., Cao, F., Li, J., Chen, X.: Developing sea cloud data system key technologies for large data analysis and mining. J. Netw. New Media **1**(6), 20–26 (2012)

3. Bressan, N., Andrew, J.: Integration of drug dosing data with physiological data streams using a cloud computing paradigm. In: 35th Annual International Conference on Engineering in Medicine and Biology Society (EMBC), pp. 4175–4178. IEEE (2013)
4. Kai, E., Ashir, A.: Technical challenges in providing remote health consultancy services for the unreached community. In: 27th International Conference on Advanced Information Networking and Applications Workshops (WAINA), pp. 1016–1020. IEEE (2013)
5. Dilsizian, S.E., Siegel, E.L.: Artificial intelligence in medicine and cardiac imaging: harnessing big data and advanced computing to provide personalized medical diagnosis and treatment. Curr. Cardiol. Rep. **16**, 441 (2013)
6. Kafali, O., Bromuri, S., Sindlar, M.: Commodity 12: a smart e-health environment for diabetes management. J. Ambient Intell. Smart Environ. **5**(1), 479–502 (2013)
7. Wu, J., Roy, J., Stewart, W.F.: Prediction modeling using EHR data: challenges, strategies, and a comparison of machine learning approaches. Med. Care **48**(6), S106–S113 (2010)
8. Jensen, P.B., Jensen, L.J., Brunak, S.: Mining electronic health records: towards better research applications and clinical care. Nat. Rev. Genet. **13**(6), 395–405 (2012)
9. Huang, Q.R., Qin, Z., Zhang, S., Chow, C.M.: Clinical patterns of obstructive sleep apnea and its co morbid conditions: a data mining approach. J. Clin. Sleep Med. **4**(6), 543 (2008)
10. Zrimec, T., Wong, J.: Improving computer aided disease detection using knowledge of disease appearance. In: Med Info 2007: Proceedings of the 12th World Congressing Health (Medical) Informatics; Building Sustainable Health Systems, p. 1324. IOS Press, Amsterdam (2007)
11. Melzer, T.R., Richard, W.: Arterial spinlabelling reveals an abnormal cerebral perfusion pattern in Parkinson's disease. Brain, awq377 (2011)
12. Xue, Y., Li, Q., Jin, L., Feng, L., Clifton, D.A., Clifford, G.D.: Detecting adolescent psychological pressures from micro-blog. In: Zhang, Y., Yao, G., He, J., Wang, L., Smalheiser, N.R., Yin, X. (eds.) HIS 2014. LNCS, vol. 8423, pp. 83–94. Springer, Heidelberg (2014)
13. Yoo, J., Yan, L., Lee, S.: A wearable ECG acquisition system with compact planar-fashionable circuit board based shirt. IEEE Trans. Inf. Technol. Biomed. **13**(6), 897–902 (2009)
14. Gargiulo, G., Bifulco, P., Cesarelli, M.: An ultra-high input impedance ECG amplifier for long-term monitoring of athletes. Med. Devices (Auckl) **3**, 1–9 (2010)
15. Yan, Y., Qin, X., Fan, J., Wang, L.: A review of big data research in medicine & healthcare. E-Sci. Technol. Appl. **5**(6), 3–16 (2014)
16. Shimmer. http://www.shimmersensing.com/

Characterizing Interference in a Campus WiFi Network via Mobile Crowd Sensing

Chengwei Zhang, Dongsheng Qiu, Shiling Mao, Xiaojun Hei(✉), and Wenqing Cheng

School of Electronic Information and Communications, Huazhong University of Science and Technology, Wuhan 430074, China
{zhangcw,qds2013,mshil,heixj,chengwq}@hust.edu.cn

Abstract. WiFi networks and smartphones have been penetrating into people's daily life pervasively. The increasingly dense deployments of WiFi APs have led to the severe spectrum usage overlap and channel interference. In this paper, we proposed a mobile crowd sensing method to characterize the interference experienced by a campus WiFi network by utilizing the powerful sensing capability of smartphone and users' mobility. We designed and implemented a mobile measurement App. This App can help the volunteers to sense the neighboring WiFi APs in the background on the Android mobile phones. The measurement data are then uploaded to the measurement repository server for further data analysis. Our measurement results showed that both 2.4 GHz and 5 GHz WiFi APs have been commonly deployed on campus, and 2.4 GHz APs dominate for around 80 % of total measured APs. The spectrum overlap and channel interference in the 2.4 GHz band is much severe than that in the 5 GHz band. The rising WiFi interference is due to the uncoordinated planning, random deployment and intensive density of WiFi networks at different locations. Our field measurement study may provide guidelines to design the next generation software-defined WiFi networks in order to achieve high performance with minimized interference.

Keywords: Mobile crowd sensing · WiFi · Spectrum interference · Internet measurement · Android system

1 Introduction

WiFi-based wireless local area networks are widely used for Internet access due to their advantages in three aspects: (1) simple technical implementation; (2) low-cost network construction; (3) high-bandwidth wireless links. A large number of WiFi hotspots have been deployed at various locations. Originally designed for single access point with limited number user devices, WiFi has also been increasingly used for Internet access in a large area with many clients, such as a hotzone. It has been envisioned that WiFi networks will be served as the major network components for constructing smart city and even smart country.

S. Guo et al. (Eds.): CollaborateCom 2015, LNICST 163, pp. 173–182, 2016.
DOI: 10.1007/978-3-319-28910-6_16

Note that the rapid penetration of smartphones has been reshaping the communication and entertainment paradigm in people's daily life. Contemporary smartphones commonly integrate many sensors: Global Navigation Satellite System (GNSS), accelerometers, gyroscopes, magnetometers, light sensors, as well as WiFi and Bluetooth transceiver modules [1]. Due to the pervasive usage of smartphones, together with the cooperative sensing capability and users' mobility, can accomplish data measurement, collection, and pre-processing through powerful sensors and microprocessors while users carry them around during their daily activities [2,3].

To date, there have been emerging a number of researches and applications heavily utilizing smartphones and user mobility, such as recording physiological measure of users [4], monitoring user behavior [5], detecting the quality of the urban environment [6], and so on. The mobile crowd sensing can overcome the limited resources of the individual smartphones, and achieve real and randomized measurement experiments rather than well planned experiments [7,8]. [9,10] studied the data transmission efficiency and energy consumption problem of mobile crowd sensing. In particular, recent measurements [11,12] have shown that the wireless networks (WiFi and 3G/4G) utilized by mobile devices consumed significant energy in data transmissions. Such field measurement studies have well motivated the design and the implementation of mobile cloud transmission systems [13,14] to transfer heavy energy-hungry services up to the clouds for mobile Apps.

In this paper, we proposed a mobile crowd sensing method for characterizing the interference of a campus WiFi network. Smartphones from volunteers in the measurement can automatically probe, maintain and upload WiFi APs' information through an augmented measurement tool, namely, WiFi Tracer [15], which is an Android application running on smartphones. In order to achieve a large scale WiFi measurement, we invited many participants as anonymous users to randomly move in various ways (driving, jogging and walking) on campus with the measurement App running on their smartphones. The major results from these experiments are summarized as follows:

1. There have been considerably high-density WiFi APs running on the campus area. Over 10000 WiFi APs and more than 7000 distinct WiFi networks have been detected. It indicates that the campus is a typical area with high-density WiFi APs, and characterizing WiFi networks will help to understand the potential interference, deployment and optimization issues for high-density WiFi networks.
2. Theoretically, the usage of WiFi frequencies and channels should be distributed evenly in 2.4 GHz and 5 GHz bands that have more than 30 free channels in total. Both 2.4 GHz and 5 GHz WiFi APs are commonly deployed in measurement areas, and 2.4 GHz APs dominate about almost 80 % of the total measured APs.
3. We also measured the public campus WLAN and analyzed its characteristics. It has shown that more than 70 % measurement areas have been covered by the public campus WLAN.

2 Crowd Sensing Platform

2.1 Platform Overview

As shown in Fig. 1, our proposed mobile crowd sensing platform is an integrated platform which consists of three major components including data acquisition, collection and analysis. The first component takes the responsibility for collecting basic information of WiFi APs and storing the results locally. Smartphones serve as WiFi probes to harvest the nearby WiFi and GPS information, and they process the original data in the local database through the WiFi Tracer tool. The second component is responsible for collecting and analyzing the data as a repository server hosted on a cloud platform. When the volunteers finish the measurements, WiFi Tracer will automatically upload the local results to the server. The third component is used to share the available WiFi information as an incentive for participants.

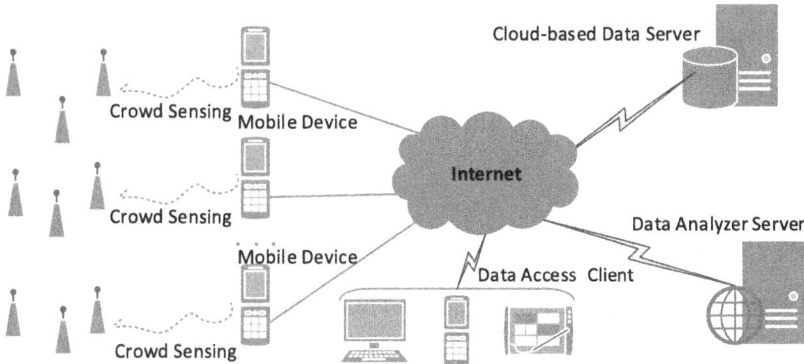

Fig. 1. WiFi measurement architecture using mobile crowd sensing

2.2 WiFi Tracer

WiFi Tracer is an Android mobile application as the terminal to implement mobile crowd sensing. In order to improve the efficiency and accuracy of measurements, we should avoid sensing the same location for multiple times unnecessarily. Hence, the tool follows a scanning procedure as shown in Fig. 2.

WiFi Tracer senses the current location of mobile device before measurement and compute the distance between the current location and the previous measurement location. If the distance between these two locations is larger than a threshold (10 m by default), the application will actively scan the WiFi APs nearby and tag this measurement with the time stamp and GPS coordinates to form the metadata of WiFi APs. The measurement results are then written into the local database through Android SQLite. WiFi Tracer tracks the

Begin: Initialization
smartphone initialized: WiFi transceiver initialized, GPS sensor initialized.
Step 1: Default parameter configuration
set $deviceInfo \leftarrow$ basic device information, $minDistance \leftarrow 10(m)$,
$period \leftarrow 10(s)$, $origPosition \leftarrow$ current GPS position.

Step 2: Scanning Phase
if $scanPeroid = peroid$ && $distance(origPosition, currPosition) > minDistance$
Activate the WiFi scanning process; proactively scan the WiFi APs nearby.
Record $scanResult : (bssid, ssid, frequency, rssi, capabilities)$,
Build entity: $o^i_{bssid} : (scanTime, scanCount, deviceInfo, scanResult, currPosition)$,
Store the data set O into the local database and upload to the remote server.
else
Keep waiting in background; then go to Step 2.
Step 3: Terminate the app, and stop all the functions.
End: Terminated.

Fig. 2. Sketch of the WiFi Tracer scanning procedure

dynamics of WiFi APs periodically (such as 10 s) if the user is moving during the measurement session.

3 Result Analysis

Mobile crowd sensing may involve many mobile devices in measurement and each device becomes a distinct end-point in experiments. User's mobility cooperating with smartphones make the whole experiment as a randomly distributed measurement process, and the data storage and computation from the server side provides convenient sharing mechanism to maintain and analyze measurement results among the measurement clients. We chose a university campus area as the main experiment area to inspect the WiFi APs and networks. We chose the well performed Android smartphones (ZTE Nubia Z7, etc.) as measurement devices which provide a well support for popular WiFi protocols such as 802.11 a/b/g/n and can work well on WiFi standard frequencies both 2.4 GHz and 5 GHz bands.

During the measuring process, participants moved on the main roads with a relatively low speed ($\leq 20\,KM/H$) and almost took 1.5 to 2 h to traverse the whole campus measurement areas. Our experiments assumed that most of indoor WiFi APs and networks were visible on the main road and could be obtained by the WiFi Tracer.

3.1 Dataset

Table 1 shows the measurement results that there are more than 10000 independent WiFi APs in measurement areas and most of the WiFi APs are private.

Private WiFi APs are WiFi networks that can share networks in small areas and require password to access successfully. Compared to the deployment of a public campus WLAN, how to reduce the interference with channel and frequency from the WiFi network has become a potential problem because there exists abundant private WiFi APs across the public campus WLAN.

Table 1. Measurement dataset

Metric	Amount
Scan times	20210
Data samples	534210
Independent areas by GPS	13065
Number of distinct WiFi APs	11380
Number of distinct WiFi Networks	7483
Number of 2.4 GHz APs	10390
Number of 5 GHz APs	1988
Number of public WiFi APs	2893

Heatmap of WiFi APs' Distribution. Figure 3 show the heatmap of the WiFi APs distribution. The red areas suggests that there are high density of WiFi APs. There are over 50 independent WiFi APs in the red area according to the parameters used in drawing this figure. When we compared the heatmap to digital maps, we found that the areas with high density of WiFi APs have a close relationship with their physical locations. The circled areas from 1 to 6 are official areas, teaching areas and living areas.

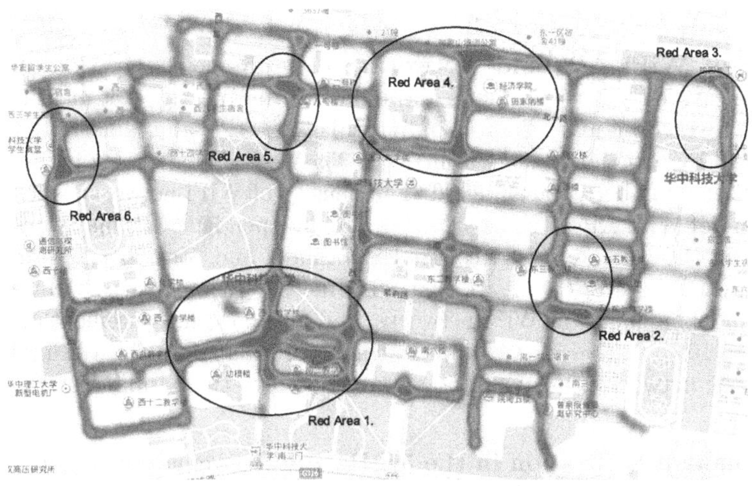

Fig. 3. WiFi AP heatmap (Color figure online)

WiFi Channel Usage. The percentage of different channels usage is depicted in Fig. 4 for both 2.4 GHz and 5 GHz WiFi APs. The results show that the 2.4 GHz band is the main working band for the WiFi networks, which dominates over 80 % over all the measured WiFi APs, while the 5 GHz band only accounts for nearly 20 %.

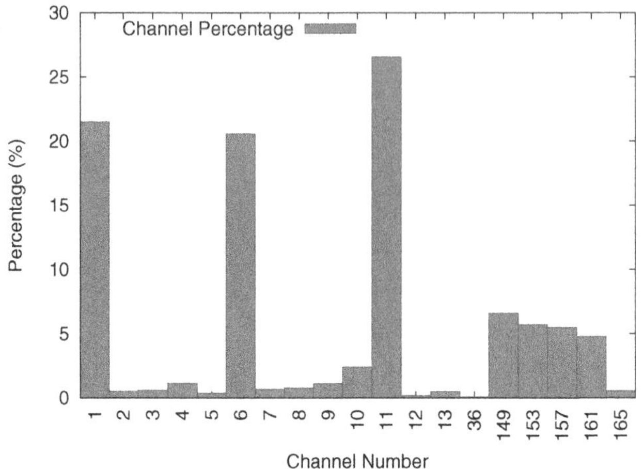

Fig. 4. WiFi channel utilization

As shown in Fig. 4, channel 1, 6 and 11 are the most popular used channels in 2.4 GHz band. WiFi manufactures normally spread the default channels of 2.4 GHz WiFi appliances in these three independent channels to avoid the adjacent channel interference in practical applications. The channels in 5 GHz band are completely isolated with each other and will not result in any adjacent channel interferences.

Density of WiFi APs and Networks. Figure 5 shows the AP density in distinct measured locations. Figure 5(a) indicates that nearly 90 % measurement areas are covered by more than 15 individual WiFi APs, and almost 70 % areas are covered by WiFi APs range from 15 to 35. At serval extremely high-density locations, the number is beyond 100. The density of WiFi networks is less than the density of WiFi APs in same areas because independent APs may work cooperatively in the Extended Service Set(ESS) model and construct a wide-range WiFi network. Figure 5(b) shows that 80 % measurement areas are covered by more than 10 independent WiFi networks, and over 65 % measurement areas are covered by 10 to 30 WiFi networks. We conjecture that both the WiFi AP density and the network density can be approximated to the normal distributions.

WiFi Channel Utilization in the 5 GHz Band. We have mainly discussed about the characteristics of 2.4 GHz WiFi APs in the previous sections. Figure 4 show that the channel utilization of WiFi APs meets the 80/20 rule, and about

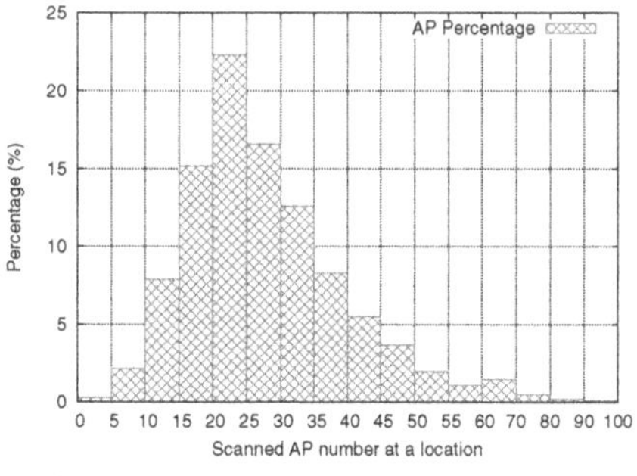

(a) Density statistics of WiFi APs

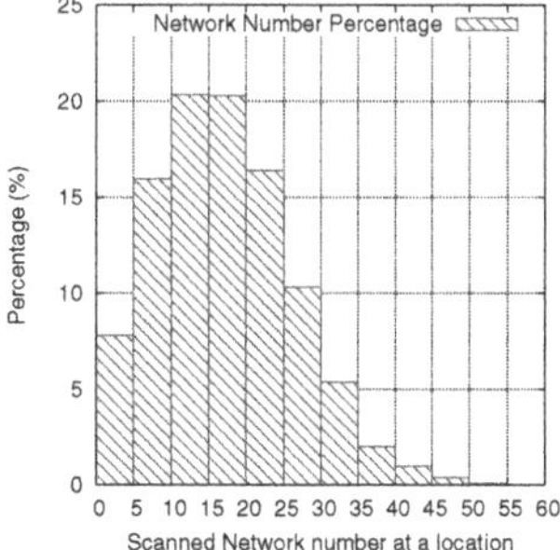

(b) Density statistics of WiFi Networks

Fig. 5. Density of WiFi APs and distinct networks

Table 2. Usage of 5 GHz WiFi APs

Type	Private APs	Public APs	Total
Number	100	1888	1988
Percentage(%)	5	95	100

20 % WiFi APs are working at the 5 GHz band. From these 5 GHz APs, Table 2 shows that only 5 % of them belong to private networks, and it usually suggests that 5 GHz WiFi APs are barely used as personal WiFi networks, even though they have better performance and less interference.

3.2 Characterizing a Public Campus WLAN

There are more than 4000 public campus WiFi APs found in our measurements. Figure 6 shows the distribution of a public campus WLAN and private networks. We observe that the public WLAN and private networks appear to be complementary from the visual display of Fig. 6(a) and (b).

Interference of Hybrid WiFi Networks. Figure 7 presents a comparison of the density of the public WLAN and private WiFi APs in the same place under this hybrid wireless network environment. Figure 7(a) shows that 80 % areas have fewer than 20 private APs, and nearly 20 % areas are covered by private APs in the range of [20, 40]. Compared to private WiFi networks, the density of the public WLAN is almost doubled in the same location. In this hybrid network environments, the public WLAN is not only affected by the private networks, but also the network itself.

We defined the **density ratio** as the number of private APs and the number of the public APs at a spot for differentiating the network interference of hybrid networks. Figure 7(b) shows the density ratio compared with the public WLAN APs in the hybrid network areas. The results show that the density ratio in

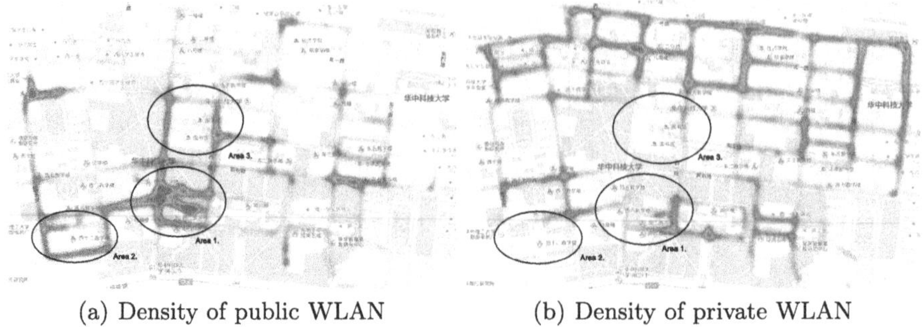

(a) Density of public WLAN (b) Density of private WLAN

Fig. 6. Spatial spread density statistics of WiFi networks

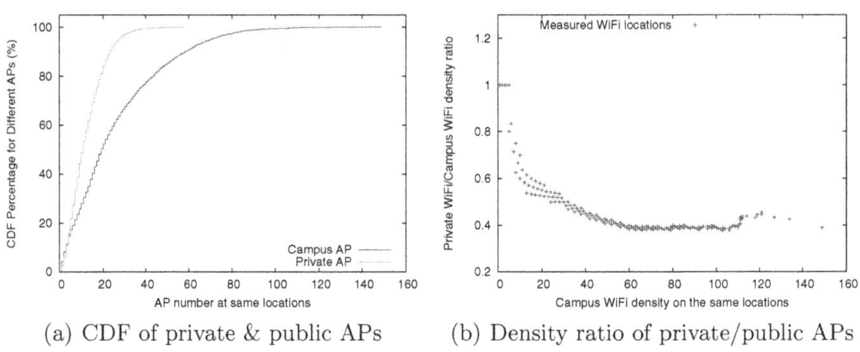

(a) CDF of private & public APs (b) Density ratio of private/public APs

Fig. 7. Public campus WLAN vs Private WLAN

nearly 90 % areas are less than 1 which suggest that the number of public APs are larger than the number of private APs in the same measurement areas. We conjecture that the public campus WiFi network suffers from the potential interference not only from the private network but also from itself due to its high density deployment.

Indoor vs. Outdoors Interference of Public WLAN. We conducted additional experiments to gain insights into the WLAN from the outdoors to the indoors. Figure 8(a) shows that about only about 20 % areas are covered with less than 20 public APs and the main density of outdoor APs are ranged from 20 % and 80 % for almost 60 % measurement areas. The density of public WLAN (i.e., the green curve in Fig. 8(a)) only shows that the adjacent channel interference among the WLAN. However, through the measurement, we found most APs of the WLAN utilize three independent main channels(1, 6, and 11) as the default working channels in the 2.4 GHz band and part of channels in the 5 GHz band. Hence, more public WLAN APs in same areas will bring forth more co-channel interferences. The density on the same channel (i.e., the red curve in Fig. 8(a)) shows the co-channel interference in the WLAN.

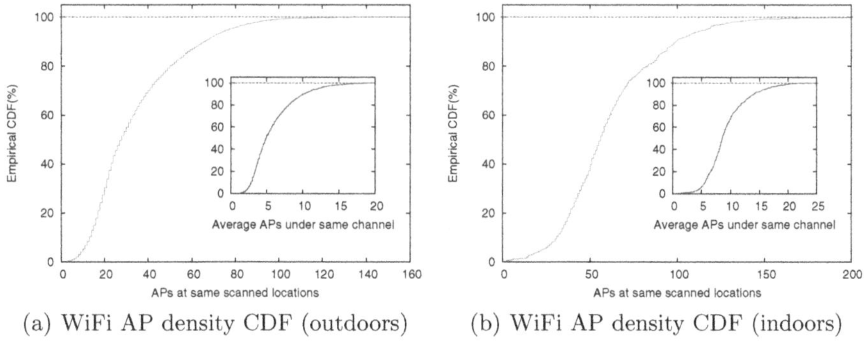

(a) WiFi AP density CDF (outdoors) (b) WiFi AP density CDF (indoors)

Fig. 8. CDF of public campus WLAN density (Color figure online)

Figure 8(b) shows that there are more serious co-channel interference issues indoors than outdoors. The results show that about 20 % areas are covered with less than 40 % public APs and over 40 % indoor locations have been detected more than 10 public APs, which are almost doubled compared with the outdoor case. Figure 8 shows that the public WLAN suffers the co-channel interferences from itself rather than private WiFi networks.

4 Conclusion

In this paper, we conducted a measurement study of characterizing the WiFi APs and networks on a campus using a mobile crowd sensing method. The results show that the deployments of the current WiFi networks have various problems due to no planning, large-scale and high-density. In both 2.4 GHz and 5 GHz bands, the utilization of the channel distributions of WiFi APs satisfies the 80/20 rule in measurement areas. Those high-densely deployed WiFi APs suffer severe interference from adjacent channels and co-channels both in 2.4 GHz and 5 GHz.

We further analyzed the characteristics of interference in the public campus WiFi WLAN and private WiFi networks. The results show that the density of public campus WiFi APs is much higher than private WiFi APs in the hybrid network areas. Hence, the campus WLAN suffers from the potential interferences not only from private networks but also from itself due to its high-density deployment in the main channels.

Our measurement results also showed that the current WiFi networks deployments are not planned at all, which led to the significant performances degradation, such as interference from other network, the competition and sharing of channels, the optimal deployment of wide-area WiFi network, and so on. It may not solve these emerging problems only depending on the standard protocols of 802.11 series in current WiFi networks; therefore, we are motivated to combine the control module and the management module using a software-defined approach to manage the interference and to enhance the performance of campus WiFi networks and private WiFi networks.

Acknowledgement. This work was supported in part by the national Natural Science Foundation of China, under Grant 61370231, in part by the Fundamental Research Funds for the Central Universities under Grant HUST:2014QN156 and 2015QN217.

References

1. Zhuang, Y., Syed, Z., Georgy, J., El-Sheimy, N.: Autonomous smartphone-based wifi positioning system by using access points localization and crowdsourcing. Pervasive Mobile Comput. **18**, 118–136 (2015)
2. Khan, W.Z., Xiang, Y., Aalsalem, M.Y., Arshad, Q.: Mobile phone sensing systems: a survey. IEEE Commun. Surv. Tutorials **15**, 402–427 (2013)
3. Lane, N., Miluzzo, E., Lu, H., Peebles, D., Choudhury, T., Campbell, A.: A survey of mobile phone sensing. IEEE Commun. Mag. **48**, 140–150 (2010)
4. Gao, C., Kong, F., Tan, J.: HealthAware: Tackling obesity with health aware smart phone systems. In: IEEE ROBIO, pp. 1549–1554 (2009)
5. Rachuri, K.: EmotionSense: a mobile phones based adaptive platform for experimental social psychology research. In: ACM UbiCompp, pp. 281–290 (2010)
6. Mun, M., et al.: PEIR, the personal environmental impact report, as a platform for participatory sensing systems research. In: ACM MobiSys (2009)
7. Ganti, R., Ye, F., Lei, H.: Mobile crowdsensing: current state and future challenges. IEEE Commun. Mag. **49**(11), 32–39 (2011)
8. Lane, N.D., Eisenman, S.B., Musolesi, M., Miluzzo, E., Campbell, A.T.: Urban sensing systems: Opportunistic or participatory? In: ACM HotMobile (2008)
9. Lane, N.D., et al.: Piggyback crowdsensing (PCS): Energy efficient crowdsourcing of mobile sensor data by exploiting smartphone app. opportunities. In: ACM Conference on Embedded Networked Sensor Systems (SenSys) (2013)
10. Xiao, Y., Simoens, P., Pillai, P., Ha, K., Satyanarayanan, M.: Lowering the barriers to large-scale mobile crowdsensing. In: ACM HotMobile (2013)
11. Shu, P., Liu, F., Jin, H., Chen, M., Wen, F., Qu, Y.: eTime: Energy-efficient transmission between cloud and mobile devices. In: IEEE INFOCOM, April 2013
12. Zhang, T., et al.: eTrain: Making wasted energy useful by utilizing heartbeats for mobile data transmissions. In: IEEE ICDCS, June 2015
13. Liu, F., et al.: Gearing resource-poor mobile devices with powerful clouds: Architectures, challenges, and applications. IEEE Wirel. Commun. **20**, 1334–1354 (2013)
14. Liu, F., Shu, P., Lui, J.C.: AppATP: an energy conserving adaptive mobile-cloud transmission protocol. IEEE Trans. Comput. **64**, 3051–3063 (2015)
15. Zhang, C., Qiu, D., Hei, X.: WiFi tracer. http://itec.hust.edu.cn/~zhangcw/WiFiTracer

On Participant Selection for Minimum Cost Participatory Urban Sensing with Guaranteed Quality of Information

Hong Yao(✉), Changkai Zhang, Chao Liu, Qingzhong Liang, Xuesong Yan, and Chengyu Hu

School of Computer Science and Technology, China University of Geosciences, Wuhan, China
yaohong@cug.edu.cn

Abstract. Exploring vehicles to conduct participatory urban sensing has become an economic and efficient sensing paradigm to pursue the smart city vision. Intuitively, having more vehicles participate in one sensing task, higher quality-of-information (QoI) can be achieved. However, more participation also implies a higher sensing cost, which include the cost pay to participated vehicles and 3G traffic cost. This paper introduces an interesting problem on how to select an appropriate set of vehicles to minimize the sensing cost while guaranteeing the required QoI. In this paper, we define a new QoI metric called coverage ratio satisfaction (CRS) with the consideration of coverage from both temporary and spatial aspects. Based on the CRS definition, we formulate the minimum cost CRS guaranteeing problem as an integer linear problem and propose a participant selection strategy called Vehicles Participant Selection (VPS). The high efficiency of VPS is extensively validated by real trace based experiments.

Keywords: Vehicular sensor network · Quality-of-Information · Coverage Ratio Satisfaction · Vehicles Participant Selection

1 Introduction

Participatory sensing is first proposed in [1], which introduces the idea of collecting and sharing environment sensory data via smartphones. As one representative participatory sensing paradigm, vehicular sensor networks (VSNs) that explores moving vehicles are regarded as a promising city sensing solution and therefore have received much attention in the literature. VSNs can be used to obtain various urban life related information (e.g., air quality, noise level, temperature, etc.) using vehicle-equipped sensors. With the rapid development in vehicular networks and cellular communications, these sensory data can be collected at a central server for further data analysis to promote the urban life quality. Unlike traditional sensor networks, VSNs do not have strong energy, storage, processing and communication constraints. In addition, they are applicable to a wide range of data collection thanks to the node mobility.

S. Guo et al. (Eds.): CollaborateCom 2015, LNICST 163, pp. 183–194, 2016.
DOI: 10.1007/978-3-319-28910-6_17

In this paper, we consider an application scenario shown in Fig. 1, where a set of vehicles randomly move in a urban area. Each vehicle is equipped with various sensors for data collection and a cellular communication module. Therefore, a vehicle can upload the collected data in real time. In order to ensure high quality-of-information (QoI), we shall ensure each sub-region is covered by a fixed amount of vehicles. Intuitively, more participants implies a higher QoI. However, this is at the expense of higher cost. For a task with given QoI requirement, there is no need to arbitrarily hire a large set of participants.

Our objective is to find a subset of participant vehicles whose coverage can best satisfy CRS metrics requirement of task in both temporal and spatial dimensions, and minimize the cost. The cost of task include two parts. One is the cost of selected vehicles, when a vehicle join the system, it will requires a reward, only satisfied, it will executes data collection task. The other is 3G network traffic costs, the more sensed data upload to server, the higher cost will cause.

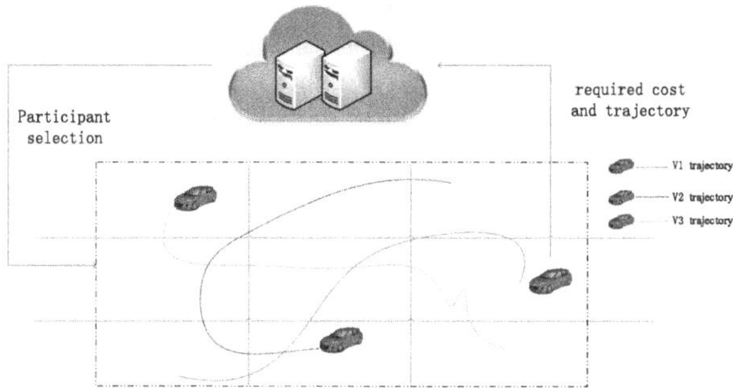

Fig. 1. The application scenario, the role of all vehicles are divided into three categories, The target area is divided into many sub-regions

The main contributions of the paper are as follows:

- We introduce the CRS metrics in terms of vehicular coverage, which is used to ensure each sub-region covered by amount of vehicles in each time slot, it can ensure the quality of monitoring task.
- Assuming knowing each users moving trajectory in advance, even though this assumption may not be realistic, the obtained solutions can be used to show potential data collection cost savings that can be brought by using collaborative sensing in the VSN, and can also serve as a benchmark for performance evaluation.
- We propose a participant selection strategy called VPS. The selected vehicles are selected based on a greedy algorithm that explicitly considers CRS metrics, and minimize the cost of the task.

The rest of the paper is organized as follows: In Sect. 2, we introduce the related research activities. Section 3 gives the system model and then formally defines the problem. In Sect. 4, we describe the details of our strategy. Evaluation results are presented in Sect. 5. The paper is concluded in Sect. 6.

2 Related Works

In this section, we discuss the related works on participatory sensing, which collected data using smartphones, and Vehicular Sensor Network.

2.1 Participatory Sensing

Participatory sensing using smartphones is a promosing method to enable the recently emerging software-defined sensing paradigm [2] as the sensing functions on smartphones can be freely customized according to the sensing needs. Many systems are designed to support data collected task with budget constraints. For Example, Z. Song et al. [3] was to find a subset of participants whose sensory data collection could best satisfy QoI requirements of multiple concurrent tasks in both temporal and spatial dimensions, with a constrained task budget. H. Xiong et al. [4] aimed to maximize the coverage quality of the sensing task while satisfying the incentive budget constraint. The object of this work is different from above works, and the definition of QoI is diffrent, too.

One of the most problem of participatory sensing with smartphones is energy constrain. In [5], Sheng et al. proposed to leverage cloud-assisted collaborative sensing to reduce sensing energy consumption for mobile phone sensing applications. In [6], Zhao et al. presented a novel fair energy-efficient allocation framework whose objective was characterized by min-max aggregate sensing time. In [7], Wang et al. proposed effSense - a novel energy-efficient and cost-effective data uploading framework leveraging the delay-tolerant mechanisms. In VSN, we will not consider the energy constrain.

2.2 Vehicular Sensor Network

Delay Tolerant Network has been widely studied [8–10], and Vehicular Sensor Network is a hot topic in it. There are a number of papers that studied monitoring task in Vehicular Sensor Network [11,12]. In [11], Devarakonda et al. presented a vehicular-based mobile approach for measuring fine-grained air quality in real-time. In [12], The objective of traffic monitoring was to achieve the traffic condition precisely and efficiently. In [13], the authors developed an efficient data collection algorithm capable of providing data redundancy elimination under network capacity constraints. In [14], Li et al. proposed a novel approach for mobile users to collect the network-wide data. In [15], Palazzi et al. presented a solution, based on vehicular sensor networks, for gathering data from a certain geographic area while satisfying with a specific delay bound. Though there are so many works have done in VSN, our work will solve the problem that select an appropriate set of vehicles to minimize the sensing cost from a different angle.

3 System Design

In this section, we introduce the system model used throughout this paper, including the system model related notations and the Coverage Ratio Satisfaction metrics.

3.1 System Model

In order to ensure the quality of monitoring task, we need to select a set of vehicles to participant in the task, which can satisfy CRS metrics requirement of task, while minimize the cost. We assume there exists a central server, a set of vehicles moving in Region $\mathcal{R}$ during time slot $\mathcal{T}$. The central server is used to select the vehicles based on our strategy and collect data. There are m participant vehicles denoted as $\mathcal{M} = \{V_1, V_2, ..., V_m\}$. We divide the target region into r sub-region, they are denoted as $\mathcal{R} = \{R_1, R_2, ..., R_r\}$. We divides the entire sensing period into a set of time slots and they are denoted as $\mathcal{T} = \{T_1, T_2, ..., T_t\}$. e_i^q denotes required cost by participant i for task q. On each virtual cube that is composed of a 2-D area and within a certain time slot, in order to ensure the quality of data collection in the task q, each sub-region should be covered by a certain number of vehicles in each time slot, the required amount of vehicles can be denoted as d_{rt}^q, $\forall r \in \mathcal{R}$, $\forall t \in \mathcal{T}$, which is given by the task publisher as a requirement. Only in each sub-region, the coverage are satisfied in each time slot, it means that the set of selected vehicles satisfy the requirement.

3.2 Coverage Ratio Satisfaction Metrics

In order to ensure the quality of information of data collection, we should make sure that each sub-region should be covered by a manageable number of vehicles. But how to estimate whether the quality of information of collected is good or not? In this section, we will solve this problem.

At first, we should know the task publisher's demand of vehicles to cover the sub-regions, we use $\mathcal{D}^q$ matrix to denote it, and d_{rt}^q,$\forall r \in \mathcal{R}$, $\forall t \in \mathcal{T}$ means the requirement amount of vehicles that cover sub-region r within time slot t for task q. Before the start of the task, each participant vehicle upload its trajectory to the central server, so we can know each vehicle's coverage and let matrix C_i^q denote the vehicle i's coverage, c_{irt}^q,$\forall i \in \mathcal{M}$, $\forall r \in \mathcal{R}$, $\forall t \in \mathcal{T}$, means vehicle i whether cover the sub-region r within a certain time slot t, where

$$c_{irt}^q = \begin{cases} 0, & \text{vehicle } i \text{ cannot cover sub-region } r \text{ within time slot } t \\ 1, & \text{otherwise} \end{cases} \tag{1}$$

When a set of vehicles are selected as SVs for task q, the subset is denoted as $\mathcal{S}$, then we let $c_{rt}^q(\mathcal{S})$, $\forall r \in \mathcal{R}$, $\forall t \in \mathcal{T}$ denote the set $\mathcal{S}$'s coverage for task q on a certain sub-region l, within a certain time slot t.

If a participant vehicle i is selected into $\mathcal{S}$, the subset's coverage will change. If the value of $c_{rt}^q(\mathcal{S})$, has reached the d_{rt}^q, it will not change. When the value of $c_{rt}^q(\mathcal{S})$ is smaller than d_{rt}^q, then the its value will increased by 1, it means that $c_{rt}^q(\mathcal{S}) \leq d_{rt}^q$.

Now that many vehicles have selected into $\mathcal{S}$, how to calculate the set $\mathcal{S}$'s coverage $C^q(\mathcal{S})$? Because the coverage is related to each vehicle, then the coverage in sub-region r within time slot t can be calculated as follows,

$$c_{rt}^{q}(\mathcal{S}) = \sum_{i \in \mathcal{S}} c_{irt}^{q} \tag{2}$$

And in the larger sense, the coverage of $\mathcal{S}$ can be calculated

$$C^{q}(\mathcal{S}) = \sum_{i \in \mathcal{S}} C_{i}^{q} \tag{3}$$

To best understand the Coverage Ratio Satisfaction Metrics, $\mathcal{P}_{rt}^{q}$ is denoted as the coverage ratio in sub-region r in time slot t for the task q.

$$\mathcal{P}_{rt}^{q}(\mathcal{S}) = \frac{c_{rt}^{q}(\mathcal{S})}{d_{rt}^{q}} \tag{4}$$

As we know, the $c_{rt}^{q}(\mathcal{S}) \leq d_{rt}^{q}$ and they are all nonnegative number, so the range of $\mathcal{P}_{rt}^{q}$ is from 0 to 1.

Proposition 1. *Given $\mathcal{S}_1 \subset \mathcal{S}_2$, we have*

$$\mathcal{P}_{rt}^{q}(\mathcal{S}_1) \leq \mathcal{P}_{rt}^{q}(\mathcal{S}_2)$$

Proof.

$$\mathcal{P}_{rt}^{q}(S_2) - \mathcal{P}_{rt}^{q}(S_1) = \frac{c_{rt}^{q}(\mathcal{S}_2)}{d_{rt}^{q}} - \frac{c_{rt}^{q}(\mathcal{S}_1)}{d_{rt}^{q}}$$

$$= \frac{c_{rt}^{q}(\mathcal{S}_2) - c_{rt}^{q}(\mathcal{S}_1)}{d_{rt}^{q}}$$

As $\mathcal{S}_1 \subset \mathcal{S}_2$, From (2) we know that,

$$c_{rt}^{q}(\mathcal{S}_2) = c_{rt}^{q}(\mathcal{S}_1) + c_{rt}^{q}(\mathcal{S}_2 - \mathcal{S}_1)$$

As $c_{rt}^{q}(\mathcal{S}_2 - \mathcal{S}_1)$ must be nonnegative number, so

$$\mathcal{P}_{rt}^{q}(\mathcal{S}_2) - \mathcal{P}_{rt}^{q}(\mathcal{S}_1) \geq 0$$

Therefore the proposition is correct.

From proposition 1, we know that if a vehicle is selected as SV, the increasing of coverage is negative. Then if the coverage is not satisfy the requirement, we need select more vehicles to sense. The ϑ_{rt}^{q} is the coverage ratio that should be satisfied in the sub-region r within time slot t, it is given by the task publisher. In order to better understand whether the requirement coverage is satisfied, we define the Coverage Ratio Satisfaction metrics as follows

- **Definition**: If $\mathcal{P}_{rt}^{q}(\mathcal{S}) \geq \vartheta_{rt}^{q}$, $\forall r \in \mathcal{R}$, $\forall t \in \mathcal{T}$ is satisfied, the set $\mathcal{S}$ satisfy the Coverage Ratio Satisfaction(CRS) metrics.

4 Problem Formulation and Solution

The goal of this paper is to find a set of participant vehicles that make the cost of task least while ensure the coverage ratio in each sub-region within any time slot, the cost include each participant vehicle's required cost and the spend to upload sensed data. We denote the optimal set of SVs as $\mathcal{S}^*$. We denote

$$x_i^q = \begin{cases} 0, & \text{vehicle i do not select as SV} \\ 1, & \text{otherwise} \end{cases} \tag{5}$$

Hence, the optimization problem is formulated as

$$\text{Minimize}: \quad \sum\nolimits_{i \in \mathcal{M}} x_i^q \cdot (e_i^q + \sum\nolimits_{r \in \mathcal{R}} \sum\nolimits_{t \in \mathcal{T}} c_{irt}^q \cdot p)$$

subject to:

$$\begin{array}{c} x_i^q = \{0, 1\}, \quad \forall i \in \mathcal{M} \\ \mathcal{P}_{rt}^q(\sum_{i \in \mathcal{M}} x_i^q) \geq \vartheta_{rt}^q, \quad \forall i \in \mathcal{M}, \forall r \in \mathcal{R}, \forall t \in \mathcal{T} \end{array} \tag{6}$$

p denotes the cost of each data uploaded to server. If the $x_i^q = 1$, the vehicle i will be selected to the $\mathcal{S}^*$.

Until now, the problem of participant selection is formalized as an optimization problem. the novel optimization problem treats the coverage ratio as constraint for selecting participants and aims at minimizing the cost of the task. But the optimization problem is an NP-hard problem, it is obviously a 0/1 knapsack problem. When the amount of participant vehicles are large enough, we need a heuristic algorithm to compute the suboptimal solution.

4.1 Proposed VPS Strategy

The objective function of (8) fits the basic form of nonlinear knapsack problem, The knapsack problem or rucksack problem is a problem in combinatorial optimization: Given a set of items, each with a mass and a value, determine the number of each item to include in a collection so that the total weight is less than or equal to a given limit and the total value is as large as possible.

The optimization target of the nonlinear knapsack problem is to find a set of vehicles, The decision problem form of the knapsack problem is NP complete, the greedy algorithms are frequently used to provide a suboptimal approximated solution. The central part of our participant selection strategy is also in line with the heuristic greedy algorithm, we need to select the maximum value of units and define this vehicle as "efficient" participant vehicle. Each participant vehicle has the efficiency, so first we need to define how to compute vehicle's efficiency. let $\mathcal{S}^*$ denote the set of participants that were selected in the previous round, then the efficiency $\varphi(\mathcal{S}^*, i)$ of a participant vehicle i in this round can be calculated by

$$\varphi(\mathcal{S}^*, i) = \frac{\sum\limits_{r \in \mathcal{R}} \sum\limits_{t \in \mathcal{T}} (c_{rt}^q(\mathcal{S}^* + i) - c_{rt}^q(\mathcal{S}^*))}{e_i^q} \tag{7}$$

The method how to calculate $\varphi(\mathcal{S}^*, i)$ will be used in the proposed strategy VPS, which select participants by rounds of iterations. The pseudo-code of VPS is given in Algorithm 1, and a detailed description is given as follows.

- *Step 1: Initialization.* At the beginning, we should input the task publisher's requirement coverage matrix $\mathcal{D}^q$, the coverage ration constrain matrix ϑ^q, the participant vehicles coverage matrix $C_i^q, \forall i \in \mathcal{M}$ and each participant vehicle's required cost $e_i^q, \forall i \in \mathcal{M}$. All participant vehicles are divided into two sets, the selected set $\mathcal{A}$ and unselected $\mathcal{B}$. At this step, all participant vehicles are put into $\mathcal{B}$ and the set $\mathcal{A}$ is empty.
- *Step 2: Selection.* In this step, we will select a vehicle from unselected set $\mathcal{B}$ to selected set $\mathcal{A}$. We need to compute each vehicle's efficiency in the set $\mathcal{B}$ and select the most efficiency vehicle to selected set $\mathcal{A}$.
- *Step 3: Looping.* Loop step 2, until the selected vehicles satisfy the CRS metrics. How to judge the selected set whether satisfied, we will show it in the Algorithm 2.

Algorithm 1. VPS Algorithm.

Require:

coverage requirement of each task $\mathcal{D}^q$;
area and time division of tasks, $\mathcal{R}$ and $\mathcal{T}$;
participant vehicles, $\mathcal{M}$;
each participant vehicle's required cost, e_i^q;
the location of participant vehicle, $C_i^q, \forall i \in \mathcal{M}$;

Ensure:

Selected participant vehicles, $\mathcal{S}^*$;

set of participant vehicles $\mathcal{B} = \mathcal{M}$, set of selected vehicles $\mathcal{A} = NULL$;
coverageLeft $\leftarrow \mathcal{D}^q$;
selectedID $\leftarrow 0$;
while $!GetRatio(coverageLeft)$ **do** :
  maxEfficiency $\leftarrow 0.0$;
  for vehicle $i \in \mathcal{B}$ **do** :
    compute i's efficiency $\varphi(\mathcal{A}, i)$ in (7);
    if $\varphi(\mathcal{A}, i) >$ *maxEfficiency*
      selectedID $= i$;
      maxEfficiency $= \varphi(\mathcal{A}, i)$;
    end if
  end for
  $\mathcal{A} \leftarrow \mathcal{A} +$ *selectedID*;
  $\mathcal{B} \leftarrow \mathcal{B} +$ *selectedID*;
  coverageLeft $\leftarrow$ *coverageLeft* $- O^q_{selectedID}$;
end while
return selected participant set $\mathcal{S}^* = \mathcal{A}$;

Algorithm 2. GetRatio Algorithm.

Require:
coverage requirement left of each task, *coverageLeft*;
the required coverage ratio, ϑ;
Ensure:
Judge whether the coverage satisfied the requirement, *true or false*;
for $r \in \mathcal{R}$ **do** :
  for $t \in \mathcal{T}$ **do** :
    if $coverageLeft_{rt}/R^q_{rt} > 1 - \vartheta^q_{rt}$
      return false;
    else
      continue;
    end if
  end for
end for
return true;

5 Performance Evaluation

In this section, we implemented the Vehicular Participant Strategy for the sensing collection task in Vehicular Sensor Network. While the amount of participant vehicles is invariable, we are interested in exploring the relationship between the coverage ratio and the total cost, the relationship between the coverage ratio and the amount of selected vehicles, the relationship between the coverage ratio and the total collected data. While the coverage ratio is invariable, we are interested in exploring the relationship between the amount of the participant vehicles and the total cost, the relationship between the amount of the participant vehicles and the amount of selected vehicles, the relationship between the amount of participant vehicles and the amount of total collected data.

5.1 Simulation Settings

We evaluate the performances of VPS using the real GPS traces collected from 300 taxis in Shanghai on February 1, 2007 [16]. The dataset record the taxis' trajectory, each record item includes many attributes, in this evaluation we only need the four attributes: time, nodeID, longitude and latitude.

We assume there is a data collected task in a region of Shanghai, the region's longitude is from 121.35 to 121.55 and its latitude is from 31.14 to 31.34. We divided the region into 16 sub-regions, and the area of those sub-regions are equal size, we also divide the sensing time into 6 time slot. In order to ensure the quality of the data collected, we also stipulate that each sub-region should be covered by a certain number of vehicles in each time slot.

We refer to the proposed scheme as VPS and to examine the system performance, we will compare it with the theory resolution and another participant selection scheme "DPS" [3]. Comparing with the theory resolution, we can know the error of our strategy "VPS". The scheme "DPS" is a dynamic participant selection strategycompare with it, we can know the advantage of our strategy "VPS".

5.2 Results and Analysis

In this section, we will give a detailed exposition about the relationship between variables and objectives through the experimental data. In order to do the experiment more convenient, we let each sub-region's requirement coverage ratio is same. In Fig.2, the variable coverage ratio range from 0.5 to 1, we know that the amount of selected vehicles is increasing while the coverage ratio is growing, in other words, if we want high coverage, we need more vehicles to sense. Compared with strategy DPS, our strategy need less selected vehicles, and the error between VPS and theory resolution is affordable.

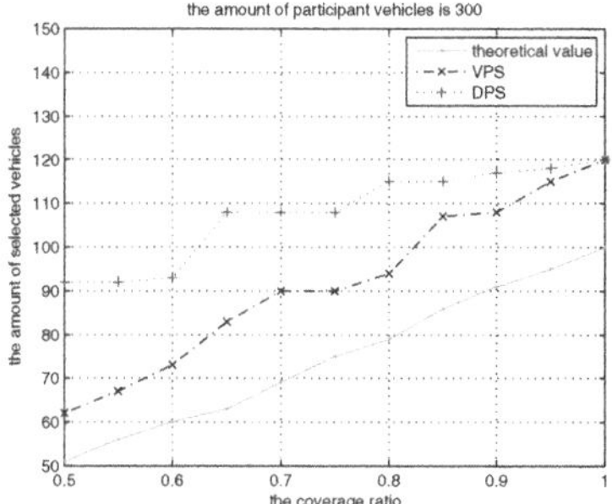

Fig. 2. The amount of selected vehicles vs. coverage ratio

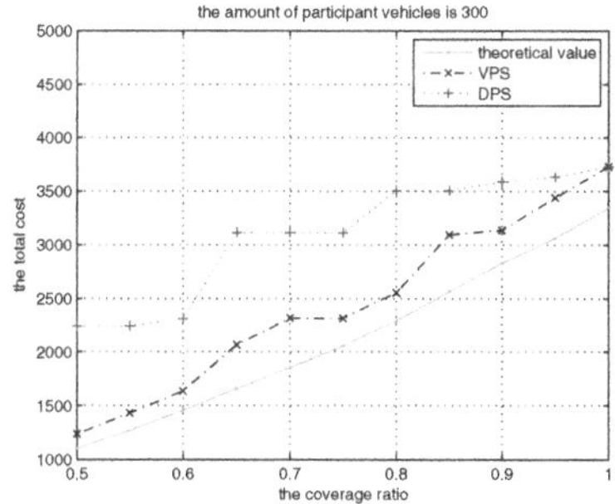

Fig. 3. The total cost vs. coverage ratio

Figure 3 shows the relationship between the coverage ratio and the cost. As the coverage ratio increased, we need pay more to satisfied the requirement. From this figure, We can clearly observe that our strategy is satisfactory, the result of our cost is less than VPS, and slightly higher than the theoretical value. Figure 4 shows that the total amount of collected data increase as the coverage ratio grow.

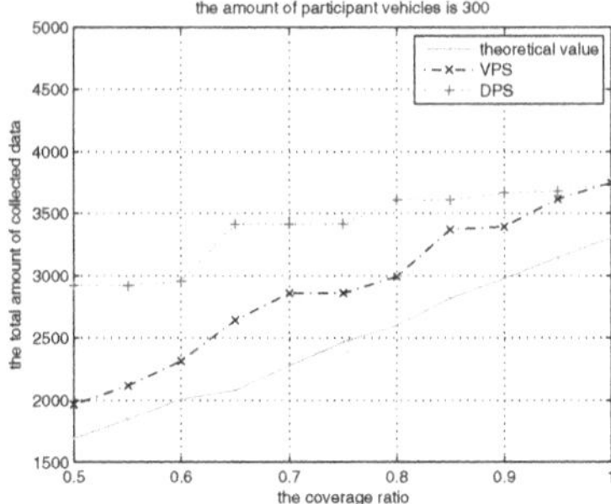

Fig. 4. The total amount of collected data vs. coverage ratio

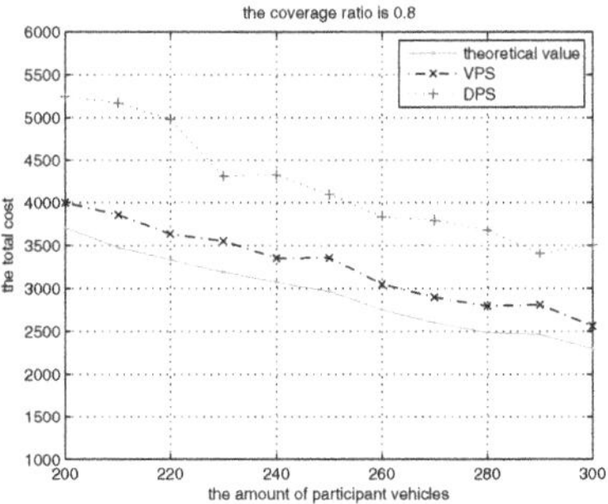

Fig. 5. The total cost vs. the amount of participant vehicles

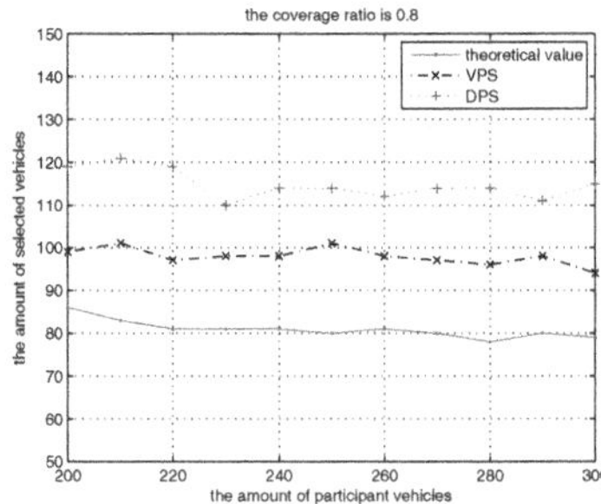

Fig. 6. The amount of selected vehicles vs. the amount of participant vehicles

As we know, if the coverage matrix and the amount of participant vehicles are certain, the coverage ratio can make much of an effect on the total cost, the amount of selected vehicles and the total amount of collected data. Now, we want to know the relationship between the amount of participant vehicles and the total cost, the amount of selected vehicles and the amount of collected data while the coverage matrix and coverage ratio is certain. Figure 5 means that the total cost will decreased while the amount of participant vehicles increased, it is easy to understand, as more vehicles participate in the task, it must be some vehicles require lower cost, so the total cost will decrease. On the other hand, it's very important to let more vehicles participate in the sensing task. Figures 6 and 7 means that as the amount of participant vehicles increased, the amount of selected vehicles and the amount of collected data maintain steady, change in a fixed interval.

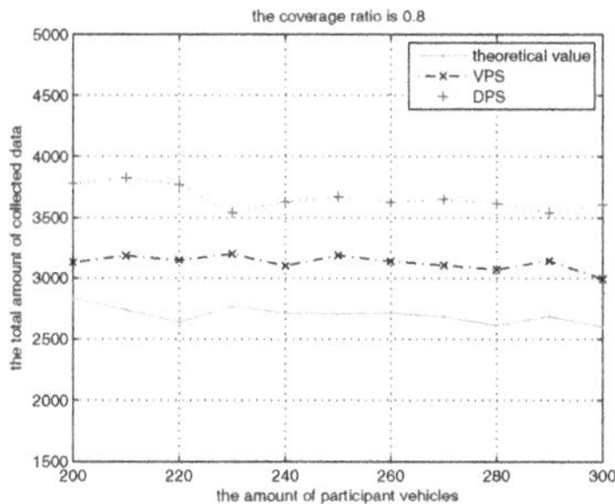

Fig. 7. The total amount of collected data vs. the amount of participant vehicles

6 Conclusion

In this paper, we define a new QoI metric called coverage ratio satisfaction (CRS) with the consideration of coverage from both temporary and spatial aspects. Based on the CRS definition, we formulate the minimum cost CRS guaranteeing problem as an integer linear problem and propose a participant selection strategy called Vehicles Participant Selection (VPS) and experiments show that it is an efficient strategy. We want to let our strategy can serve as a benchmark for performance evaluation. In the future work, we want to let the selection strategy be distributed instead of centralized.

Acknowledgements. This research was supported in part by the NSF of China (Grant No. 61402425, 61272470, 61305087,61440060),the China Postdoctoral Science Foundation funded project(2014M562086), the Fundamental Research Funds for National University, China University of Geosciences (Wuhan) (Grant No. CUG14065, CUGL150830, CUG120114).

References

1. Burke, J.A., Estrin, D., Hansen, M., Parker, A.: Participatory sensing. Center for Embedded Network Sensing (2006)
2. Zeng, D., Li, P., Guo, S., Miyazaki, T., Hu, J., Xiang, Y.: Energy minimization in multi-task software-defined sensor networks. IEEE Trans. Comput. **64**(11), 3128–3139 (2015)

3. Song, Z., Liu, C.H., Wu, J., Ma, J., Wang, W.: QoI-Aware multitask-oriented dynamic participant selection with budget constraints. IEEE Trans. Veh. Technol. **63**(9), 4618–4632 (2014)
4. Xiong, H., Zhang, D., Chen, G., Wang, L., Gauthier, V.: Crowdtasker: Maximizing coverage quality in piggyback crowdsensing under budget constraint. In: Proceedings of the 2015 IEEE International Conference on Pervasive Computing and Communications (PerCom) (2015)
5. Sheng, X., Tang, J.: Energy-efficient collaborative sensing with mobile phones. In: INFOCOM, Proceedings IEEE, pp. 1916–1924. IEEE (2012)
6. Zhao, Q., Zhu, Y., Zhu, H., Li, B.: Fair energy-efficient sensing task allocation in participatory sensing with smartphones. In: INFOCOM, Proceedings IEEE, pp. 1366–1374. IEEE (2014)
7. Wang, L., Zhang, D.: Effsense: energy-efficient and cost-effective data uploading in mobile crowdsensing. In: Proceedings of the ACM Conference on Pervasive and Ubiquitous Computing Adjunct Publication, pp. 1075–1086. ACM (2013)
8. Zeng, D., Guo, S., Barnawi, A., Yu, S., Stojmenovic, I.: An improved stochastic modeling of opportunistic routing in vehicular CPS. IEEE Trans. Comput. **64**(7), 1819–1829 (2015)
9. Zeng, D., Guo, S., Hu, J.: Reliable bulk-data dissemination in delay tolerant networks. IEEE Trans. Parall. Distrib. Syst. **25**(8), 2180–2189 (2014)
10. Yao, H., Zeng, D., Huang, H., Guo, S., Barnawi, A., Stojmenovic, I.: Opportunistic offloading of deadline-constrained bulk cellular traffic in vehicular DTNs. IEEE Trans. Comput. **64**(12), 3515–3527 (2015)
11. Devarakonda, S., Sevusu, P., Liu, H., Liu, R: Real-time air quality monitoring through mobile sensing in metropolitan areas. In: Proceedings of the 2nd ACM SIGKDD International Workshop on Urban Computing, pp. 15. ACM (2013)
12. Du, R., Chen, C., Yang, B., Lu, N., Guan, X., Shen, X.: Effective urban traffic monitoring by vehicular sensor networks. IEEE Trans. Veh. Technol. **64**(1), 273–286 (2015)
13. Bruno, R., Nurchis, M.: Robust and efficient data collection schemes for vehicular multimedia sensor networks. In: IEEE 14th International Symposium and Workshops on a World of Wireless, Mobile and Multimedia Networks (WoWMoM), pp. 1–10. IEEE (2013)
14. Li, Z., Liu, Y., Li, M., Wang, J.: Exploiting ubiquitous data collection for mobile users in wireless sensor networks. IEEE Trans. Parall. Distrib. Syst. **24**(2), 312–326 (2013)
15. Palazzi, C.E., Pezzoni, F., Ruiz, P.M.: Delay-bounded data gathering in urban vehicular sensor networks. Pervasive Mob. Comput. **8**(2), 180–193 (2012)
16. Center, S.G.C.: Shanghai taxi trace data (2012). http://wirelesslab.sjtu.edu.cn

λ-CoAP: An Internet of Things and Cloud Computing Integration Based on the Lambda Architecture and CoAP

Manuel Díaz, Cristian Martín(✉), and Bartolomé Rubio

Department of Languages and Computer Science, University of Málaga, Boulevar Louis Pasteur 35, 29071 Málaga, Spain
{mdr,cmf,tolo}@lcc.uma.es

Abstract. The Internet of Things (IoT) is an emerging technology that is growing continuously thanks to the number of devices deployed and data generated. Nevertheless, an upper layer to abstract the limitations of storing, processing, battery and networking is becoming a mandatory need in this field. Cloud Computing is an especially suitable technology that can supplement this field in the limitations mentioned. However, the current platforms are not prepared for querying large amounts of data with arbitrary functions in real-time, which are necessary requirements for real-time systems. This paper presents λ-CoAP architecture, a novel paradigm not introduced yet to the best of our knowledge, which proposes an integration of Cloud Computing and Internet of Things through the Lambda Architecture (LA) and a Constrained Application Protocol (CoAP) middleware. The λ-CoAP architecture has the purpose to query, process and analyze large amounts of IoT data with arbitrary functions in real-time. On the other hand, the CoAP middleware is a lightweight middleware that can be deployed in resource constrained devices and allows the way of the IoT towards the Web of Things. Moreover, the λ-CoAP also contains a set of components with well defined interfaces for querying, managing, and actuating over the system.

Keywords: Internet of Things · Lambda Architecture · Coap middleware · Cloud computing

1 Introduction

The Internet of Things (IoT) [1] has received a lot of attention in recent years, thanks to the continuous research in this field, the technological advances and the large amount of systems, components, software and devices release every day. The IoT is composed of a set of interconnected things (mobile devices, RFID tags, sensors, smart-phones, cameras, etc.) which have the ability to sense, communicate and/or actuate over the Internet. Moreover, thanks to the IoT capacity for adapting on many situations, it has carried the IoT suitable for monitoring, control and manage in many areas such as Smart Ambient and Monitoring.

S. Guo et al. (Eds.): CollaborateCom 2015, LNICST 163, pp. 195–206, 2016.
DOI: 10.1007/978-3-319-28910-6_18

Nowadays, it is possible to acquire an embedded personal computer for a few dollars [2] and check the free car parks in real-time in your city, something unthinkable just a few years ago. All of this has been originated from the IoT, and it is now one of the most interesting fields of research that will be present to help us everyday.

However, the devices involved in the IoT have serious constraints with respect to processing, storing and networking. These issues has originated integrations with new paradigms like Cloud Computing, known as Cloud of Things [3], which has solved such IoT limitations. Cloud Computing enables an on demand access to a pool of configurable resources providing virtually unlimited capabilities in terms of storage and processing power [4], which are the main drawbacks of the IoT. Even though the integration with Cloud Computing provides the IoT the requirements already mentioned, the current need for extracting knowledge of the data in real-time imply to think beyond. Moreover, there are a large amounts of heterogeneous devices deployed around the world, so they also generate large amounts of data which will keep on growing in the coming years [5]. Cloud Computing can solve the above requirements, but the needs for extracting knowledge with large amounts of data in real-time like in critical systems, means that Cloud Computing might be unsuitable for certain situations due to high latency.

The Lambda Architecture (LA) [6] is a novel paradigm introduced by Nathan Marz composed by Cloud Computing components—a distributed queue, batch and stream processing and a distributed database—designed to offer arbitrary and predicted queries over arbitrary real-time data. The key idea in the LA is the precomputed view, which contains the knowledge consequence of applying functions over the system data. The data in LA is split in two ways: historical data, which contains all data generated in the system, and real-time data with the stream data received. The LA also decomposes the paradigm in three layers: the batch layer, the real-time layer and the serving layer. All data received is delivered to a distributed queue which replies it into the real-time layer for processing and generating the real-time views and the batch layer which stores it in the master data and generates the batch views with the historical data. The LA therefore offers new opportunities for processing and analysis large amounts of arbitrary data in real-time.

Nevertheless, due to the heterogeneity of devices which compose the IoT, which have different functionalities, capabilities and programming languages among other things, an abstraction layer is necessary to abstract that heterogeneity offering a unique way to interconnect anything. Through a middleware, the IoT can hide communication and low-level acquisition aspects in anything [7]. Currently, there are a lot of Web services that work over the Internet for sharing and exchanging a large amount of data and services. So allowing a compatible middleware with the current systems and the Internet, the IoT leads to a part of the Internet, also known as Web of Things (WoT) [8], where the current Web services will be enriched with physical smart objects. Moreover, the Web-enabled applications are available on many platforms with Internet connection, from computer to smart phone, PDAs and tablets, so the WoT will also enable the IoT on many platforms. However, Web services usually work over protocols such as HTTP and TCP, which are too heavy for resource constrained devices. Taking into account that, the Internet Engineering Task Force (IETF) launched the Constrained Application Protocol (CoAP) [9,10]. CoAP is a web transfer protocol designed for resource constrained devices that work over UDP. CoAP follows the same style that RESTFul Web services, supporting the Uniform Resource Identifier (URI) and a HTTP model, but it uses UDP thereby reducing the transfer overhead and header of TCP. Furthermore, CoAP also supports asynchronous communication and multicast, not available in TCP and desirable in resource constrained devices with power, battery and network limitations. CoAP was not created as a common middleware, but nevertheless we propose a middleware based on CoAP for providing a layer to abstract communication, low-level acquisition and discovering aspects over the IoT. The IETF also defines the guidelines for HTTP-CoAP mapping, so the CoAP middleware is therefore a promising IoT middleware for integrating the IoT into the Web.

In this paper, we introduce λ-CoAP, an architecture for integrating the IoT and Cloud Computing through the LA and a CoAP middleware, with real-time and mobility requirements and resource embedded devices. The λ-CoAP architecture constitutes a novel paradigm not introduced yet to the best of our knowledge, which has several purposes: bring the IoT to the WoT; improve the IoT with the necessary capacities in terms of storage, processing and networking provided by the LA; and last but not least, define a framework for analysis and actuating over large amounts of real-time data in IoT environments.

The rest of the paper is structured as follows. In Sect. 2 a state of the art of the components of the architecture is presented. Section 3 presents the general scheme of the proposed architecture. Finally, some conclusions and future work are presented in Sect. 4.

2 Related Work

For a better organization of the λ-CoAP architecture requirements, related work is divided in three categories taking into account the main requirements proposed in this article. Firstly, we summarize different Cloud Platforms related to those that constitute the LA. Next, several middleware for the IoT are summarized. And lastly, we have summarized related work about the Smart CoAP Gateways.

2.1 Cloud Platforms

Batch Processing. The components responsible of generating the batch views in the LA are the batch processing components. They allow the execution of a large amount of jobs without manual intervention, achieving a greater distribution and high throughput. Apache Hadoop [11] is a well-known batch processing platform for storing and processing large amounts of data. Apache Hadoop is composed by three main components: Hadoop Distributed File System (HDFS),

Map Reduce and Yet Another Resource Negotiator (YARN). HDFS is the distributed file system of Apache Hadoop, responsible for replicating and balancing the data over the slaves deployed, achieving high bandwidth, reliability and scalability. On the other hand, Map Reduce and YARN are Hadoop components responsible for processing jobs and managing the resource management respectively. Therefore, Apache Hadoop is a suitable component, compatible with multiple Cloud platforms, for generating batch views in the LA.

Apache Spark [12] is another batch processing platform for processing and analysis large amounts of data. In contrast to Apache Hadoop, Apache Spark does not contain its own file system, but trusts on different data stores such as HDFS, Apache Cassandra, Apache HBase and Amazon S3. Apache Spark follows a different approach than Apache Hadoop. Apache Spark knows the high latency due to reload continuous data from disk, and keeps it in memory for reducing the latency. Although Apache Spark is a desirable component to achieve high performance in a processing system, in the LA the latency requirements are addressed by the real-time layer, so it is not necessary. Moreover, Apache Hadoop presents more integration compatibility with other Cloud platforms.

Real-Time Processing. Real-time processing components are those located in the real-time layer, and are responsible for processing and analysis the stream data provided by the distributed queue. Apache Storm [14] is an open source distributed system for real-time processing. Apache Storm has an architecture based on directed graphs, where the edges represent the flow data between the vertices deployed, which are the computational components. The design based on directed graphs contribute to provide fault-tolerant and replication in addition to enable several layers to abstract the processing. Moreover, Apache Storm also offers semantics guarantees with 'at least once' and 'at most once' data processing. Also together with the integration with Apache Kafka and several data stores, lead to Apache Storm to be a suitable component for the real-time layer of the LA.

Apache Spark Streaming [15] is also an open source streaming processing component. Apache Spark Streaming does not act like Apache Storm, since it processes the stream data and then stores them in a specific format. Apache Spark Streaming is also integrated with Apache Spark, so they can reuse the same functions and data representation enabling a hybrid architecture with real-time and batch processing. However, due to needs of integration with several components which form the LA, Apache Storm is more suitable for this purpose.

Distributed Databases. The serving layer is perhaps the main component of the LA, since it is responsible for serving and merging the real-time and batch views. To support the serving layer a distributed database is necessary for serving and querying data as soon as possible. Apache HBase [16] is an open source distributed database suitable for random access and read/write large amounts of data. Apache HBase uses HDFS as a storage system, where all data is stored in tables like traditional Relational Database Management Systems (RDBMS).

The Apache HBase tables are composed by multiples rows, where each rows can store a set of mixed and indeterminate key-values. Apache HBase also supports fault-tolerant, replication and load-balancing and is properly integrated with Apache Hadoop.

Nonetheless, platforms such as Apache HBase and Apache Hadoop do not guarantee how quickly data can be stored and accessed, which are the main features in the LA. Druid [17,18] is an open source distributed column-oriented database for storing and querying data in real-time. Druid was created in order to resolve problems about applications which require low latency on ingestion and query data. The key idea of Druid is to persist data on memory for quick access. The historical data is persisted and obtained from the deep storage when real-time data changes to historical. Moreover, Druid has integrations with external Cloud platforms such as Apache Kafka [13], Apache Storm and Apache Hadoop, so the serving layer will be properly constituted with Druid.

2.2 IoT Middleware

The IoT middleware contributes to abstract the processes of communication, low-level acquisition and discovering in the IoT devices. Furthermore, it also keeps away the heterogeneity in the IoT devices, showing each device like a unified middleware.

LooCI [19] is a middleware for building component-based applications in Wireless Sensor Network (WSN). The component infrastructure allows mechanisms for deploying and managing components in runtime. LooCI also provides interoperability across various platforms: a Java micro edition for constrained devices known as Squawk, the OS for the IoT Contiki, and the OSGi.

On the other hand, the OMG Data-Distribution Service for Real-Time Systems (DDS) [20] is a centric publish/subscribe middleware for real-time and embedded systems. All data in DDS is exchanged between consumers and producers through typed data topics providing a level of safety.

However, the latter middlewares do not focus on offering interoperability with the Internet, and its system requirements can be too heavy for resource constrained devices, in contrast to the header of the CoAP middleware that only requires 4 bytes. In addition, the real-time requirement is only addressed by DDS, but its protocol stack can be too heavy for embedded devices too. Therefore, the CoAP middleware is a lightweight middleware suitable for embedded devices with real-time requirements for the λ-CoAP architecture.

2.3 Smart CoAP Gateway

For a HTTP-CoAP mapping, the integration between the CoAP devices and the LA, besides minimizing the overload in constrained devices, it is necessary to have a smart gateway that acts as an intermediate among the Web, the LA and CoAP devices. The Smart Gateway acts as a cross-layer proxy between HTTP and CoAP devices, creating a barrier to protect the embedded devices in case of an overload of requests. In addition, the Smart Gateway is also responsible for transmitting the IoT data generated by the CoAP devices for further storing, processing and analysis. Furthermore, through the Smart Gateway, the great number of web applications deployed could make use of the physical devices deployed achieving a cyber-physical environment.

Ludovici and Calveras [21] present a HTTP-CoAP proxy to leverage the interconnection of 6LowPAN WSN with HTTP long-polling requests. Ludovici and Calveras know of the performance loss while doing continuous HTTP requests, so a WebSocket communication is proposed to improve it. In [22], a proxy is presented to interconnect a ZigBee—a wireless communication protocol for embedded devices—CoAP WSN with HTTP in order to enable an UPnP system. However, these works focus on proxies with specific communications for embedded devices such as 6LowPAN and ZigBee, and are not focus on integration with Cloud Computing components. Our Smart Gateway aims to abstract different communications (Ethernet and ZigBee) in order to build a Smart Gateway suitable for WSN as for mobile devices like smart-phones.

3 The λ-CoAP Architecture

The λ-CoAP is a novel architecture designed to offer a general framework for processing, storing, analysis and obtaining conclusions of IoT data in real-time. The λ-CoAP is the result of combining current components of Cloud Computing for abstracting the limitations of the IoT devices, with an IoT middleware suitable for resource constraint devices. The λ-CoAP architecture also includes the adoption of smart gateways, which has been established in order to abstract and protect the IoT devices from external sources, but also offers a new way to integrate the IoT in the WoT. Furthermore, the λ-CoAP also presents mechanisms for querying data and generating actions over the IoT as well as a Web UI where the users registered will can query and manage the system.

Figure 1 shows the general architecture of the λ-CoAP. It is composed by three differentiated components: a Cloud, the Smart Gateways and end devices. The Cloud is responsible for allocating and serving the components of the LA—Apache Hadoop, Apache Storm, Apache Kafka and Druid—and other components which compose the architecture: the Actions Component, a Web UI, a Querying Interface and optional Smart Gateways. The Smart Gateways can be deployed locally for abstracting local IoT deployments like a smart-house, in addition to cloud deployment for mobile devices. Lastly, the end devices incorporate a middleware based on CoAP whose main function is to abstract the communications with the Smart Gateways for querying data or actuation over them as well as discovering and low-level acquisition aspects. The following sections describe each component belonging to the λ-CoAP architecture.

3.1 Lambda Architecture

As introduced, the LA is a paradigm composed by several Cloud Computing components in order to enable a framework for processing, analysis, storing

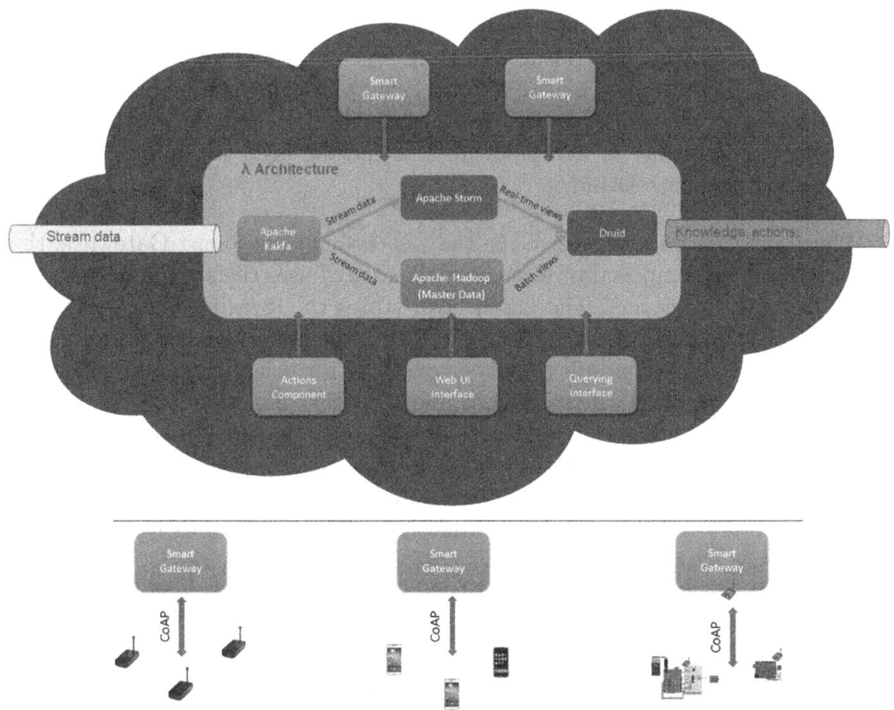

Fig. 1. The λ-CoAP Architecture

and querying arbitrary data with arbitrary functions in real-time. Immutable data—data that does not change as time passes, only can be queried or added—besides the precomputed views are key concepts in the LA.

All data received in the LA is stored in the master data and it is converted into another form during the processing, so the initial data received never changes over time. The latter prevents human errors such as accidental deletions and updates. Also, Cloud Computing LA components replicate the data and offer mechanisms to high availability and fault-tolerant, so the probability of data lost is small. Generating arbitrary functions and complex analysis over large amounts of data may require a considerable latency, an issue for real-time systems. Precomputed views have been designed to have available the complex analysis required besides extracting knowledge over the system data. The LA is decomposed in the following layers for such purposes:

- **Batch layer:** responsible for processing the historical data and generating the batch precomputed views through batch processing. The batch layer also stores all data of the system in an immutable form, known as master data, so it allows generating new precomputed views with new functions at any time. The batch layer is composed by the batch processing platform Apache Hadoop.

- **Real-time layer:** makes up the high latency of the batch layer, processing the stream data and generating real-time precomputed views. The real-time layer is composed by the real-time processing platform Apache Storm.
- **Serving layer:** responsible for abstracting the batch and real-time views offering a unique way to access them. The serving layer is composed by the distributed database Druid.

When a stream data is received in the LA through the Smart Gateways, the distributed queue composed by Apache Kafka distributes the stream data to the batch and real-time layers. The batch layer stores the stream data received by Apache Kafka and generates the batch views with the historical data periodically. The batch layer makes complex analysis over the historical data and generates actions for the IoT about such analysis. On the other hand, the real-time layer generates the real-time views and actions with the stream data received. All actions both the generated by the real-time layer and the batch layer are sent to the Actions Component which is responsible to communicate with the Smart Gateways in order to actuate over the underlying IoT devices. Lastly, the serving layer merge the batch and real-time views for the coming queries.

3.2 Smart Gateway

The Smart Gateway is the component responsible for abstracting the IoT in addition to connect it with the LA. The Smart Gateway is also responsible for incorporating a cross-layer proxy to interconnect the IoT with the Web. There are two ways of Smart Gateway deployment: a cloud and local deployment. The local deployment is intent to abstract local deployments like WSN or smart-home. On the other hand, the cloud deployment is intent to integrate mobile devices without a local Smart Gateway. The local Smart Gateways uses the ZigBee protocol and Ethernet/Wifi/UMTS for devices which support it, for the communication with the IoT devices. The cloud deployments trust only on the Ethernet/Wifi/UMTS module installed in each component, so a ZigBee network is not available. Moreover, the adoption of a lightweight protocol for resource constrained devices like ZigBee, which does not trust in UDP, has only been done to the best of our knowledge in a UPnP system in [22]. Each Smart Gateway is composed by the following components:

- **LA Connector:** connects the Smart Gateway with the LA. When a stream provided by the Smart Gateway is received, the LA Connector sends it to Apache Kafka for further processing of the LA.
- **Web Server:** is responsible for managing the HTTP requests of external sources such as an action provided of the LA and a query of a client. The Web Server checks firstly on the Database Cache if the data required is available. If the data required is not present in the Database Cache, the Web Server obtains the address of the device associated to the request, and makes a CoAP request with it to obtain or act over the device that is sent to the CoAP Connector.

- **CoAP Connector:** receives requests from the Web Server to request data or actuate over a device. The CoAP Connector also connects the CoAP middlewares with the Smart Gateways to obtain the data or send the actions requested.
- **Database Cache:** has two main functions, in fact, it is both a cache and a lightweight database. On the one hand, the Database Cache stores information about end devices and its resources. On the other hand, the Database Cache also stores data of devices in order to provide a cache and protects the end devices of overload of requests.

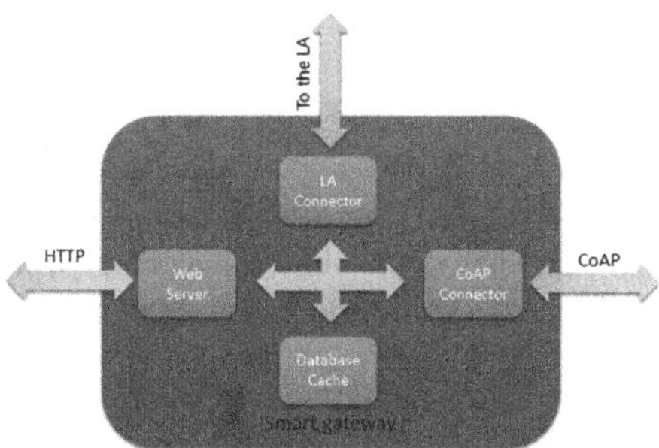

Fig. 2. Smart Gateway

Figure 2 shows the architecture of the Smart Gateway. When a CoAP middleware is deployed in the system, it sends a broadcast message in local deployments in order to inform the rest of the network that is deployed. The Smart Gateway, upon the reception of the broadcast message, registers the device on its database and makes a request to the CoAP Connector for obtaining its resources provided. Once the Smart Gateway receives the requested message, by default the Smart Gateway subscribes to all resources contained in the CoAP middleware through the observe CoAP option. The Smart Gateway also stores information about CoAP resources in order to inform the HTTP clients with the resources provided by the CoAP middleware and translate operations. The CoAP middleware also sends broadcast messages periodically in order to inform the other components that are alive. In cloud deployments, there are not broadcast messages, but the end devices also inform to the Cloud Smart Gateway that they are deployed/alive. Every time that an observed CoAP data is received in the CoAP connector, it is transferred to the LA Connector for sending it to the LA.

3.3 CoAP Middleware

The CoAP middleware is responsible for abstracting communication, low-level acquisition and discovering aspects in the IoT devices. The CoAP middleware provides an abstract layer for accessing low-level components like sensors as well as actuating over the actuators components in the IoT devices. It depends on the networking established, the CoAP middleware can be installed in a WSN through the ZigBee protocol besides to be installed in mobiles devices through Ethernet/Wifi/UMTS.

The CoAP middleware also manages CoAP resources which can be identified by an URI. CoAP resources are components responsible for the abstract operations in the IoT devices such as obtaining the value of a specific sensor and performing the action over an actuator component. Querying the underlying sensors installed in each device is performed through a resource with CoAP GET requests, whereas actuating over a components is performed through a resource with CoAP POST requests. The CoAP requests are generated by the CoAP Connector of the Smart Gateways based on the HTTP requests. Therefore, through the Smart Gateways, users can query and actuate over the IoT by means of HTTP GET and POST operations.

The discovering process is initiated when a new CoAP middleware is deployed in the system. The discovering process has been designed to help the Smart Gateways to know how many CoAP middlewares are deployed, which are alive and which are its resources. Moreover, the discovering process also informs the rest of the network the status of the middleware, allowing it to create distributed CoAP resources among several CoAP middlewares.

3.4 External Components

In order to provide a unified way to actuate, query and manage the system, the λ-CoAP also incorporates the following components:

- **Cloud Smart Gateways:** are Smart Gateways deployed in the Cloud which manage and abstract the underlying IoT mobiles devices. Cloud Smart Gateways can be deployed based on the system needs, so there may be from 0 to n deployments.
- **Actions Component:** provides an API RESTFul for receiving the result actions generated by the LA. The Actions Component establishes the communications with the respective Smart Gateway in order to actuate over the action required CoAP resource.
- **Web UI interface:** provides a Web UI where the users registered can manage, query and monitor the λ-CoAP architecture.
- **Querying Interface:** provides an API RESTFul to query all data and conclusions belong to the LA.

The adoption of API RESTFul interfaces also allows that external systems can integrate the λ-CoAP architecture in their business models.

4 Conclusions and Future Work

This work presents a novel architecture to integrate the Internet of Things and Cloud Computing with real-time requirements, called the λ-CoAP architecture.

The λ-CoAP architecture contributes to solve the problems of processing, analysis and storing large amounts of IoT data with arbitrary functions through a paradigm known as the LA. The λ-CoAP architecture also supports the variety, velocity and volume of data generated by the IoT, allowing the known Big Data paradigm.

The λ-CoAP architecture proposes a CoAP middleware in order to abstract the low-level aspects of the IoT and provides a lightweight way to actuate and send IoT data. Moreover, the IoT is abstracted through Smart Gateways, which provide a cross-proxy between HTTP and CoAP, allowing the access to the IoT through normal HTTP requests. In fact, the latter also contributes to carry the IoT towards the WoT. The Smart Gateways also take into account the mobility of the IoT, and supports mobile devices as local deployments. Finally, the architecture is composed of external components for querying, actuating and managing the system through well defined interfaces.

Therefore, we think that the λ-CoAP architecture is a promising architecture for the IoT with real-time and mobility requirements, that can be applied in many areas both with smart-phone networks and with WSNs. We are currently involved in the development of the architecture in order to evaluate the performance and real-time requirements on an IoT deployment.

Acknowledgment. This work was funded by the Spanish projects TIC-1572 ("MIsT-Ica: Critical Infrastructures Monitoring based on Wireless Technologies") and TIN2014-52034-R ("An MDE Framework for the Design and Integration of Critical Infrastructure Management Systems").

Author Contributions

All authors contributed to the conception of the proposal, defined the methodology and contributed to writing and revising the article.

Conflicts of Interest

The authors declare that there is no conflict of interest regarding the publication of this manuscript.

References

1. Ashton, K.: That 'internet of things' thing. J. RFID **22**, 97–114 (2009)
2. C.H.I.P.: The World's First 9 dollars Computer. http://nextthing.co/
3. Aazam, M., Khan, I., Alsaffar, A.A., Huh, E.N.: Cloud of things: integrating internet of things and cloud computing and the issues involved. In: 11th International Bhurban Conference on Applied Sciences and Technology (IBCAST), Anchorage, Alaska USA, pp. 414–419. IEEE (2014)

4. Botta, A., de Donato, W., Persico, V., Pescap, A.: On the integration of cloud computing and internet of things. In: 2nd International Conference on Future Internet of Things and Cloud (FiCloud-2014), Barcelona Spain, pp. 23–30. IEEE (2014)
5. Zaslavsky, A., Perera, C., Georgakopoulos, D.: Sensing as a service and big data. In: International Conference on Advances in Cloud Computing (ACC-2012), Bangalore India, pp. 21–29 (2012)
6. Marz, N., Warren, J.: Big Data: Principles and Best Practices of Scalable Realtime Data Systems. Manning Publications Co., Stamford (2015)
7. Calbimonte, J.P., Sarni, S., Eberle, J., Aberer, K.: XGSN: an open-source semantic sensing middleware for the web of things. In: 13th International Semantic Web Conference 7th International Workshop on Semantic Sensor Networks (SSN2014), Riva del Garda, Trentino Italy (2014)
8. Zeng, D., Guo, S., Cheng, Z.: The web of things: a survey. J. of Commun. **6**, 424–438 (2011)
9. Bormann, C., Castellani, A.P., Shelby, Z.: Coap: An application protocol for billions of tiny internet nodes. J. Internet Comput. **16**, 62–67 (2012)
10. Shelby, Z., Klaus, H., Carsten, B.: The Constrained Application Protocol (CoAP). https://tools.ietf.org/html/rfc7252/
11. Shvachko, K., Kuang, H., Radia, S., Chansler, R.: The hadoop distributed file system. In: 26th Symposium on Mass Storage Systems and Technologies (MSST), pp. 1–10. IEEE, Incline Villiage, Nevada USA (2010)
12. Zaharia, M., Chowdhury, M., Franklin, M.J., Shenker, S., Stoica, I.: Spark: cluster computing with working sets. In: 2nd USENIX Conference on Hot Topics in Cloud Computing, p. 10. Boston, MA USA (2010)
13. Apache Kafka. http://kafka.apache.org/
14. Toshniwal, A., Taneja, S., Shukla, A., Ramasamy, K., Patel, J.M., Kulkarni, S., et al.: Storm@ twitter. In: 2014 ACM SIGMOD International Conference on Management of Data, pp. 147–156. ACM, Snowbird, Utah USA (2014)
15. Apache Spark Streaming. https://spark.apache.org/streaming/
16. Apache HBase. http://hbase.apache.org/
17. Yang, F., Tschetter, E., Léauté, X., Ray, N., Merlino, G., Ganguli, D.: Druid: A real-time analytical data store. In: 2014 ACM SIGMOD International Conference on Management of Data, pp. 157–168. ACM, Snowbird, Utah USA (2014)
18. Druid. http://druid.io/
19. Hughes, D., Man, K.L., Shen, Z., Kim, K.K.: A loosely-coupled binding model for Wireless Sensor Networks. In: 2012 International SoC Design Conference (ISOCC), Jeju Island, Korea (South), pp. 273–276. IEEE (2012)
20. The OMG Data-Distribution Service for Real-Time Systems (DDS). http://portals.omg.org/dds/
21. Ludovici, A., Calveras, A.: A proxy design to leverage the interconnection of CoAP wireless sensor networks with web applications. J. Sensors. **15**, 1217–1244 (2015)
22. Mitsugi, J., Yonemura, S., Hada, H., Inaba, T.: Bridging upnp and zigbee with coap: protocol and its performance evaluation. In: Proceedings of the Workshop on Internet of Things and Service Platforms, p. 1. ACM, Tokyo Japan (2011)

A Framework for Multiscale-, QoC- and Privacy-aware Context Dissemination in the Internet of Things

Sophie Chabridon[1](✉), Denis Conan[1], Thierry Desprats[2], Mohamed Mbarki[3], Chantal Taconet[1], Léon Lim[1], Pierrick Marie[2], and Sam Rottenberg[1]

[1] SAMOVAR, Télécom SudParis, CNRS, Université Paris-Saclay, 9 Rue Charles Fourier, 91011 évry Cedex, France
{Sophie.Chabridon,Denis.Conan,Chantal.Taconet,Leon.Lim, Sam.Rottenberg}@telecom-sudparis.eu

[2] Université de Toulouse, IRIT UMR, 5505 Toulouse, France
{Thierry.Desprats,Pierrick.Marie}@irit.fr

[3] ARTAL Technologies, 227 Rue Pierre-Gilles de Gennes, 31681 Labège, France
Mohamed.Mbarki@artal.fr

Abstract. The tremendous amount of context information that can be generated by the Internet of Things (IoT) calls for new solutions able to dig for the relevant information fitting applications' needs. This paper proposes to leverage multiscale-, Quality of Context (QoC)- and privacy-awareness for the efficient filtering of context information disseminated between the decoupled producers and consumers of the IoT. We first discuss some specific challenges that must be addressed by next generation context managers, including multiscalability, distributed push and pull communications, and the consideration of both QoC and privacy constraints. We then answer these challenges with a new context dissemination framework involving visibility and forwarding filters and illustrate it through the implementation of a collaborative social welfare scenario.

Keywords: Context management · Internet of Things · Context dissemination · Multiscalability · Quality of context · Privacy · Distributed event-based system

1 Introduction

The Internet of Things (IoT) is characterized by the extreme heterogeneity of the things it may interconnect and by their spontaneous interaction mode [1]. This leverages the adaptation capability of new context-aware applications. They are no more limited to their perceived ambient environment but they can collect context information from sources situated at other remote spaces and possibly at other scales too. In this article, we present our vision of multiscale context management systems combining components at different scales from local to remote ambient spaces and from the Cloud. This vision comes with new opportunities but also with new challenges. To master the tremendous amount of highly

S. Guo et al. (Eds.): CollaborateCom 2015, LNICST 163, pp. 207–218, 2016.
DOI: 10.1007/978-3-319-28910-6_19

dynamic and uncertain information collected from the IoT, new solutions are required to reason at the relevant scale and to manipulate context information of sufficient quality. This quality level should be considered jointly with privacy for not disclosing more information than necessary [7].

Our contributions are threefold: (i) multiscale context dissemination through distributed push and pull communication modes with (ii) joint management of the quality of context (QoC) and (iii) privacy protection.

The remainder of this paper is structured as follows. Section 2 defines the required properties of a new generation of context managers for the IoT and overviews the current state of the art. Section 3 describes the characteristics of our proposed framework for answering the requirements raised by context dissemination in the IoT. We then present a qualitative evaluation of our framework in Sect. 4.3. We conclude with a summary and an outline of further research in Sect. 5.

2 Toward a New Generation of Context Managers

2.1 Requirements for Context Management over the IoT

With the IoT, the need for distributing context management components raises dramatically. Indeed, a huge number of things can be connected to the global network infrastructure at any time during their life cycle either temporarily or permanently. Moreover, some things are situated in fixed locations while others are mobile. Finally, heterogeneity is the rule as small things may collaborate with powerful systems following the concept of mobile cloud computing [10]. **(R1) Distributed context management should be deployable on various network infrastructures exposing multiple scales**. Things are no longer considered only as context producers. They are independent actors that can also autonomously exchange, store and process information as well as interact to cooperatively compute useful data for human users, without involving them. Regarding the usefulness of context data for applications, one solution consists in describing context quality through meta-data: QoC is related to any information that describes the quality of context data [6]. **(R2) The choice of the relevant QoC metadata should be open and flexible**. Privacy preservation is another important concern of the public for the acceptance of the IoT [14]. **(R3) The knowledge provided by context data and their associated QoC metadata should respect the privacy of the context owners and not reveal more information than necessary**.

2.2 Existing Solutions for Context Dissemination

At first glance, context data dissemination can be addressed by existing solutions to the general problem of data distribution, that is by using a middleware providing some type of coordination models [12]: transactional, RPC-like, tuple-space, message-oriented, content-based, peer-to-peer or publish/subscribe middleware. However, context data distribution possesses original needs, which can be expressed in the concept of "uninformed" and "informed" context data distribution, that is whether the routing according to context needs is performed blindly or not [5]. The solution presented in this paper specifically targets three issues of informed context data distribution: (i) context data production/consumption decoupling with enforcement of context data visibility scopes, (ii) QoC-based context data distribution, and (iii) preservation of context owners' privacy. We review below related works regarding these three issues.

Following the publish/subscribe communication model [9], distributed event-based systems (DEBS) [17] are becoming popular as an enabler for context data dissemination in the IoT: Their interaction pattern decouples in space and time the things that produce events from applications that consume these events. With the concept of "scope" introduced in [11], the visibility of a notification can be limited to a subset of the consumers. In this paper, we argue that the system concept of scale matches with the DEBS concept of scope, and we propose multiscoping —i.e. distributed routing is impacted by the visibility of notifications that are analysed according to several dimensions. The REBECA [11] system implements monoscoping where only one scope graph is used at a time. Here we extend this concept to multiscoping and we allow the interoperability with scope-agnostic applications. [2] or [13] propose techniques for rewiring the broker overlay in order to avoid involving pure forwarder brokers. However, as highlighted by [3], a bad placement may result in a high number of messages being propagated between brokers. We favor a more distributed solution in which brokers can manage visibility filters.

[19] motivates the need for context managers to take QoC into account by application adaptation, middleware efficiency and users' privacy enforcement. In their proposed solution, all the parties should have an agreement in advance about the QoC they provide and require before sharing their context information. This mechanism needs further enhancement for the case of the IoT where the parties do not know each other in advance. Moreover, a common definition of the list of criteria used to qualify the context information within the context managers is still an open problem [5]. We therefore propose the unified QOCIM meta-model [16] allowing application developers to represent their own meta-data about QoC.

Concerning privacy protection in the IoT, most of the works offer confidentiality and anonymity using encryption mechanisms [4], k-anonymity or l-diversity models [20,22]. Our approach is complementary by granting access to consumers based on their intended use of context data expressed in contracts.

3 A Framework for Multiscale Context Management with QoC- and Privacy-awareness

Unlike large scale distribution focusing on a quantitative issue, multiscale distribution mainly addresses the heterogeneity of a system. We define *multiscalability* as the ability to cover several scales in at least one viewpoint which is associated to at least one dimension [18]. A *viewpoint* leads to a particular architectural view of a system which can be studied independently. A *dimension* corresponds to a measurable characteristic, numerical or semantic, of a system view for a given viewpoint. Using a measure, a dimension can then be divided using an ordered set of *scales*. Some examples of viewpoint are device (with the dimensions of storage capacity and processing power) and geography (with the dimensions of distance and adminstration area).

3.1 Main Components of the Global Architecture

Figure 1 illustrates the main architectural components of our context management infrastructure that provides context data dissemination between all categories of producers and consumers. A component can be either a collector or a capsule. A context collector is an element that provides raw context data and corresponds to a producer. A context capsule is a functional element of the context manager. It plays both the consumer and producer roles. Context-aware applications are clients that consume context information. A brokering service, distributed over the underlying physical network infrastructure, supports an efficient propagation of context data. It ensures the context delivery to the relevant context consumers. It may be deployed on several brokering overlay networks.

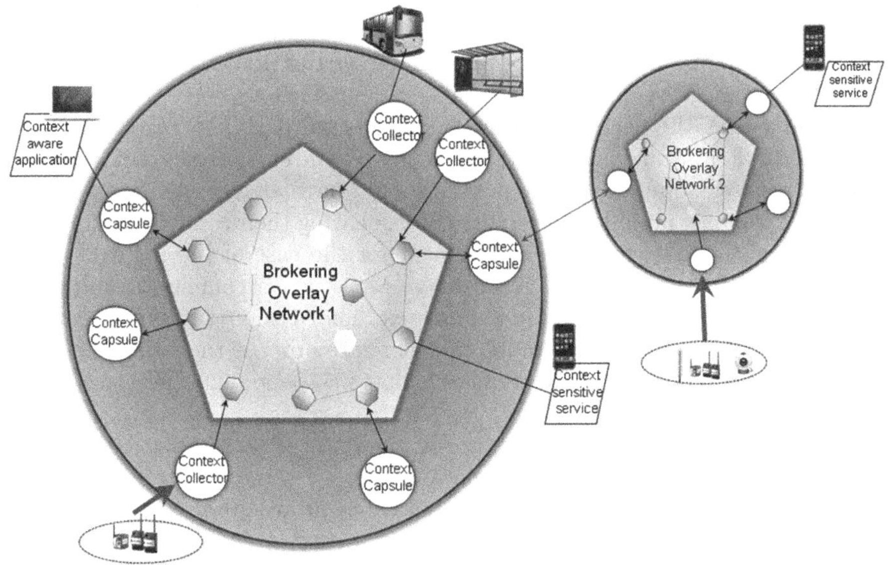

Fig. 1. Generic infrastructure with different types of overlay network

3.2 Distribution of Context Information with Multiscoping Using MuDEBS

We have developed the MuDEBS framework[1] as a Multiscale Distributed Event-Based System (DEBS). It allows to distribute context information in the IoT,

[1] https://fusionforge.int-evry.fr/www/mudebs/.

which is made up of brokers interconnected to build an overlay network of brokers. Clients of the system (producers and/or consumers of context data) also take part to the overlay network by being attached to brokers (every client is attached to one broker called the access broker). All these components (brokers and clients) communicate by asynchronous message passing. In order to ease the work of application designers, filters are content-based—i.e. they are constraints expressed on the whole content of notifications [9]. In addition, in order to remain as open and interoperable as possible, we assume a semi-structured data model *à la* XML.

The concept of "scope" is used in the field of DEBS to put the concept of visibility of notifications forward [11]. The visibility of a notification limits the set of consumers that may get access to this notification. We associate the system concept of scale instance (of multiscale distributed systems) with the concept of scope (of DEBS), and we go further by abstracting the customisability of DEBS with multiscoping [15]. Therefore, we complement the API of regular DEBS with the management of multiscoping. Figure 2 illustrates a scope graph for the *administration area* dimension and its projection onto the overlay network of brokers.

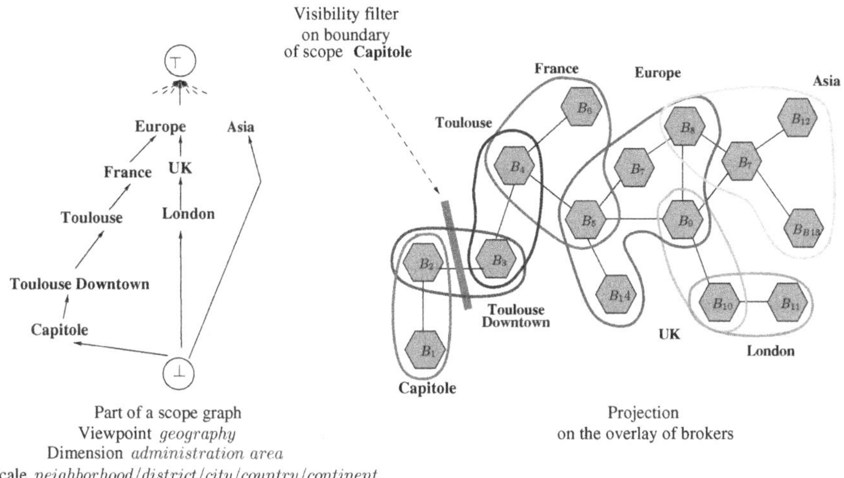

Fig. 2. Projection of a scope graph onto the overlay network of brokers

3.3 Contractualizing Multiscale-, QoC- and Privacy-awareness

The decoupling of context consumers and producers inherent to the IoT calls for new solutions for handling QoC and protecting the privacy of the persons concerned by the context data being collected. We handle this decoupling by using contracts where QoC, privacy and multiscale requirements and/or guarantees are stated. This contract model is implemented as part of the MUCONTEXT framework[2]. We define two kinds of context contract, one for the context producer

[2] https://fusionforge.int-evry.fr/www/mucontext/.

side and one for the context consumer side. On one hand, a context producer contract includes clauses about the production of context data: (1) the privacy requirements, in the form of an XACML policy [21], stating context data they accept to provide to a context manager and how these data may be shared, (2) the QoC guarantees defining the level of QoC, compliant with QoCIM [16], they are committed to provide and (3) possibly multiscale requirements identifying in what scopes the context data should be visible. On the other hand, context consumers, encompassing context-aware applications and context end-users, describe their QoC and multiscale requirements, and privacy guarantees, in the form of ABAC (Attribute-Based Access Control) information [8], in context consumer contracts.

4 Qualitative Validation

We have experimented the MUDEBS and MUCONTEXT frameworks through the implementation of the 4ME (*Mobile, MultiModal, Multiscale Experience*) application as part of the INCOME project[3]. 4ME provides collaborative services to mobile users in major urban cities. A network of MUDEBS brokers is deployed in those cities. End users define their general privacy rules. They have the ability to adjust those rules for each application.

We describe in this section how to implement and deploy 4ME and give some lessons learned in this development.

4.1 Illustrative Scenario

A social welfare association proposes leisure activities to its members (students, employees, etc.) and provide them with the 4ME collaborative context-aware application they can use on their smartphone. 4ME allows members to register/unregister to activities, get in touch with members sharing common activities, be aware of their current location and arrange to meet on the road while heading to the activities'premises in the city.

The *Easy Cooking* activity takes place on the last Friday of each month in the *Montaudran* district in the city of Toulouse, and the *Play Soccer* activity is proposed every Friday in the neighborhood of the *Capitole* place of the *Toulouse Downtown* district. Both activities are scheduled from 12:30pm to 1:30pm. A member can register to several activities, change its activity registrations, but cannot be registered to two activities at the same time slot.

The progress of an instance of the scenario is the following. Julian has registered this week to the soccer activity. It is already 12:15pm when he gets out of a meeting. He launches the 4ME app to determine whether he can meet another participant on his way to the activity's premises. As Julian has previously chosen the soccer activity, his 4ME app is subscribed and receives the notifications of the *Play soccer* scope. Each member enrolled in an activity publishes his/her

[3] http://anr-income.fr.

current position in the appropriate scope. The MUDEBS framework is responsible for managing the spread of each position and its delivery in the form of a notification to all members belonging to the same scope with the appropriate QoC according to the privacy rules. Julian therefore gets notified of the positions of the members of the *Play soccer* group. He notes that no member is nearby and that he is already late and will not be able to arrive on time. Julian then decides to cancel his participation to the *Play soccer* activity. He checks the status of the *Easy Cooking* activity (the activity's premises are nearer) and learns that there are remaining places. He decides to enroll in this activity, and his agenda gets updated. Following this change in his agenda, the 4ME app unsubscribes from the *Play soccer* scope and subscribes to the *Easy Cooking* scope. Likewise, his position is not visible anymore to members of the *Play soccer* group and is henceforth visible to members of the *Easy Cooking* group. Julian is no longer notified of the positions of members of the *Play soccer* group. He is now notified of the positions of members of the *Easy Cooking* group. Julian sees that Corina is on the way and that she is nearby. He therefore decides to contact her in order to go to the activity's premises with her. The *Easy Cooking* teacher, with a simple look to the position of the participants on his tablet, is aware of their future arrival time.

4.2 Scenario Implementation

We show in this section some details of our implementation of the illustrative scenario. We show how filtering mechanisms are installed for this usecase.

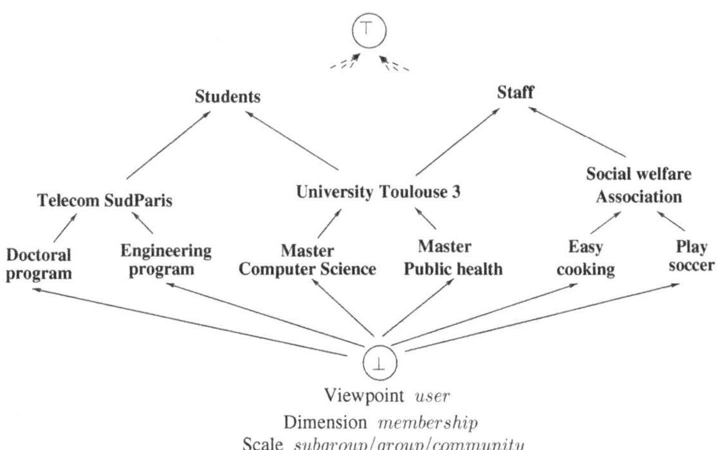

Fig. 3. Scope graph for *Membership* dimension of *User* viewpoint

Deployment and Administration of the MuDEBS Framework. In a first place, the context management administrator defines the different scope graphs corresponding to the multiscale characterization involved in the application. The scenario considers the *geography* and the *user* viewpoints. For each of these viewpoints, the scenario implies only one dimension, *administrative area* dimension and the *membership* dimension respectively.

Figure 2 (see Sect. 3.2) shows a scope graph for the *administrative area* dimension and its projection as an overlay on the network of brokers. Figure 3 shows the scope graph for the *membership* dimension.

In order to reduce the message traffic and to increase the scalability of the platform, the administrator may configure generic visibility filters. In our example, the administrator has chosen to limit the broadcast of messages inside a city. So the location notifications produced in the city of Toulouse are not forwarded to brokers associated by the projection to other cities.

For our experiment, we have deployed a network of 28 brokers. An excerpt of the deployment script is given in Listing 1.

Listing 1. Filtering on scope

```
startbroker --uri $B1_URI #start broker 1
startbroker --uri $B2_URI #start broker 2
#connect two brokers
broker --uri $B1_URI --command connect --neigh $B2_URI
# define scope projection and install visibility filters
broker --uri $B1_URI --command joinscope --dimension
    $ADMIN_AREA --subscope $P0 --superscope $FRANCE --
    mapupfile $MAPUP_FILTER --mapdownfile $MADOWN_FILTER
```

Implementation of the 4ME Application. Two components are installed on each end user mobile phone: a collector that publishes the position of the user with various QoC levels, and the 4ME application. MUDEBS provides an API to write collectors and applications (see Listing 2). To publish positions, the collector (1) advertises and then (2) publishes. To receive positions, 4ME (3) subscribes and then (4) receives position.

Listing 2. MuDEBS API

```
1 advertise(advertise_filter, XACML_policy, SCOPES);
2 push(report);
3 subscribe(subscribe_filter, ABAC_request, SCOPES);
4 pull(report)
```

On each mobile phone, collectors are started by the 4ME application. A first one is started half an hour before the activity with a hundred meters accuracy, a second one is started when the user arrives in the district of the activity premises with a ten meter accuracy. The collector advertises with the privacy policies defined by the end user through an XACML description. The collector defines with an advertisement filter the QoC of the publication. The advertisement may define for each dimension the scope of the publications. For the scenario, the scope is restricted to the membership dimension in order to limit the diffusion to the users who share the same activity, there is no additional restriction on the geography dimension.

The 4ME application is started on each mobile phone. It is configured differently on Corina and Julian's phones and on the teacher tablet. Indeed, Corina and Julian require positions with a good accuracy in order to be able to meet on the road, while the teacher needs to receive the position of all the meeting participants even with a lower accuracy. 4ME sends a subscription with a specific filter indicating the relevant scopes and with the definition of the purpose of the subscription through an ABAC description. An excerpt of Corina's subscription filter is given in Listing 3. Line 3 chooses the observation to receive the users positions, line 5 chooses the QoC criterion corresponding to accuracy (with identifier 4.1), and line 7 defines the required accuracy value.

Before the publication of the positions, MUDEBS must first of all determine whether the ABAC information does match the privacy policy associated with an advertisement in order to authorise or not access to the publication message and determine the required associated QoC level.

Listing 3. Filter with QoC guarantees

```
1 // Constraint on context data including QoC-value constraint
2 if (xpath.evaluate("//observable[uri='#location'] and
3                     //qocindicator[@id='4' and
4                     qoccriterion[@id='[4.1]']/
5                     qocmetricdefinition[@id='4.1']
6                     and qocmetricvalue[@value<='10']]",
7                     doc, XPathConstants.NODESET).length == 0) {
8                           return true;}
```

Figure 4 shows the screen of Corina when Julian enters the district of the activity premises.

4.3 Lessons Learned

4ME has been implemented as an evaluation prototype by the industrial partner of the project. MUDEBS is able to filter publications for different purposes. Scale filtering is achieved easily with MUDEBS through a graph of scopes, either for administration purpose (visibility filter), or for application specific purpose. This does not require any additional development by using the subscription/advertisement scope parameter. MUCONTEXT allows decoupled producers and consumers to express their requirements in terms of QoC and privacy. Subscription filters enable developers to specify various QoC requirements and allow applications to receive information with the appropriate QoC level. Privacy concerns are taken into account as early as possible in the design of applications through the use of the XACML standard. In this experiment, the industrial partner has been able to define easily all the appropriate filters.

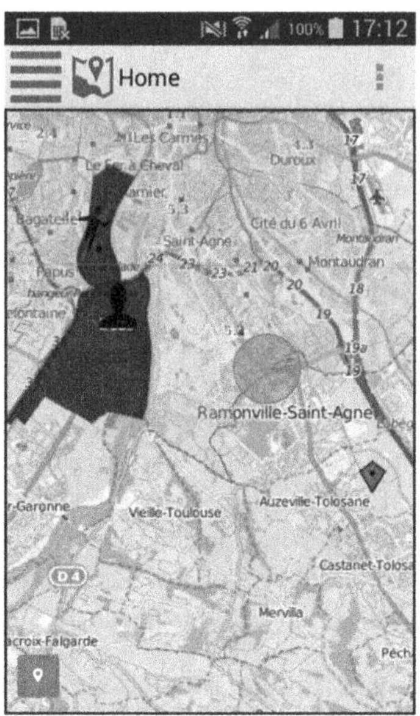

Fig. 4. On the way to a social activity - Screen copy

5 Conclusion

The new challenges brought by the IoT in terms of spontaneous interaction, instability, amount of transient context data, call for innovative solutions that can reason at the relevant scales. We identified three requirements to be fulfilled by the new generation of context managers for enabling their deployment at multiple scales over the IoT. We then described the key features proposed by the INCOME project to address these requirements in an integrated way: (i) An open architecture hosting entities of various power and size encompassing context producers, context processors and context consumers. (ii) Distributed push and pull communication modes well adapted to the spatio-temporal decoupling of these entities while guaranteeing context data delivery thanks to specific advertisement and subscription filters, and thanks to efficient routing algorithms. (iii) An uniform contract modeling approach for specifying QoC criteria, privacy properties and multiscale dimensions that allows generic, configurable and intelligent routing filters. Such filters avoid superfluous context propagations in the brokering overlay network by first checking contract compliance. Facing the big amount of data generated by the IoT, this will preserve performance. We have presented the 4ME application for collaborative social welfare activities and the lessons learned in the development of a real scenario.[4]

[4] http://anr-income.fr.

Acknowledgments. This work is part of the French National Research Agency (ANR) project INCOME (ANR-11-INFR-009, 2012-2015). The authors thank all the members of the project who contributed directly or indirectly to this article.

References

1. Atzori, L., Iera, A., Morabito, G.: The internet of things: a survey. Comput. Netw. **54**(15), 2787–2805 (2010)
2. Baldoni, R., Beraldi, R., Querzoni, L., Virgillito, A.: Efficient publish/subscribe through a self-organizing broker overlay and its application to SIENA. Comput. J. **50**(4), 444–459 (2007)
3. Barazzutti, R., Felber, P., Fetzer, C., Onica, E., Pineau, J.-F., Pasin, M., Rivière, É., Weigert, S.: StreamHub: a massively parallel architecture for high-performance content-based publish/subscribe. In: Proceedings of the ACM DEBS, July 2013
4. Barazzutti, R., Felber, P., Mercier, H., Onica, E., Rivière, E.: Thrifty privacy: Efficient support for privacy-preserving publish/subscribe. In: 6th ACM International Conference on Distributed Event-Based Systems, pp. 225–236. ACM, New York (2012)
5. Bellavista, P., Corradi, A., Fanelli, M., Foschini, L.: A survey of context data distribution for mobile ubiquitous systems. ACM Comput. Surv. **44**(4), 24:1–24:45 (2012)
6. Buchholz, T., Kupper, A., Schiffers, M.: Quality of context information: What it is and why we Need it. In: 10th International Workshop of the HP OpenView University Association (HPOVUA), Geneva, Switzerland, July 2003
7. Chabridon, S., Laborde, R., Desprats, T., Oglaza, A., Marie, P., Machara Marquez, S.: A survey on addressing privacy together with quality of context for context management in the internet of things. Ann. Telecommun. **69**, 1–2 (2014)
8. Covington, M.J., Sastry, M.R.: A contextual attribute-based access control model. In: On the Move to Meaningful Internet Systems, pp. 1996–2006 (2006)
9. Eugster, P.T., Felber, P.A., Guerraoui, R., Kermarrec, A.-M.: The many faces of publish/subscribe. ACM Comput. Surv. **35**(2), 41–88 (2003)
10. Fernando, N., Loke, S.W., Rahayu, W.: Mobile cloud computing: A survey. Future Gener. Comput. Syst. Elsevier **29**(1), 84–106 (2013)
11. Fiege, L., Cilia, M., Mühl, B.C.: Publish-subscribe grows up,: Support for management, visibility control, and heterogeneity. IEEE Internet Comput. **10**(1), 48–55 (2006)
12. Issarny, V., Caporuscio, M., Georgantas, N.: A perspective on the future of middleware-based software engineering. In: Proceedings of the Conference on Future of Software Engineering, Minneapolis, USA, pp. 244–258, May 2007
13. Sherafat Kazemzadeh, R., Jacobsen, H.-A.: Opportunistic multipath forwarding in content-based publish/subscribe overlays. In: Narasimhan, P., Triantafillou, P. (eds.) Middleware 2012. LNCS, vol. 7662, pp. 249–270. Springer, Heidelberg (2012)
14. Langheinrich, M.: Privacy by design-principles of privacy-aware ubiquitous systems. In: Abowd, G.D., Brumitt, B., Shafer, S. (eds.) UbiComp 2001. LNCS, vol. 2201, pp. 273–291. Springer, Heidelberg (2001)
15. Lim, L., Conan, D.: Distributed event-based system with multiscoping for multiscalability. In: Proceedings of the 9th Workshop on Middleware for Next Generation Internet Computing, MW4NG 2014, p. 3: Observation of strains. Infect Dis Ther. 3(1), 35–43.: 1–3: 6. ACM, New York 2014 (2011)

16. Marie, P., Desprats, T., Chabridon, S., Sibilla, M.: QoCIM: A meta-model for quality of context. In: Brézillon, P., Blackburn, P., Dapoigny, R. (eds.) CONTEXT 2013. LNCS, vol. 8175, pp. 302–315. Springer, Heidelberg (2013)
17. Mühl, G., Fiege, L., Pietzuch, P.R.: Distributed Event-Based Systems. Springer, Heidelberg (2006)
18. Rottenberg, S., Leriche, S., Taconet, C., Lecocq, C., Desprats, T., MuSCa: A multi-scale characterization framework for complex distributed systems. In: 4th FedCSIS Workshop on Model Driven Approaches in System Development (MDASD), Warsaw, Poland, September 2014
19. Sheikh, K., Wegdam, M., Van Sinderen, M.: Middleware support for quality of context in pervasive context-aware systems. In: 5th IEEE Conference on Pervasive Computing and Communications - Workshops, March 2007
20. Weixiong, R., Lei, C., Sasu, T.: Toward efficient filter privacy-aware content-based pub/sub systems. IEEE Trans. Knowl. Data Eng. **25**(11), 2644–2657 (2013)
21. eXtensible Access Control Markup Language (XACML) Version 3.0. http://docs.oasis-open.org/xacml/3.0/xacml-3.0-core-spec-os-en.html, January 2013
22. Zhou, Y., Shou, L., Shang, X., Chen, K.: Dissemination of anonymized streaming data. In: 9th ACM International Conference on Distributed Event-Based Systems (DEBS 2015), Oslo, Norway, pp. 104–115, July 2015

Security

SSG: Sensor Security Guard for Android Smartphones

Bodong Li(✉), Yuanyuan Zhang, Chen Lyu, Juanru Li, and Dawu Gu

Lab of Cryptology and Computer Security,
Shanghai Jiao Tong University, Shanghai, China
{uchihal,yyjess,chen_lv,jarod,dwgu}@sjtu.edu.cn
http://loccs.sjtu.edu.cn/wiki/doku.php

Abstract. The smartphone sensors provide extraordinary user experience in various Android apps, e.g. sport apps, gravity sensing games. Recent works have been proposed to launch powerful sensor-based attacks such as location tracing and sound eavesdropping. The use of sensors does not require any permission in Android apps, so these attacks are very difficult to be noticed by the app users. Furthermore, the combination of various kinds of sensors generates numerous types of attacks which are hard to be systematically studied.

To better address the attacks, we have developed a taxonomy on sensor-based attacks from five aspects. In this work, we propose a sensor API hooking and information filtering framework, *Sensor Security Guard* (SSG). Unlike any rough hooking framework, this system provides fine-grained processing for different security levels set by the users, or by default. The sensor data is blocked, forged or processed under different mode strategies and then returned to the apps. In addition, according to the taxonomy, SSG develops fine-grained corresponding countermeasures. We evaluate the usability of SSG on 30 popular apps chosen from Google Market. SSG does not cause any crash of either the Android system or the apps while working. The result indicated that SSG could significantly preserve the users' privacy with acceptable energy lost.

Keywords: Hook · Sensor API · Android · Security

1 Introduction

In recent years, the popularity of the Android smartphones provides extraordinary user experience with the assist of various built-in sensors on the devices that are able to measure various motion, orientation, and ambient conditions. Numerous Android apps are utilizing sensors nowadays, such as games, IMs and sport-related apps. For example, a three-dimensional accelerometer commonly

Major program of Shanghai Science and Technology Commission (Grant No: 15511103002): Research on Mobile Smart Device Application Security Testing and Evaluating.

S. Guo et al. (Eds.): CollaborateCom 2015, LNICST 163, pp. 221–233, 2016.
DOI: 10.1007/978-3-319-28910-6_20

known as a motion sensor, is now deployed in Nike+ running application [2] to record and calculate the running distance.

When users are enjoying these sensor-aided apps, the information collected from the sensors might be revealing the privacy secretly at mean time. A few embedded hardware including GPS sensor, microphone and camera have attracted most interests in privacy protection research, for they provide users' precise physical location, voice or photos, straightforwardly. But the privacy leaked from the integrated sensors such as orientation sensors, magnetometers, accelerometers, etc., are barely noticed nor studied. For example, the information gathered by accelerometer is the smartphone's acceleration at a point in time. It seems irrelevant to user privacy, however, an attacker can derive the possible moving direction on top of it [9]. Even worse, the Android apps do not require any permissions to use such motion sensors (accelerometer and gyroscope).

Such stealthy use of the sensors might cheat most users that the sensors are quite safe. However, it has brought five grave privacy leak issues on identity theft, location tracing, password eavesdropping, etc. For example, with long-term sensor data collecting and analysis, users' identities could be inferred from gait patterns [11,15]. By gathering sensitive information, a malicious app could also disclose personal location tracing [9,10,13], past speeches [6,12] and inputs to keyboard [3,5,14]. Furthermore, an attacker is able to identify a user's mobile device by measuring anomalies of sensors [4,7,8].

To better address the security issues, we first classify the attacks that are forged on top of the sensors into five categories by the compromised resource/privacy. Previous works on Android sensor information abuse are still interested in privacy related information as location, password, user identity, etc. Accordingly, we propose five threat categories, (1) location tracing, (2) sound eavesdropping, (3) keystroke monitoring, (4) device fingerprint distinguishing, and (5) user identity pinpointing. The characteristics of the threats are discrete, and the exploit methods vary from each other. Usually, most attacks exploit more than one sensors, as conspiracy attacks.

In order to design an all-in-one solution to protect privacy from sensor-based attacks, we propose *Sensor Security Guard* (SSG), a sensor API hooking and sensitive information filtering framework for the Android platform. For most malicious apps are the culprits for abusing the sensors, so we put SSG right below the application layer in the Android architecture to monitor all potential malicious behavior from above. SSG provides security modes and black/white list mechanism to grant flexible access permissions to the apps. For highly suspicious apps, the access to the sensors are totally prohibited. For normal apps, we use the SSG filters to roughen the sampling from the sensors and return it to the apps. This mechanism ensures the apps cannot calculate accurate results for deriving any privacy from the sensor data.

The main contributions of this work are as follows:

(1) *Sensor Security Guard.* We propose and implement a sensor API hooking and sensitive information filtering framework SSG for the Android apps. It's easy to deploy into the system and barely cause performance loss.

To the best of our knowledge, SSG is the very first sensor protection system for the Android platform.

(2) *Sensor-based attack classification.* The research on sensor-based attacks is so far discrete. Other than focusing on the sensors' functions, we propose a way to classify the attacks according to the resource/privacy the attackers are obtaining from the sensors. Besides proposing the attack categories, we also design five submodules based on the taxonomy for the SSG to handle the corresponding threats from the malicious apps.

2 Attack Classification

Each attack would involve more than one sensor. With more sensors, the attack is able to collect more types of information to encompass a precise result. But, no matter how the exploited sensors vary in each attacking scenario, an attack is always focusing on one kind of privacy/sensitive information. Hereby, we classify the attacks according to the types of attack targets they aim at.

- *Location tracing.* The adversary makes use of the sensor data to locate the device without the aid of GPS and network. There are several studies on using motion sensor data to detect user locations [9,10,13]. According to [9], accelerometers can be used to locate a device owner within a 200 m radius of the true location.
- *Sound eavesdropping.* Without access to the microphone on the device, the adversary is still able to collect sound sampling from the gyroscope sensor. From previous works [6,12], motion sensors will leak sound information. Michalevsky et al. [12] show that the gyroscopes data is sufficient to identify speaker information and even parse speech using signal processing and machine learning.
- *Keystroke monitoring.* The adversary is able to infer user's inputs with the help of sensors. For example, photometer is a light-sensitive sensor. One of the attacks is to infer the keystrokes by measuring the change of the light when the shadow of the figure projecting on the device/photometer. When we make an input with the soft keyboard of the mobile, a great deal of information is passed to the sensors, not only the motion sensors, but also photometers, etc. Similar attacks are introduced in the research like [3,5,14]. Besides photometers, the motion sensors are also adopted in such attacks with a high success rate.
- *Device-fingerprinting distinguishing.* With the sensor data, the adversary can get a unique device fingerprint. Some works [4,7,8] show that the sensors can also be used to uniquely identify a phone by measuring anomalies in the signals which are the results from manufacturing imperfections. Das et al. [7] not only proposed the method to get a device fingerprint with sensors, but also give the techniques to mitigate such device fingerprinting.
- *User-Identity pinpointing.* The adversary may profile the users using sensor data, even identify the users. According to [11,15], with the motion sensor's data, we can profile the mobile user and reveal the identity.

3 Design of SSG

To avoid the complex mixed sensor attacks in the above scenarios, the naive solution is to block all the sensor data at all time. In this case, a sensor API hooking technique is enough for it intercepts all the information from the sensors. The Android system provides a sensor framework for the developers to access sensor resource. By inserting a hooking module on top of the sensor framework and cut off the sensor data for the apps up-above, API hooking is capable of blocking the potential sensor-based attacks. But, this mechanism is quite rough.

First challenge of designing such type of framework is to filter the suspicious applications accessing the sensor data. For example, a benign sportive app only starts the get-sensor-data process when it's needed, and finishes it immediately when the collecting is over, while a malicious app would keep collecting sensor data as long as it needs. The app filter should be capable to cover the known and unknown attacks of various types. Fortunately, with the attack classification we provided in Sect. 2, the attacks usually fall into one of the categories.

Another challenge is providing forged data to the apps who overclaim the sensor sampling. It's tightly integrated with the previous challenge. When the security framework identifies the property of the app, it determines a proper accuracy for the purpose of the app.

SSG provides a refined security solution to meet the challenges above. It is capable of processing the corresponding sensor data by the types of the attacks and the credibility of the apps. The overall architecture is shown in Fig. 1. It is composed of two modules: (1) a front-end apk file called *SSG Manager*, and (2) a back-end data interception module *Hook Module.*

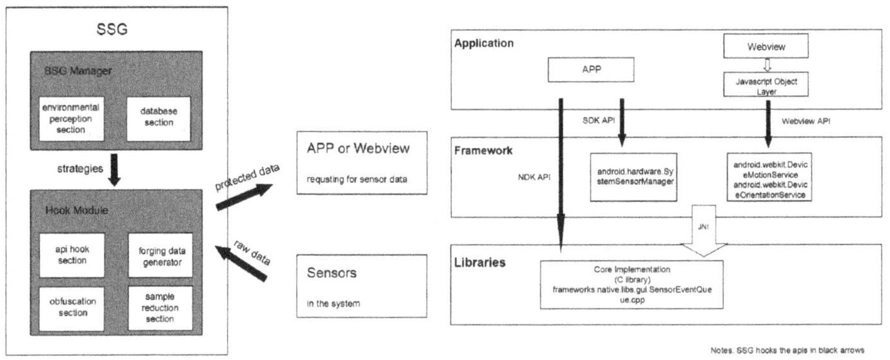

Fig. 1. Architecture of SSG

Fig. 2. Sensor data sources in Android

3.1 SSG Manager

The front-end *SSG Manager* decides how to process the sensor data according to the apps, a.k.a. the data processing strategy provider. *SSG Manager* has two tasks: (1) The app user decides how to apply the strategy. We provide three security modes for the apps, and pass the right to the users who can make the decisions through a graphic user interface. (2) It chooses the protection strategies accordingly by perceiving the status of the smartphone, see Table 1. For instance, when the user inputs password from the keyboard, any access to the pressure and sound related sensor data is forbidden.

Based on the attack classification, we have collected most threat scenarios and provided corresponding countermeasures. It is implemented in the submodule *Environmental Perception Section.*

SSG manager also maintains the black/white list of the application, in the submodule *Database Section.* The database is built on the choice of the user– put an app into black or white list. If the user could not decide by herself at the moment, SSG manager will decide the security strategy based on the environmental information. This database is growing with the time. Maintaining such a database on the cloud-end is efficient to respond to emerging attacks.

3.2 Hook Module

The *Hook Module* works as a sentry. By hooking the sensor APIs, implemented by submodule *API Hook Section*, it passes on the data collection requirements from the apps and WebView, then gathers all the data from the sensors underneath. Besides, *Hook Module* provides the optional functionality of roughening the sampling data from the sensors in three submodules *Forging Data Generator*, *Obfuscation Section* and *Sample Reduction Section.* By doing so, we interrupt the accuracy of the data that is required to recover the privacy/sensitive information.

3.3 SSG Work Flow

A typical processes of SSG is as follows: when the system launches, SSG traverses all the apps that are using the sensors. The user can manually configure the security mode for each app. There are three modes: *Secure Mode*, *Free Mode* and *Normal Mode.*

When the user requires a highly secure operation (such as online payment, private phone call), he can choose the *Secure Mode* for the specific app. Then, all types of sensors' data are forged by *Hook Module* and provided to all the apps that are using sensor data at this moment. For example, during an online payment transaction, *Secure Mode* disables the access to the sensor system-wide, so that the malicious apps, if any, running at the background cannot gather any sensor data.

If the user chooses *Free Mode* when he is using a sensor-related app in a less privacy-sensitive environment. When an app or a WebView asks for any type of sensors data, SSG will provide the raw sampling data without any process. However, in this mode, the user is at high information leak risk on his own choice.

At last, all the other apps will be under *Normal Mode* by default. SSG provides an even fine-grained black/white list for each app. If it's the first time that an app asks for sensor data, SSG will ask the user to put this app into black list, white list or neither. SSG provides raw data for the apps in the white list. On the contrary, the apps in the black list are provided with the forging data from *Hook Module*. If the apps are on neither lists, SSG will provide context-sensitive protection strategies according to the state given in Table 1. By perceiving the mobile context, SSG applies different countermeasures against various threat scenarios. Detailed description can be found in Sect. 5.1.

4 Implementation

At designing stage, SSG consists of two major modules: *Hook Module* and *SSG Manager*. In *Hook Module*, there are four submodules: *API Hook Section*, *Forging Data Generator*, *Obfuscation Section*, and *sample Reduction Section. SSG Manager* is composed of *Environmental Perception Section* and *Database Section.*

We implement SSG in Android 4.2.2 on the device of Nexus 4. The *Hook Module* relies on Cydia Substrate [1], and should be pre-put into the system image or installed with root privilege. For the *SSG Manager*, we develop an app which should be installed as a common one. Next, we will come to the specific introduction of each section's implementation.

4.1 Hook Module

API Hook Section. Figure 2 indicates the residence of SSG in the Android architecture. The Android system provides two ways to access the sensors data on the device: Application and WebView.

Application. Most of local apps will access sensors by using the Android sensor framework, or from NDK using C or C++. An app can get an instance of *android.hardware.Sensor* by the method *getDefaultSensor* of the package *android.hardware.SensorManager*. Then call the method *SensorManager.registerListener*, which will attach *android.hardware.SensorEventListener* to the *Sensor*. At last, we achieve *SensorEventListener*'s callback function *onSensorChanged* to obtain the sensor data. In this way, we can access all kinds of sensors available on the device. *hardware/libhardware/include/hardware/sensor.h* shows the API provided by the NDK. */frameworks/native/libs/gui/ SensorEventQueue.cpp*, *Sensor.cpp* and *SensorManager.cpp* give details of the API methods. We can get a Sensor instance by *SensorManager.getDefaultSensor.* Then we attach *SensorEventQueue* to *Sensor* and obtain the data from method *SensorEventQueue.read.*

WebView. In a WebView, we can access the sensor with Javascript handler: *window.ondevicemotion* and the event object: *event.accelerationGravity*, *event.accelerationIncludingGravity* and *event.rotationRate*. In this way, we can only access limited kinds of sensors.

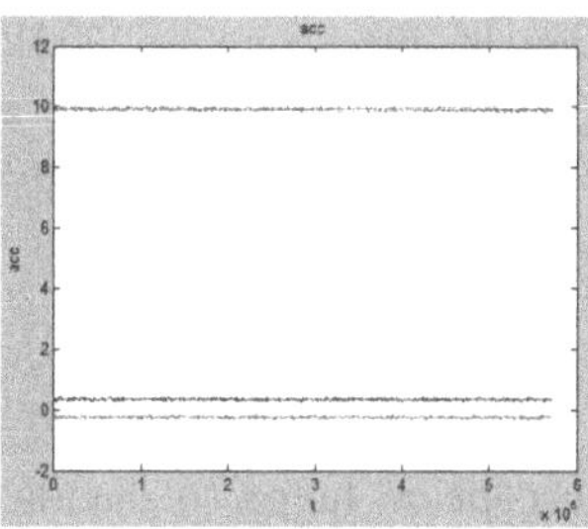

Fig. 3. Raw data of accelerometer while the device is static

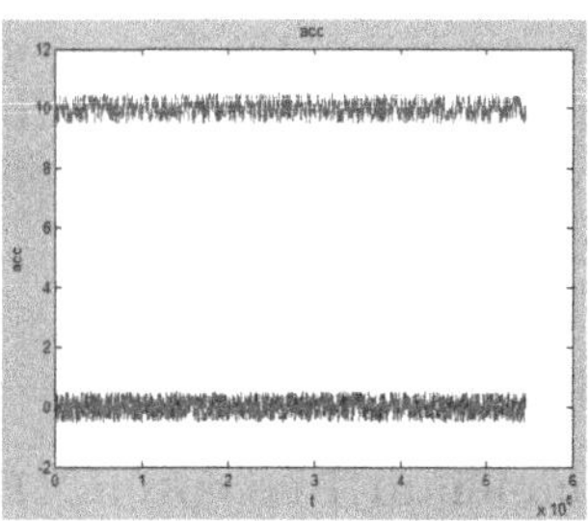

Fig. 4. Forging data of accelerometer

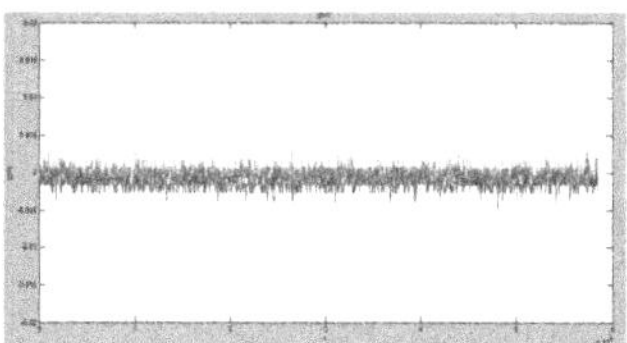

Fig. 5. Raw data of gyroscope while the device is static

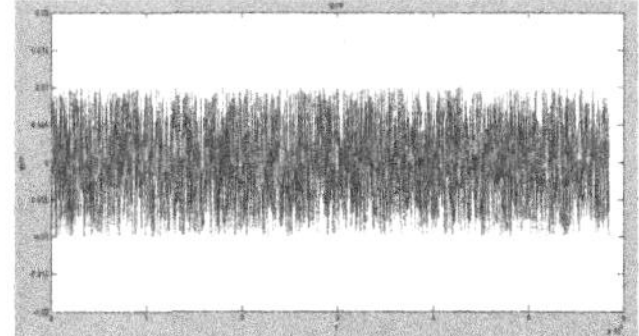

Fig. 6. Forging data of gyroscope

Forging Data Generator. SSG replaces the raw sensor data with forging data under different strategy choices. The forging data would better not contain any information about the specific device, the user or the ambient information at the moment. For various sensors, different rules are formulated. SSG forges the data which makes the device looks static. For example, the forging accelerometer data: axis x, axis y, will be limited in the range [0.5, −0.5], and axis z will be limited in range [9.5, 10.5]. The forging gyroscope data: x,y, and z will be limited in range [0.01, -0.01]. We show the forging data examples in Figs. 3, 4, 5 and 6.

Obfuscation. In order to increase the difficulty of obtaining the fingerprint information and reduce the accuracy rate, SSG chooses Anupam Das Basic Obfuscation [7] to add noise and hide the anomalies. The details of the obfuscation is same as the paper [7]'s Basic Obfuscation. We also compute $a_O = a_M * g_O + o_O$, where g_O and o_O are the obfuscation gain and offset, respectively. We choose a range of [−0.5, 0.5] for the accelerometer offset, [−0.1, 0.1] for the gyroscope offset, and [0.95, 1.05] for the gain.

Sampling Reduction. In order to prevent high frequency signals leak from the gyroscope and accelerometer, SSG limits the data acquisition frequency of the two sensors. Consider that a high frequency may provide the attacker accurate information, SSG decreases the highest sampling rate by adding 0.02 s delay at least. As we know, the highest sampling frequency of gyroscope is 200 Hz in Android, so the least delay will be 0.005 s. After decreasing the sampling rate, we know that the least delay in SSG is 0.025 s, so the highest frequency can only reach 40 Hz.

4.2 SSG Manager

Environmental Perception. Environmental perception helps to decide the security strategy of the apps that are under *Normal Mode* in *SSG Manager*, most security strategies depend on the actual smartphone environment as listed in Table 1. According to the actual environment, SSG takes different measures to protect. The environment perception is important and its responsibility is to perceive the mobile environment, and pass the strategy related with the environment to the *Hook Module.*

Table 1. Environmental factors monitored by SSG

Perceived behavior	Method	Permission
velocity of the device	API: android.location.LocationManager. requestLocationUpdates	ACCESS_COARSE_LOCATION ACCESS_FINE_LOCATION
Call state of the device	API: android.telephony.TelephonyManager. getCallState() Broadcast Receiver Intent.ACTION_NEW_OUTGOING_CALL	READ_PHONE_STATE
Soft keyboard state of the device	Hook: android.inputmethodservice. InputMethodService.showWindow android.inputmethodservice. InputMethodService.doHideWindow	Root
Screen state of the device	API: android.os.PowerManager.isScreenOn(); android.app.KeyguardManager. inKeyguardRestrictedInputMode()	None

Database Section: Black/White List Managing. This section is responsible for the storage of user configuration rules and the current use states of sensors. All data is stored in the *SSG Manager*'s database (SQLite3). When an app requests sensor data for the first time, the SSG will ask the user whether needs to protect the sensor data. At this point, the user has three options, as shown in Fig. 7:

1. Set this request free — Add the app to the white list, provide real data later.
2. Block this request — Add the app to the black list, provide forging data later.
3. Let SSG to help me — Add security strategy to the app, provide different strategies according to the different environment.

In addition to the black and white list, this section will also store the use states of the sensors. Record form is as follows:

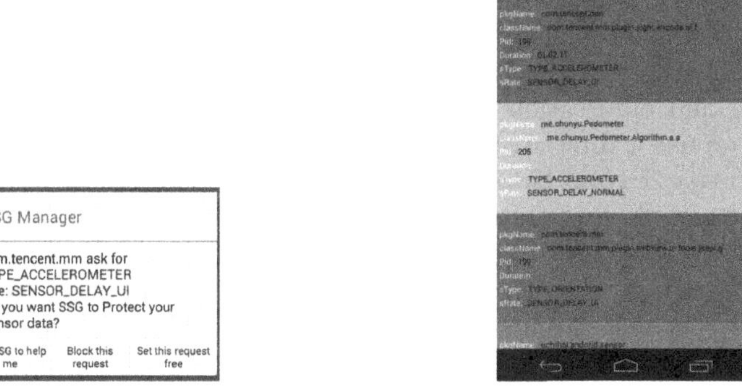

Fig. 7. SSG Manager's toast

Fig. 8. SSG Manager's information interface

pkg name:class name:pid:start time:sensor type:sensor rate

E.g. : *com.tencent.mm:com.tencent.mm.plugin.sight.encode.ui.f:199:1439374 073896:1:2*

These status records will be displayed to the user through the *SSG Manager*'s graphic user interface as shown in Fig. 8.

5 Evaluation

5.1 Security

- **Location Protection.** A benign app only starts the get-sensor-data process when it's needed, and will finish it immediately when the collecting is over. According to our observation, the limited time is suggested to be no more than 20 min [9]. In our experiments, when the device velocity is over 20 km/h, SSG starts to provide forging velocity data periodically.
- **Sound Noising.** When the smarphone is at a call state, SSG provides forging data to all non-system apps. The forging data contains no useful information obviously, and it will not affect any app's function. If the phone is not in a call state, SSG will limit the sensors with a sampling frequency under 160 Hz in default. According to the Nyquist sampling theorem, a sampling frequency f enables us to reconstruct signals at frequencies of upto f/2. So we can say that we can only completely reconstruct signals under 80 Hz from the gyroscope data which will not contain any information about the human speech.
- **Keystroke Shield.** We find that when the soft keyboard is on or the phone is in a waiting-for-unlocking state, no sensor is required by any app in general. SSG will provide forging data in such cases and will not affect any app's function.

- **Device-Fingerprinting Blurring.** According to [4,7,8], attacker can get a unique fingerprinting with the sensor data because that sensor may have anomalies in the signals and different devices may have different features of anomalies. The paper gives two ways to mitigate such device fingerprinting: calibrating and obfuscation. Das et al. have verified its effectiveness in his paper, so we use it directly, not to prove.
- **User-Identity Protection.** Identity attack has the same features as the location attack. So the strategy that limit the time of sensor data collection is equally effective here. In particular, most apps shouldn't use the sensors in the background. Therefore, if the app is pushed to the back ground, SSG will minus the limited time(e.g. default 10 mins). This will make the data collecting work much more difficult.

5.2 Usability

First, we validate that SSG can effectively provide the sensor data to the common apps and verify that it will not cause the apps to crash. We select 30 apps with high download rates in 6 categories from the app markets. Check app's use state of sensors by static analysis. Then manually install, run and verify the apps on Nexus 4. The results in Table 2 show that every app can run normally without any crash.

Table 2. Selected apps in 30 test experiment objects

App	Sensors used
Wechat	*accelerometer,orientation,proximity*
QQ	*accelerometer,gyroscope,light,pressure,proximity,gravity*
BaiduMap	*accelerometer,magnetic-field,orientation,gyroscope, pressure,gravity,linear-acceleration,rotation-vector*
AutonaviMap	*accelerometer,magnetic-field,orientation,gyroscope, pressure*
TencentMap	*accelerometer,gyroscope,light,pressure, gravity*
SogouMap	*accelerometer,magnetic-field,orientation,gyroscope, rotation-vector*
TencentPao	*accelerometer,step-counter*
SSGame	*accelerometer,gyroscope,light,gravity*
Kuwo	*accelerometer,magnetic-field,light*
zhanqiAndroid	*accelerometer,gyroscope,proximity,linear-acceleration*
Dongdong	*orientation,proximity,step-counter*
Runtastic	*accelerometer,magnetic-field,orientation,proximity*
XiaomiHealth	*accelerometer,orientation,step-counter*
Bamboo	*accelerometer,magnetic-field,orientation,light, pressure,proximity,step-counter*
Taobao	*accelerometer,gyroscope,gravity*

5.3 Effectiveness

To evaluate whether the sensor data provided by SSG can hide the user privacy, we consider 3 scenarios: inputting, calling, moving.

For input, we manually type some characters using system soft keyboard. Meanwhile, we collect and record the raw sensor data provided by system and the data provided by SSG respectively. Then we transform the data into images by Matlab as shown in Figs. 9 and 12. For phone call, we manually use the phone to make a call and record the raw sensor data and forging data respectively as before. The result is shown as in Figs. 10 and 13. For device moving, we drive at speeds of over 20 km an hour with the phone in the car and test two cases: In one hand, we test the case when the duration of get-sensor-data process is over the limited time as shown in Fig. 11. In another, we turn on the GPS of the phone and test the case with the duration within the limited range as shown in Fig. 14. SSG has succeeded in smoothening the spiky curves. Therefore, the attackers are not able to extract any useful information.

5.4 Cost

There are two reasons to explain that SSG will not have too much energy cost: For one thing, there is no complex calculations in SSG and the energy cost of SSG

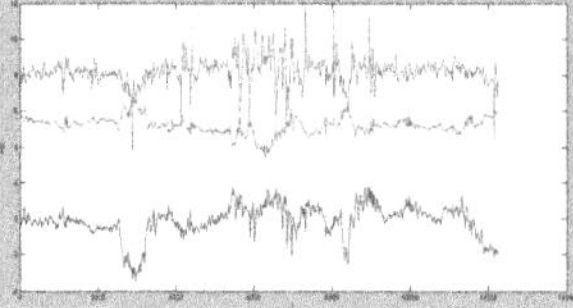

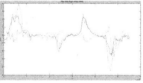

Fig. 9. Raw data of accelerometer on input

Fig. 10. Raw data of gyroscope on call

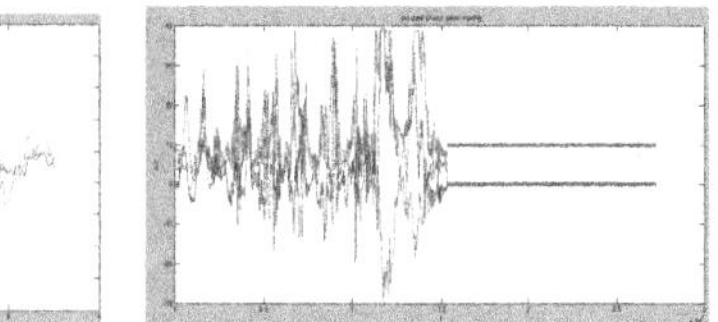

Fig. 11. Forging data of acceleometer when the duration of get-sensor-data process is over the limited time

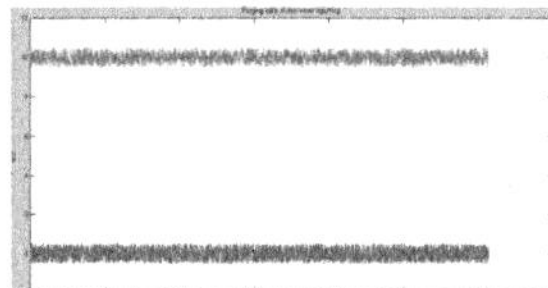

Fig. 12. Forging data of accelerometer on input

Fig. 13. Forging data of gyroscope on call

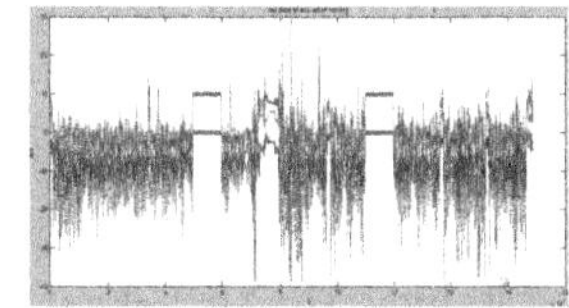

Fig. 14. Forging data of accelerometer while driving at speeds of over 20 kilometers an hour

is almost as much as a common app's. For another, SSG works only when some apps are requesting for sensor data. And some functions of SSG (e.g. Generating forging data) need certain context (e.g. The keyboard is on, the phone is in a calling state and so on). However, the time when sensors are working has a really small proportion of the total time, not to mention the certain context.

To evaluate the energy overhead, we develop a test app to request for sensor (accelerometer) data continuously. Then we install the test app into the Nexus 4 device with the battery in a full state. There is nothing installed and running in the device but SSG and the test app. We consider three scenarios: no sensor access, one sustained load of sensor (accelerometer) access, one sustained load of sensor (accelerometer) access with SSG providing forging data. We compare the time when the battery is running down. During the experiment, We tried to shut down all the power consumption sections of the device,such as screen, WiFi, GPS,MONET and so on. The results show that there is nearly no difference whether the SSG is on. The experimental data can't point account for the actual energy cost by the SSG, however, to a certain extent, it can be explained that SSG will not have a high energy cost.

6 Conclusion

In this paper, we analysised the security problems in the sensors of Android and firstly proposed the concept of sensor protection.Then we proposed SSG(sensor security guarder)–a hook-based sensor protection framework for Android smartphones which can practically, effectively and efficiently protect the sensors from kinds of attacks including location attack, speech attack, keystroke attack, device-fingerprinting attack and user-identity attack. We fully implemented SSG in Android 4.2.2 on Nexus 4. It's not difficult to deploy and compatible with all the 30 test-apps which all have sensor-related functions and high download rates. We have measured the protection effects of SSG in three scenarios: inputting, calling, moving. The results showed that SSG has an obviously protective effect and incurs acceptable energy.

References

1. Cydia substrate. http://www.cydiasubstrate.com/
2. Nike+ running applications. http://www.nike.com/us/en_us/c/running/nikeplus/gps-app
3. Al-Haiqi, A., Ismail, M., Nordin, R.: On the best sensor for keystrokes inference attack on android. Procedia Technology (2013)
4. Bojinov, H., Michalevsky, Y., Nakibly, G., Boneh, D.: Mobile device identification via sensor fingerprinting (2014). arXiv:1408.1416
5. Cai, L., Chen, H.: Touchlogger: inferring keystrokes on touch screen from smartphonemotion. In: 6th Proceedings of HotSec (2011)
6. Currie, D.: Shedding some light on voice authentication (2009)
7. A. Das, N. Borisov, and M. Caesar.Exploring ways to mitigate sensor-based smartphone fingerprinting.arXiv preprint arXiv:1503.01874, 2015

8. Dey, S., Roy, N., Xu, W., Choudhury, R.R., Nelakuditi, S.: Accelprint: imperfections of accelerometers make smartphones trackable. In: 21st Proceedings of the Network and Distributed System Security Symposium (NDSS) (2014)
9. Han, J., Owusu, E., Nguyen, L.T., Perrig, A., Zhang, J.: Accomplice: location inference using accelerometers on smartphones. In: 4th Proceedings of Communication Systems and Networks (COMSNETS) (2012)
10. Lee, S.-W., Mase, K.: Activity and location recognition using wearable sensors. IEEE Pervasive Comput. (2002)
11. Mäntyjärvi, J., Lindholm, M., Vildjiounaite, E., Mäkelä, S.-M., Ailisto. H.: Identifying users of portable devices from gait pattern with accelerometers. In: 30th Proceedings of Acoustics, Speech, and Signal Processing (ICASSP 2005) (2005)
12. Michalevsky, Y., Boneh, D., Nakibly, G.: Gyrophone: recognizing speech from gyroscope signals. In: 23rd Proceedings of USENIX Security Symposium. USENIX Association (2014)
13. Mohan, P., Padmanabhan, V.N., Ramjee, R.: Nericell: rich monitoring of road and traffic conditions using mobilesmartphones. In: 6th Proceedings of ACM Conference on Embedded Network Sensor Systems (2008)
14. Spreitzer, R.: Pin skimming: exploiting the ambient-light sensor in mobile devices. In: 4th Proceedings of ACM Workshop on Security and Privacy in Smartphones & Mobile Devices (2014)
15. Wang, H., Lymberopoulos, D., Liu, J.: Sensor-based user authentication. In: Abdelzaher, T., Pereira, N., Tovar, E. (eds.) EWSN 2015. LNCS, vol. 8965, pp. 168–185. Springer, Heidelberg (2015)

Fast Secure Scalar Product Protocol with (almost) Optimal Efficiency

Youwen Zhu(✉), Zhikuan Wang, Bilal Hassan, Yue Zhang, Jian Wang, and Cheng Qian

College of Computer Science and Technology,
Nanjing University of Aeronautics and Astronautics, Nanjing 210016, China
zhuyw@nuaa.edu.cn

Abstract. Secure scalar product protocol has wide applications for privacy-preservation in collaborative computation. In this paper, we propose a new secure scalar product protocol, which does not employ any public-key encryption and third party. Compared to scalar product computation without privacy-preservation, our proposed scheme introduces no extra communication overheads and little extra computation cost. That is, the new scheme can achieve almost optimal running efficiency, and thus is much applicable to privacy-preservation for large-scale data in collaborative computation. Theoretical analysis and evaluation indicate the security and efficiency of our scheme.

Keywords: Privacy preserving · Collaborative computation · Security · Scalar product protocol

1 Introduction

With the rapid development of computing devices and transmission mediums, distributed collaborative computation has become more and more popular, in which independent individuals/organizations could collaborate with each other to perform various computations on the union of data they hold such that they can achieve a comprehensive computation result.

Nevertheless, this collaborative computation paradigm also introduces several challenges, especially the data security and privacy concerns. For example, a company would like to evaluate the prospect of a project. To obtain an accurate result, the company might need the data of other institutions. Nevertheless, the other institutions may not want to disclose their, because their data might contain valuable business information and sensitive personal information, the disclosure of which will result in big losses or even violate some relevant law and regulation [1,2]. To respond this embarrassing situation, various privacy-preserving approaches have been put forward. Since being introduced to privacy preserving collaborative data mining by Lindell and Pinkas [3], secure multi-party computation (SMC) [4,5] is shown to be a useful instrument for preserving data privacy

S. Guo et al. (Eds.): CollaborateCom 2015, LNICST 163, pp. 234–242, 2016.
DOI: 10.1007/978-3-319-28910-6_21

in collaborative computation. SMC enables two or more participants to implement the collaborative computation on their dataset without revealing the data of a participant to anybody else, including other participants. That is, SMC can currently support collaborative computation and privacy-preservation.

For two n-dimensional vectors $\boldsymbol{x} = (x_1, x_2, \cdots, x_n)$ and $\boldsymbol{y} = (y_1, y_2, \cdots, y_n)$, the scalar product of them is the sum $\sum_{i=1}^{n} x_i y_i$, which is also called dot product. The scalar product computation is a common step in many applications, such as computing Euclidean distance [6], item similarity [7], or trust value [8]. While the vectors $\boldsymbol{x}$ and $\boldsymbol{y}$ are holden by two different parties, it is a challenging problem to compute the scalar product of them without violating the privacy of any data. As one of most significant SMC protocols, scalar product protocol (SPP) aims at completing the challenging privacy preserving scalar product computation, i.e., computing the dot product and currently keeping each input vector private to its owner throughout the computation. SPP has been widely used in various privacy-preserving collaborative computation [6,9–13]. As being a fundamental role, an efficient SPP can boost the practical process of privacy preserving distributed collaborative computation.

Up to now, many schemes [14–20] have been proposed to perform the privacy preserving scalar product computation. Du and Zhan presented two schemes in [14]: dot product protocol employing a commodity server and scalar product protocol using random invertible matrix. Nevertheless, the former one requiring a third party, i.e., the commodity server, which will bring about fully privacy disclosure once the third party colludes with any participant. The latter does not need the third party, but takes $O(n^2)$ computation time which is not suitable for large-scale computation. Through algebraic transformation, another scalar product protocol was introduced in [15]. As yet, the scheme in [15] also needs $O(n^2)$ time. In [17,18], Zhu et al. discussed the relation of secure scalar product protocol and privacy preserving add to multiply protocol, but did not provide efficient solution for them. Based on the additively homomorphic encryption system, three solutions for securely computing dot product of private vectors are given in [16,19,21], respectively. As well known, homomorphic encryption system is quite expensive in real-world applications. Recently, a secret sharing-based scalar product protocol was presented by Shaneck and Kim [20]. Unfortunately, the solution also employs a third party, and while the third party colludes with a participant it will reveal the private data of the other participant. Lately, Zhu et al. [22,23] proposed an efficient approach to securely compute the scalar product while the dimension n is even. The state-of-the-art scheme can achieve $O(n)$ complexity without requiring any third party and public key encryption system.

In this paper, we investigate the fundamental and widely-used SPP. We observe that both computation cost and communication overheads of Zhu et al.'s scheme [22,23] can be dramatically reduced while sacrificing no security. Then, we proposed a new solution to SPP. Comparing with the state-of-the-art SPP scheme (which is also the fastest existing one) in [22,23], our proposed scheme requires less than half cost in computation and communication both, but keeps the same security. Generally, our main contributions in this paper are as follows.

- We present a new approach to preform scalar product computation on two private vectors of independent participants and currently preserve the data privacy of each party. We can dramatically reduce the computation and communication cost by more than 50 % while achieving the same security, compared to the sate-of-the-art one in [22,23].
- We take no extra communication overheads and little extra computation cost, comparing with computing the scalar product without any privacy-preservation. That is, we can attain almost optimal efficiency.
- Through theoretical analysis and evaluation, we indicate the security, correctness, and efficiency of our proposed scheme.

The rest of the paper is organized as follows. Section 2 introduces our system model, and discusses the state-of-the-art scheme. Then, Sect. 3 proposes our new scheme. Section 4 evaluates our proposed scheme through theoretical analysis and simulation experiments. At last, Sect. 5 concludes the paper.

2 System Model and Preliminaries

2.1 System Model

We consider a distributed collaborative computation model consisting of two participants: Alice and Bob. Here, Alice privately holds a vector $\boldsymbol{x} = (x_1, x_2, \cdots, x_n)$ and Bob has the other private vector $\boldsymbol{y} = (y_1, y_2, \cdots, y_n)$. In this paper, we assume n to be an even integer, i.e., we focus on the even-dimension SPP. Without loss of generality, suppose $n = 2 * k$ where k is a positive integer. It should be pointed out that any even-dimension SPP can be transformed into a general SPP, through the hybrid method in [23].

The object of SPP is that Alice attains a private number u and Bob receives a confidential output v while the private vectors are not disclosed to the other participant or anybody else. Besides, the output numbers u and v should satisfy the following Eq. (1).

$$\boldsymbol{x} \cdot \boldsymbol{y} = u + v \tag{1}$$

That is, $u + v = \sum_{i=1}^{n} x_i y_i$.

2.2 Threat Model

Generally speaking, SMC has two assumptions for the participant behaviors: semi-honest model, and malicious model. A semi-honest participant is also called to be honest-but-curious. Under the semi-honest model, each participant is assumed to correctly follow the steps of SMC protocol, but may keep a record about what he legally received to find out as much other participants' confidential information as possible. In contrast, a malicious participant might do anything in the collaborative computation. The work [4] has proved that any SMC protocol in semi-honest model can be transformed into a secure computation protocol in malicious model.

In this paper, we assume the participants to be semi-honest, i.e., they will exactly implement the protocol according to the specified steps. We also suppose the communication channels between the participants are secure and authenticated, which can be realized by conventional cryptography.

2.3 Discussion of the Sate-of-the-ART Scheme

Latley, Zhu et al. [22,23] put forward an efficient SPP (called EDSPP) for even-dimension private vectors, the detailed steps of which are shown in Protocol 1. In Step 1 of the protocol, for each $j = 1$ to k, the participants will totally generate 4 random numbers, complete 12 additions (including subtractions) and 6 multiplications, and send 6 numbers. Step 2 of the protocol contains $2k$ additions. Therefore, EDSPP will generate $4k$ random numbers, require $14k$ additions and $6k$ multiplications, and send $6k$ numbers.

The work [22,23] has shown that EDSPP will disclose $(x_{2j-1} + x_{2j})$ to Bob, and reveal $(y_{2j-1} - y_{2j})$ to Alice. Though the disclosed summation might reveal partial information about private input, the security still can be acceptable in some real-world applications shown in [22,23]. In this paper, we will propose a new even-dimension SPP with much higher efficiency and the same security.

Protocol 1. Even-Dimension Scalar Product Protocol (EDSPP) in [22]

Input: Alice has a private $2k$-dimension vector $\boldsymbol{x} = (x_1, x_2, \cdots, x_{2k})$ and Bob holds another confidential $2k$-dimension vector $\boldsymbol{y} = (y_1, y_2, \cdots, y_{2k})$. ($k \in \mathbb{Z}^+$, $x_i, y_i \in \mathbb{R}, i = 1, 2, \cdots, 2k$)

Output: Alice obtains private output u and Bob securely gets v which meet $u + v = \boldsymbol{x} \cdot \boldsymbol{y} = \sum_{i=1}^{2k} x_i y_i$.

Step 1:

for $j = 1$ to k **do**

  Step 1.1: Alice locally generates two random real numbers a_j and c_j such that $a_j + c_j \neq 0$. Then, she computes $p_j = a_j + c_j$, $x'_{2j-1} = x_{2j-1} + a_j$ and $x'_{2j} = x_{2j} + c_j$, and sends $\{p_j, x'_{2j-1}, x'_{2j}\}$ to Bob by a secure channel. Bob randomly generates two real numbers b_j and d_j which meet $b_j - d_j \neq 0$, and computes $q_j = b_j - d_j$, $y'_{2j-1} = b_j - y_{2j-1}$ and $y'_{2j} = d_j - y_{2j}$. Then, he securely sends $\{q_j, y'_{2j-1}, y'_{2j}\}$ to Alice.

  Step 1.2: Alice locally calculates

$$u_j = y'_{2j-1}(x_{2j-1} + 2a_j) + y'_{2j}(x_{2j} + 2c_j) + q_j(a_j + 2c_j)$$

  and Bob, by himself, computes

$$v_j = x'_{2j-1}(2y_{2j-1} - b_j) + x'_{2j}(2y_{2j} - d_j) + p_j(d_j - 2b_j).$$

end for

Step 2: Alice obtains $u = \sum_{j=1}^{k} u_j$ and Bob gets $v = \sum_{j=1}^{k} v_j$.

---

3 Our New Scheme

In this paper, we focus on securely computing the scalar product of two private even-dimension vectors. For simplicity of presentation, we will introduce our scheme by using two 2-dimensional vectors (i.e., $n = 2$). Our complete solution for any $2k$-dimensional vectors ($n = 2k,\ k > 0$) will be presented in the last part of this section.

While $n = 2$, Alice holds $\boldsymbol{x} = (x_1, x_2)$ and Bob has $\boldsymbol{y} = (y_1, y_2)$. To compute u and v which meets $u + v = \boldsymbol{x} \cdot \boldsymbol{y} = x_1 y_1 + x_2 + y_2$, Alice and Bob can exchange one dimension with each other. Concretely, Alice sends x_2 to Bob, and Bob shares y_1 with Alice, then Alice can set $u = x_1 y_1$ and Bob can attain $v = x_2 y_2$. However, the simple interchange will violate the privacy of x_2 and y_1. Our secure scheme is achieved by improving the above simple approach.

We first transform the problem as follows. Let X be the 1×2 matrix (x_1, x_2), and Y be the 2×1 matrix $(y_1, y_2)^T$. Then, $\boldsymbol{x} \cdot \boldsymbol{y} = XY$.

Further, while M is a 2×2 invertible matrix, we have $\boldsymbol{x} \cdot \boldsymbol{y} = XY = (XM)(M^{-1}Y)$. Let $X' = XM$ and $Y' = M^{-1}Y$. If Alice and Bob shares the first dimension of X' and the second dimension of Y' with each other respectively, they can attain u and v. Through selecting appropriate matrix M, we can also preserve the privacy of both participants.

Here, we set the 2×2 matrix

$$M = \begin{bmatrix} 1 & 1 \\ 1 & 0 \end{bmatrix},$$

and correspondingly

$$M^{-1} = \begin{bmatrix} 0 & 1 \\ 1 & -1 \end{bmatrix}.$$

Hence, $X' = XM = (x_1 + x_2,\ x_1)$ and $Y' = M^{-1}Y = (y_2,\ y_1 - y_2)^T$. Let Alice share $(x_1 + x_2)$ with Bob, and Bob give $(y_1 - y_2)$ to Alice. After that, Alice and Bob computes $u = x_1(y_1 - y_2)$ and $v = (x_1 + x_2)y_2$, respectively. Then, we have $u + v = (XM)(M^{-1}Y) = \boldsymbol{x} \cdot \boldsymbol{y}$. That is, we can complete the scalar product computation with merely disclosing $(x_1 + x_2)$ and $(y_1 - y_2)$, which achieves the same security with the work in [22,23]. More importantly, we require much less computation and communication cost.

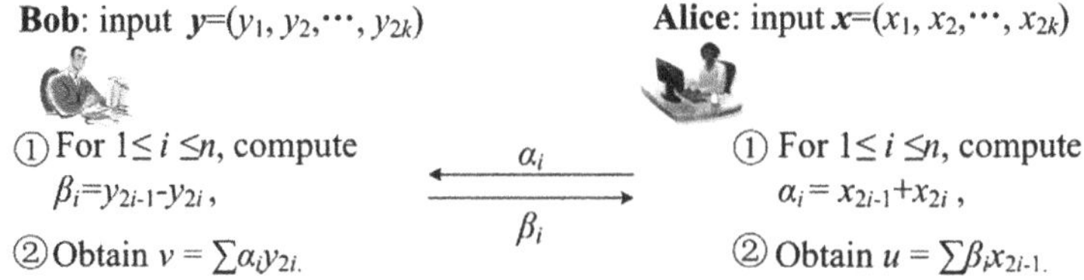

Fig. 1. Our Efficient Even-Dimension Scalar Product Protocol (ESPP)

Our complete scheme, called Efficient Even-Dimension Scalar Product Protocol (ESPP), is formally described in Protocol 2 . To vividly show our method, we also present our scheme in Fig. 1.

Protocol 2. Efficient Even-Dimension Scalar Product Protocol (ESPP)

Input: Alice's private $2k$-dimension vector $\boldsymbol{x} = (x_1, x_2, \cdots, x_{2k})$,
Bob's confidential $2k$-dimension vector $\boldsymbol{y} = (y_1, y_2, \cdots, y_{2k})$.
($k \in \mathbb{Z}^+$, for all $j \in [1, 2k]$, $x_j, y_j \in \mathbb{R}$)
Output: Alice obtains private output $u \in \mathbb{R}$ and Bob securely gets $v \in \mathbb{R}$ which meet $u + v = \boldsymbol{x} \cdot \boldsymbol{y}$, i.e., $u + v = \sum_{j=1}^{2k} x_j y_j$.

Steps:
Alice and Bob set the initial values $u = 0$ and $v = 0$.
for $i = 1$ to k **do**
    Alice computes $\alpha_i = x_{2i-1} + x_{2i}$, and Bob simultaneously sets $\beta_i = y_{2i-1} - y_{2i}$.
    Then, Alice and Bob send α_i and β_i to each other.
    At last, Alice locally calculates $u = u + x_{2i-1}\beta_i$, and Bob computes $v = v + \alpha_i y_{2i}$.
end for

---

4 Evaluation

4.1 Correctness

We consider the correctness of our scheme as follows.

For each $i = 1$ to k in Protocol 2 , we always have

$$\begin{aligned} x_{2i-1}\beta_i + \alpha_i y_{2i} &= x_{2i-1}(y_{2i-1} - y_{2i}) + (x_{2i-1} + x_{2i})y_{2i} \\ &= x_{2i-1}y_{2i-1} + x_{2i}y_{2i}. \end{aligned}$$

Thus, $u + v = \sum_{i=1}^{k}(x_{2i-1}y_{2i-1} + x_{2i}y_{2i})$ in our Protocol 2 .

That is,

$$u + v = \sum_{j=1}^{2k} x_j y_j = \boldsymbol{x} \cdot \boldsymbol{y},$$

which completes our proof.

4.2 Security

It is easy to see that our scheme discloses nothing but $(x_{2i-1} + x_{2i})$ and $(y_{2i-1} - y_{2i})$. Thus, our scheme can achieve the same security with the existing work in [22,23]. The security has been analyzed by [22,23] in detail, and therefore we do not provide more detail about the security here.

Table 1. Comparison of cost

	EDSPP [22,23]	Non Privacy-preservation	Our Scheme
Addition	$14k$	$2k$	$4k$
Multiplication	$6k$	$2k$	$2k$
Communication	$6k\mathcal{B}$	$2k\mathcal{B}$	$2k\mathcal{B}$

4.3 Efficiency

Our protocol requires 4 additions and 2 multiplications, and sends 2 numbers. Thus, we need $4k$ additions and $2k$ multiplications, and sends $2k$ numbers in total.

Assume the bit length of each number is $\mathcal{B}$. In Table 1, we compare the cost of EDSPP in [22,23], our scheme, and the scalar product computation without privacy-preservation. It shows that our scheme is much more efficient than EDSPP [22,23], in both computation cost and communication overheads. Comparing with scalar product computation without privacy-preservation, our scheme introduces no extra cost apart from a few additions. Therefore, our scheme can achieve almost optimal efficiency for privacy-preserving distributed collaborative scalar product computation.

5 Conclusion

In this paper, we proposed a new even-dimension scalar product protocol, ESPP. Our proposed scheme can attain the same security with the state-of-the-art solution, while dramatically reducing the computation cost and communication overheads. Additionally, our scheme introduces no extra cost apart from a few additions, comparing with scalar product computation without privacy-preservation. It indicates that our scheme can achieve almost optimal efficiency for privacy-preserving distributed collaborative scalar product computation.

For the future work, we will devote to the formally secure SPP with high efficiency.

Acknowledgement. This work is partly supported by the Fundamental Research Funds for the Central Universities (No. NZ2015108), the Natural Science Foundation of Jiangsu Province of China (No. BK20150760), the China Postdoctoral Science Foundation funded project (No. 2015M571752), and the Jiangsu Planned Projects for Postdoctoral Research Funds (No. 1402033C). We want to thank Prof. Wei Yang for his helpful discussion with us.

References

1. HIPAA: The health insurance portability and accountability act of 1996, October 1998. http://www.ocius.biz/hipaa.html
2. Cios, K.J., Moore, G.W.: Uniqueness of medical data mining. Artif. Intell. Med. **26**(1–2), 1–24 (2002)

3. Lindell, Y., Pinkas, B.: Privacy preserving data mining. J. Cryptology **15**(3), 177–206 (2002)
4. Goldreich, O.: Foundations of Cryptography: Volume II, Basic Applications. Cambridge University Press, Cambridge (2004)
5. Lindell, Y., Pinkas, B.: Secure multiparty computation for privacy-preserving data mining. J. Priv. Confidentiality **1**(1), 59–98 (2009)
6. Xiao, M., Huang, L., Xu, H., Wang, Y., Pei, Z.: Privacy preserving hop-distance computation in wireless sensor networks. Chin. J. Electron. **19**(1), 191–194 (2010)
7. Agrawal, R., Imieliski, T., Swami, T.: Mining association rules between sets of items in large databases. In: Proceedings of the ACM SIGMOD International Conference on Management of Data, pp. 207–216 (1993)
8. Yuan, X., Huang, L., Yang, W.: Privacy preserving computation of trust-value in wireless sensor networks. In: IEEE 3rd International Conference on Communication Software and Networks, pp. 573–576 (2011)
9. Murugesan, M., Jiang, W., Clifton, C., Si, L., Vaidya, J.: Efficient privacy-preserving similar document detection. VLDB J. **19**(4), 457–475 (2010)
10. Chen, T., Zhong, S.: Privacy-preserving back-propagation neural network learning. IEEE Trans. Neural Netw. **20**(10), 1554–1564 (2009)
11. Bansal, A., Chen, T., Zhong, S.: Privacy preserving back-propagation neural network learning over arbitrarily partitioned data. Neural Comput. Appl. **20**(1), 143–150 (2011)
12. Zhu, Y., Huang, L., Dong, L., Yang, W.: Privacy-preserving text information hiding detecting algorithm. J. Electron. Inf. Technol. **33**(2), 278–283 (2011)
13. Smaragdis, P., Shashanka, M.: A framework for secure speech recognition. IEEE Trans. Audio Speech Lang. Process. **15**(4), 1404–1413 (2007)
14. Du, W., Zhan, Z.: A practical approach to solve secure multi-party computation problems. In: 2002 Workshop on New Security Paradigms, pp. 127–135. ACM, New York (2002)
15. Vaidya, J., Clifton, C.: Privacy preserving association rule mining in vertically partitioned data. In: 8th ACM SIGKDD International Conference on Knowledge Discovery and Data Mining, pp. 639–644. ACM, New York (2002)
16. Goethals, B., Laur, S., Lipmaa, H., Mielikainen, T.: On private scalar product computation for privacy-preserving data mining. In: 7th Annual International Conference on Information Security and Cryptology, pp. 104–120 (2004)
17. Zhu, Y., Huang, L., Yang, W.: Relation of PPAtMP and scalar product protocol and their applications. In: IEEE symposium on Computers and Communications, pp. 184–189 (2010)
18. Zhu, Y., Huang, L., Yang, W., Li, D., Luo, Y., Dong, F.: Three new approaches to privacy-preserving add to multiply protocol and its application. In: Second International Workshop on Knowledge Discovery and Data Mining, pp. 554–558 (2009)
19. Amirbekyan, A., Estivill-Castro, V.: A new efficient privacy-preserving scalar product protocol. In: Sixth Australasian Conference on Data Mining and Analytics, vol. 70, pp. 209–214. Australian Computer Society (2007)
20. Shaneck, M., Kim, Y.: Efficient cryptographic primitives for private data mining. In: 2010 43rd Hawaii International Conference on System Sciences, pp. 1–9. IEEE Computer Society (2010)
21. Dong, C., Chen, L.: A fast secure dot product protocol with application to privacy preserving association rule mining. In: Tseng, V.S., Ho, T.B., Zhou, Z.-H., Chen, A.L.P., Kao, H.-Y. (eds.) PAKDD 2014, Part I. LNCS, vol. 8443, pp. 606–617. Springer, Heidelberg (2014)

22. Zhu, Y., Takagi, T., Huang, L.: Efficient secure primitive for privacy preserving distributed computations. In: Hanaoka, G., Yamauchi, T. (eds.) IWSEC 2012. LNCS, vol. 7631, pp. 233–243. Springer, Heidelberg (2012)
23. Zhu, Y., Takagi, T.: Efficient scalar product protocol and its privacy-preserving application. Int. J. Electron. Secur. Digit. Forensics **7**(1), 1–19 (2015)

Efficient Secure Authenticated Key Exchange Without NAXOS' Approach Based on Decision Linear Problem

Mojahed Ismail Mohamed[1,2(✉)], Xiaofen Wang[1], and Xiaosong Zhang[1]

[1] School of Computer Science and Engineering, University of Electronic Science and Technology of China, Chengdu, China
mmmmoj@hotmail.com, wangxuedou@sina.com, johnsonzxs@uestc.edu.cn
[2] Department of Electronic Engineering, Karary University, Omdurman, Sudan

Abstract. LaMacchia, Lauter and Mityagin [4] presents significant security model for Authenticated Key Exchange (AKE) protocols (eCK) which it is extending for Canetti-Krawczyk model (CK). They contrived a protocol secured in that model called NAXOS. eCK model allows adversary to obtain ephemeral secret information corresponding to the test session which complexify the security proof. To vanquish this NAXOS combines an ephemeral private key with a static private key to generate an ephemeral public in the form $X = g^{H(x,a)}$. As a consequence, the discrete logarithm of an ephemeral public key is hidden via an additional random oracle. In this paper we present AKE protocol secure in eCK model under Decision Linear assumption(DLIN) without using NAXOS trick with a fastened reduction, which reduce the risk of leaking the static private key, that because of the derivation of the ephemeral public key is independent from the static private key. This is in contrast to protocols that use the NAXOS' approach. And minimize the use of the random oracle, by applying it only to the session key derivation. Moreover, each ephemeral and static key has its particular generator which gives tight security for the protocol.

Keywords: eCK model · AKE · Decision Linear assumption · NAXOS' approach

1 Introduction

An Authenticated Key Exchange protocol (AKE) allows two parties to end up with a shared secret key in secure and authenticated manner. The authentication problem deals with restraining adversary that actively controls the communication links used by legitimated parties. They may modify and delete messages in transit, and even inject false one or may controls the delays of messages.

In 1993, Bellare and Rogaway [1] provided the first formal treatment of entity authentication and authenticated key distribution appropriate to the distributed environment. In 1998, Bellare,Canetti, Mihir and Krawczyk [2] provided model

S. Guo et al. (Eds.): CollaborateCom 2015, LNICST 163, pp. 243–256, 2016.
DOI: 10.1007/978-3-319-28910-6_22

for studying session-oriented security protocols. They also introduce the "authenticator" techniques that allow for greatly simplifying the analysis of protocols. In addition, they proposed a definition of security of KE protocols rooted in the simulatability approach used to define security of multiparty computation. In 2002 Canetti and Krawczyk [3] presented their security model which had extended by LaMacchia, Lauter and Mityagin [4] model and proposed NAXOS protocol which is secure under their model. That model capture attacks resulting from leakage of ephemeral and long-term secret keys, defined by an experiment in which the adversary is given many corruption power for various key exchange sessions and most solve a challenge on a test session. This model doesn't give an adversary capability to trivially break an AKE protocol.

To acquire eCK security, NAXOS need that the ephemeral public key X is computed from an exponent result from hashing an ephemeral private key x and the static private key a, more precisely $X = g^{H(x,a)}$ instead of $X = g^x$. In this paper generating ephemeral public key as $X = g^{H(x,a)}$ is called NAXOS's approach. In NAXOS's approach no one is capable to query the discrete logarithm of an ephemeral public key X without the pair (x, a); thus the discrete logarithm of X is hidden via an additional random oracle. Using NAXOS' approach many protocols [5–8] were claimed secure in the eCK model under the random oracle assumption. In the standard model, eCK-secure protocols were claimed secure in the eCK model as Okamoto [9]; they uses pseudo-random functions instead of hash functions.

Motivating Problem. (1) Design AKE-secure protocol without NAXOS trick to achieve two goals: (i) To reduce the risk of leaking the static private key, since the derivation of the ephemeral public key is independent from the static private key. This is in contrast to protocols that use the NAXOS' approach. (ii) Minimize the use of the random oracle, by applying it only to the session key derivation. Kim, Minkyu, Atsushi Fujioka, and Berkant Ustaolu [10] proposed two strongly secure authenticated key exchange without NAXOS approach, one of their protocol supposed to be secure under the GDH assumption and the other under the CDH assumption in random oracle model. (2) Design AKE-secure protocol secure under Decision Linear Assumption. Boneh, Boyen, and Shacham [11] introduced a decisional assumption, called Linear, intended to take the place of DDH in groups - in particular, bilinear groups [12] - where DDH is easy. For this setting, the Linear problem has desirable properties, as Boneh, Boyen and Shacham show: it is hard if DDH is hard, but, at least in generic groups [13], remains hard even if DDH is easy.

Contributions. We presents a concrete and practical AKE protocol that is eCK secure under Decisional linear assumption in the random oracle model. Our protocol does not rely on any NAXOS trick that yields a more efficient solution when it is implemented with secure device. We give tight proofs reducing eCK security of our protocol to break the used cryptographic primitives under random oracle.

In our protocol the ephemeral public key is containing of each peers generator, which result in two different discrete logarithm problem with two different generators, which increase the complexity.

In derivation of session key, each party will compute shared secret from ephemeral keys and static keys.

Organization. Section 2 reviews security definitions and state the hard problem. Section 3 gives brief for the eCK model. Section 4 proposes AKE-secure protocol with its security results. Section 5 compares our protocol with other related AKE protocols and shows its efficiency. And finally we draw the conclusion in Sect. 6.

2 Preliminaries

In this section we review security definitions we will use to construct our protocol.

2.1 The Decision Linear Diffie-Hellman Assumption

Let G be a cyclic group of prime order p and along with arbitrary generators u, v and h where

$$g, u, v, h \in G :< g >= G; u = g^{\alpha}; v = g^{\beta}; g^{\delta} = h; \alpha, \beta, \delta \in \mathbb{Z}_p^* \tag{1}$$

consider the following problem:

Decision Linear Problem in G [11]**.** Given $u, v, h, u^a, v^b, h^c \in G$ as input, output yes if $a + b = c$ and no otherwise.

One can easily show that an algorithm for solving Decision Linear in G gives an algorithm for solving DDH in G. The converse is believed to be false. That is, it is believed that Decision Linear is a hard problem even in bilinear groups where DDH is easy. More precisely, we define the advantage of an algorithm $\mathcal{A}$ in deciding the Decision Linear problem in G as

$$\begin{aligned} AdvLinear_{\mathcal{A}} \overset{\text{def}}{=\!=} \Big| &\Pr\left[\mathcal{A}(u, v, h, u^a, v^b, h^{a+b}) = yes : u, v, h \leftarrow_{\$} G; a, b \leftarrow_{\$} \mathbb{Z}_p\right] \\ &- \Pr\left[\mathcal{A}(u, v, h, u^a, v^b, \gamma) = yes : u, v, \gamma \leftarrow_{\$} G; a, b \leftarrow_{\$} \mathbb{Z}_p\right]\Big| \end{aligned} \tag{2}$$

The probability is over the uniform random choice of the parameters to $\mathcal{A}$, and over the coin tosses of $\mathcal{A}$. We say that an algorithm $\mathcal{A}(t, \epsilon)$-decides Decision Linear in G if $\mathcal{A}$ runs in time at most t, and $AdvLinear_{\mathcal{A}}$ is at least ϵ.

Definition 2.1. *We say that the (t, ϵ)-Decision Linear Assumption (DLIN) holds in G if no t-time algorithm has advantage at least ϵ in solving the Decision Linear problem in G.*

2.2 Linear Diffie-Hellman

Let $dl_u, dl_v : G \to \mathbb{Z}_p$ be the discrete logarithm (DL) functions which takes an input $X, Y \in G$ and returns $x, y \to \mathbb{Z}_p$ such that $X = v^x$ and $Y = u^y$. Define the Linear Diffie-Hellman functions $ldh : G^2 \to G$ as $ldh(A, B) = A^{dl_v(X)}B^{dl_u(Y)}$,$ldh(X, Y) = X^{dl_v(A)}Y^{dl_u(B)}$, and Decisional Linear predicate $DLIN_{u,v,h} : G^3 \to \{0, 1\}$ as a function which takes an input $(A, B, Z) \in G^3$ and returns 1 if

$$Z = A^{dl_v(X)}B^{dl_u(Y)} = h^{dl_v(X)+dl_u(Y)} \tag{3}$$

or in input $(X, Y, Z) \in G^3$ and returns 1 if

$$Z = X^{dl_v(A)}Y^{dl_u(B)} = h^{dl_v(X)+dl_u(Y)} \tag{4}$$

3 Security Model

In this section, eCK model is outlined [17]. In eCK model there are n different parties $P = P_1, \ldots, P_n$ running the KE protocol Π. Each party is possesses a pair of long-term static (private/public) keys together with a corresponding certificate issued by certifying authority. The protocol Π is executed between two parties, say $\mathcal{A}$ and $\mathcal{B}$, whose static public key are A and B respectively. These two parties exchange their ephemeral public keys X and Y, and obtain the same final session key.

Sessions. A party is activated by an outside call or an incoming message to execute the protocol Π. Each program of executing Π is modeled as an interactive probabilistic polynomial-time machine. We call a session an invocation of an instance of Π within a party. We assume that $\mathcal{A}$ is the session initiator and $\mathcal{B}$ is the session responder. Then $\mathcal{A}$ is activated by the outside call $(\mathcal{A}, \mathcal{B})$ or the incoming message $(\mathcal{A}, \mathcal{B}, Y)$. When activated by $(\mathcal{A}, \mathcal{B})$, $\mathcal{A}$ prepares an ephemeral public key X and stores a separate session state which includes all session-specific ephemeral information. The session identifier (denoted by sid) in $\mathcal{A}$ is initialized with $(\mathcal{A}, \mathcal{B}, X, -, \mathcal{I})$. After $\mathcal{A}$ is activated by $(\mathcal{A}, \mathcal{B}, Y)$ (receiving an appropriate message from responder), the session identifier is updated to $(\mathcal{A}, \mathcal{B}, X, Y, \mathcal{I})$. Similarly, the responder $\mathcal{B}$ is activated by the incoming message $(\mathcal{B}, \mathcal{A}, X)$. When activated, $\mathcal{B}$ also prepares an ephemeral public key Y and stores a separate session state, and the corresponding session identifier is $(\mathcal{B}, \mathcal{A}, Y, X, \mathcal{R})$. A $(\mathcal{B}, \mathcal{A}, Y, X, \mathcal{R})$ (if it exists) is said to be matching to the session $(\mathcal{A}, \mathcal{B}, X, Y, \mathcal{I})$ or $(\mathcal{A}, \mathcal{B}, X, -, \mathcal{I})$. For a session $(\mathcal{A}, \mathcal{B}, *, *, role)$, $\mathcal{A}$ is called the owner of the session while $\mathcal{B}$ is called the peer of the session. We say sid is complete if there is no symbol in sid.

Adversaries. The adversary $\mathcal{M}$ is also modeled as a probabilistic polynomial-time machine. $\mathcal{M}$ controls the whole communications between parties by sending arbitrary messages to the intended party on behalf of another party and receiving the outgoing message from the communicating parties. In order to capture the possible attacks, $\mathcal{M}$ is allowed to make the following queries as well as H queries of (hash) random oracles.

EstablishParty($\mathcal{U}$): $\mathcal{M}$ Registers an arbitrary party $\mathcal{U}$ not in P, whose static public key is on $\mathcal{M}$s own choice. We call this kind of new registered parties dishonest ($\mathcal{M}$ totally controls the dishonest parties), while the parties in P are honest. We require that when $\mathcal{M}$ makes such query, the certifying authority should verify that the submitted static public key is in the appropriate group (to avoid small subgroup attack) and the proof that $\mathcal{M}$ knows the corresponding static private key.

Send($\mathcal{A}$,m): $\mathcal{M}$ sends the message m to party $\mathcal{A}$. Upon invocation $\mathcal{A}$ by m, the adversary obtains the outgoing message of $\mathcal{A}$.

EphemeralKeyReveal(sid): $\mathcal{M}$ obtains the ephemeral private key stored in the session state of session *sid*.

StaticKeyReveal(P_i): $\mathcal{M}$ learns the long-term static private key of an honest party P_i. In this case, P_i no longer seems honest.

SessionKeyReveal(sid): $\mathcal{M}$ obtains the session key for the session *sid* if the session has accepted, otherwise $\mathcal{M}$ obtains nothing.

Experiment. $\mathcal{M}$ is given the set P of honest parties, and makes whichever queries he wants. The final aim of the adversary is to distinguish a session key from a random string of the same length. Thus $\mathcal{M}$ selects a complete and fresh session *sid*, and makes a special query *Test(sid)*. This query can be queried only once, and the session *sid* is called test session. On this query, a coin b is flipped, if $b = 1$ $\mathcal{M}$ is given the real session key held by *sid*, otherwise $\mathcal{M}$ is given a random key drawn from the key space at random. $\mathcal{M}$ wins the experiment if he guesses the correct value of b. Of course, $\mathcal{M}$ can continue to make the above queries after the *Test* query; however the test session should remain fresh throughout the whole experiment.

Definition 3.1 (Fresh session). *Let sid be a complete session, owned by honest $\mathcal{A}$ with honest peer $\mathcal{B}$. If the matching session of sid exists, we let $\overline{sid}$ denote the session identifier of its matching session. sid is said to be fresh if none of the following events occurs:*

1. *$\mathcal{M}$ makes a **SessionKeyReveal(sid)** query or a **SessionKeyReveal($\overline{sid}$)** query if $\overline{sid}$ exists.*
2. *If $\overline{sid}$ exists, $\mathcal{M}$ makes either of the following queries:*
   (a) *Both **StaticKeyReveal($\mathcal{A}$)** and **EphemeralKeyReveal(sid)**, or*
   (b) *Both **StaticKeyReveal($\mathcal{B}$)** and **EphemeralKeyReveal($\overline{sid}$)**.*
3. *If $\overline{sid}$ does not exist, $\mathcal{M}$ makes either of the following queries:*

(a) Both ***StaticKeyReveal***$(\mathcal{A})$ *and* ***EphemeralKeyReveal***(sid), *or*
(b) ***StaticKeyReveal***$(\mathcal{B})$.

The eCK security notion can be described now.

Definition 3.2 (eCK security). *The advantage of the adversary $\mathcal{M}$ in the above experiment with respect to the protocol Π is defined as (b is the guessed value of coin by $\mathcal{M}$):*

$$Adv_{\Pi}^{AKE}(\mathcal{M}) = |2\Pr[b' = b] - 1| \tag{5}$$

The protocol Π is said to be secure if the following conditions hold:

1. *If two honest parties complete matching sessions, then they will both compute the same session key, except with a negligible probability.*
2. *The advantage of the adversary $\mathcal{M}$ is negligible.*

4 Protocol

Parameters. Let k to be defined as security parameter and G be as a cyclic group and g be its generator with order a k-bit prime p. Let users public key is a triple of generators $u, v, h \in G$. Parties $\mathcal{A}'s$,$\mathcal{B}'s$ static private key is $a, b \in \mathbb{Z}_p^*$,respectvly. Where $\mathcal{A}'s$ public key is $A = u^a$,$\mathcal{B}'s$ public key is $B = v^b$. Let $H : \{0,1\}^* \rightarrow \{0,1\}^k$ to be a hash function,for security proof will be modeled as a random oracle.

4.1 Protocol Description

As follow description, $\mathcal{A}$ is the session initiator and $\mathcal{B}$ is the session responder.

1. $\mathcal{A}$ chooses randomly $x \in_R \mathbb{Z}_p^*$ as an ephemeral private key, computing $X = v^x$ as the ephemeral public key and then sends ($\mathcal{B}$,$\mathcal{A}$,X) to $\mathcal{B}$.
2. When $\mathcal{B}$ receiving ($\mathcal{B}$,$\mathcal{A}$,X), will verifies that $X \in G$. if so, will chooses randomly $y \in_R \mathbb{Z}_p^*$ as an ephemeral private key, computing $Y = u^y$ as the ephemeral public key and then sends ($\mathcal{A}$,$\mathcal{B}$,X,Y) to $\mathcal{A}$. Then $\mathcal{B}$ computing the shared secret $Z = X^b A^y$, the session $SK = H(Z, X, Y, \mathcal{A}, \mathcal{B})$ and competes the session.
3. When $\mathcal{A}$ receiving ($\mathcal{A}$,$\mathcal{B}$,X,Y), will checks whether he owns a session id with identifier *sid* ($\mathcal{A}$,$\mathcal{B}$,X,$\times$). if so, he verifies that $Y \in G$. if so, he computing the shared secret $Z = Y^a B^x$, the session $SK = H(Z, X, Y, \mathcal{A}, \mathcal{B})$ and competes the session.

The two parties will compute the shared secret

$$\mathcal{B} : Z = X^b A^y = v^{x^b} u^{a^y} = h^{xb+ya} \tag{6}$$

$$\mathcal{A} : Z = Y^a B^x = u^{y^a} v^{b^x} = h^{xb+ya} \tag{7}$$

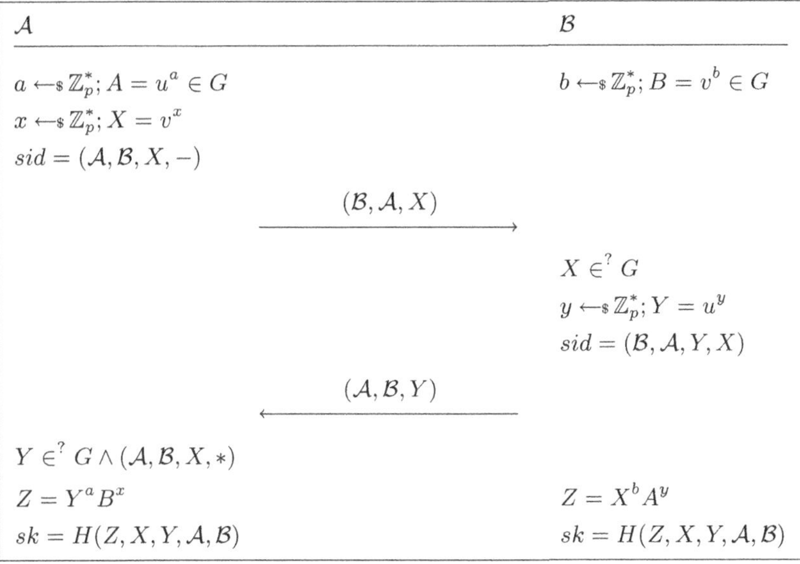

Fig. 1. Our Protocol

4.2 Protocol Security

Theorem 4.1. *If the DLIN assumption holds in G and H is modeled as a random oracle, the Protocol Π is eCK-secure.*

Proof. Let $\mathcal{M}$ be PPTadversary against protocol Π, then we assume $Adv_{\Pi}^{AKE}(\mathcal{M})$ is non-negligible. While H is modeled as a random oracle, there are only three ways for the adversary $\mathcal{M}$ to distinguish a session key - from a random string - of the test session.

- E1. Guessing attack: $\mathcal{M}$ will guesses the session key correctly.
- E2. Key replication attack: $\mathcal{M}$ success in creating a session with the same key to the test session and not matching to the test session.
- E3. Forging attack: $\mathcal{M}$ success in computing the value Z, and then makes queries to H with corresponding tuples $(Z, X, Y, \mathcal{A}, \mathcal{B})$.

The probability of E1 is $\mathcal{O}(1/2^k)$, which is negligible since H is a random oracle. E2 is same to computing an H-collision; thus the probability of E2 to occur is $\mathcal{O}((s(k)^2/2^k))$, and it is a negligible probability. Thus events E1 and E2 can be omitted.

$$Adv_{\Pi}^{AKE}(\mathcal{M}) \leq \Pr[E3] \tag{8}$$

Now, we consider the following sub-events of E3.

- Event1. E3 occurs without existing of matching session for the test session.
- Event2. E3 occurs with existing of matching session for the test session.

Then

$$\Pr[E3] = \Pr[Event1] + \Pr[Event2] \tag{9}$$

We can get the following sub-events of Event1 so that Event1 = Evenl.1 ∨ Event1.2.

- Event1.1. Event1 ∨ $\neg EphemeralKeyReveal(sid)$.
- Event1.2. Event1 ∨ $\neg StaticKeyReveal(owner)$.

Also we can get the following sub-events of Event2 so that Event2 = Event2.1 ∨ Event2.2 ∨ Event2.3 ∨ Event2.4.

- Event2.1. Event2 ∨ $\neg EphemeralKeyReveal(sid)$ ∨ $\neg EphemeralKeyReveal(\overline{sid})$.
- Event2.2. Event2 ∨ $\neg StaticKeyReveal(owner)$ ∨ $\neg StaticKeyReveal(peer)$.
- Event2.3. Event2 ∨ $\neg EphemeralKeyReveal(sid)$ ∨ $\neg StaticKeyReveal(peer)$.
- Event2.4. Event2 ∨ $\neg StaticKeyReveal(owner)$ ∨ $\neg EphemeralKeyReveal(\overline{sid})$.

We get

$$\Pr[Event1] \leq \Pr[Event1.1] + \Pr[Event1.2] \tag{10}$$

$$\Pr[Event2] \leq \Pr[Event2.1] + \Pr[Event2.2] + \Pr[Event2.3] + \Pr[Event2.4] \tag{11}$$

We will construct a solver for The Decision Linear Problem (DLIN) $\mathcal{S}$ that uses protocol Π and adversary $\mathcal{M}$. The solver $\mathcal{S}$ is given (U, V, Z), where U, V and Z are selected uniform randomly in G, access to $DLIN_{u,v,h}(.,.,.)$ oracle to solve Decision Linear problem. Without loss of generality, we denote $\mathcal{A}$ as the test session owner and $\mathcal{B}$ as the responder, and we assume that $\mathcal{A}$ to be the initiator.

Event1.1. We will use $\mathcal{M}$ to construct a DLOG solver $\mathcal{D}$ and DLIN solver $\mathcal{S}$ with non-negligible probability to succeeds. $n(k)$ honest parties will prepared by $\mathcal{S}$, then $\mathcal{S}$ will selects party $\mathcal{B}$ to assigns static public key B^* with v^{b*} where $b*$ is unknown. Random static public and private key pairs will be assigned to the remaining $n(k)-1$ parties. A session sid belongs to $\mathcal{A}$ will be chosen by $\mathcal{S}$. $\mathcal{S}$ will follows the protocol when activating honest parties and will responds faithfully to all queries as he knows static private keys of at least one peer. When the session be sid which has the ephemeral public key U setting by $\mathcal{S}$.

While $\mathcal{S}$ has know idea about the static private key of $\mathcal{B}$, it will be difficult to the simulator to responding queries related to $\mathcal{B}$. Precisely, $\mathcal{M}$ has difficult to compute shared secrets Z but may have to answer SessionKeyReveal queries for sessions owned by $\mathcal{S}$ with peer $\mathcal{C}$. To obtain session keys of these session, $\mathcal{M}$ computes the shared secrets Z and query H. $\mathcal{S}$ will fail its simulation when those two values did not coincide. To overcome this, R^{list} will be prepared by $\mathcal{S}$

with entries of the form $(P_i, P_j, W, W', SK) \in \{0,1\}^* \times \{0,1\}^* \times G^2 \times \{0,1\}^k$, this list will be used later in responses to H and SessionKeyReveal queries.

We will show the behavior of $\mathcal{S}$ when $\mathcal{M}$ sends queries related to $\mathcal{B}$. Party $\mathcal{B}$ generates Y. As we know if $(\mathcal{C}, \mathcal{B}, X, Y, \mathcal{I})(\mathcal{B}, \mathcal{C}, Y, X, \mathcal{R})$ is the session identifier, then $\mathcal{B}$ is the session responder $(\mathcal{I},\mathcal{R})$.

- Send($\mathcal{B}$,$\mathcal{C}$): y will be selected randomly by $\mathcal{S}$ to compute $Y = u^y$. then $sid = (\mathcal{B}, \mathcal{C}, Y, *, \mathcal{R})$ will be new session. $(\mathcal{C}, \mathcal{B}, Y)$ will be sent to $\mathcal{M}$.
- Send($\mathcal{B}$,$\mathcal{C}$,X): y will be selected randomly by $\mathcal{S}$ to compute $Y = u^y$. then $sid = (\mathcal{B}, \mathcal{C}, Y, X, \mathcal{R})$ will be new session. $(\mathcal{C}, \mathcal{B}, Y)$ will be sent to $\mathcal{M}$.
- Send($\mathcal{B}$,$\mathcal{C}$,Y,X): $\mathcal{S}$ will checks whether $\mathcal{B}$ owns session with $sid = (\mathcal{B}, \mathcal{C}, Y, *, \mathcal{R})$. if there is no session with this identifier then abort; otherwise, $\mathcal{S}$ will update the session identifier $sid = (\mathcal{B}, \mathcal{C}, Y, X, \mathcal{R})$.
- $H(.)$: $\mathcal{S}$ prepares an initially empty list H^{list} in the form $(\hat{Z}, W, W', P_i, P_j, SK) \in G^3 \times \{0,1\}^* \times \{0,1\}^* \times \{0,1\}^k$ and will simulate a random oracle usually. If the query in the form $(\hat{Z}, X, Y, \mathcal{C}, \mathcal{B})$ and $(\hat{Z}, Y, X, \mathcal{B}, \mathcal{C})$ then $\mathcal{S}$ will response with one of the following.
  1. if $(\hat{Z}, X, Y, \mathcal{C}, \mathcal{B}, SK) \vee (\hat{Z}, Y, X, \mathcal{B}, \mathcal{C}, SK) \in H^{list}$ for some SK, then $\mathcal{S}$ return SK to $\mathcal{M}$.
  2. Otherwise, $\mathcal{S}$ checks if there exist $(X, Y, \mathcal{C}, \mathcal{B}, SK) \vee (Y, X, \mathcal{B}, \mathcal{C}, SK) \in R^{list}$ such that $DLIN_{u,v,h}(XA, YB, \hat{Z}) = 1$. If such relation exist, $\mathcal{S}$ returns SK from R^{list}, and stores the new tuple $(X, Y, \mathcal{C}, \mathcal{B}, SK) \wedge (Y, X, \mathcal{B}, \mathcal{C}, SK)$ in H^{list}.
  3. If neither of the above two cases hold, then $\mathcal{S}$ chooses $SK \in_R \{0,1\}^k$ at random, returns it to $\mathcal{M}$ and stores the new tuple $(X, Y, \mathcal{C}, \mathcal{B}, SK) \wedge (Y, X, \mathcal{B}, \mathcal{C}, SK)$ in H^{list}.
- SessionKeyReveal($\mathcal{B}, \mathcal{C}, Y, X$) or SessionKeyReveal($\mathcal{C}, \mathcal{B}, X, Y$): An initially empty list R^{list} will be prepared by $\mathcal{S}$ in the form $(P_i, P_j, W, W', SK) \in \{0,1\}^* \times \{0,1\}^* \times G^2 \times \{0,1\}^k$.
  When SessionKeyReveal($\mathcal{B}, \mathcal{C}, Y, X$) or SessionKeyReveal($\mathcal{C}, \mathcal{B}, X, Y$) is queried, $\mathcal{S}$ will response with one of the following.
  1. If there is no session with identifier $(\mathcal{C}, \mathcal{B}, X, Y)$ or $(\mathcal{B}, \mathcal{C}, Y, X)$ the query is aborted.
  2. If $(\mathcal{B}, \mathcal{C}, Y, X, SK) \vee (\mathcal{C}, \mathcal{B}, X, Y, SK) \in R^{list}$ for some SK, $\mathcal{S}$ returns SK to $\mathcal{M}$.
  3. Otherwise, go through H^{list} to find $(\hat{Z}, X, Y, \mathcal{C}, \mathcal{B}, SK)$ or $(\hat{Z}, Y, X, \mathcal{B}, \mathcal{C}, SK)$ satisfying $DLIN_{u,v,h}(XA, YB, \hat{Z}) = 1$. If such tuple is exist, $\mathcal{S}$ returns SK, and stores the new tuple $(\mathcal{B}, \mathcal{C}, Y, X, SK) \vee (\mathcal{C}, \mathcal{B}, X, Y, SK)$ in R^{list}.
  4. If none of the above three cases hold, the $\mathcal{S}$ choose $SK \in_R \{0,1\}^k$ at random, returns it to $\mathcal{M}$ and stores the new tuple $(\mathcal{B}, \mathcal{C}, Y, X, SK) \vee (\mathcal{C}, \mathcal{B}, X, Y, SK)$ in R^{list}.
- EphemeralKeyReveal(.): $\mathcal{S}$ faithfully will respond to the query.
- StaticKeyReveal($\mathcal{B}$) or EstablishParty($\mathcal{B}$): $\mathcal{S}$ aborts.
- Test(sid): if $sid \neq \overline{sid}$, $\mathcal{S}$ aborts. Otherwise, $\mathcal{S}$ randomly choose $\zeta \in \{0,1\}^k$ at random, returns it to adversary $\mathcal{M}$.

When event Event1.1 occurs and the session sid^* selected by $\mathcal{M}$ as the test session corresponding to peer $\mathcal{B}$, then no failure in the simulation will be happened. Now let's take U and V as incoming ephemeral public key and outgoing ephemeral public key for the test session. Let $\mathcal{B}$'s public key to be B^* ($b^* \equiv dl_v(B^*) mod p$). Now to let $\mathcal{M}$ with non-negligible probability he must had queried H with inputs $\hat{Z} = U^a B^{*^{x^*}}$ ($x^* \equiv dl_v(U) mod p$). But as long the ephemeral public key of sid^* is V, then $\mathcal{M}$ runs $StaticKeyReveal(\mathcal{A})$, $SessionKeyReveal(sid^*)$ and get a, Z^* respectively, then $\mathcal{M}$ computes $B^{*^{x^*}} = \frac{Z^*}{U^a}$ which solve the linear DH of (V, B^*) and computes U^a which solve the linear DH of (U, A).

As we have previously that $\mathcal{M}$ has probability greater than $\frac{1}{2} + \mathcal{O}\left(\frac{q^2(k)}{p}\right)$ can solve DLIN, and at least $\frac{1}{s(k)n(k)}$ the test session is sid^* with peer $\mathcal{B}$ ($\frac{1}{n(k)}$ to pick the correct party $\mathcal{B}$ and $\frac{1}{s(k)}$ to pick the correct session). Thus, the advantage of $\mathcal{S}$ is

$$\begin{aligned} Adv^{DLIN}(\mathcal{S}) &\geq \left(\frac{1}{s(k)n(k)}.Adv_{\Pi}^{AKE}(\mathcal{M}) - Adv^{DLOG}(\mathcal{D})\right) \\ &\geq \frac{1}{2} + \mathcal{O}\left(\frac{q^2(k)}{p}\right) \end{aligned} \tag{12}$$

Event1.2. In this event $n(k)$ honest parties will be prepared by $\mathcal{S}$, and two of them will be selected distinctly. Assume $\mathcal{A}$ and $\mathcal{B}$ the two parties selected distinctly, where U and V corresponds to their static public keys respectively. Then the rest of $n(k) - 2$ parties will assigned to random static and private key pairs. $\mathcal{M}$ will follow the protocol description whenever he activates sessions corresponding to any honest party except $\mathcal{A}$ and $\mathcal{B}$. When he activates sessions corresponding to $\mathcal{A}$ and $\mathcal{B}$, then he will do as in Event1.1.

When the session sid^* selected by $\mathcal{M}$ as the test session corresponding to peer $\mathcal{A}$ and $\mathcal{B}$, let $\mathcal{M}$ with non-negligible probability he must had queried H with inputs $Z = Y^{dl_u(A=U)} B^x$.

To do so, $\mathcal{M}$ runs $EphemeralKeyReveal(sid^*)$, $SessionKeyReveal(sid^*)$ and get x, Z^* respectively, then $\mathcal{M}$ computes $Y^{a^*} = \frac{Z^*}{B^x}$ which solve the linear DH of (Y, A) and computes B^x which solve the linear DH of (X, B).

As we have previously that $\mathcal{M}$ has probability greater than $\frac{1}{2} + \mathcal{O}\left(\frac{q^2(k)}{p}\right)$ can solve DLIN, and at least $\frac{1}{s(k)n^2(k)}$ the test session is sid^* with owner $\mathcal{A}$ and peer $\mathcal{B}$ ($\frac{1}{n(k)}$ to pick the correct party $\mathcal{A}$ and $\frac{1}{n(k)}$ to pick the correct party $\mathcal{B}$ $\frac{1}{s(k)}$ to pick the correct session). Thus, the advantage of $\mathcal{S}$ is

$$\begin{aligned} Adv^{DLIN}(\mathcal{S}) &\geq \left(\frac{1}{s(k)n^2(k)}.Adv_{\Pi}^{AKE}(\mathcal{M}) - Adv^{DLOG}(\mathcal{D})\right) \\ &\geq \frac{1}{2} + \mathcal{O}\left(\frac{q^2(k)}{p}\right) \end{aligned} \tag{13}$$

Event2.1. In this event $n(k)$ honest parties will be prepared by $\mathcal{S}$ with random static public/private keys. Two session sid, sid^* corresponding to $\mathcal{A}$ as the owner of *sid* and $\mathcal{B}$ as the owner of *sid** by $\mathcal{S}$. Let V,U be the ephemeral public key of *sid*,*sid** respectively.

When Event2.1 occurs, there is no failure in the simulation and $\mathcal{M}$ must success with non-negligible probability to query H with $Z = U^a B^{dl_v(V)}$.

To do so, $\mathcal{M}$ runs $StaticKeyReveal(\mathcal{A}), SessionKeyReveal(sid^*)$ and get a, Z^* respectively, then $\mathcal{M}$ computes $B*^{X^*} = \frac{Z^*}{U^a}$ which solve the linear DH of (V, B^*) and computes U^a which solve the linear DH of (U, A).

As we have previously that $\mathcal{M}$ has probability greater than $\frac{1}{2}+\mathcal{O}\left(\frac{q^2(k)}{p}\right)$ can solve DLIN, and at least $\frac{1}{s^2(k)}$ the test session is *sid** with its matching session *sid* ($\frac{1}{s(k)}$ to pick the *sid* for party $\mathcal{A}$ and $\frac{1}{s^2(k)}$ to pick its matching session *sid** for party $\mathcal{B}$). Thus, the advantage of $\mathcal{S}$ is

$$Adv^{DLIN}(\mathcal{S}) \geq \left(\frac{1}{s^2(k)}.Adv_{\Pi}^{AKE}(\mathcal{M}) - Adv^{DLOG}(\mathcal{D})\right) \geq \frac{1}{2} + \mathcal{O}\left(\frac{q^2(k)}{p}\right) \tag{14}$$

Event2.2. For Event2.2 $\mathcal{S}$s simulation is similar to Event1.2. Hence:

As we have previously that $\mathcal{M}$ has probability greater than $\frac{1}{2}+\mathcal{O}\left(\frac{q^2(k)}{p}\right)$ can solve DLIN, and at least $\frac{1}{s(k)n^2(k)}$ the test session is *sid** with owner $\mathcal{A}$ and peer $\mathcal{B}$ ($\frac{1}{n(k)}$ to pick the correct party $\mathcal{A}$ and $\frac{1}{n(k)}$ to pick the correct party $\mathcal{B}$ $\frac{1}{s(k)}$ to pick the correct session). Thus, the advantage of $\mathcal{S}$ is

$$Adv^{DLIN}(\mathcal{S}) \geq \left(\frac{1}{s(k)n^2(k)}.Adv_{\Pi}^{AKE}(\mathcal{M}) - Adv^{DLOG}(\mathcal{D})\right) \geq \frac{1}{2} + \mathcal{O}\left(\frac{q^2(k)}{p}\right) \tag{15}$$

Event2.3 and Event2.4. For event2.3, event2.4 $\mathcal{S}$s simulation is similar to Event1.1. Hence:

As we have previously that $\mathcal{M}$ has probability greater than $\frac{1}{2}+\mathcal{O}\left(\frac{q^2(k)}{p}\right)$ can solve DLIN, and at least $\frac{1}{s(k)n(k)}$ the test session is *sid** with peer $\mathcal{B}$ ($\frac{1}{n(k)}$ to pick the correct party $\mathcal{B}$ and $\frac{1}{s(k)}$ to pick the correct session). Thus, the advantage of $\mathcal{S}$ is

$$Adv^{DLIN}(\mathcal{S}) \geq \left(\frac{1}{s(k)n(k)}.Adv_{\Pi}^{AKE}(\mathcal{M}) - Adv^{DLOG}(\mathcal{D})\right) \geq \frac{1}{2} + \mathcal{O}\left(\frac{q^2(k)}{p}\right) \tag{16}$$

Recombining Eqs. (12), (13), (14), (15) and (16), $\mathcal{S}$'s advantage will be

$$Adv^{DLIN}(\mathcal{S}) \geq max \left\{ \begin{array}{r} \frac{1}{s(k)n(k)}.Adv_{\Pi}^{AKE}(\mathcal{M}) - Adv^{DLOG}(\mathcal{D}), \\ \frac{1}{s(k)n^2(k)}.Adv_{\Pi}^{AKE}(\mathcal{M}) - Adv^{DLOG}(\mathcal{D}), \\ \frac{1}{s^2(k)}.Adv_{\Pi}^{AKE}(\mathcal{M}) - Adv^{DLOG}(\mathcal{D}), \\ \frac{1}{2} + \mathcal{O}\left(\frac{q^2(k)}{p}\right) \end{array} \right\} \quad (17)$$

While $Adv_{\Pi}^{AKE}(\mathcal{M})$ is non-negligible then Pr[E3] is non-negligible, and hence from (9),(10) and (11), with non-negligible probability one of these events will happen Event1.1, ..., Event2.4, and therefore $Adv^{GDH}(\mathcal{S})$ is non-negligible. $\mathcal{S}$, $\mathcal{D}$ and H simulation will take polynomially bounded time, $\mathcal{O}(k)$ and $t(k), n(k), s(k), h(k), q(k)$ are polynomial in k. Therefore, $Adv_{\Pi}^{AKE}(\mathcal{M})$ has polynomially bounded running time. Hence, $\mathcal{S}$ is a polynomial-time algorithm that solves the $DLIN$ problem in G with non-negligible, which contradicts the assumed security of $DLIN$ problem in G. This completes the argument.

5 Efficiency

Comparison between our protocol with other related AKE protocols in terms of based assumption, computational efficiency and security model will be discussed in this section. In Table 1 number of exponentiation in G (E), number of static public keys (SPK) and number of ephemeral public key (EPK). Table 1 shows the group exponentiations count; Okamoto's protocol is secure in the standard model, but the proof relies on an existence of PRF family. In the security proof of HMQV and CMQV, the reduction argument is less tight since the Forking Lemma [14] is essential for the arguments. KFU [10]-P1 use two static public key in computation. Our protocol in Table 1, have tighter security reductions and do not use the Forking Lemma and just use one static public key in computation.

Table 1. Protocols Comparison

Protocol	Computation	Security model	Assumption	NAXOS approch	SPK/EPK
Okamoto [9]	8E	eCK	Standard	Yes	2/3
HMQV [15]	2.5E	CK, wPFS,KCI, LEP	GDH, KEA1, RO	No	1/1
CMQV [5]	3E	eCK	RO, GDH	Yes	1/1
NAXOS [15]	4E	eCK	RO, GDH	Yes	1/1
NETS [8]	3E	eCK	RO, GDH	Yes	1/1
SMEN [16]	6E	eCK	RO, GDH	No	2/2
KFU [10]	3E	eCK	RO, GDH	No	2/1
Our	3E	eCK	DLIN, RO	No	1/1

It clear that our protocol has same computation efficiency and security model with NETS, CMQV and KFU-P1, but it differs from them in base assumption. Moreover our protocol and KFU distinguish with no NAXOS' approach. But KFU use two static public key in computation.

Our work showed possibility of constructing eCK-secure AKE protocols not relaying on NAXOS' approach, thus we showed that our protocol is secure though revealing of ephemeral private key while leaking of the static private key is not decrease which give it more practically advance.

Moreover, our protocols uses single random oracle which is opposed to two of HMQV and CMQV and which gives it advance on them. We only use random oracle in the session key derivation.

In addition, our protocol uses decision linear assumption with tight security proof.

6 Conclusions

In this paper we present new efficient eCK-secure AKE protocol without relying on NAXOS approach. We presents secure protocol in eCK model under Decision Linear assumption(DLIN) without using NAXOS trick with a fastened reduction.Our protocol reduce the risk of leaking the static private key, that because of the derivation of the ephemeral public key is independent from the static private key. Moreover, each ephemeral and static key has its particular generator which gives tight security for the protocol. Our protocol has strong definition with more efficiency and minimizing uses of random oracle, by applying it only to the session key derivation. Moreover, we present AKE-secure protocol rely on decision linear assumption with tight security proof.

References

1. Bellare, M., Rogaway, P.: Entity authentication and key distribution. In: Stinson, D.R. (ed.) CRYPTO 1993. LNCS, vol. 773, pp. 232–249. Springer, Heidelberg (1994)
2. Bellare, M., Canetti, R., Krawczyk, H.: A modular approach to the design and analysis of authentication and key exchange protocols. In: Proceedings of the Thirtieth Annual ACM Symposium on Theory of Computing. ACM (1998)
3. Canetti, R., Krawczyk, H.: Analysis of key-exchange protocols and their use for building secure channels. In: Pfitzmann, B. (ed.) EUROCRYPT 2001. LNCS, vol. 2045, pp. 453–474. Springer, Heidelberg (2001)
4. Lauter, K., Mityagin, A., LaMacchia, B.A.: Stronger security of authenticated key exchange. In: Susilo, W., Liu, J.K., Mu, Y. (eds.) ProvSec 2007. LNCS, vol. 4784, pp. 1–16. Springer, Heidelberg (2007)
5. Ustaoglu, B.: Obtaining a secure and efficient key agreement protocol for (H)MQV and NAXOS. Des. Codes Crypt. **46**(3), 329–342 (2008). http://www.eprint.iacr.org/2007/123
6. Huang, H., Cao, Z.: Strongly secure authenticated key exchange protocol based on computational Diffie-Hellman problem. In: Inscrypt (2008)

7. Lee, J., Park, J.: Authenticated key exchange secure under the computational Diffie-Hellman assumption. http://www.eprint.iacr.org/2008/344
8. Lee, J., Park, C.: An efficient key exchange protocol with a tight security reduction. http://www.eprint.iacr.org/2008/345
9. Okamoto, T.: Authenticated key exchange and key encapsulation in the standard model. In: Kurosawa, K. (ed.) ASIACRYPT 2007. LNCS, vol. 4833, pp. 474–484. Springer, Heidelberg (2007)
10. Kim, M., Fujioka, A., Ustaoğlu, B.: Strongly secure authenticated key exchange without NAXOS' approach. In: Takagi, T., Mambo, M. (eds.) Advances in Information and Computer Security. LNCS, vol. 5824, pp. 174–191. Springer, Heidelberg (2009)
11. Boneh, D., Boyen, X., Shacham, H.: Short group signatures. In: Franklin, M. (ed.) CRYPTO 2004. LNCS, vol. 3152, pp. 41–55. Springer, Heidelberg (2004)
12. Joux, A., Nguyen, K.: Separating decision Diffie-Hellman from computational Diffie-Hellman in cryptographic groups. J. Cryptology **16**(4), 239–247 (2003)
13. Shoup, V.: Lower bounds for discrete logarithms and related problems. In: Fumy, W. (ed.) EUROCRYPT 1997. LNCS, vol. 1233, pp. 256–266. Springer, Heidelberg (1997)
14. Pointcheval, D., Stern, J.: Security arguments for digital signatures and blind signatures. J. Cryptology **13**(3), 361–396 (2000)
15. Krawczyk, H.: HMQV: a high-performance secure Diffie-Hellman protocol. In: Shoup, V. (ed.) CRYPTO 2005. LNCS, vol. 3621, pp. 546–566. Springer, Heidelberg (2005)
16. Wu, J., Ustaoglu, B.: Efficient Key Exchange with Tight Security Reduction. Technical report CACR 2009–23, University of Waterloo (2009). http://www.cacr.math.uwaterloo.ca/techreports/2009/cacr200923.pdf
17. Li, H., ChuanKun, W.: CMQV+: an authenticated key exchange protocol from CMQV. Sci. China Inf. Sci. **55**(7), 1666–1674 (2012)

Towards Secure Distributed Hash Table

Zhe Wang(✉) and Naftaly H. Minsky

Rutgers University, Piscataway, NJ 08854, USA
{zhewang,minsky}@cs.rutgers.edu

Abstract. A distributed hash table (DHT) provides decentralized lookup service for distributed applications. All current implementations of DHT are achieved by the individual components being run by the participants of the application in question. Namely, the correctness of the DHT relies on that all the participants follow the same protocol. Unfortunately, this aspect of the current approach makes DHT seriously vulnerable to attacks. Such security and fault tolerance concerns about DHT prompted several attempts to improve the vulnerability of DHT. However, all the proposed solutions also rely on the code to be executed correctly. We present in this paper a novel way for implementing DHT, giving rise to an architecture we call GDHT, for Governed Distributed Hash Table. GDHT implements the required protocol with a powerful means for establishing policies governing the behaviors of the participants of DHT. By carrying out the protocol by an equally distributed middleware, the correctness of the execution of routing algorithm is guaranteed. Moreover, the execution of the security module and improvements on routing algorithm can also be ensured.

Keywords: Distributed hash table · Fault tolerance · Collaboration · Security · Governed · Chord · Sybil attack · Routing attack

1 Introduction

A *distributed hash table* (DHT) is a distributed group of components that collaborate in forming a decentralized lookup service for distributed, mostly P2P type, applications. It has been used for a variety of applications, such P2P file sharing systems [4], distributed file systems [5], domain name services [10], instant messaging [12], and recently, distributed online social networks [17,18]. The concept of DHT has many different implementations, such as Chord [14], Pastry [13], CAN [11] and Kademlia [8], which are based on different coordination protocols that all the components of a given DHT must observe.

All current implementations of DHT have this in common: the individual components of a DHT must be run by the participants of the application in question—henceforth to be referred to simply as the participants—who use their component as a gateway to the DHT at large. Unfortunately, this aspect of the current approach to the implementation of DHTs makes it seriously vulnerable to attacks. Although all the participants get the software of the DHT components, for them to run it locally, there is no guarantee that everyone is going to

S. Guo et al. (Eds.): CollaborateCom 2015, LNICST 163, pp. 257–266, 2016.
DOI: 10.1007/978-3-319-28910-6_23

follow the required protocol—particularly because in many applications of DHT the participants are unknown and cannot be trusted. For example, a malicious participant may change the code to forward a lookup request to a wrong node, or to claim it is responsible for the requested key and then respond with bogus result, or simply deny the existence of certain key.

This is a well known problem, which has been studied by several researchers. This research has been reviewed in [15], which discusses several types of attacks on a DHT, and describes protective measures against them, by changing the DHT protocol in various ways. But since such a changed protocol is to be executed locally, the protective measures built into it are themselves vulnerable to malicious attacks by some participants.

The Contribution of this Paper: We address this issue by taking the responsibility of carrying out the DHT protocol in question away from the untrusted participants, entrusting it to a trustworthy middleware used to govern the interaction of the participants with the DHT. The resulting architecture is called GDHT, for Governed DHT. And the middleware on which it is based is called law-governed interaction, or LGI. This middleware is decentralized, and thus scalable, and stateful—it needs to be stateful to be able to handle the highly stateful nature of the various DHT protocols. As a proof of concept we describe here the implementation of GDHT for the Chord version of DHT.

The rest of this paper is organized as follows: Sect. 2 discusses the attack models that the DHTs are mostly vulnerable to, and the proposed approaches for resolving them. Section 3 introduces the model of GDHT. Section 4 describes our implemented Chord version of GDHT that demonstrates how this abstract model can be used for a concrete application. And we conclude in Sect. 5.

2 Attack Models and the Limitations of Current Solutions

While the users of DHT benefit from the availability and scalability the DHT provides, they also face certain security and fault tolerance issues, especially when the information and resources, which are stored and transmitted in participants of DHT, are critical and sensitive. Because the implementations of DHT are usually distributed through releasing a suite of software for downloading. The participants get the software and run it locally. They rely on that all the participants follow the same protocol, by running the same code of software. However, since the software is run at each participant's computer, there is no guarantee that everyone is going to follow the same protocol. For example, a malicious participant may change the code to forward a lookup request to a wrong node, or to claim it is responsible for the requested key and then respond with bogus result, or simply deny the existence of certain key.

There are a wide range of attacks that malicious participants could exploit and launch on the software to gain illicit benefit. Several attack models focus on the nature of DHT participants or the routing between them. Chief among them are *routing attack* and *the Sybil attack*. Basically, these attacks try to create malicious nodes (numerously) and then deceive the benign nodes collaboratively.

In the rest of this section, we are going to first describe the two attack models, analyze the solutions that researchers proposed, and then show their limitations.

2.1 Routing Attack

A routing attack is generally an attempt to prevent the routing of a lookup request from being successful [15]. For example, a malicious participant can refuse to forward lookup requests. Or it can forward the request to a non-existing or another compromised participant. Moreover, it could pretend to be responsible for certain key. It's also possible that the malicious participant routes requests normally, but denies the existence of a valid key or to respond with bogus result.

The approaches of defending routing attacks can be generalized to two main categories—redundant routing [3,7] and redundant storage [12]. Redundant routing employs either mechanisms like wide path or multiple routing table, while redundant storage replicates the data (or metadata of the location). Both methods are very costly as they increase the overhead of each routing hop or the numbers of transmission operations and the actual storage space—not to mention the synchronization issue between replicas. Even so, the cost is not the major problem. What is worse is that the redundancy cannot guarantee the success of the routing. Those solutions are feasible only when a reasonably low fraction f of participants are malicious [15]. We are going to show, in next section that a Sybil attack easily breaks these defenses by effectively increasing f.

We also demonstrate, in our implementation in Sect. 4, that how our model can enforce everyone to follow the same protocol, while not assuming there is only very small percentage of malicious participants.

2.2 Sybil Attack

A Sybil attack exploits the fact that in a distributed system, if the system fails to guarantee that each logical identity refers to a single remote physical entity, an attacker could create a large number of identities and dominate the overlay network by fooling the protocols and subverting mechanisms based on redundancy. The Sybil attack does not damage the DHT by itself, but can be used as a vector to create a majority of colluding malicious participants of it [15]. This attack is not specific to DHTs, but it is important because DHTs are vulnerable to it and the attack can be used to facilitate the execution of many other attacks. For example, if there are many malicious identities in the system, it becomes easier to pollute the routing tables of honest participants, and control the majority of the replicas for a given key.

A general solution to the Sybil attack is to use certification [3,15]. It assumes the existence of a trusted certification authority (CA) to make sure that one physical entity can only acquire one valid identifier. However, the proposed approaches failed to guarantee that every participant is going to check the certificate. Therefore, the malicious participants can subvert this mechanism and create large amount of identities, even when the majority of participants are still willing to check the certificate. We are going to show, in our implementation in Sect. 4, that how our model can enforce everyone's certificate gets checked.

Another group of solutions rely on binding certain metrics to an identifier [1, 6,16,19]. Nevertheless, these solutions are either too rigid when relying on static information (e.g. IPs, network characteristics, geographic coordinates) or hardly working when relying on relatively dynamic metrics (e.g. network performance, social informations). Moreover, some approaches proposed to use computational puzzles [2], which try to limit the number of fake identities generated by malicious participants by having honest participants request each other to solve puzzles that require a significant amount of computational resources. The idea is to limit the capability of a malicious participant to generate multiple identities. However, similar to the certification solution, since it consumes a lot of resources, they cannot guarantee that everyone is willing to participate in this mechanism. They also need our model to enforce everyone to follow the protocol.

3 A Model of Governed Distributed Hash Table (GDHT)

We introduce here a model of a DHT that enables the regulation of a DHT via enforced protocol that can establish its overall structure and behavior. We call this model GDHT (for *Governed Distributed Hash Table*).

The model employs our previous work—the Law-Governed Interaction (LGI). LGI is a middleware that can govern the interaction (via message exchange) between distributed *actors*, by enforcing an explicitly specified law about such interaction. A detailed presentation of LGI can be found in its manual [9]—which describes the release of an implementation of the main parts of LGI.

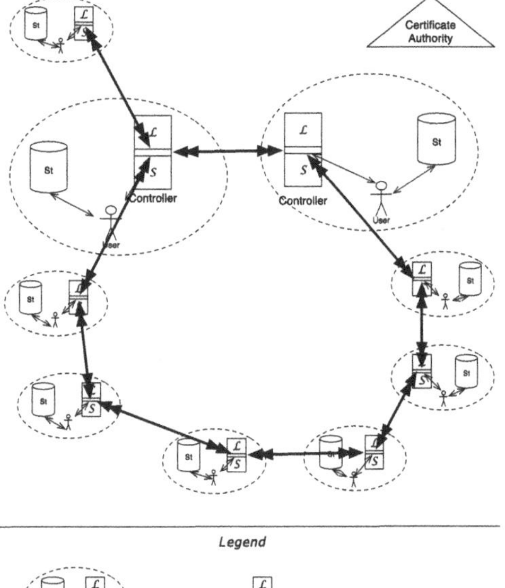

Fig. 1. The anatomy of a GDHT

The GDHT model is *generic*, and rather abstract, in the sense that it does not have any built-in communal structure. But it can support a wide range of different types of DHTs, whose structure and behavior is determined by the laws chosen for them. We do, however, present a concrete implementation of a specific Chord protocol, in Sect. 4, to show our model can be easily used for building variety of DHTs.

This section is organized as follows. Section 3.1 is a definition of this model; Sect. 3.2 describes the launching of a GDHT; and Sect. 3.3 discusses the manner in which such a DHT operates.

3.1 A Definition of a GDHT

A GDHT-community D is defined as a 4-tuple $\langle P, \mathcal{L}, C, S \rangle$, where P is the set of participants of D; $\mathcal{L}$ is the law that governs this GDHT, and is often denoted by $\mathcal{L}_D$; C is a set of generic LGI controllers that serves as the middleware trusted to enforce any law $\mathcal{L}$ loaded into them; and S, called the *support* of D, is a set of components that provides various services to D, and is mostly specific to it. We now elaborate on this definition of the GDHT model by providing some details about its four elements, and about the relations among them. This overall structure of a GDHT is depicted schematically in Fig. 1.

The Set P of Participants of a GDHT: An individual participant x of a GDHT D is a triple $\langle user, mediator, storage \rangle$, where *user* is usually a human, operating via some kind of computational platform, like a computer or smart phone; *mediator* is one of the LGI-controllers in C that mediates all interactions between x and other participants of D; and *storage*, is the repository of resources that the participant is responsible for.

The Law $\mathcal{L}_D$ of GDHT-community D: This law endows a GDHT-community with its overall structure, in particular by controlling its membership, as well as the interactive behavior of its participants. The generality of LGI laws endows this model with great deal of generality regarding the nature of the GDHT governed by it. In particular, suitable laws can make a GDHT-community behave like Chord, or like Kademlia, or any other DHT.

The Set C of Controllers: C is meant to be the *trusted computing base* (TCB) of a GDHT. Every user can create its own controller, using the software provided by the released LGI middleware. But if malicious corruption of controllers by their users is of concern, then it is better for the participants to adopt controllers created and maintained by a trusted *controller service* (CoS), so that they can authenticate each other as bona fide LGI controllers. For such a CoS to be trusted to provide genuine controllers, this service needs to be managed by a trusted organization. It should be pointed out that the organization that maintains the CoS does not have the access to the data exchanged between the participants for several reasons. First each individual controller has access only to very small part of the exchanges, and even these are maintained for just a fleeting moment.

The Support S of a Given GDHT D: A GDHT D may require various services that are not themselves participant of D; and most of them are not defined by the generic GDHT model. Such services may be designed specifically for the DHT at hand, or may exist independently of it. Participant of D interacts with such services subject to law $\mathcal{L}_D$, while the services themselves may not communicate subject to this or other LGI-law. A certification authority (CA) is such an example that may belong to S, which is used for the key authentication.

Note that the existence of central support service would not compromise significantly the scalability of a GDHT, if it is offline or used relatively rarely. And it would not compromise significantly the privacy of a GDHT, if it does not contain sensitive information.

3.2 The Launching of a GDHT

A specific GDHT D is launched by constructing its *foundation*, and then having individual participants join it incrementally. The foundation of D consists of: (1) the law $\mathcal{L}_D$ under which this GDHT is to operate; (2) the controller service CoS, whose controllers would enforce this law; and (3) the support S to be used by this particular GDHT. Each of these parts of the foundation of D can be either built specifically for it, or selected from existing such items. In particular, the controller service CoS may be managed and maintained specifically for D, but it may already exist, serving many different GDHTs, as well as other applications. And some, or all, parts of the *support* S of D—such as its CA—may have an independent existence, serving other applications.

Once the foundation of D exists, anybody can attempt to join it as a participant via the following three steps: First, the user needs to deploy its private storage. Second, the user needs to acquire an LGI-controller from the CoS used by D, and instruct this controller to download law $\mathcal{L}_D$ from the law server. Finally, the user should *adopt* this controller as its mediator.

Note, however, that the adoption is governed by law $\mathcal{L}_D$, which may require, among other things, certain certificates to be provided by the user. If the user does not satisfy the requirements of law $\mathcal{L}_D$ then the adoption will fail. This is one way to control the membership of a given DHT and defend the Sybil attack.

3.3 The Operation of a GDHT

Consider a participant x of D sending a message m, for example a lookup request, to another participant y. The message first arrives at the controller of x, which operates under law $\mathcal{L}_D$. If this controller forwards the message m to y—note that it may decide to block it—then m first arrives at the controller of y, which decides what to do with it according to law $\mathcal{L}_D$. In other words, participants of a GDHT interact with each other via their controllers, and the controllers communicate with each other subject to the law $\mathcal{L}_D$ of the DHT.

Figure 1 may help understand the situation. This figure depicts several participants, represented by ovals, each of which encloses the three components of a participant: the user, its mediator (controller), and its storage. The interaction between participants is depicted by the thick arrows. The component parts of a participant interact with each other as depicted by the thin arrows.

4 The Implementation of Chord GDHT

In this section, we are going to show our implementation of GDHT. It is an implementation of Chord, with two security enhancements—certification and redundant routing. The reason we chose Chord is for the sake of simplicity. Although it is not an optimal protocol, it is quite simple and easy to read. By demonstrating our implementation of Chord, we show that our GDHT model is capable of building arbitrary type of DHTs, as long as the protocol is specified in law. Similarly, we chose certification as an example to show our capability of implementing the security features, which are discussed in Sect. 2.

4.1 Chord Overview

Chord is one of DHT protocols, introduced by [14]. A DHT assigns keys to different nodes (participants); a node stores the values for all the keys for which it is responsible. The protocol regulates how keys are assigned to nodes and how find out the value for certain key by locating the node responsible for it. Nodes and keys are both assigned an m-bit identifier using consistent hashing, which is critical to the performance and correctness of Chord. Both keys and nodes are distributed in the same identifier space with very low possibility of collision. Moreover, it also enables nodes to join and leave the network without disruption.

Nodes and keys are arranged in an identifier circle that has at most 2^n nodes. (n is large enough to avoid collision.) Each node has a successor and a predecessor. The successor is the next node in the identifier circle in a clockwise direction. The predecessor is counter-clockwise. If there is a node for each possible ID, the successor of node 0 is node 1, and the predecessor of node 0 is node 2^n - 1; however, normally there are "holes" in the sequence. The concept of successor can be used for keys as well. The successor node of a key k is the first node whose ID equals to k or follows k in the identifier circle, denoted by *successor(k)*. Every key is stored at its successor node, so looking up a key k is to query *successor(k)* [14].

4.2 The Law of Chord GDHT

Rule $\mathcal{R}1$ shows how a user joins a GDHT. There are two cases of joining a DHT: (1) if a participant x knows some other participant y in the DHT already, then x will query for its successor from y; (2) otherwise, x is the creator of this DHT, then it will set its successor as itself. x, whether it is the creator, will also set obligations to periodically check the liveness of its successor and predecessor, and update its finger table. We will show later how to achieve when time is due.

The key of a participant is determined by the hash of its name. Here we assume that each participant has unique name. If the uniqueness of names cannot be guaranteed, the use of other unique ID (e.g. social security number or driver license number) should be applied. To prevent malicious participants providing multiple fake names to launch the Sybil attack, the controller will check the certificate which certifies the authenticity of the name (Fig. 2).

```
R1.
    UPON adopted(Arg, X, cert(issuer(CA),subj(X),attr([name(X)])))
         DO[add(Key(hash(X)));
         imposeObligation(stabilize, 1, min),
         imposeObligation(fix_fingers, 1, min),
         imposeObligation(check_predecessor, 1, min)]
         IF Arg = nil
         DO[ add(Predecessor(nil)),
         add(Successor(Self))]
         ELSE
         DO[ add(Predecessor(nil)),
         forward(Self, find_successor(Key@CS, Self, Successor@CS), Arg)]
R2.
    UPON arrived(X, find_successor(id, callback_id, callback_var), Y)
         IF id in (Self, Successor@CS]
         DO[forward(Self, found_successor(Successor@CS, callback_var), callback_id)]
         ELSE
         DO[next_hop = closest_preceding_node(id),
         forward(Self, find_successor(id, callback_id, callback_var), next_hop)]
R3.
    UPON arrived(X, get_predecessor, Y)
         DO[forward(Self, predecessor(Predecessor@CS), X)]
R4.
    UPON obligationDue(stabilize)
         DO[forward(Self, get_predecessor, Successor@CS),
         imposeObligation(stabilize, 1, min)]
R5.
    UPON arrived(X, predecessor, Y)
         IF predecessor in (Key@CS, Successor@CS)
         DO[add(Successor(predecessor)),
         forward(Self, notify(Key@CS), Successor@CS)]
R6.
    UPON arrived(X, notify(id), Y)
         IF Predecessor@CS = nil
         or id in (Predecessor@CS, Key@CS)
         DO[add(Predecessor(id))]
R7.
    UPON obligationDue(fix_fingers)
         DO[imposeObligation(fix_fingers, 1, min),
         update_finger_table(next++, find_successor(Key@CS + 2^next-1))]
R8.
    UPON obligationDue(check_predecessor)
         IF Predecessor@CS is Unreachable
         DO[add(Predecessor(nil))]
```

Fig. 2. Law $\mathcal{L}_D$: Implementation of chord GDHT

Once a participant is asked about the successor of a key, according to Rule $\mathcal{R}2$ it will first check whether its successor is responsible for that key. If so, it will return its successor, otherwise, it will search its local finger table for the highest predecessor of that key, and then ask it for the successor of that key.

Rule $\mathcal{R}3$ simply shows when a participant receives a query about its predecessor, it will respond with it.

Every participant runs a function called *stabilize* periodically to learn about newly joined participants. Rule $\mathcal{R}4$ and Rule $\mathcal{R}5$ show that a participant x calls its successor y periodically about its predecessor, if y's predecessor is not x but some participant z between them, meaning z is a newly joined participant, x will notify z that it is z's predecessor. In the case that x is a newly joined participant, it will notify its successor y that it is y's predecessor. Rule $\mathcal{R}6$ shows that when notified by another participant that it is its predecessor, mostly because that participant just joined, it will update its predecessor in control state.

Each participant periodically calls a function named *fix fingers* to make sure the finger table entries are updated. This is how new joined nodes initialize the finger tables, and how existing nodes add new nodes into their own finger tables. Rule $\mathcal{R}7$ shows that a participant will periodically check each entry in its finger table and update accordingly.

Each participant also runs a function called *check predecessor* periodically, to cleanup the participant's predecessor reference if its predecessor becomes unavailable; this enables the node to accept a new predecessor when notified. Rule $\mathcal{R}8$ shows that a participant will periodically check the liveness of its predecessor.

4.3 Additional Security Features

As we mentioned in Sect. 2, there are several protective measures proposed to resolve the vulnerability of DHT from different aspects, by means of changing the DHT protocol. But since such a changed protocol is still to be executed locally, the protective measures themselves are also vulnerable to malicious attacks.

However, if certain changes of the protocol can be written into $\mathcal{L}_D$ and carried out by the controllers of GDHT, it would be a very good supplement to the Chord version of GDHT, from both security and fault tolerance perspectives. In our implementation, we employed redundant routing and certification as examples for handling routing attack and the Sybil attack. Due to lack of space, we only showed how to enforce the use of certification above. Most of proposed approaches can be implemented under GDHT and they rely on GDHT to guarantee the executions.

5 Conclusion

This paper addresses the vulnerability to security and fault tolerance posed by the nature of DHT. Namely, the correctness of the DHT relies on that all the participants follow the same protocol. Unfortunately, this cannot be guaranteed by the current approach of implementing DHTs. These risks prompted several attempts to enhance the DHT protocols. However, these solutions are to be executed locally, making themselves vulnerable to malicious attacks.

We address this issue by carrying out the DHT protocol away from the untrusted participants, entrusting it to a trustworthy middleware used to govern the interaction of the participants with the DHT. The architecture is called GDHT, for Governed DHT, which is decentralized, scalable, and stateful. As a proof of concept we implemented the Chord version of GDHT, with some security enhancements. The overhead added by employing GDHT is quite negligible, comparing to the enhancements from security and fault tolerance aspects.

References

1. Bazzi, R.A., Konjevod, G.: On the establishment of distinct identities in overlay networks. In: Distributed Computing, vol. 19 (2007)
2. Borisov, N.: Computational puzzles as sybil defenses. In: 2006 Sixth IEEE International Conference on Peer-to-Peer Computing, P2P 2006. IEEE (2006)
3. Castro, M., Druschel, P., Ganesh, A., Rowstron, A., Wallach, D.S.: Secure routing for structured peer-to-peer overlay networks. ACM SIGOPS Operating Syst. Rev. **36**, 299–314 (2002)
4. Cohen, B.: Incentives build robustness in bittorrent. In: Workshop on Economics of Peer-to-Peer systems, vol. 6 (2003)
5. Dabek, F., Kaashoek, F., Karger, D., Morris, R., Stoica, I.: Wide-area cooperative storage with CFS. ACM SIGOPS Operating Syst. Rev. **35**, 202–215 (2001)
6. Danezis, G., Lesniewski-Laas, C., Kaashoek, M.F., Anderson, R.: Sybil-resistant DHT routing. In: di Vimercati, S.C., Syverson, P.F., Gollmann, D. (eds.) ESORICS 2005. LNCS, vol. 3679, pp. 305–318. Springer, Heidelberg (2005)
7. Hildrum, K., Kubiatowicz, J.D.: Asymptotically efficient approaches to fault-tolerance in peer-to-peer networks. In: Fich, F.E. (ed.) DISC 2003. LNCS, vol. 2848, pp. 321–336. Springer, Heidelberg (2003)
8. Maymounkov, P., Mazières, D.: Kademlia: A Peer-to-Peer information system based on the XOR metric. In: Druschel, P., Kaashoek, M.F., Rowstron, A. (eds.) IPTPS 2002. LNCS, vol. 2429, pp. 53–65. Springer, Heidelberg (2002)
9. Minsky, N.H.: Law Governed Interaction (LGI): A Distributed Coordination and Control Mechanism (An Introduction, and a Reference Manual), Rutgers, February 2006. http://www.moses.rutgers.edu/
10. Pappas, V., Massey, D., Terzis, A., Zhang, L.: A comparative study of the DNS design with DHT-based alternatives. In: INFOCOM (2006)
11. Ratnasamy, S., Francis, P., Handley, M., Karp, R., Shenker, S.: A scalable content-addressable network, vol. 31. ACM (2001)
12. Rhea, S., Godfrey, B., Karp, B., Kubiatowicz, J., Ratnasamy, S., Shenker, S., Stoica, I., Harlan, Y.: OpenDHT: a public DHT service and its uses. In: ACM SIGCOMM Computer Communication Review, vol. 35 (2005)
13. Rowstron, A., Druschel, P.: Pastry: scalable, decentralized object location, and routing for large-scale peer-to-peer systems. In: Guerraoui, R. (ed.) Middleware 2001. LNCS, vol. 2218, p. 329. Springer, Heidelberg (2001)
14. Stoica, I., Morris, R., Liben-Nowell, D., Karger, D., Kaashoek, F., Dabek, F., Balakrishnan, H.: Chord: a scalable peer-to-peer lookup protocol for internet applications. IEEE/ACM Trans. Netw. **11**, 17–32 (2003)
15. Urdaneta, G., Pierre, G., Van Steen, M.: A survey of DHT security techniques. ACM Comput. Surv. (CSUR), 43 (2011)
16. Wang, H., Zhu, Y., Hu, Y.: An efficient and secure peer-to-peer overlay network. In: 2005 IEEE Conference on Local Computer Networks 30th Anniversary. IEEE (2005)
17. Wang, Z., Minsky, N.: Establishing global policies over decentralized online social networks. In: Proceedings of the 9th IEEE International Workshop on Trusted Collaboration, October 2014
18. Wang, Z., Minsky, N.: Regularity based decentralized social networks. In: Proceedings of the 9th International Conference on Risks and Security of Internet and Systems (CRiSIS2014), October 2014
19. Haifeng, Y., Kaminsky, M., Gibbons, P.B., Flaxman, A.: Sybilguard: defending against sybil attacks via social networks. ACM SIGCOMM Comput. Commun. Rev. **36**, 267–278 (2006)

An Anomaly Detection Model for Network Intrusions Using One-Class SVM and Scaling Strategy

Ming Zhang(✉), Boyi Xu, and Dongxia Wang

National Key Laboratory of Science and Technology on Information System Security, Beijing Institute of System Engineering, Beijing, China
{mingle_cheung, boyi_xu}@yeah.net, WDX_76738@126.COM

Abstract. Intrusion detection acts as an effective countermeasure to solve the network security problems. Support Vector Machine (SVM) is one of the widely used intrusion detection techniques. However, the commonly used two-class SVM algorithms are facing difficulties of constructing the training dataset. That is because in many real application scenarios, normal connection records are easy to be obtained, but attack records are not so. We propose an anomaly detection model for network intrusions by using one-class SVM and scaling strategy. The one-class SVM adopts only normal network connection records as the training dataset. The scaling strategy guarantees that the variability of feature values can reflect their importance, thus improving the detection accuracy significantly. Experimental results on KDDCUP99 dataset show that compared to Probabilistic Neural Network (PNN) and C-SVM, our one-class SVM based model achieves higher detection rates and yields average better performance in terms of precision, recall and F-value.

Keywords: Intrusion detection · Anomaly detection · One-class SVM · Scaling strategy

1 Introduction

The Internet has brought with endless joy and great convenience. Especially, with the rapid growth of Web applications, everything seems so easy. However, in recent years, "attack", "intrusion" and other similar words frequently appear in people's eyes. We are suffering from increasing network threats. The well-known internet security corporation, Symantec, reminds in its annual Internet Security Threat Report (ISTR) that cybercrime remains prevalent and damaging threats from cybercriminals continue to loom over businesses and consumers [1]. Another Web security company, Cenzic, reported in 2014 that 96 % of the tested internet applications had vulnerabilities with a median of 14 per application, resulting in that hackers are increasingly focusing on and are succeeding with layer 7 (application layer) attacks [2]. These reports show that network security should not be ignored and effective security measures are much needed.

Among the important ways to solve security problems, intrusion detection is an effective and high-profile method. Intrusion detection was first introduced by Anderson

S. Guo et al. (Eds.): CollaborateCom 2015, LNICST 163, pp. 267–278, 2016.
DOI: 10.1007/978-3-319-28910-6_24

in [3]. Later, lots of researches have been carried out [4]. Generally, there are two main approaches to conduct intrusion detection: signature-based detection (misuse detection) and anomaly-based detection. The signature-based detection model has a good prior knowledge of known attacks, but seldom involves new types of attacks. Hence, in practice, it could miss a significant amount of real attacks [5]. By contrary, the anomaly detection creates a profile from normal behaviors and any violation will be reported as an intrusion. Theoretically, it is capable of detecting both known and unknown attacks. Under the current complicated network environment, the anomaly detection is much more required and has a better application foreground. In this paper, we focus on the anomaly detection.

With the network improving at an unprecedented pace, the traditional intrusion detection approaches are faced with more and more challenges. So a lot of new techniques have been introduced to conduct intrusion detection [6], among which the Support Vector Machine (SVM) is one of the widely used techniques [7, 8]. Whereas in the actual intrusion detection scenarios, the conventional two-class SVM algorithms may face some minor problems. For example, in many cases, normal network records can be obtained easily, but intrusion records are not so. So it is difficult to construct the training dataset. Actually, the intrusion detection is not a straightforward binary classification problem. The attacks can be divided into many categories. Given this, we propose to adopt the one-class SVM, which uses the normal connection records as the training dataset and can recognize normal from various attacks, to create anomaly detection model for network intrusions. Besides, the scaling strategy is introduced to improve the detection accuracy.

The rest of this paper is organized as follows. In Sect. 2, we introduce some related work about the intrusion detection. In Sect. 3, we first present the framework of our one-class SVM based intrusion detection model, and then discuss the implementation details. Experimental results and performance comparison are described in Sect. 4. Finally, Sect. 5 concludes this paper.

2 Related Work

The research on intrusion detection began from Anderson's famous literature [3]. In [3], the author proposed a model established from statistics of users' normal behaviors, so as to find the "masquerader" that deviates from the established normal model, which laid the foundation of intrusion detection and revealed the basic idea of anomaly detection. Later researches on anomaly detection also employ various statistical methods including multivariate statistics [9], Bayesian analysis [10], principal component analysis [11], and frequency and simple significance tests [12]. The signature-based detection (also called misuse detection) was first introduced by Denning in [13]. The author proposed an intrusion detection model that can be regarded as a rule-based pattern matching system. Both the misuse detection and statistics based anomaly detection have some limitations, such as low intelligence and poor ability to adapt to various application scenarios. And when encountering with larger datasets, the detection results would become worse [14].

To solve the limitations of above models, a number of machine learning techniques have been used [15, 16], of which the most widely used techniques may be Artificial Neural Networks (ANNs) [17] and Support Vector Machines (SVMs) [18]. A common practice is to use ANN and SVM to construct the hybrid model to detect intrusions [19, 20]. In this paper, our work relates to SVM and ANN is used as a comparison.

Multi-class SVM is also an alternative in intrusion detection. In [21], the author applied multi-class SVM classifiers, using one-against-one method, for anomaly as well as misuse detection to identify attacks precisely by type. But like the two-class SVM, the multi-class SVM is also faced with the difficulties to construct the training dataset.

Some other studies concern combining cluster algorithms with SVM techniques. In [22, 23], a hierarchical clustering method was applied to preprocess the originally enormous dataset to provide a reduced dataset for the SVM training. Thus the intrusion detection system could greatly shorten the training time. In this paper, we are more concerned about how to improve the detection accuracy, and seldom care about the learning speed. But the clustering method to reduce the dataset can also be used in our model.

Based on the related work, we propose an anomaly detection model for network intrusions by using one-class SVM and scaling strategy. One-class SVM can overcome the difficulties that the common two-class SVM and multi-class SVM encounter. Scaling strategy can greatly improve the detection accuracy.

3 One-Class SVM Based Anomaly Detection

In this section, we expound our one-class SVM based intrusion detection model. We first present the framework of the model, and then discuss how each constituent module works.

3.1 Framework of One-Class SVM Model

Our one-class SVM based intrusion detection model consists of the following three modules, as illustrated in Fig. 1

Module I: Feature extracting module. Feature extracting is the necessary step to make the detection module work correctly. Our intrusion detection model integrates a feature extracting module mainly to extract useful features from the raw data and then generates manageable formatted data for the detection module.

Module II: Scaling module. As an enhancing module, the scaling module normalized the data before inputting them to the detection module. In many circumstances, scaling the feature values to a small range can help to get better detection results and avoid numerical difficulties during the calculation.

Module III: One-class SVM module. Working as the detection module, one-class SVM involves two processes. The training process accepts the normalized training data and then generates a decision model. The testing process takes both the decision model and the normalized testing data as inputs, and then produces the detection results.

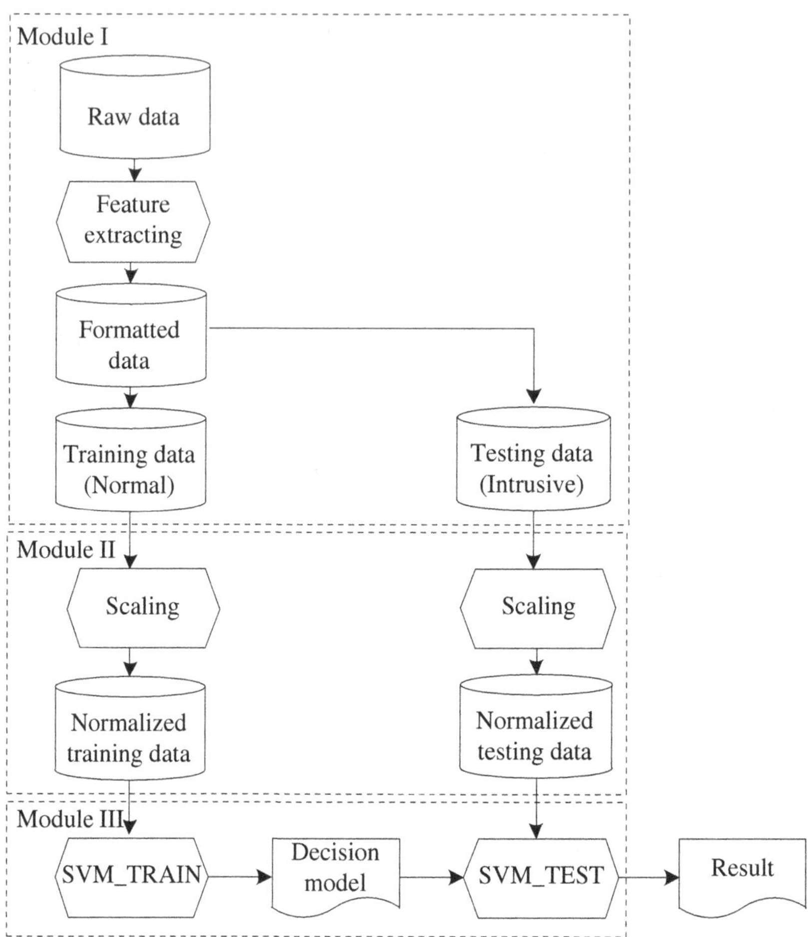

Fig. 1. Framework of one-class SVM based model

3.2 Feature Extracting Module

Almost no intrusion detection model can distinguish between intrusive connections and normal connections directly from original packets. They must be inputted with formatted data. Feature extracting is to obtain useful information from raw data and then format it, so that it can be interpreted by the detection module. There is no permanent standard to extract features. It may be better to extract features based on the actual network environment to find whether some attacks are hidden in connections. Extracting proper features helps the detection module to make more accurate predictions. In terms of network intrusions, some frequently-used features need paying attention to, such as the length (number of the seconds) of the connection, the type of the protocol, e.g. tcp, udp, etc., the number of data bytes transferred, the number of "root" accesses and so forth. In our one-class SVM based detection model, the feature extracting module takes the raw data as inputs, and then extracts expected features to form the formatted data. Moreover, the feature extracting module is charged with dividing the formatted data into two divisions, the training data and the testing data. This process is fairly simple. The normal records comprise the training data and the rest (intrusive) records comprise the testing data. This relates to the detection mechanism of one-class SVM (detailed later).

3.3 Scaling Module

Scaling a value means to add or subtract a constant and then multiply or divide by a constant, to make the value lie in an expected range. So it is also called "normalizing". Scaling before applying one-class SVM is very important. The main advantage of scaling is to avoid features in greater numeric ranges dominating those in smaller numeric ranges. In intrusion detection models, we extract features from many aspects. These features may have great difference in numerical values. For example, the feature, length of the connection, may have a range of 0 to 10, while another feature, number of data bytes transferred, can have a range of 0 to 65535. Then the contribution of the first feature to the detection result will be swamped by the second. So it is crucial to scale the feature values so that their variability reflects their importance. Another advantage is to avoid numerical difficulties during the calculation. Because kernel functions used in one-class SVM usually need complex calculations of feature vectors, and large feature values might cause numerical problems. It is recommended to scale the feature values to a small range. In our one-class SVM based detection model, the scaling module scales both training and testing data to the same range [0, 1]. We use the following min-max normalization method.

$$x^* = \frac{x - min}{max - min}, \tag{1}$$

where x is the initial feature value, x^* is the new scaled value, *min* denotes the minimum value of the same features and *max* denotes the maximum value.

3.4 One-Class SVM Module

Here, we adopt the one-class SVM proposed by Scholkopf [24]. First, consider the training dataset:

$$D = \{(\boldsymbol{x}_i, y_i) | \boldsymbol{x}_i \in \mathbb{R}^n, y_i = +1\}_{i=1}^{l}, \tag{2}$$

where $\boldsymbol{x}_i$ is the feature vector with dimension n, $y_i = +1$ means all the training patterns are normal observations, and l is the number of training patterns.

The algorithm basically separates all the training data points from the origin. Suppose the hyperplane has the form:

$$w \cdot \phi(\boldsymbol{x}) - \rho = 0, \tag{3}$$

then the distance from the hyperplane to the origin is $\frac{\rho}{\|w\|}$. Maximizing the distance results to solving the following quadratic programming problem:

$$\min_{w,\xi,\rho} \frac{1}{2}\|w\|^2 + \frac{1}{vl}\sum_{i=1}^{l}\xi_i - \rho, \quad \text{s.t. } w \cdot \phi(\boldsymbol{x}_i) \geq \rho - \xi_i, \xi_i \geq 0. \tag{4}$$

Here, $\phi(\boldsymbol{x}_i)$ is the feature mapping function that maps $\boldsymbol{x}_i$ from its input space to a feature space, ξ_i is the slack variable for outlier $\boldsymbol{x}_i$ that allows it to lie on the other side of the decision boundary (hyperplane), and $v \in (0, 1]$ is the regularization parameter that is an upper bound on the fraction of outliers and a lower bound on the fraction of support vectors.

For convenience, we can introduce the kernel function, which is defined as follows:

$$k(\boldsymbol{x}_i, \boldsymbol{x}) = \phi(\boldsymbol{x}_i)\phi(\boldsymbol{x}). \tag{5}$$

For the one-class SVM used in our detection model, we use the Gaussian kernel function:

$$k(\boldsymbol{x}_i, \boldsymbol{x}) = e^{-\gamma\|\boldsymbol{x}_i - \boldsymbol{x}\|^2}. \tag{6}$$

After introducing the kernel function, we can get the following dual form of the primal quadratic programming problem:

$$\min_{\boldsymbol{\alpha}} \frac{1}{2}\sum_{i,j=1}^{l}\alpha_i\alpha_j k(\boldsymbol{x}_i, \boldsymbol{x}_j) \quad \text{s.t. } 0 \leq \alpha_i \leq \frac{1}{vl}, \sum_{i=1}^{l}\alpha_i = 1. \tag{7}$$

The answer to the dual problem (Eq. 7) is also the answer to the primal quadratic programming problem (Eq. 4). Furthermore, solving the dual problem is much easier and more feasible. We use the SMO (Sequential Minimal Optimization) algorithm [25] to solve the dual problem. Once solving the problem, we can get the following decision function:

$$f(\boldsymbol{x}) = \operatorname{sgn}\left(\sum_{i=1}^{l}\alpha_i k(\boldsymbol{x}_i, \boldsymbol{x}) - \rho\right). \tag{8}$$

That is, if $w \cdot \phi(\boldsymbol{x}) - \rho \geq 0$, $\boldsymbol{x}$ is regarded as a normal event, otherwise, it is declared as intrusive.

4 Experiments and Discussions

To evaluate the performance of our one-class SVM based intrusion detection model, we conducted a series of experiments on KDDCUP99 [26] dataset.

4.1 Data Preparation

In 1998, DARPA Intrusion Detection Evaluation Program was prepared and managed by MIT Lincoln Labs. A standard dataset [27] was provided. The KDDCUP99 dataset used in our experiments is a version of this dataset.

The raw training data contains about five million TCP connection records from seven weeks of network traffic. Similarly, the two weeks of testing data yields around three million records. Each connection record has 41 derived features that help in distinguishing normal connections from attacks, and is labeled as either normal, or as an attack, with exactly one specific attack type. Attacks fall into four main categories: DOS, Probe, R2L and U2R.

In experiments, we used stratified random sampling to reduce the size of dataset. For one-class SVM used in our intrusion detection model, the training data must contain only normal patterns and does not contain any attacks. So we selected a random sample of normal records in the raw training data. The sampling proportion is about 3 %. To test the model's ability to detect different kinds of attacks, we randomly selected different types of records in the raw testing data. The sampling proportion is about 1 %. Some types of attacks such as R2L and U2R were totally selected due to their low proportion in KDDCUP99 dataset. Finally, 32426 normal connection records in the raw training data and 31415 connection records in the raw testing data were randomly selected. Table 1 shows the details about different categories of records. "Other" indicates the new types of attacks not present in the four main categories.

Table 1. Number and distribution of training and testing data

Category	Training dataset		Testing dataset	
Normal	32426	100 %	6060	19.29 %
DOS	/	/	22429	71.40 %
Probe	/	/	315	1.00 %
R2L	/	/	622	1.98 %
U2R	/	/	39	0.12 %
Other	/	/	1950	6.21 %
Total	32426	100 %	31415	100 %

4.2 Evaluation Criteria

In order to evaluate the performance of IDS, some accepted measurements are proposed. We use *TP*, *FN*, *TN* and *FP* to represent the number of true positives, false negatives, true negatives and false positives, respectively. Usually, we use the detection rate to evaluate the IDS' ability to detect real attacks. For some category of attacks, the detection rate is the fraction of detected attacks accounting for the total ones. In addition to the detection rate, another three criteria are also widely used for performance evaluation, especially for performance comparison. They are precision, recall and F-value. Precision is the fraction of true positives in total determined positives (i.e. the sum of true positives and false positives). Recall has the same formula as the detection rate. F-value considers both the precision and the recall to compute the evaluation value. The precision, recall and F-value are defined as follows.

$$Precision = \frac{TP}{TP + FP} \tag{9}$$

$$Recall = \frac{TP}{TP + FN} \tag{10}$$

$$F - value = \frac{2 * Recall * Precision}{Recall + Precision} \tag{11}$$

4.3 Results and Discussions

In this section, we compare our one-class SVM based model with other two well-knowns, probabilistic neural network (PNN) [28] and C-SVM (proposed by Cortes and Vapnik in [29]), given that they both adopt the radial basis function (Gaussian function or Gaussian kernel) as the one-class SVM does and are often used to detect intrusions due to their good classification performance. PNN used in our experiments is taken from the MATLAB R2013b toolbox and C-SVM from the software LIBSVM [30]. Because the training data used by PNN and C-SVM must contain both normal and abnormal records, we conducted a stratified random sampling for the raw training data in KDDCUP99 with the proportion around 1 %. The final training data contains 49567 records, including 9728 Normals (19.63 %), 39167 DOSs (79.02 %), 412 Probes (0.83 %), 208 R2Ls (0.42 %), and 52 U2Rs (0.10 %). The three models use the same testing data as described in Sect. 4.1.

In experiments, the parameter γ (gamma) in radial basis function was set to 0.5, the cost parameter c in C-SVM was set to 1 and the parameter v (nu) in one-class SVM was set to 0.05. First, we compare and discuss the detection rates of these three models for different categories of attacks. The results are shown in Table 2 and Fig. 2, and are produced in this way—first, any attack that can be detected by one-class SVM is declared abnormal without any distinction, then we compute the detection rate for different category of attacks according to the labels in the testing data. We can see that for DOS attacks, the three models get perfect results (all above 99 %). For Probe attacks, one-class SVM can reach the top detection rate 100 %, while the detection rates of PNN and C-SVM are relatively lower, respectively 98.73 % and 86.98 %. We should note that for R2L, U2R and "Other" categories of attacks, the results of all the three models are not very satisfactory. We believe one of the main reasons is that the number of attacks in these three categories is relatively small (see Table 1), so the test results have some limitations. Another reason may be that the attacks are too covert to be detected by the models. But even so, the detection results of one-class SVM are

Table 2. Detection rates of different models

	PNN	C-SVM	One-class SVM
DOS	0.9979	0.9958	0.9950
Probe	0.9873	0.8698	1.0000
R2L	0.0804	0.0322	0.2685
U2R	0.1284	0.4872	0.6923
Other	0.0687	0.1421	0.2067

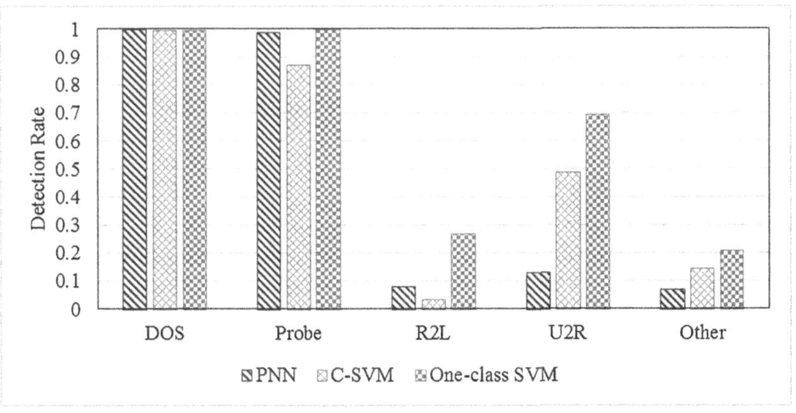

Fig. 2. Detection rate comparison of different models

considerably better than two others'. Furthermore, for PNN and C-SVM, the "Other" category of attacks are new attacks not present in their training data, so it is especially difficult for them to detect such attacks. But for one-class SVM, the new attacks receive the same treatment as with other categories of attacks, without any difference.

Next, we use three other criteria, precision, recall and F-value to conduct performance comparison. The results are shown in Table 3 and Fig. 3. As illustrated by Fig. 3, one-class SVM produces a slightly lower precision than PNN and C-SVM. But the precisions of all the three models are very high (above 99 %). Apparently, the recall and F-value of one-class SVM are higher than others'.

Table 3. Precision, recall and f-value of different models

	PNN	C-SVM	One-class SVM
Precision	0.9988	0.9957	0.9903
Recall	0.8916	0.9041	0.9161
F-value	0.9422	0.9477	0.9518

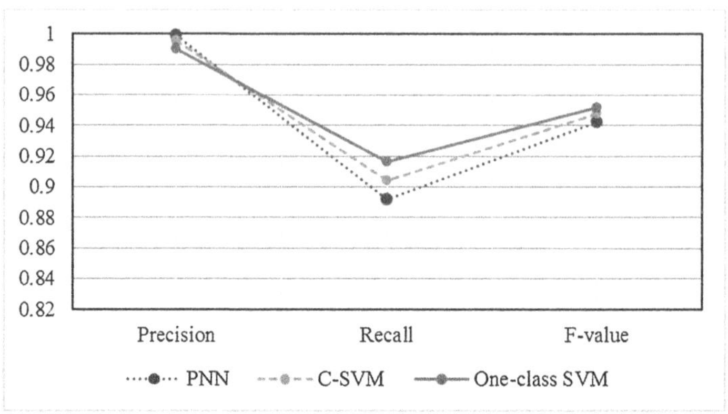

Fig. 3. Performance comparison of different models

5 Conclusion

We propose a novel anomaly detection model for network intrusions by using one-class SVM and scaling strategy. One-class SVM is a one-versus-rest classifier, which is very suitable for anomaly detection. Although the commonly used two-class SVM algorithms have been applied in intrusion detection, they are facing the difficulties of constructing the training dataset. That is because in many true application scenarios, it is easy to obtain normal connection records, but difficult to obtain attack records, or the number of attack records is very limited. Whereas to a great extent, the distribution of training records affects the detection results of the two-class SVM. Hence, we propose to use one-class SVM, which adopts only the normal network connection records as the training data, to conduct the anomaly detection. The scaling strategy scales the feature values to a small range so that their variability reflects their importance, thus greatly improving the detection accuracy and avoiding numerical difficulties during the calculation. The experimental results on KDDCUP99 dataset show that compared to PNN and C-SVM, our one-class SVM achieves higher detection rates for different categories of attacks and has an average better performance in terms of precision, recall and F-value. The deficiency lies in that both our one-class SVM based and other two models show relatively low detection rates for low-frequent attacks, such as R2L and U2R. Affecting the accuracy of results, the insufficient number of data is partially to blame. But the detection model could also be enhanced. We leave this as future work.

Acknowledgement. The work of this paper is supported by the National Natural Science Foundation of China Project under grant No. 61271252.

References

1. Symantec Enterprise.: Internet Security Threat Report 2014. http://www.symantec.com/content/en/us/enterprise/other_resources/b-istr_main_report_v19_21291018.en-us.pdf. accessed 15 April 2015

2. Cenzic.: Application Vulnerability Trends Report 2014. http://www.cenzic.com/downloads/Cenzic_Vulnerability_Report_2014.pdf. accessed 15 April 2015
3. Anderson, J.P.: Computer security threat monitoring and surveillance. vol. 17. Technical report, James P. Anderson Company, Fort Washington, Pennsylvania (1980)
4. Axelsson, S.: Intrusion detection systems: A survey and taxonomy. vol. 99. Technical report, 2000
5. Kruegel, C., Tóth, T.: Using decision trees to improve signature-based intrusion detection. In: Vigna, G., Kruegel, C., Jonsson, E. (eds.) RAID 2003. LNCS, vol. 2820, pp. 173–191. Springer, Heidelberg (2003)
6. Patcha, A., Park, J.-M.: An overview of anomaly detection techniques: existing solutions and latest technological trends. Comput. Netw. **51**(12), 3448–3470 (2007)
7. Li, Y., Li, W., Wu, G.: An intrusion detection approach using SVM and multiple kernel method. Int. J Adv. Comput. Technol. IJACT **4**(1), 463–469 (2012)
8. Li, Y., et al.: An efficient intrusion detection system based on support vector machines and gradually feature removal method. Expert Syst. Appl. **39**(1), 424–430 (2012)
9. Taylor, C., Alves-Foss, J.: Low cost network intrusion detection (2000)
10. Barbara, D., Wu, N., Jajodia, S.: Detecting novel network intrusions using Bayes estimators. In: SDM (2001)
11. Shyu, M.-L., et al.: A novel anomaly detection scheme based on principal component classifier. Miami Univ Coral Gables FL Dept of Electrical and Computer Engineering (2003)
12. Qin, M., Hwang, K.: Frequent episode rules for intrusive anomaly detection with internet datamining. In: USENIX Security Symposium (2004)
13. Denning, D.E.: An intrusion-detection model. IEEE Trans. Softw. Eng. **2**, 222–232 (1987)
14. Wang, G., et al.: A new approach to intrusion detection using artificial neural networks and fuzzy clustering. Expert Syst. Appl. **37**(9), 6225–6232 (2010)
15. Sinclair, C., Pierce, L., Matzner, S.: An application of machine learning to network intrusion detection. In: 15th Annual Computer Security Applications Conference (ACSAC 1999) Proceedings. IEEE (1999)
16. Tsai, C.-F., et al.: Intrusion detection by machine learning: a review. Expert Syst. Appl. **36** (10), 11994–12000 (2009)
17. Ryan, J., Lin, M.-J., Miikkulainen, R.: Intrusion detection with neural networks. In: Advances in neural information processing systems 943–949 (1998)
18. Kim, D.S., Park, J.S.: Network-based intrusion detection with support vector machines. In: Kahng, H.-K. (ed.) ICOIN 2003. LNCS, vol. 2662, pp. 747–756. Springer, Heidelberg (2003)
19. Sung, A.H., Mukkamala, S.: Identifying important features for intrusion detection using support vector machines and neural networks. In: 2003 Symposium on Applications and the Internet, Proceedings, pp. 209–216. IEEE (2003)
20. Mukkamala, S., Janoski, G., Sung, A.: Intrusion detection using neural networks and support vector machines. In: Proceedings of the 2002 International Joint Conference on Neural Networks, IJCNN 2002. vol. 2. IEEE (2002)
21. Ambwani, T.: Multi class support vector machine implementation to intrusion detection. In: Proceedings of the International Joint Conference on Neural Networks, vol. 3. IEEE (2003)
22. Khan, L., Awad, M., Thuraisingham, B.: A new intrusion detection system using support vector machines and hierarchical clustering. Int. J. Very Large Data Bases **16**(4), 507–521 (2007)
23. Horng, S.-J., et al.: A novel intrusion detection system based on hierarchical clustering and support vector machines. Expert Syst. Appl. **38**(1), 306–313 (2011)
24. Schölkopf, B., et al.: Estimating the support of a high-dimensional distribution. Neural Comput. **13**(7), 1443–1471 (2001)

25. Platt, J.: Sequential minimal optimization: a fast algorithm for training support vector machines (1998)
26. UCI KDD Archive.: KDDCUP99 dataset. http://kdd.ics.uci.edu/databases/kddcup99/. accessed 15 April 2015
27. MIT Lincoln Laboratory.: DARPA Intrusion Detection Data Sets. http://www.ll.mit.edu/mission/communications/cyber/CSTcorpora/ideval/data/index.html. accessed 15 April 2015
28. Specht, D.F.: Probabilistic neural networks. Neural Netw. **3**(1), 109–118 (1990)
29. Cortes, C., Vapnik, V.: Support-vector networks. Mach. Learn. **20**(3), 273–297 (1995)
30. Chang, C.-C., Lin, C.-J.: LIBSVM : a library for support vector machines. ACM Trans. Intell. Syst. Technol. **2**, 27:1–27:27 (2011). http://www.csie.ntu.edu.tw/~cjlin/libsvm

Short Paper

Layered Consistency Management for Advanced Collaborative Compound Document Authoring

Johannes Klein(✉), Jean Botev, and Steffen Rothkugel

Faculty of Science, Technology and Communication, University of Luxembourg, 1359 Luxembourg, Luxembourg
{johannes.klein,jean.botev,steffen.rothkugel}@uni.lu

Abstract. In distributed collaborative document authoring environments, the preservation of a globally consistent data state is an important factor. However, synchronization conflicts are unavoidable and constitute a serious challenge. Our advanced compound document system provides the basis for a novel consistency management approach, in particular regarding autonomous conflict detection and resolution. Current techniques to achieve and maintain global consistency in distributed environments almost exclusively utilize file-based data structures, thereby limiting the accessibility to supplementary information.

In this paper, we present a layer-based consistency management approach harnessing a fine-granular, graph-based data representation and relational dependencies. We discuss the application of concurrent conflict detection and resolution modules designed to preserve user intent while avoiding workflow interruptions. The combination of an advanced compound document system with autonomous, layer-based consistency management has the potential to notably increase reliability and facilitate the collaborative authoring process.

Keywords: Compound document systems · Document engineering · Distributed authoring · Collaboration · Consistency management · Conflict detection and resolution · Intention preservation

1 Introduction

Global data consistency in a distributed document authoring system is commonly ensured by either utilizing a conflict-free or commutative replicated data type [1], operational transformation algorithms [2], or by employing conflict detection and resolution schemes [3,4]. The latter use optimistic synchronization and eventual consistency [1,5], as conflicts are expected to only occur rarely. This assumption allows for highly responsive implementations with locally issued commands being applied instantaneously. Assuming a conflict-free application, the commands are afterwards distributed to the remote sites. In case of a conflict, an autonomous resolution is aspired. Eventually, the distributed system will reach a consistent state in which possible conflicts have been resolved and no new commands are pending.

S. Guo et al. (Eds.): CollaborateCom 2015, LNICST 163, pp. 281–288, 2016.
DOI: 10.1007/978-3-319-28910-6_25

However, for most systems, conflict detection and resolution is more complex and error-prone. In part, this can be attributed to relying on established file-based data structures, which complicate or do not provide access to further information. Particularly approaches based on intention preservation [2,6] require supplementary data as a prerequisite to determine a collaborator's intent. Therefore, we utilize an advanced Compound Document System (aCDS) [7] as a basis for consistency management in a distributed document authoring environment. The aCDS's fine-grained, graph-based structure facilitates storing the data while allowing for an accurate attribution of metadata to elements of arbitrary size and complexity. Moreover, element-centric attributes as well as intra- and inter-document relations, both user-generated or created by the system, are supported. These relations are particularly useful for intention preservation features as they allow for more comprehensive capturing of an edit's circumstances. The modular design of the aCDS furthermore facilitates the maintainability and a straightforward extensibility of the system.

These properties form the basis for the layered consistency management (LCM) approach proposed in this paper. LCM utilizes the native data representation to partition conflict detection and resolution functionality according to the unique structure of the data in the aCDS. Instead of employing the detection and resolution concepts on a block of data, the functionality is distributed among several specialized consistency management modules. These are selected based on the type of edited data and their location in the aCDS graph representation.

Currently, LCM is being integrated into our aCDS. In order to facilitate global information exchange through inter-document relations, a central server connects the distributed collaborators. Furthermore, a master copy of all compound documents is kept server-side, allowing for the application of all commands issued throughout the system and ensuring a consistent document representation. In the following section, we present the aCDS and its graph-based data structure. A discussion of the LCM approach and its close integration with the aCDS's specific representation of data follow in Sect. 3. Related work is reviewed in Sect. 4 before concluding this paper with a brief summary in Sect. 5.

2 Compound Documents

This section introduces the core concepts employed in the aCDS. In particular, we will discuss interdependencies between the underlying data representation and the information managed therein, which is fundamental to our consistency management approach.

2.1 The Advanced Compound Document System

Compound document systems transparently integrate different, application-specific documents or document parts, and have been a recurring subject of research in the past decades [8]. They offer a wide range of exciting possibilities with regard to the creation and management of complex documents. The aCDS developed by our group [7] serves as the basis for our collaborative authoring system. Its combination of fine-grained data representation, inherent modularity and deep integration of relations and attributes make it an ideal candidate for distributed and collaborative document authoring. It allows for in-place editing of various data types and its modularity enables simple extensibility. Harnessing these features for a real-time collaboration environment while maintaining its advanced editing capabilities, responsiveness, and resilience to conflict, is the main objective of this work.

A graph-based structure stores the main data in dedicated nodes and the concomitant metadata in associated nodes and edges. The granularity of the data is, in contrast to file-based approaches, not predefined but directly related to user operations and the layout of the document. This allows for a precise representation of the compound document and its accompanying information. For example, a copy-and-paste command not only makes the elements available in other parts of the document, but it preserves the implicit relations between source and copy for subsequent use. File-based systems generally fail to maintain this relational information beyond the execution of the command.

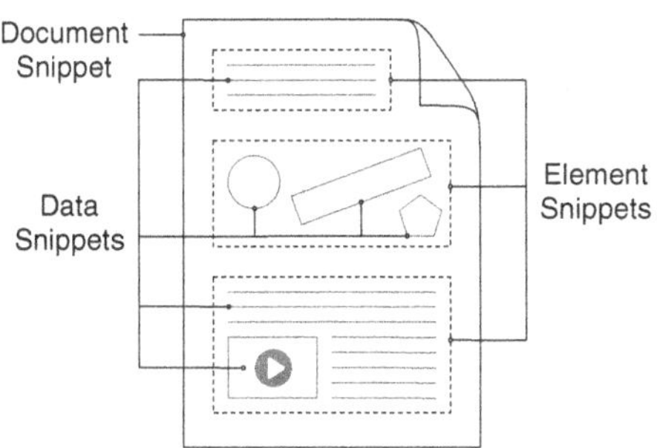

Fig. 1. aCDS data representation

The data representation of the aCDS is schematically depicted in Fig. 1. Every compound document is defined by its Document, Element, and Data Snippets along with their positions in the graph, contents, and relations. Each data type has specialized modules handling its peculiarities and defining its representation. All nodes form a parent-child relationship, therefore enabling straightforward navigation and data retrieval through the graph structure.

Intra- and inter-document relations between the elements of an aCDS are either created explicitly by users invoking commands or implicitly by analyzing their behavior. Similarly, attributes containing additional information can be specified manually by the user or automatically by the system. Manually defined attributes provide valuable information about a user's intentions and document perception, e.g., alternate element versions or source references, which would be otherwise complex to establish. The system itself utilizes attributes to store for instance the last editors or the dataset memberships of an element.

3 Layered Consistency Management

File-based approaches mostly include documents as single entities into the synchronization process, thereby leaving the data's inherent structure unused for a more precise and partitioned procedure. In contrast, and due to the specific properties of our aCDS, we are able to utilize said information in the proposed, layered consistency management (LCM) concept. This enables the analysis of individual elements, supplemented by their relational dependencies, metadata, attributes, and type-specific syntactic and semantic information.

The finer-grained data representation permits the precise localization of conflict-related data, thereby limiting the necessary processing tasks. Moreover, the concurrent application of specialized consistency management modules enables the independent analysis of subsets of an element's data, while also providing the basis for parallel task execution.

Our conflict management is logically partitioned into three distinct layers, directly related to the data representation of the aCDS as depicted in Fig. 1. The first two layers contain structural information and metadata whereas the bottom layer stores the actual data of an element. Document Snippets, which are located on the first layer, include the element's metadata and relational information. Particularly the latter are of great importance regarding the detection and resolution of conflicts involving the main data. On the second layer, Element Snippets store information about the structural representation of the element's graph and serve as an insertion point for other documents. As the structural and visual representation of a document are closely related, this data is utilized for, e.g., conflict analysis involving layout complications. The third layer comprises the actual data stored in Data Snippets with type-specific formats defined by the respective LCM modules.

The distribution of the consistency management logic over specialized modules in combination with the layered data representation allows for reusability and synergy effects. For instance, an elementary module capable of detecting conflicts in XML-based elements is combined with other modules enabling a dedicated analysis of a vector graphics element. Furthermore, the evaluation of one conflict can be limited to a single module and one layer, or, in a more complex scenario, include multiple different layers and modules.

LCM allows for the application of intention preservation techniques in a distributed environment by combining layer-based synchronization with the utilization of supplementary metadata. This reduces the need for manual conflict resolution and keeps workflow interruptions at a minimum [9]. Constant interference can lead to user dissatisfaction, isolation from the collaboration environment and eventually leaving the collaborator excluded from the group. Automatic consistency management is essential as synchronization conflicts are inevitable [10]. Still, manual conflict resolution is unavoidable, e.g., in case of concurrent edits of the same element. LCM enables supporting users involved in the resolution process with comprehensive data about the conflict which is generated utilizing all information available.

3.1 Layer-Based Conflict Detection

Consistency management is a multi-step process beginning with the local detection of synchronization conflicts. A conflict is introduced by the application of either a local or remote command to a data state dissimilar to the one it was initially invoked upon. Various factors, e.g., network latency, add time between invocation and application, thereby increasing the potential for encountering different data states for remotely received commands. Two distinct conflict areas are detected: issues with command application and ambiguous outcomes. They leave the data in a potentially inconsistent state or violate the user's intent. The conflict detection process can be classified into the following scenarios D.1 – D.4:

D.1 – A command has been executed without issues and the data remains consistent. The next command can be safely applied.

D.2 – A command has been executed raising at least one conflict which is limited to a single layer of the data structure. The corresponding conflict detection module analyzes the problem as a basis for the resolution process.

D.3 – A command has been executed raising numerous conflicts on multiple layers of the data structure. The corresponding conflict detection modules concurrently analyze each affected layer before individually providing the gathered information to the relevant resolution modules. The necessity to cumulate the conflict data is assessed during resolution, as it still may be possible all problems are isolated and can be concurrently resolved.

D.4 – A command is able to execute without conflict, but with ambiguous results. To guarantee the selection of a state conforming to global consistency constraints, each possible data state must be analyzed individually. The corresponding modules concurrently gather the related information on the affected layers and provide it to the relevant resolution modules. This information includes the circumstances of the application and all possible resulting data states.

The utilization of the aCDS's data structure facilitates the comprehensive conflict detection and analysis capabilities of LCM and provides the basis for the following, autonomous resolution process.

3.2 Layer-Based Conflict Resolution

In the second LCM phase, concurrently operating conflict detection modules utilize local and global data sources. These sources include information gathered during the detection process as well as data from related, but remote documents. Furthermore, the necessity for user involvement is established. The scenarios discussed in Sect. 3.1 lead to the conflict resolution approaches R.1 – R.4:

R.1 – Successful resolution is facilitated by solely utilizing the conflicting data. Distributed systems relying on a file-based data representation generally apply corresponding approaches.

R.2 – In addition to data experiencing the conflict, resolution requires the utilization of supplementary information still available on site. This includes related information from other local elements or documents and attributes.

R.3 – In contrast to R.2, sufficient information to resolve the conflict is not available locally. Still, relational dependencies indicate the presence of useful data on remote sites which can be accessed over the network. Although the inclusion of remote information is more time-consuming than purely local resolution, user involvement can still be avoided.

R.4 – The system is unable to perform an autonomous conflict resolution. Therefore, manual resolution by the collaborators is unavoidable. All available information, including the output of the detection modules, is processed and comprehensively presented to the users tasked with the solution. The preparation of a precise problem description not only expedites the process and thereby reduces the individual's workflow interruption but also enables proper resolution. These conflict resolution approaches rely heavily on the supplementary information available as part of our aCDS. Each approach involves one or multiple layers of the data structure into the resolution process. Concurrent and linked execution of the layer-specific modules is determined by the individual conflicts' requirements. With the exception of approach R.4, all resolve the corresponding conflict scenarios autonomously.

3.3 Local Concurrency Handling

Eventually, a site within the collaboration environment is already executing a command when it either receives another remote command or a new one is issued locally by the user. In this case, and regardless of any ongoing conflict resolution process, the current command execution is finished before the next is initialized. The sites therefore maintain FIFO queues storing all pending commands, ensuring a globally consistent state for command execution. This is necessary for relational dependencies to be able to provide reliable and up-to-date information.

4 Related Work

As opposed to consistency management approaches in distributed collaboration environments which rely mainly on file-based data structures [11], our LCM employs a more fine-grained representation based on compound documents.

One possible solution is to rule out conflicts by design by utilizing conflict-free replicated data types [1]. This requires further dedicated structures such as tombstones which retain elements for reference even after their deletion, a concept not needed when implementing LCM. Tombstones either result in an unbounded growth of the data structure as, e.g., observable in WOOT [12], or they require the use of garbage collection as applied in the Treedoc [13] implementation. Without tombstones, a linear or even sublinear space complexity with regard to the number of insert operations is achievable, as demonstrated by, e.g., LSEQ [11]. LCM, however, stores supplemental information such as relational dependencies and attributes only during the existence of the corresponding element. Thereby, the need for garbage collection is eliminated while preventing an unbounded growth of the data structure.

Another possible approach is the application of operational transformation as employed by, e.g., dOPT and GOT [2]. Similar to LCM, causality, intention, and global consistency are preserved in the presence of synchronization conflicts. As this is achieved through the conversion of the initial commands according to the requirements of the remote site's data state, transformation needs to be realized via commutative functions. Even for functions treating only character-wise primitives, formal proof of correctness is very difficult and error-prone [14]. In contrast, LCM not only allows for operations of arbitrary complexity but also utilizes the meta-information inherent to these operations. This information is not only applicable to conflicts concerning the local data state but can also be employed for resolution processes on remote sites.

Similar to LCM, the model of eventual consistency [1,5] is employed by these approaches. Therefore, a globally consistent data state is not guaranteed at all times.

5 Conclusion

Consistency management is central to distributed document authoring and a prerequisite for providing the user with a globally synchronized and unintrusive environment. The combination of our advanced Compound Document System and the layered consistency management concept introduced in this paper allow for the comprehensive utilization of relational dependencies and metadata to achieve autonomous consistency management and intention preservation. Specialized functional modules based on the data type enable concurrent conflict detection and resolution, prevent the processing of unrelated information and provide the user with thorough information about a conflict in case manual conflict resolution is required.

The fine-granular data structure inherently supports the utilization of supplementary contextual information as well as of data explicitly and implicitly generated by the use of the collaboration environment. This allows for a responsive, reliable, and extensible system supporting the collaborator's efforts while limiting workflow interruptions through largely autonomous consistency management. We are currently preparing a study to assess further usability and performance aspects of the LCM approach.

References

1. Shapiro, M., Preguiça, N., Baquero, C., Zawirski, M.: Conflict-free replicated data types. In: Défago, X., Petit, F., Villain, V. (eds.) SSS 2011. LNCS, vol. 6976, pp. 386–400. Springer, Heidelberg (2011)
2. Sun, C., and Ellis, C. A.: Operational transformation in real-time group editors: issues, algorithms, and achievements. In: Proceedings of the ACM 1998 Conference on Computer Supported Collaborative Work (CSCW 1998), pp. 59–68, Seattle (1998)
3. Zheng, Y., Shen, H., and Sun, C.: Agile semantic conflict detection in real-time collaborative systems. In: Proceedings of the 2009 International Symposium on Collaborative Technologies and Systems (CTS 2009), pp. 139–146, Baltimore (2009)
4. Sun, D., Sun., Xia, S., and Shen, H.: Creative conflict resolution in collaborative editing systems. In: Proceedings of the ACM 2012 Conference on Computer Supported Collaborative Work (CSCW 2012), pp. 1411–1420, Seattle (2012)
5. Saito, Y., Shapiro, M.: Optimistic replication. ACM Comput. Surv. **37**(1), 42–81 (2005)
6. Sun, C., Chen, D.: Consistency maintenance in real-time collaborative graphics editing systems. ACM Trans. Comput. Hum. Interact. **9**(1), 1–41 (2002)
7. Kirsch, L., Botev, J., Rothkugel, S.: The snippet platform architecture - dynamic and interactive compound documents. Int. J. Future Comput. Commun. **3**(3), 161–167 (2013)
8. Ter Hofte, G., Van Der Lugt, H.: CoCoDoc: a framework for collaborative compound document editing based on OpenDoc and CORBA. In: Proceedings of the IFIP/IEEE International Conference on Open Distributed Processing and Distributed Platforms, pp. 15–33, Toronto (1997)
9. Hudson, J. M., Christensen, J., Kellogg, W. A., Erickson, T.: "I'd Be Overwhelmed, But It's Just One More Thing To Do:" availability and interruption in research management. In: Proceedings of the CHI 2002 Conference on Human Factors in Computing Systems, pp. 97–104, Minneapolis (2002)
10. Jambon, F.: Error recovery representations in interactive system development. In: Proceedings of the 3rd Annual ERCIM Workshop on "User Interfaces for All", pp. 177–182, Obernai (1997)
11. Nédelec, B., Molli, P., Mostéfaoui, A., Desmontils, E.: LSEQ: an adaptive structure for sequences in distributed collaborative editing. In: Proceedings of the ACM Symposium on Document Engineering 2013 (DocEng 2013), pp. 37–46, Florence (2013)
12. Oster, G., Urso, P., Molli, P., Imine, A.: Data consistency for P2P collaborative editing. In: Proceedings of the 2006 ACM Conference on Computer Supported Cooperative Work (CSCW 2006), pp. 259–268, Banff (2006)
13. Preguiça, N.M., Marquès, J.M., Shapiro, M., Letia, M.: A commutative replicated data type for cooperative editing. In: Proceedings of the 29th IEEE International Conference on Distributed Computing Systems (ICDCS 2009), pp. 395–403, Montreal (2009)
14. Li, D., Li, R.: An admissibility-based operational transformation framework for collaborative editing systems. Int. J. Comput. Support. Collaborative Work (CSCW) **19**(1), 1–43 (2010)

On Ambiguity Issues of Converting LaTeX Mathematical Formula to Content MathML

Kai Wang, Xinfu Li(✉), and Xuedong Tian

Hebei Key Laboratory of Machine Learning and Computational Intelligence, College of Computer Science and Technology, Hebei University, Shijiazhuang, China
mc_lxf@126.com

Abstract. Facing the demand of providing retrieval result with rich semantic information for users in math searching, mathematical formulas of LaTeX are usually converted to Content MathML. For the problem of ambiguity formulas in the process of conversion, a method of semantic disambiguation for mathematics formulas which is based on the operator context was proposed. At first, ambiguity operator was found according to the ambiguity operator mapping table. Then, the ambiguity operator context is got through the array traversal. At last, the specific meaning was conjectured according to the ambiguity operator context. The experimental results show that compared with the type-system the method can make up for its disadvantages in simple formulas aspect and gets a higher average accuracy. In practical application, this method can effectively solve the problem of ambiguity formulas in the process of conversion.

Keywords: Mathematic formula conversion · LaTeX · Content MathML · Ambiguity formula · Semantic of formula

1 Introduction

Mathematical formula is more and more widely used on the Web. As the basis of mathematical formula retrieval system, format conversion is particularly important. The forms of LaTeX and MathML (Mathematical Markup Language) [1] formulas have been rapidly developed with their unique characteristics. Therefore, the issue of converting LaTeX mathematics formulas to Content MathML becomes a top priority in related fields. It would be an enormous job to systematically codify most of mathematics by hand – a task that can never be complete. The key problem is how to solve the problem of ambiguity formula.

Many scholars had done related research for mathematical formula tree structure, format conversion and ambiguity formula. Guan [2] extracted the tree structure of MathML formula and realized the related operations. Nie et al. [3] put forward an algorithm based on index and had carried on the concrete analysis about the tree structure of LaTeX formula. Zhang [4] used the principle of list and stack and combined with the operator priority realized the conversion of Infix to Content MathML. Zhao [5] proposed a method with higher recall ratio and precision ratio about the standardization of mathematical formula and semantic retrieval. However, there is no

S. Guo et al. (Eds.): CollaborateCom 2015, LNICST 163, pp. 289–295, 2016.
DOI: 10.1007/978-3-319-28910-6_26

study for the problem of ambiguity formula. Ting Zhang et al. [6] invented a formula translator called MathEdit. They fulfilled the conversion among Presentation MathML, Content MathML and Infix, which provided a great convenience for different forms of mathematical formula input, output, and storage. Su [7] came up with a kind of method based on the binary representation of the complexity of computation and realized the conversion among several common mathematical formula formats. The literature [8, 9] respectively introduced a method of conversion, that is the Presentation MathML to LaTeX and LaTeX to Presentation MathML. Doush et al. [10] put forward a framework of adding semantic information in the mathematical expression and realized the conversion of Presentation MathML to Content MathML using a method of RDFa (Resource Description Framework in attributes). Cai et al. [11] studied the problem of ambiguity mathematical formula transformation about Presentation MathML to Content MathML. The problem of LaTeX mathematical formula to the Content MathML ambiguity transformation was not involved.

According to the inspiration of scholars both at home and abroad, an ambiguity conjecture method for mathematical formulas based on operator context was proposed to deal with the ambiguity problems in the process of conversion about LaTeX mathematical formula to Content MathML.

2 Ambiguity Mathematical Formula

Some mathematical symbols of LaTeX have several meanings although they have unique representation. We need to clarify their specific meaning in the process of conversion. This kind of formulas with ambiguity operators are called ambiguity mathematical formula. LaTeX and Content MathML mapping table is listed in Table 1.

Table 1. LaTeX and content MathML mapping table

<table>
<tr><th>Ambiguity operator</th><th>LaTeX</th><th>Meaning</th><th>Content MathML</th></tr>
<tr><td>×</td><td>\times</td><td>product</td><td><times/></td></tr>
<tr><td></td><td></td><td>vector product</td><td><vectorproduct/></td></tr>
<tr><td></td><td></td><td>cartesian product</td><td><cartesianproduct/></td></tr>
<tr><td>superscript(T)</td><td>^T</td><td>power</td><td><power/> … < ci > T</ci></td></tr>
<tr><td></td><td></td><td>transposition</td><td><transpose/> … < ci > T</ci></td></tr>
<tr><td>superscript(-1)</td><td>^{-1}</td><td>power</td><td><power/> … < minus/>
<cn > -1 </cn></td></tr>
<tr><td></td><td></td><td>inverse function
inverse of a matrix</td><td><inverse/></td></tr>
<tr><td>| |</td><td>\[\left|{}
\right|\]</td><td>absolute</td><td><abs/></td></tr>
<tr><td></td><td></td><td>aggregative card</td><td><card/></td></tr>
<tr><td>{ }</td><td>\[\left\{{}
\right\}\]</td><td>set</td><td><set></td></tr>
<tr><td></td><td></td><td>grouping</td><td><apply></td></tr>
</table>

(*Continued*)

Table 1. (*Continued*)

Ambiguity operator	LaTeX	Meaning	Content MathML
[ ]	\[\left[{ } \right]\]	closed interval	<interval>
		grouping	<apply>
( )	\[\left({ } \right)\]	open interval	<interval>
		list	<list>
		grouping	<apply>
		vector	<vector>
d*	d*	differential coefficient	<diff/>
		integral	<int/> <bvar>

3 Ambiguity Conjecture Method

This paper proposes an ambiguity conjecture method for mathematical formula based on operator context. When finding ambiguity operator extracts its context first, then according to the different forms of contexts to conjecture the specific meaning of the operator in the process of conversion.

Using MathType to get LaTeX mathematical formula first, then tokenizing the formula into the smallest item and saving them to array. If it is an ambiguity operator it's position and context could be retrieved from the array. There are kinds of contexts. Some common forms are shown in Table 2.

Table 2. Some common forms of the context of ambiguity operator

Order	Context forms	Examples	Specific examples	Meaning
1	uppercase	A,B et al.	$A \times B$	product or vector product or cartesian product
2	lowercase	a, b et al.	$a \times b$	product
3	number	1,123 et al.	123×456	product
4	expression	$x + y$, $a*b$ et al.	$(x + y) \times z$	product
5	Greek letter	α, βet al	$\alpha \times \beta$	product or vector product
6	special form	Null, "T" et al.	A^T	power or transposition
7	function	sin x, f (x) et al.	$\sin x \times \cos x$	product

The algorithm based on operator context is designed according to the same ambiguity operator has different meanings with different context and combines the ambiguity mathematical properties of the operator itself. A program flow chart is shown in Fig. 1.

Using pseudo code to describe the context algorithm:

```
IF the operator is "\times" THEN
         DO getting "above" and "below";
IF above is "uppercase" and below is "uppercase" THEN
          DO related translation;
ELSE IF above is "number" and below is "lowercase" THEN
          DO related translation;
ELSE IF the operator is "^" THEN
           DO getting "above" and "below";
IF above is "function" and below is "T" THEN
           DO related translation;
ELSE IF above is "expression" and below is "number"
THEN
           DO related translation;
END
```

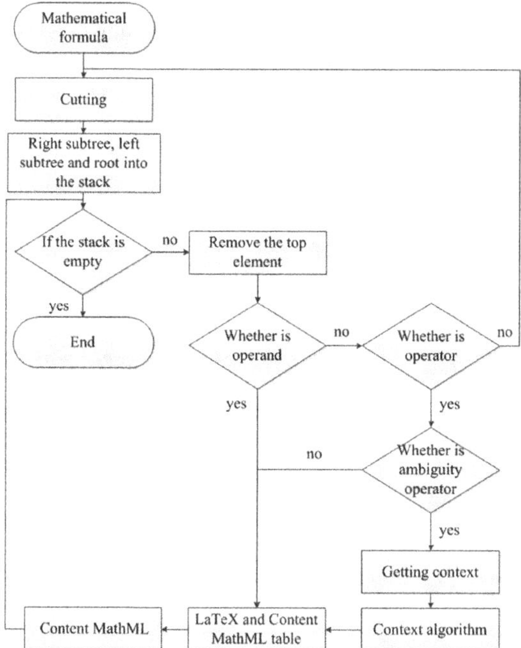

Fig. 1. Program flow chart

4 Experimental Results and Analysis

In order to verify the validity of the method, this paper gets the ambiguity mathematical formulas from the public data set [12]. There are 483,874 mathematical formulas in total. This paper using the simple random sampling extracts 1,000 ambiguity formulas to carry out the experiment and artificially contrast. The experimental result is shown in Table 3.

Table 3. Results of the experiment

Type	Meaning	Total formulas	Correct formulas	Accuracy ratio (%)	Simple formula	Correct formulas	Accuracy ratio (%)
×	product	723	660	91.3	216	149	69.0
	matrix product	231	183	79.2			
	cartesian product	46	35	76.1			
^{T}	power	463	423	91.4	240	170	70.8
	transform	537	483	89.9			
^{-1}	power	189	176	93.1	35	28	80.0
	inverse matrix	48	45	93.8			
	inverse function	30	24	80.0			
| |	absolute	903	815	90.3	178	129	72.5
	card	97	76	78.4			
{ }	set	135	112	83.0	–	–	–
	grouping	865	787	91.0			
[ ]	closed interval	117	110	94.0	–	–	–
	grouping	883	770	87.2			
( )	open interval	106	96	90.6	–	–	–
	grouping	782	702	89.8			
	list	23	11	47.8			
	vector	89	55	61.8			
d*	integral	763	721	94.5	–	–	–
	differential coefficient	237	220	92.8			

In the experiment, there are 7,267 ambiguity mathematical formulas of LaTeX in total. The average conversion accuracy is 89.5 %. However, the simple formulas of accuracy ratio are far below the value.

Through the analysis of the results is not hard to find that the formulas of incorrectly conjecturing most are simple ambiguity formulas which led to a low accuracy of simple ambiguity formulas. Simple ambiguity formulas have in common is that their context is too single, so it is different to judge the true meaning of ambiguity operator. If natural language context of formula can be combined, the ambiguity mathematical formula accuracy ratio can be improved in the actual process of conversion.

5 Conclusion

This paper analyzed a problem about ambiguity formulas in the process of LaTeX to Content MathML conversion. The experimental results show that compared with the type-system the method makes up for its disadvantages in dealing with simple formulas and has a higher average accuracy. In practical application, this method can effectively solve the problem of ambiguity formulas in the process of conversion.

There is no denying that the deficiencies are in the system due to insufficient time. The method is simple and needs to do a lot of test. The next step will focus on how to combine natural language context to further improve the ambiguity mathematical formula transformational accuracy ratio. LaTeX mathematics formula to Content MathML is still in the immature stage and needs to do more researches.

Acknowledgments. This work is supported by National Natural Science Foundation of China (No. 61375075), Natural Science Foundation of Hebei Province (No. F2013201134).

References

1. W3C Math Working Group. Mathematical Markup Language (MathML) version 3.0 2nd edn. W3C Recommendation, 10 April 2014. http://www.w3.org/TR/MathML/
2. Guan, M.: The research of mathematical formula indexing based on MathML. Hebei University, Hebei (2013)
3. Nie, J., Chen, T., Fu, H.: Research and implementation of internet mathematic formula search engine based on Latex. J. Comput. Appl. **30**(2), 312–313 (2010)
4. Zhang, T.: Research and Implementation of Web-based mathematical expressions translation. Lanzhou University, Lanzhou (2009)
5. Zhao, L.: Research on the method and technology of mathematical formulas semantic retrieving based on ontology. Nankai University, Tianjin (2011)
6. Zhang, T., Li, L., Su, W., et al.: A mathematical formula converter based on mathedit. Comput. Appl. Softw. **27**(1), 14–16 (2010)
7. Su, W.: Research on web-based input and accessibility of mathematical expressions. Lanzhou University, Lanzhou (2010)
8. Stamerjohanns, H., Ginev, D., David, C., Misev, D., Zamdzhiev, V., Kohlhase, M.: Mathml-aware article conversion from LaTeX (English). In: Petr, S. (ed.) Towards a Digital Mathematics Library, Grand Bend, 8–9 July 2009, pp. 109–120. Masaryk University Press, Brno (2009)
9. Woodall, D.R.: LaTeX MathML: translating LaTeX math notation dynamically to presentation MathML (2010)

10. Doush, I.A., Alkhateeb, F., Maghayreh, E.A.: Towards meaningful mathematical expressions in e-learning. In: Proceedings of the 1st International Conference on Intelligent Semantic Web-Services and Applications, Amman (2010)
11. Cai, C., Su, W., Li, L.: On key issues of converting presentation mathematics formulas to content. Comput. Appl. Softw. **29**(8), 30–33 (2012)
12. NICIR 11 Math Wikipedia Task. http://ntcir11-wmc.nii.ac.jp/index.php/NTCIR-11-Math-Wikipedia-Task

LTMF: Local-Based Tag Integration Model for Recommendation

Deyuan Zheng[1], Huan Huo[1(✉)], Shang-ye Chen[2], Biao Xu[1], and Liang Liu[1]

[1] University of Shanghai for Science and Technology, Shanghai 200093, China
huo_huan@yahoo.com
[2] School of Information and Technology, Northwest University, Xian 710127, China

Abstract. There are two primary approaches to collaborative filtering: memory- based and model-based. The traditional techniques fail to integrate with these two approaches and also can't fully utilize the tag features which data contains. Based on mining local information, this paper combines neighborhood method and matrix factorization technique. By taking fuller consideration of the tag features, we propose an algorithm named LTMF (Local-Tag MF). After the real data validation, this model performs better than other state-of-art algorithms.

1 Introduction

As one of the two main collaborative filtering techniques, memory-based method is to calculate the similarity to find the neighbors of users or items and produce clusters to complete the recommendation. The model-based method typically adopts the view called latent factor model, which assumes that the users or items are composed of latent factors. By extracting the latent factor from user vector or item vector through mathematic method, we can find the user with matching items to complete the recommendation.

Traditional memory-based model and model-based method barely can be combined. Moreover, most algorithms do not fully consider tags, which can aggravate the sparsity problem of rating matrices. Also, without fully using the tags, it will result the "cold starting" problem. We must explore the local structure and similarity to analyze the connections between data that not explicit annotated. [1] considered the tag features, and [2] introduced the mix-recommendation. However, these new techniques still fail to fully take account of data?s potentials and latent information.

This paper takes full account of data information, builds model from two sides. First exploring the implicit local structure by clustering algorithm, then making use of data tags to build new matrices. At last, we propose LTMF model which is better than above.

2 Related Work

There are many mature research about latent factor on collaborative filtering. Memory- based algorithm [3,4] mainly calculated the similarity between users and articles and then predict the missing values based on the existing rating matrices. [5] made a further study on sparse matrix completion algorithm. [6] proposed some methods consider KNN to this kind of problem. Among

S. Guo et al. (Eds.): CollaborateCom 2015, LNICST 163, pp. 296–302, 2016.
DOI: 10.1007/978-3-319-28910-6_27

model-based algorithms, [7] made an improvement on SVD which is called LFM algorithm and applied it on collaborative filtering. [8] proposed PMF by adding probabilistic dimension into LFM.

2.1 Probabilistic Matrix Factorization

The framework of PMF algorithm is shown as formula 1:

$$p(R|U,V,\sigma_R^2) = \Pi_{u=1}^{M}\Pi_{i=1}^{N}[N(R_{u,i}|U_u^T V_i, \sigma_R^2)]^{I_{u,i}^R} \tag{1}$$

$N(x|\mu,\sigma^2)$ denotes Probability Density Function of normal distribution with μ as the mathematical expectation of rating matrix and σ^2 as the variance. $I_{u,i}^R$ is the indicator that equals to 1 if user u rated item i and equals to 0 otherwise. Formulas 2 and 3 assume that the mathematical expectation of user and item is 0, and the variances are σ_U^2 and σ_V^2 respectively:

$$p(U|\sigma_U^2) = \Pi_{u=1}^{M} N(U_u|0,\sigma_U^2 I) \tag{2}$$

$$p(U|\sigma_V^2) = \Pi_{i=1}^{N} N(V_i|0,\sigma_V^2 I) \tag{3}$$

The loss function is defined as:

$$E = \frac{1}{2}\sum_{u=1}^{M}\sum_{i=1}^{N} I_{ui}^R (R_{ui} - U_u^T V_i)^2 + \frac{\lambda_U}{2}\sum_{u=1}^{M}||U_u||_F^2 + \frac{\lambda_V}{2}\sum_{i=1}^{N}||V_i||_F^2 \tag{4}$$

where $\lambda_U = \sigma_R/\sigma_U$, $\lambda_V = \sigma_R/\sigma_V$. The core of PMF and LFM is quite similar. But considering the randomness of latent factor, PMF always outperforms LFM. PMF is generally trained by SGD algorithm like LFM.

2.2 Other Work

Many data with tags are embedded on the Internet. [9] proposed a tag-based algorithm for recommendation. [10] used the item's type information to solve the problem of sparse and cold start. [1] proposed Tag-LFM to construct a new matrix with taking full advantage of tag features. [11] went a step further with a MF model based on local similarity named SBMF (Similarity-Based Matrix Factorization) algorithm. Most of these algorithms refer to matrix construction. A typical technique is shown in Fig. 1.

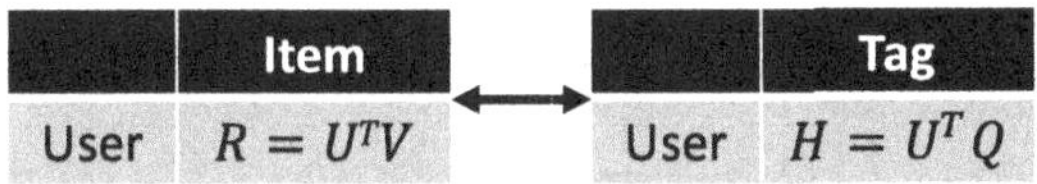

Fig. 1. New matrix construction

We assume that H is a matrix constructed by data tags. Then it is feasible to bridge the two matrices by using common user vectors or item vectors in rating matrix R and constructed matrix H. At last we can model the algorithm with more information.

3 Building LTMF Algorithm

3.1 Preparing Work

We design an algorithm to generate user cluster and item cluster. The details are shown as Algorithm 1, θ is the threshold that we can decide:

Algorithm 1. Clustering Algorithm

Compute rating frequency of user f_u and item f_i
Sort users and items based on f_u and f_i in reverse order
Compute cosine similarity of users and items
$t \leftarrow 1$, $U \leftarrow \phi$, $I \leftarrow \phi$
for $j = 1, 2, \cdots$ **do**
  if $u_j \notin U$ **then**
    $U_t \leftarrow u_j \cup u_k | s_{u_j,u_k} > \theta_j, u_k \notin U$
    $U \leftarrow U_t \cup U, t \leftarrow t + 1$
  end if
end for
The same as cluster I

In this section, we use clusters that have built before to construct local cluster as (user cluster)-(item) preference matrix and (item cluster)-(user) preference matrix by adding the local preferences into the model separately. $X_{u,i}$ and $Y_{u,i}$ can be represented as (user cluster)-(item) and (item cluster)-(user) preference, the details are shown in formulas 5 and 6 :

$$X_{u,i} = \sum_{k \in U} \frac{w_{r_{k,j}} r_{k,j}}{|u|} = (\sum_{k \in U} \frac{w_{p_k} p_k^T}{|U|}) q_j + \omega_U \tag{5}$$

$$Y_{u,i} = \sum_{k \in I} \frac{w_{r_{i,k}} r_{i,kj}}{|I|} = P_i^T (\sum_{k \in I} \frac{w_{q_k} q_k^T}{|I|}) q_j + \omega_I \tag{6}$$

where r is the rating, w is the weight of the corresponding latent factors. $\omega \sim N(0, \sigma^2)$, p and q denote the latent factor of user and item separately.

We use $G_{i,t}$ and $H_{u,t}$ to denote item-tag matrix and user-tag matrix. $G_{i,t}$ is 1 if item i contains tag t, otherwise is 0, same as $H_{u,t}$. Then we construct (user cluster)- (tag) matrix and (item-cluster)-(tag) matrix by using $X_{u,i}$?? and $Y_{u,i}$: The details are shown as formulas 7 and 8:

$$P_{u,t} = \frac{1}{N} \sum X_{u,i} \times G_{i,t} \tag{7}$$

$$Q_{u,t} = \frac{1}{N} \sum Y_{u,i} \times H_{i,t} \tag{8}$$

Now we can combine $R_{u,i}$, $P_{u,t}$ and $Q_{i,t}$ to build LTMF model.

3.2 Building Models

Rating matrix R_{ui} is formed by latent factor matrix U and V. By the definition of $X_{u,i}$ and $Y_{u,i}$, we know that $X_{u,i}$ and $Y_{u,i}$ are the functions of U and V. So

$P_{u,t}$, $Q_{i,t}$ are also the functions of U, V and the tag latent factor T, short for $P_{u,t} = f(U_u^T)T_t$, $Q_{i,t} = g(V_i^T)T_t$. The loss function of LTMF can be organized as formula 9:

$$E = \frac{1}{2}\sum_{u=1}^{M}\sum_{i=1}^{N} I_{ui}^{R}(R_{ui} - U_u^T V_i)^2 + \frac{\alpha}{2}\sum_{u=1}^{M}\sum_{t=1}^{K}(P_{ut} - f(U_u^T)T_t)^2 + \frac{\beta}{2}\sum_{i=1}^{N}\sum_{t=1}^{K} (Q_{i,t} - g(V_i^T)T_t)^2 + \frac{\lambda_U}{2}\sum_{u=1}^{M}||U_u||_F^2 + \frac{\lambda_V}{2}\sum_{i=1}^{N}||V_i||_F^2 + \frac{\lambda_T}{2}\sum_{t=1}^{K}||T_t||_F^2 \tag{9}$$

where $\omega_U = \sigma_R/\sigma_U$, $\omega_V = \sigma_R/\sigma_V$, α and β are the regularization coefficients, K is number of tags, $\lambda_U = \omega_U + \varphi_U$, $\lambda_V = \omega_V + \tau_V$, $\lambda_T = \varphi_T + \tau_T$.

3.3 SGD Training Algorithm

We use SGD algorithm to train the loss function of LTMF model, the detail is shown in Algorithm 2:

Algorithm 2. SGD training algorithm

Input: Rating Matrix R, Cluster Preference Matrix P, Q, Latent Factor Dimension F, Learning Rate η, Scale Factor α and β, Regularization Coefficients λ_U, λ_V, λ_T
Output: U, V

Randomly initialize U, V and T with small numbers
while error on validation set decrease **do**
  $\nabla_U E = I(U^T V - R)V + \alpha f'(f(U^T)T - P)T + \lambda_U U$
  $\nabla_V E = [I(U^T V - R)]^T U + \beta g'(g(V^T)T - Q)T + \lambda_V V$
  $\nabla_T E = \alpha f(f(U^T)T - P) + \beta g(g(V^T)T - Q) + \lambda_T T$
  Set $\eta = 0.08$
  while $E(U - \eta \nabla_U E, V - \eta \nabla_V E, T - \eta \nabla_T E) > E(U, V, T)$ **do**
    Set $\eta = \eta/2$
  end while
  $U = U - \eta \nabla_U E$
  $V = V - \eta \nabla_V E$
  $T = T - \eta \nabla_T E$
end while
return U, V

4 Experimental Evaluation

4.1 Datasets Description and Compared Models

To evaluate the performance of this algorithm, we use the data provided by http://www.dianping.com/. This datasets contain the information that LTMF algorithm demanded. All the items contain one tag or more, such as district, type of services, subway and same as the user data. This dataset contains 862328 ratings, 28518 items, 127150 users and 47509 tags. Every item or user has one or more tag feature vectors, it equals to 1 if contains the tag otherwise equals to 0.

To demonstrate the performance of LTMF, various methods are studied as baseline. These compared methods are: 1.KNN (memory-based neighbor model algorithm); 2. PMF (model-based matrix factorization algorithm); 3. Tag-LFM (combine tag feature MF algorithm); 4. SBMF (combine neighbor model MF algorithm). This paper uses RMSE to evaluate the performance and applies 5-fold cross validation.

In the experimental process, α and β are used to balance the impact of local structure and tag features on the model. When other parameters are fixed, setting $\alpha = 0.8$ and $\beta = 0.7$ will minimize the RMSE. $\lambda_U = \omega_U + \varphi_U$, $\lambda_V = \omega_V + \tau_V$, $\lambda_T = \varphi_T + \tau_T$, and $\omega_U = \sigma_R/\sigma_U$, $\omega_V = \sigma_R/\sigma_V$. This indicates that λ_U, λ_V and λ_T are compound parameters. But it is practical to set these parameters to a relatively small value,such as $\lambda_U = \lambda_V = \lambda_T = 0.001$.Then we can regulate these values by cross validation in experiments. And the results show that it is acceptable.

4.2 Performance Evaluation

The above Figs. 2 and 3 obviously indicate that with the number of iterations increasing, LTMF performs better than other algorithms.

Figures 4 and 5 show that in a practical environment (means that the number of iterations and the number of observed ratings are relatively more), the model with higher latent factor dimensionality generally performs better.

Figure 6 demonstrates that the algorithms performance is proportional to the number of observed ratings. LTMF combine the existing methods to create

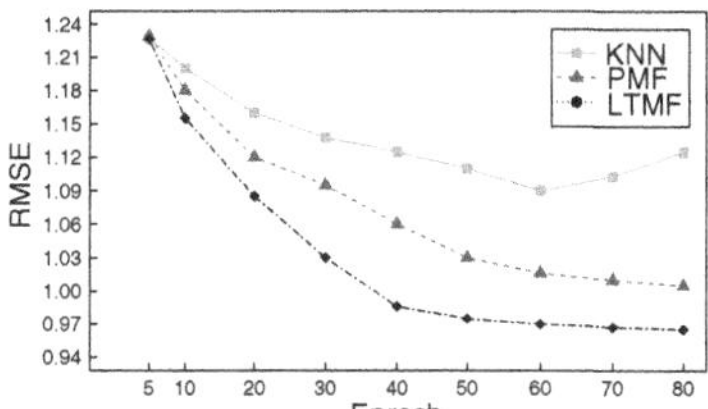

Fig. 2. Impact of number of iterations compared with basic models

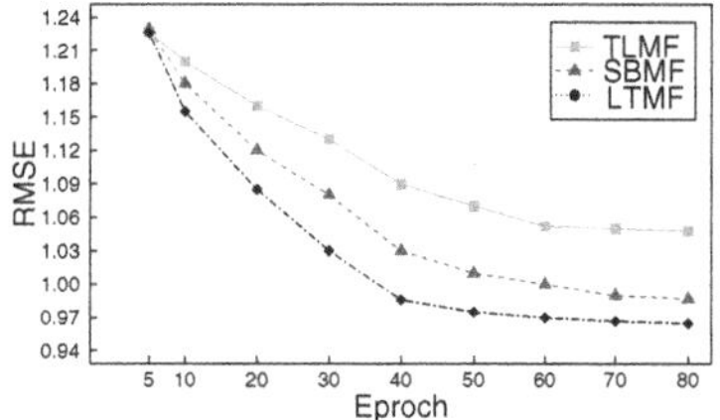

Fig. 3. Impact of number of iterations compared with advanced models

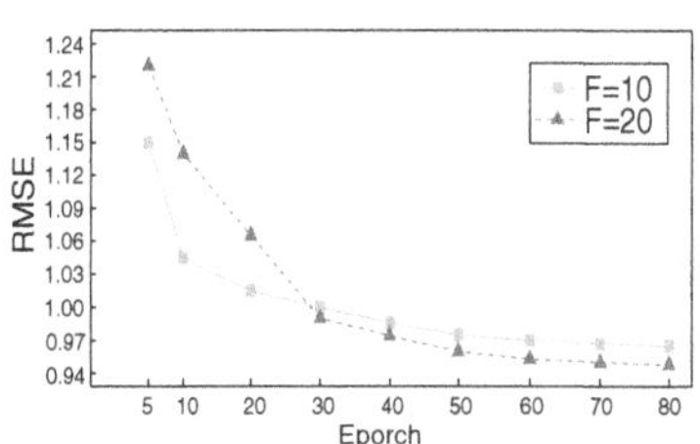

Fig. 4. Impact of latent factor dimensionality with number of iterations

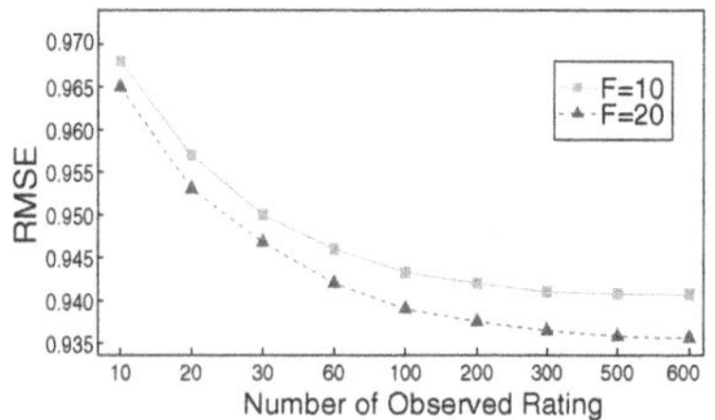

Fig. 5. Impact of latent factor dimensionality with observed ratings

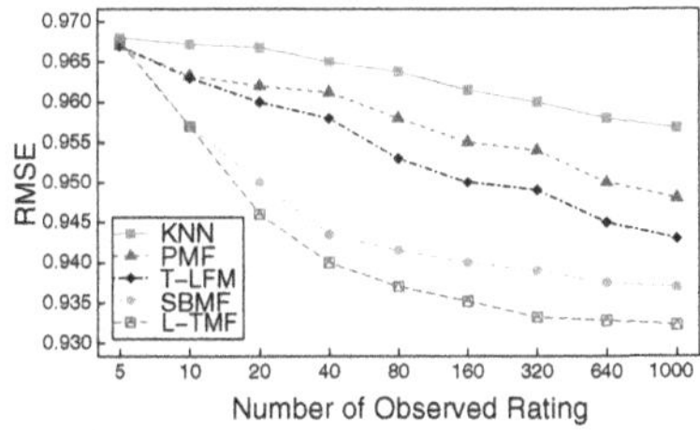

Fig. 6. Impact of observed ratings

a new one. But each stage of the algorithm can be computed separately. So the complexity of LTMF is linear growth, it is quite acceptable when the number of observed ratings increase rapidly.

5 Conclusion

This paper proposes LTMF algorithm and shows that integrating with more information can improve interpretability and performance. But due to constructing new matrices, LTMF can only be applied to the scenarios that contain the information which the algorithm demanded. And also LTMF has more parameters than other traditional models. In the future, we will study on how to tune the parameters more effective and explore other local information such as social networks.

Acknowledgment. This work is supported by National Natural Science Foundation of China (61003031, 61202376), Shanghai Engineering Research Center Project ($GCZX$14014), Shanghai Key Science and Technology Project in IT(14511107902), Shanghai Leading Academic Discipline Project($XTKX$2012) and Hujiang Research Center Special Foundation(C14001).

References

1. Kim, B.S., Kim, H., Lee, J., Lee, J.-H.: Improving a recommender system by collective matrix factorization with tag information. In: 2014 Joint 7th International Conference on Soft Computing and Intelligent Systems (SCIS), and 15th International Symposium on Advanced Intelligent Systems (ISIS), pp. 980–984. IEEE (2014)
2. Grivolla, J., Badia, T., Campo, D., Sonsona, M., Pulido, J.-M.: A hybrid recommender combining user, item and interaction data. In: 2014 International Conference on Computational Science and Computational Intelligence (CSCI), vol. 1, pp. 297–301. IEEE (2014)
3. Si, L., Jin, R.: Unified filtering by combining collaborative filtering and content-based filtering via mixture model and exponential model. In: Proceedings of the Thirteenth ACM International Conference on Information and Knowledge Management, pp. 156–157. ACM (2004)
4. Wang, J., De Vries, A.P., Reinders, M.J.: Unifying user-based and item-based collaborative filtering approaches by similarity fusion. In: Proceedings of the 29th Annual International ACM SIGIR Conference on Research and Development in Information Retrieval, pp. 501–508. ACM (2006)

5. Insuwan, W., Suksawatchon, U., Suksawatchon, J.: Improving missing values imputation in collaborative filtering with user-preference genre and singular value decomposition. In: 2014 6th International Conference on Knowledge and Smart Technology (KST), pp. 87–92. IEEE (2014)
6. Bell, R.M., Koren, Y.: Scalable collaborative filtering with jointly derived neighborhood interpolation weights. In: 2007 Seventh IEEE International Conference on Data Mining ICDM 2007, pp. 43–52. IEEE (2007)
7. Funk, S.: Netflix update: Try this at home, December 2006
8. Mnih, A., Salakhutdinov, R.: Probabilistic matrix factorization. In: Advances in Neural Information Processing Systems, pp. 1257–1264 (2007)
9. Chatti, M.A., Dakova, S., Thus, H., Schroeder, U.: Tag-based collaborative filtering recommendation in personal learning environments. IEEE Trans. Learn. Technol. **6**(4), 337–349 (2013)
10. Pirasteh, P., Jung, J.J., Hwang, D.: Item-based collaborative filtering with attribute correlation: a case study on movie recommendation. In: Nguyen, N.T., Attachoo, B., Trawiński, B., Somboonviwat, K. (eds.) ACIIDS 2014, Part II. LNCS, vol. 8398, pp. 245–252. Springer, Heidelberg (2014)
11. Wang, X., Xu, C.: SBMF: Similarity-based matrix factorization for collaborative recommendation. In: 2014 IEEE 26th International Conference on Tools with Artificial Intelligence (ICTAI), pp. 379–383. IEEE (2014)

A Privacy-Friendly Model for an Efficient and Effective Activity Scheduling Inside Dynamic Virtual Organizations

Salvatore F. Pileggi(✉)

INRIA and UPMC-LIP6, Paris, France
flavio.pileggi@lip6.fr
http://www.flaviopileggi.net

Abstract. The cooperation among people is one of the key factors for most processes and activities. The efficiency and the effectiveness of the cooperation has an intrinsic value, which significantly affects performances and outcomes. Open communities, as well as spontaneous or predefined virtual organizations, are demanding for a more solid and consistent support for activity scheduling and managing in a context of flexibility and respect of the individual needs. This paper proposes a privacy-friendly model to support virtual organizations in the scheduling and management of their most valuable resource: the time.

Keywords: Collaborative application · Distributed computing · Privacy · Organisational model

1 Introduction

The efficiency and the effectiveness of the cooperation among people has an intrinsic value, which significantly affects performances and outcomes of many processes and activities, at a quantitative and at a qualitative level [1]. Classic models used in the real world by companies have evolved at a theoretical level to integrate a more flexible philosophy (e.g. [2]). More recently, some of those models have started to be considered also in practice, as many companies are progressively leaving from classic schemas to evolve towards novel approaches where individual needs and effectiveness converge under the realistic assumption that the personal and the collective development come together. Indeed, open communities, as well as spontaneous or predefined virtual organizations, are demanding for a more solid and consistent support for activity scheduling and management in a context of flexibility and respect of individual needs. This paper focuses on activity scheduling and proposes a privacy-friendly model, called *Optimistic Scheduling* due to the implicit optimism that drives interactions among people to manage their most valuable resource: the time. The most novel solutions on the market offer features that the current reference tools (e.g. *Google Calendar*) are missing. The most dominating trends appear in coherence with the

S. Guo et al. (Eds.): CollaborateCom 2015, LNICST 163, pp. 303–308, 2016.
DOI: 10.1007/978-3-319-28910-6_28

current technological climate [3] which pushes towards a progressive socialization of tools and applications. Simple observations clearly show an unpredictable human behaviour, even in simple or well-known situations. Therefore, the model is analysed and evaluated by simulation as the function of complex user behaviours. An empirical overview of collaborative tools demonstrates as the simplest approaches (e.g. [4]) usually reach the best results, meaning products are well accepted by users and, indeed, are more usable in practice. Proposing a completely generic tool is hard and, in some case, not effective. In this work, the community is understood as a whole, meaning that users can interact each others at a global level. However, the ideal application domain assumes a *virtual organization* model, where existing and relatively static real groups (e.g. companies, institutions, teams, groups of friends) are integrated with dynamic groups that can change along the time (e.g. cooperative projects) or that are defined on the fly as the function of concrete tasks or activities. It is also assumed that users inside groups are peers. That is not always realistic as groups are often organized according to some structure or hierarchy. Moreover, it is supposed that a shared activity inside a dynamic group requires the participation of all the members. This ideal case could not suit real virtual organizations. Finally, individual preferences have a priority over groups (in contrast with most current approaches). This should push the cooperation and should optimize the use of the time.

2 Beyond the State of the Art: Overcoming a Simple Use Case

The schedule of a shared event is commonly performed according to two different approaches:

- *Scheduling by invitation* implies the organizer sending a specific invitation to the interested participants by using some shared channel (e.g. email, message, sms). This is the simplest and most used method. But it is also very vulnerable as the synchronization schema among the users is weak. First of all, the event cannot be considered as committed if confirmations are not received from all group members. If at least one of the expected participants rejects the invitation, the organizer needs to restart the process sending a new invitation. Furthermore, a missed response from at least one member can generate misunderstandings (not received? Not seen? Not interested? Unable to respond?), requires further actions from the organizer (e.g. reminders) and can lead to a potential deadlock.
- *Scheduling by poll* is the most common alternative. The organizer proposes a set of possible slots and participants are asked to express their preferences. Having a poll of possible options reduces significantly the vulnerability of the model as the organizer has to set up a new poll only if there is no agreement. Unfortunately, a lack of response from some member proposes the same problems discussed above. Furthermore, once a member has expressed his preferences, he should wait for the final confirmation from the organizer before

using the time slots he potentially accepted with an evident inefficiency in the management of time.

Both methods have a further common weakness: what if a group member changes his plans after a commitment? The process should start over!

3 Optimistic Scheduling: Efficient and Effective Time Sharing Inside Virtual Organizations

Each community member has his own calendar TS_P that is considered a private asset as no-one else in the community has access to it. On this personal calendar, each user i performs a preliminary filtering as he sets a priori the slots that can be used for a personal activity (ts_P) or a shared activity (ts_S), defining his personal space K_i. An example of preliminary filtering is represented by a calendar that only includes normal work hours and that doesn't include leaves or other absences known a priori. The whole space K of slots is given merging users' spaces according to Eq. 1. On that filtered calendar, a user i can schedule personal activities (Eq. 2) for any available slot $k \in K_i$. According to the same logic, a user can try to schedule a shared event (Eq. 3) involving other members (group).

$$K = \bigcup_i K_i \quad \forall i \tag{1}$$

$$TS_P^i(t) = \sum_k ts_P^i(k,t) \tag{2}$$

$$TS_S^i(t) = \sum_g \sum_k ts_S^g(k,t), \quad i \in g \tag{3}$$

$$TS^i(t) = TS_P^i(t) \cup TS_S^i(t) \tag{4}$$

The full activity set TS for a community member i is given by merging his personal activities (TS_P) and the shared activities (TS_S) as in Eq. 4. The whole potentially shared time can be at least equal to K, assuming people have no personal activities scheduled (Eq. 5). Users can only see their own calendars. In order to get an effective guide to schedule shared events, users can access, for any defined group they are joining, a shared structure FTS obtained by merging the personal calendars and returning the anonymized complementary set according to Eq. 6. That anonymized structure shows (Fig. 4) the slots that can be used, inside a certain group, to schedule a shared event. This simple operation allows, in fact, users to automatically understand the availability of a certain group in the respect of the members' privacy. Assuming a significant group size, inferring information is not easy, so the privacy is completely preserved. By using those structures, whichever member in a group can schedule a shared activity for a dynamic or static group with high probability of success (Fig. 4). The semantic of the model implicitly defines the main global invariant (a logical assertion that is held to always be true during a certain phase of execution of a program [5]): if a time slot ts is used by a member i of a group g for a personal purpose, then that slot cannot be used for a shared activity inside any group i is member of (Eq. 7).

$$\bigcup_i TS^i(t) = K \Rightarrow TS^i_P(t) = \emptyset, \forall i \quad (5) \qquad FTS^g(t) = K - \bigcup_i TS^i(t), i \in g \quad (6)$$

$$\exists ts^i_P(k_a, t) \quad \Rightarrow \quad \nexists ts^g_S(k_a, t), \quad i \in g, \quad k_a \in K \quad \forall t \qquad (7)$$

The model works assuming multiple simultaneous groups, providing an individual-specific view of each group in a privacy-friendly context. As individual needs have a priority on groups activity, users can still schedule their own activities also for slots that are already currently in use as shared resources. In this case the invariant defined by the Eq. 7 is not respected determining a non-valid state for the system that, coherently with the assumptions, reacts (for example cancelling the shared event and notifying the interested members about).

4 Model Analysis

The most significant issue for the analysis and the full understanding of this model is the definition of realistic user behaviours, being aware that people are or can be unpredictable. In this study, the synthetic actor that emulates users assumes a linear logic implementing three different behaviours:

- *Constructive.* The user is "cooperative" and, therefore, acts according to a logic that facilitates the successful scheduling of shared initiatives. A constructive user schedules his activities only in slots not currently in use for shared events and uses shared slots only if there is no other choice.
- *Disruptive.* This is the opposite of the previous as he schedules personal activities prioritizing the slots currently occupied by shared events. This behaviour causes the continuous reorganization of the shared events. It is not necessarily reproducing a malicious user, as it could also emulate an involuntary "noise" caused by random circumstances or periodic conflicts on the schedule.
- *Random/Independent.* Between the two extremes (constructive and disruptive) there is an infinite range of behaviours, including an independent user that acts according to a pseudo-random logic that doesn't take into account the existence of groups.

The metric to evaluate the model performance (Eq. 8) is directly proportional to the number of shared activities successfully scheduled and inversely proportional to the number of shared activities cancelled upon request of users.

$$\alpha(t) = \frac{1 + \sum_i TS^i_S(t)}{\sum_i TS^i_S(t) + \sum_i TS^i_S(t)_{|c}} \quad (8) \qquad \frac{d}{dt}TS^i(t) > 0 \quad (9)$$

The simulations are assuming a finite *sliding window* of size m to reproduce the time. At the time t, users can only schedule between the slot *t+1* and the slot *t+m*. The logic transition from *t* to *t+1* implies the slot *t* no more available (past) and a new free slot *t+m+1* available. Furthermore, the experiment also assumes that the number of scheduled events tends to increase in the time (Eq. 9), meaning users scheduling a higher number of events than the number of events cancelled or consumed. For simplicity atomic slots don't overlap each others (Eq. 10).

$$ts^{i}_{P/S}(k_1, t) \cap ts^{i}_{P/S}(k_2, t) = \emptyset, \quad \forall k_1, k_2 \in K, \forall i \tag{10}$$

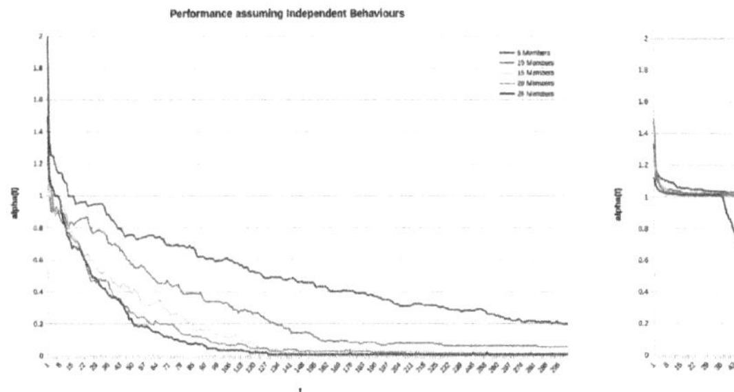

Fig. 1. Independent behaviour.

Fig. 2. Cooperative behaviour.

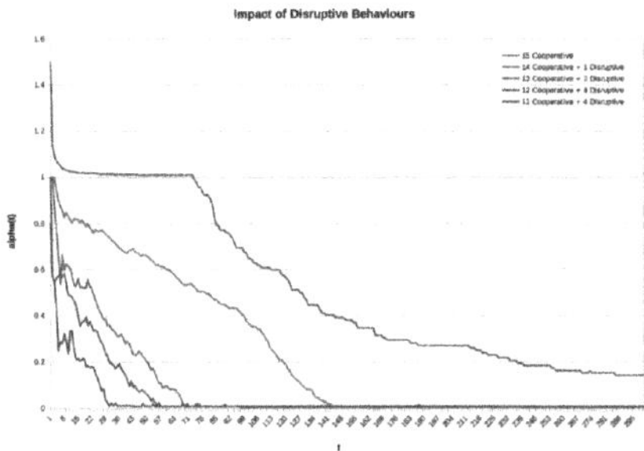

Fig. 3. Impact of disruptive behaviours.

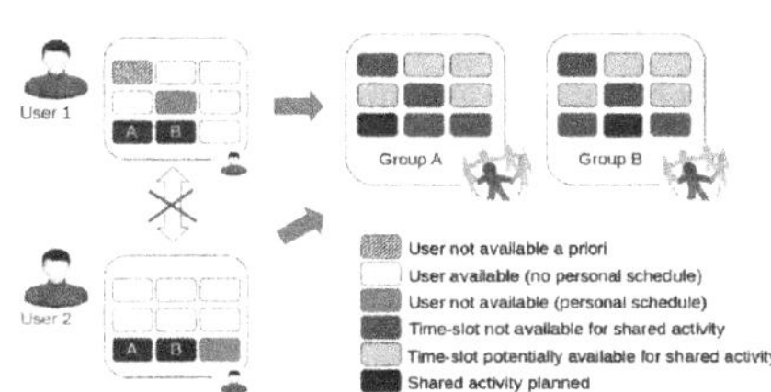

Fig. 4. Potentially shared time, shared activities and multiple groups.

The simulations assume a sliding window of 12 weeks to schedule activities and members averagely available 35 h (slots) per week, as in a common work calendar. The calendar is empty when the simulation starts, so there is a transitory period. The members schedule averagely an activity per day and the 25 % of the planned activities are shared. The simulation ends when the system is saturated (no more possibility to schedule events) or when the system has reached stationary/stable conditions. Figure 1 shows the performance decreasing as the function of the group size assuming independent behaviours. That is a very good approximation of performance inside a virtual organization where users are not acting according to this model. Figure 2 proposes the same statistics but assuming a cooperative behaviour. Is emulates a community that acts according to the proposed model. Performances are evidently higher than the previous and decrease only for the natural saturation of the system determined by the quantitative behaviour (Eq. 9). The chart in Fig. 3 provides an overview of the potential impact of disruptive behaviours on the whole performance. As showed, if one or more members is acting according to a disruptive behaviour, then performances quickly decrease and the system tends after a very short time to the saturation. Disruptive behaviours are part of real life and have to be taken into account at the time of designing real tools. They are easy to detect in common mechanisms (such as invitation and polls) due to the explicit character of the interactions. On the contrary, disruptive behaviours are hidden in a privacy-friendly context. At a model level, the global invariants (Eq. 7) can be relaxed to mitigate the effect of disruptive behaviours. This approach introduces at least one significant and critical trade-off between effectiveness and privacy/simplicity. Indeed, assuming that a slot inside a group can be used simultaneously for a personal and a shared activity protects the system from disruptive behaviours but also introduces ambiguities in the understanding and the management of the system state. Considering anonymous non-availabilities, the organizer cannot know who is missed, so the further steps of the activity planning could be negatively affected. On the other hand, concessions about privacy could invalidate most premises and, consequently, modify significantly the whole model focus. Anyway, integrating a complex could lead to applications that miss their aimed simplicity.

Acknowledgements. This research is supported in part by European FP7 project SyncFree (grant agreement 609551).

References

1. Wagner, J.A.: Studies of individualism-collectivism: effects on cooperation in groups. Acad. Manage. J. **38**(1), 152–173 (1995)
2. Jones, G.R., George, J.M.: The experience and evolution of trust: implications for cooperation and teamwork. Acad. Manage. Rev. **23**(3), 531–546 (1998)
3. Pileggi, S.F., Fernandez-Llatas, C., Traver, V.: When the social meets the semantic: social semantic web or web 2.5. Future Internet **4**(3), 852–864 (2012)
4. Raman, M.: Wiki technology as a "free" collaborative tool within an organizational setting. Inf. Syst. Manage. **23**(4), 59–66 (2006)
5. Shapiro, M., Preguiça, N., Baquero, C., Zawirski, M.: Conflict-free replicated data types. In: Défago, X., Petit, F., Villain, V. (eds.) SSS 2011. LNCS, vol. 6976, pp. 386–400. Springer, Heidelberg (2011)

A Discovery Method of Service Bottleneck for Distributed Service

Jie Wang[1], Tao Li[1,2](✉), Hao Wang[1], and Tong Zhang[1]

[1] School of Computer Science and Technology, Wuhan University of Science and Technology, Wuhan 430065, Hubei, China
{909901326,1593487967,zt1996816}@qq.com, litaowust@163.com

[2] Hubei Province Key Laboratory of Intelligent Information Processing and Real-Time Industrial System, Wuhan 430065, Hubei, China

Abstract. In order to deal with the large scale access to billions of users currently, large internet companies have adopted the distributed service of parallel processing to support it. The uncertainty of user behavior and software multi-tier architecture led to the distributed service behavior of uncertainty and complex dynamic combination between services, so it is difficult to detect the service bottleneck of distributed service. In this paper, we propose a service bottleneck discovery model of distributed service which is based on the two layer structure: the analysis based on the behavior attribute of the service and the relationship between the services.

Keywords: Distributed services · Bottlenecks · Relationship · Behavior attribute

1 Introduction

Big data, Mobile Internet, Mobile client application and Internet applications have gathered a huge amount of users. In order to timely response to the large crowd access and request, as well as provide efficient service quality, large Internet companies are adopting the distributed service system of concurrent processing as a solution.

The random behavior of massive users leads to the uncertainty of service behavior. This has brought a huge challenge to the whole service system. It can't find deep level issues by the direct influence factors such as hard disk resource, memory capacity, CPU utilization, service time, call number, network bandwidth, I/O and so on. The paper [1] introduced several methods of bottleneck discovery: the use of continuous time Markov chain to analyze the availability of resources, and through the average rate of service arrival and service rate of services to analyze the possible bottlenecks in workflow; analyze the behavior characteristics of multi level Internet application, propose a analysis model based on closed alignment network, each queue in the model corresponds to the different levels of the application, according to captured the behavior attribute of the model, then it can be used to predict the performance of the Internet and bottleneck positioning.

S. Guo et al. (Eds.): CollaborateCom 2015, LNICST 163, pp. 309–316, 2016.
DOI: 10.1007/978-3-319-28910-6_29

For different applications of distributed servers, of course, the factors that affect the quality of service are different. Some software can't simulate the real behavior of mass users by stressing testing, no fine grained analysis and deep excavation so that it can't predict and implement feedback in advance. The current research is based on load balancing to solve the problem of distributed server bottleneck, do a lot of redundant work in advance. In this paper, a new model for bottleneck discovery of distributed service is proposed. The model is designed for the two layer architecture: analysis of dynamic service behavior attributes and based on service dependencies, the validity of the model is verified in experiments and it has a certain value for the bottleneck discovery.

2 Theoretical Model and Analysis

At present, there is not a clear definition of the service bottleneck for distributed service. In order to make experiment and theory, we make a definition of service bottleneck: Under normal condition, the effect of service quality is caused by the mass increase of the service behavior, the dynamic combination of service behavior and the transfer of large-scale in short time. In this paper, a new model for service discovery of distributed service is proposed. The model is designed for the two layer architecture: analysis of dynamic service behavior attributes and based on service dependencies. When the two methods of analysis results are consistent, we believe the result is valid, that is this service is most likely to affect the quality of service in the entire service implementation process. This service has led to a large increase in time for the user-oriented services, which makes the resource utilization rate of the background server increased dramatically, even the service will run out.

2.1 Analysis of Dynamic Service Behavior Attributes

In the analysis of dynamic service behavior attributes, we are mainly to find a service bottleneck possible based on the correlation between data and the degree of data fitting in the verification of the uncertainty of distributed behavior. In the paper [2], a detailed description of the behavior of distributed services is that the dynamic behavior of the service is described by the **9** tuple of a service origin log. Those are Token, Invoking Service, Service Invoked, Location, Elapsed Time, Times Tamp, Input, Output and Status. In this paper, we use the method of service behavior collection in document [2]. The **9** tuple are the input data of the experimental model. The main work is recording statistics the counts of service-invoking, elapsed time of service- executing, invoked service and service invoked. Then use mathematical functions to explain the uncertainty of service behavior by optimization and processing of elapsed time and counts. In this paper, we first construct an uncertainty verification model of distributed service behavior to explain the real existence of bottlenecks. Then find the bottleneck or bottleneck area and lay a solid foundation for the follow-up to solve the bottleneck problem. Figure 1 as a model for uncertainty verification:

This experiment is based on the number of service calls and service time consuming statistical processing. In order to be closer to the actual operation of the distributed service, experiments are divided into two steps to verify the uncertainty

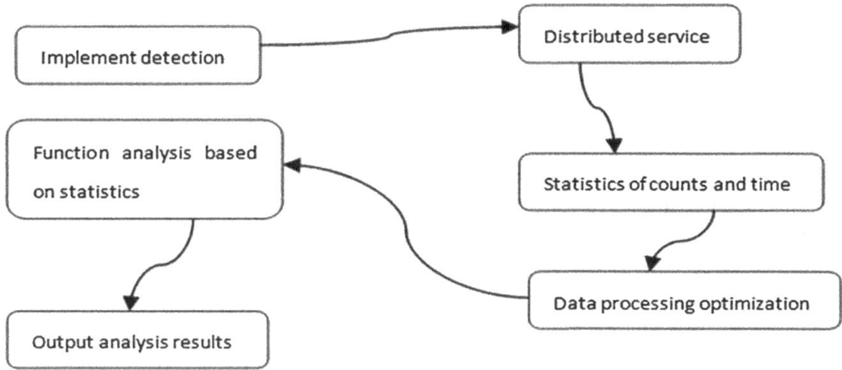

Fig. 1. Behavior uncertainty verification model of distributed services

behavior of distributed service: number of static service calls and dynamic random allocation service counts. Different results for different data processing, we introduce a concept of relative distance between data for these two variables of counts and time [3]. We deal with the data between different units by the "**relative distance**". The last we can use the **N** function to characterize relationship of counts and elapsed time by uniform amplification or reduction.

We illustrate the behavior of the distributed service by two results: correlation and function fitting degree between counts and time. Process two different units data, then analyses the results of several experimental data, we get a conclusion the correlation of their data **T** is close to **1**, the higher the correlation is. The **+1** indicates a complete positive correlation, the **–1** said total negative correlation. The experiment found the correlation between the two data is not consistent, there are complete positive correlation and complete negative correlation in two cases, so the behavior of the service is dynamic and its behavior is not determined. The fitting degree of function is developed from the data dependence, two data must be guaranteed to be relevant, the fitting function is effective. When the fitting function **R** was close to **1**, the representation of the two data can be replaced by the function expressions and the effect is remarkable. When the fitting function level was close to **0**, characterization of the two data can't be expressed by function.

The main purpose of this experiment is to analyze the service dynamic behavior attribute, then to find the service bottleneck of distributed services. In the experiment, we used the data correlation and the function fitting degree to analyze and discovery service bottleneck points. When a service is invoked by a large of users, the behavior are completely contrary to normal state or has special behavior, we think the service is a service bottleneck. The following is the algorithm process of dynamic service behavior property analysis.

2.2 Analysis of Dynamic Service Dependency

Define a series of cloud services as **S** = {**S1, S2, …, Sn**}, invoking between services such as **S1** invoke **S2**, remember as **S1->S2**, make **S1->S2** intitule path or service dependency. But it is not a complete path only as a part of the path, the full path to the implementation of the service is that **Sj** is no longer dependent on other services. We sort of total counts and total time for complete paths, find maximum complete path **L1** of total counts and longest complete path **L2** of total time. When **L1** and **L2** are consistent, we believe that the bottleneck is in this path. That is to say that the maximum complete path of total counts and longest complete path of total time are likely to be the **"bottleneck path"**. The behavior of distributed service is not deterministic, so we know when services execute at different times, different number of user access and different resource allocation schemes etc., the number of **"bottlenecks path"** is dynamically changing. When the **"bottleneck path"** is more and connected to each other, we think that the service bottleneck of distributed service constitutes a **"bottleneck area"**. The **"bottleneck area"** is also a way to find the service bottleneck and the solution to the service bottleneck. In this experiment, because of the specific service relationship and service's quantity is not very many, yet not use of **"bottleneck area"** to discover and solve problems.

After analyzing the **"bottleneck path"**, counts and time of each service in this path are analyzed. We make a sort of counts and time respectively by the proportion of sum time and sum counts for various services, then find the maximum value of the two sort, the service is likely to be a **"bottleneck service"**. Make data analysis combine with the first step experiment, we can find out which service is the bottleneck by comparing the correlation of data and the degree of function fitting. The following is the algorithm flow of service dependency:

3 Experimental Results and Analysis

3.1 Experimental Data Sources

In this experiment, the research object is login and elective service of students. Figure 2 shows the service flow. In order to simulate the real environment of student selection services, the Eclipse generated the real data scaling of a certain multiple by random to achieve the effect of the real environment.

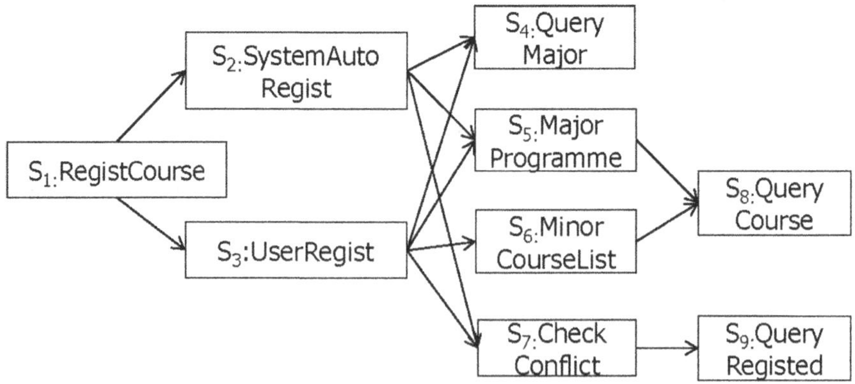

Fig. 2. The service flow chart of login and elective in the course for students

3.2 Experimental Procedures and Results Analysis

These nine nodes were recorded as services **S1–S9**, we take the service **S1** for example. Take six different invoking counts (10, 15, 20, 25, 30, 35 Unit: ten thousand). It is difficult to find the relationship between counts and time when data volume is relatively small in the experiment and the error is relatively large.

3.2.1 Behavior Attribute Analysis Based on Dynamic Service Behavior

A Counts of Static Service Invoked. Figure 3 is the data correlation between count and time of individual services. Figure 4 is function fitting degree, their horizontal coordinates are **S1–S9** these nine services, the longitudinal coordinates are the data correlation degree and the function fitting degree.

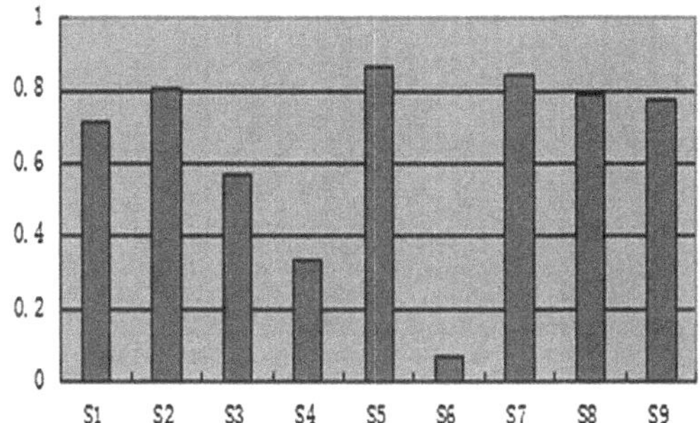

Fig. 3. The data correlation between count and time

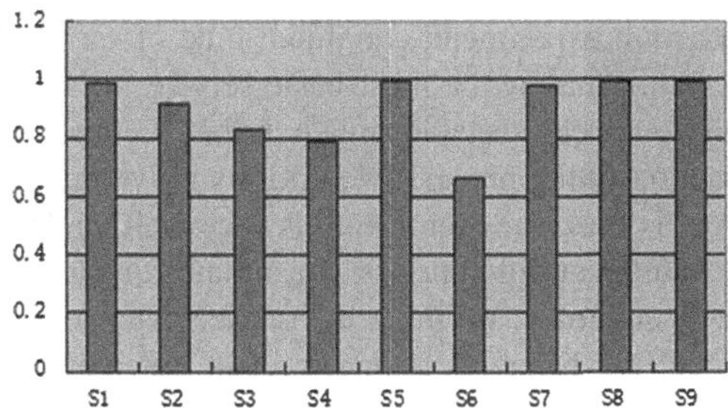

Fig. 4. Function fitting degree

B Dynamic Random Allocation Service Invoked Count. Figure 5 is the data correlation between count and time of individual services. Figure 6 is function fitting degree. Their horizontal coordinates are **S1–S9** these nine services, the longitudinal coordinates are the data correlation degree and the function fitting degree.

C Experimental Summary. In comparison to the experimental data chart, we find that the transformation of **S1–S9** is obviously different in both static and dynamic two

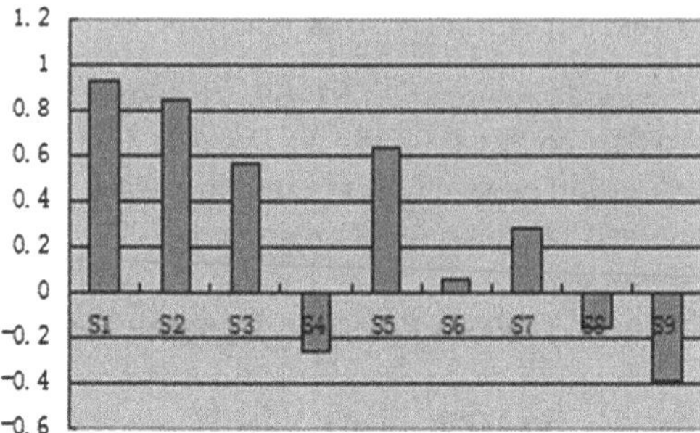

Fig. 5. The data correlation

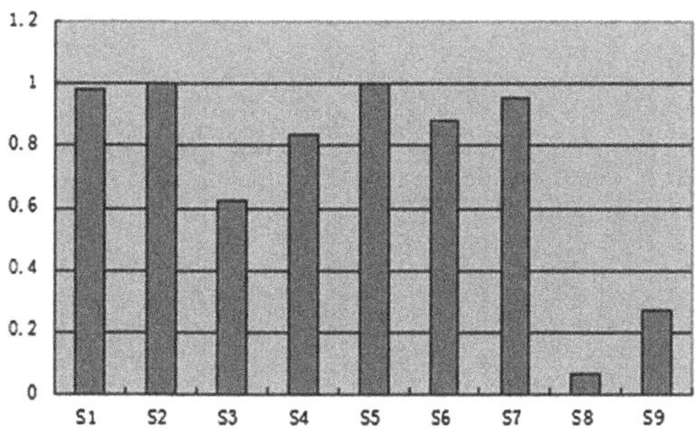

Fig. 6. Function fitting degree

different cases, the count of the invoked service in particular. In static service invocation experiments, we find counts and time to be positive correlation, but in the dynamic service invocation experiment, count and time of service **S4, S8, S9** to negative correlation. We think that as the most basic service in large-scale dynamic call situation is very likely to appear unstable situation, that becomes the bottleneck of the cloud services. In function fitting process, we do it by polynomial regression analysis, when the order number is four, function fitting is very well, under static and dynamic two cases, there is a significant difference of consuming function between the number of individual service. In summary, we think the service behavior of distributed service is dynamically changed and behavior is uncertain in different circumstances, so we must do a good job on the distributed service bottleneck detection, and research solutions in real life.

3.2.2 Analysis of Search Ranking Based on Path

The complete path of this experiment are **S1->S2->S4, S1->S2->S5->S9, S1->S2->S7->S8, S1->S3->S4, S1->S3->S5->S9, S1->S2->S6->S9, S1->S3->S7->S8**. Figure 7 is total count for each complete path chart, Fig. 8 is total time for each complete path chart.

From the chart, we can see when service S1 is invoked, the full path of the highest for the total count invoked is **L1 = S1->S3->S5->S9**, the full path of the longest for the

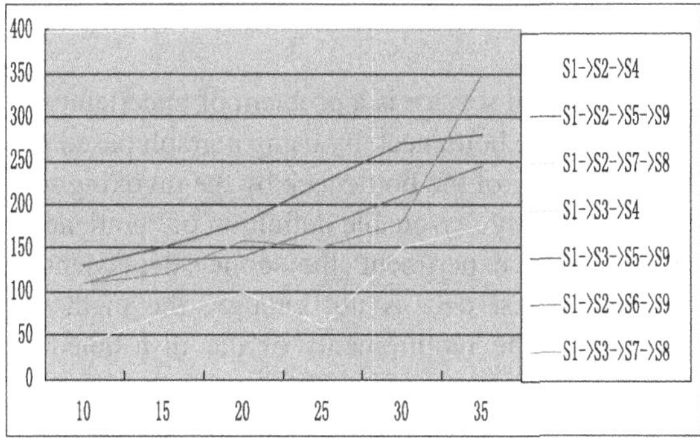

Fig. 7. Total count for each complete path

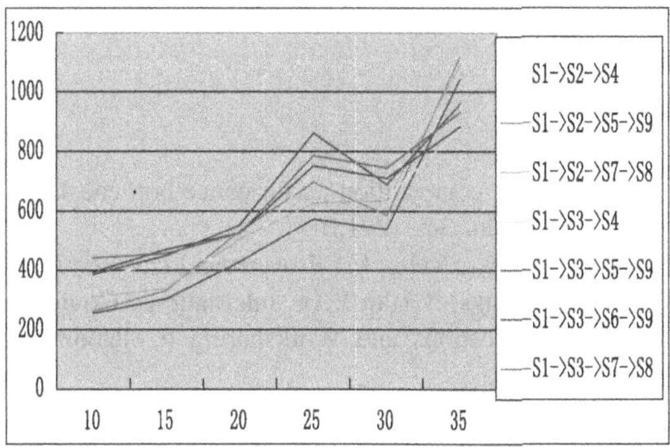

Fig. 8. Total time for each complete path

total time is **L2 = S1->S3->S5->S9**. That is **L1 = L2**, that is also the path **L1** and **L2** overlap. This also validates our hypothesis: if the maximum path and the longest path are the same path in service execution, we think this path is the **"bottleneck path"** which we are finding, the corresponding service bottleneck points are also in this path. After the contrast of the data again, we found out the maximum count of services is the service **S9** and the longest time of services is the service **S1** at the service **S1** transferring. We believe that service bottlenecks are likely to occur in service **S1** and service **S9** when users are dynamically invoked this service cosmically in the implementation of distributed services. At the same time, we find that service **"bottleneck path"** more than one when the amount of data is growing, but they are always related with the most basic and the bottom of the service. When the service bottleneck occurs, it is likely to be transferred from the dependency relationship between services, that is the **"bottleneck transmit effect"**.

4 Conclusion

Service bottleneck of distributed service is a problem of uncertainty, we can predict the possible emergence of a service bottleneck by using a graph based path search method. Improve the detection efficiency of the bottleneck by the invoking relationship between the services and make a relatively reasonable definition of "bottleneck problem". There are still some problems in the experiment: the service dependent relationship is not enough complexity and the test data is not enough, the method still needs to be strengthened. We will meet the requirements of the distributed service bottleneck detection efficiency in future research and study.

Acknowledgement. Jie Wang, Tao Li, Tong Zhang and Hao Wang are partially supported by the National Natural Science Foundation of China (Grant Nos. 61273225). Humanities and Social Sciences Foundation of Education Ministry of Hubei province (Grant Nos.2012D111).

References

1. He, Y., Shen, H.: A web service composition performance bottleneck locating strategy based on stochastic Petri net. J. Comput. Sci. (2013)
2. Li, T., Liu, L., Zhang, X., Xu, K., Yang, C.: ProvenanceLens: service provenance management in the cloun. In: Proceedings of 10th IEEE International Conference on Collaborative Computing: Networking, Applications and Worksharing (CollaborateCom 2014), pp. 3–5 (2014)
3. Hu, Z., Liu, X.: A practical data fusion algorithm. Autom. Instr. **2**(1), 1–3 (2005)
4. Zhang, X.: Java Program Design and Development, pp. 1–245. Electronics Industry Press, Beijing (2010)
5. Wu, W., Yan, Y.: Data Structure (C language), pp. 1–230. Tsinghua University Press, Beijing (2011)
6. Yang, H.: Analysis of large scale network traffic bottlenecks. National Defense Science and Technology University, pp. 43–48 (2007)
7. Department of mathematics, Tongji University. Advanced Mathematics. Higher Education Press (1996)

A Collaborative Rear-End Collision Warning Algorithm in Vehicular Ad Hoc Networks

Binbin Zhou(✉), Hexin Lv, Huafeng Chen, and Ping Xu

College of Information and Science Technology, Zhejiang Shuren University, Hangzhou, China
bbzhou1987@163.com, {hexin10241024,xpcs2007}@sina.com, 7071024@qq.com

Abstract. How to solve rear-end collision warning problem has become an increasingly tough task nowadays. Numerous studies have been investigated on this field in past decades, either time-consuming or with strict assumptions. In this paper, we have proposed a collaborative rear-end collision warning algorithm (CORECWA), to assess traffic risk in accordance with real-time traffic data detected, transmitted and processed, by vehicles and infrastructures in vehicular ad hoc networks (VANETs) collaboratively. CORECWA considers some influential factors, including space headway between the two preceding and following vehicles, velocity of these two vehicles, drivers' behavior characteristics, to evaluate the current traffic risk of the following vehicle. Experiments results demonstrate that CORECWA can gain better performance, compared with a well-acknowledged algorithm *HONDA* algorithm.

Keywords: Rear-end collision warning · Vehicular ad hoc networks · Traffic risk assessment

1 Introduction

Traffic collision has become a huge problem worldwide that brings inestimable economic and social losses. Rear-end traffic collision make up nearly 30 % traffic accidents in China according to a survey in 2012 [1], which refer to a vehicle can not control its velocity effectively to avoid bumping against the preceding vehicle. Hence, when to warn the drivers in advance the emergency and how to warn them have attracted numerous researchers' attention. This problem involves many issues, including real-time traffic data collection, data collaborative transmission and processing, decision making and so forth.

In the past decades, a large number of studies have been carried out in rear-end traffic collision problem. Previous work can be classified into two groups, including artificial intelligent methods and mathematical methods. Lots of researchers have proposed AI techniques to study drivers' behavior (i.e. perception reaction time) which can help determine when to warn the drivers in emergent moment in advance. A driving-assistance system has been developed and drivers' behavior can be identified to help generate traffic collision warning

S. Guo et al. (Eds.): CollaborateCom 2015, LNICST 163, pp. 317–322, 2016.
DOI: 10.1007/978-3-319-28910-6_30

message [2]. Fuzzy theory and BPNN have been utilized to develop approaches to generate warning notice in advance and determine minimum traffic safety distance between the preceding vehicle and following vehicle [3,4]. On the other hand, numerous scholars have developed mathematical approaches to determine the minimum traffic safety distance or minimum traffic safety time with the consideration of perception reaction time, which can be treated as the threshold value in the algorithm design [3,5–10].

In this paper, we propose a COllaborative REar-end Collision Warning Algorithm (CORECWA), to develop warning message and remind the drivers when neccessary, with the collaborative work of vehicles and infrastructures in vehicular ad hoc networks. Real-time traffic are detected, such as velocity, position, acceleration and so forth. These traffic data are transmitted and processed collaboratively, to help the following vehicle make decision whether to generate warning message and remind the driver. Experiments are conducted to evaluate CORECWA's performance with a public available dataset, and the results show that our CORECWA would gain better performance compared with *HONDA* algorithm.

The remainder of this paper is organized as follows. In Sect. 2, we formulate the rear-end collision warning problem, and propose CORECWA algorithm in Sect. 3. Experiments and analysis are presented in Sect. 4, and Sect. 5 concludes this paper.

2 Problem Formulation

To model the rear-end collision warning problem, a typical scenario (presented in Fig. 1) should be taken into consideration [11]. The road can be covered by the four roadside units (RSUs), and all the vehicles in this road can communicate with each other and RSUs.

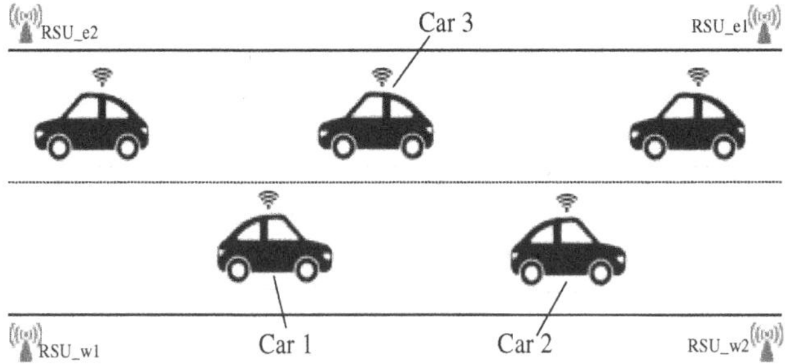

Fig. 1. A typical traffic scenario

Our problem is to find the preceding vehicle of a certain vehicle and evaluate traffic risk of this certain vehicle according to the traffic data collected collaboratively. Here, $TR(V)$ is defined as traffic risk of vehicle V. Our objective is to compute $TR(V)$ based on the real-time traffic data, and then determine a maximum value $Thresh(V)$ (shown in Eq. 1) as threshold of $TR(V)$ whether to warn drivers the emergency.It is obvious that distance computation is very critical. $Dst(V_1, V_2)$ is defined as the distance between V_1 and V_2. Moreover, $vlc(V)$ is defined as V' speed.

$$Max \quad Thresh(V) \tag{1}$$

3 Our Collaborative Rear-end Collision Warning Algorithm

In this section, we propose a COllaborative REar-end Collision Warning Algorithm (CORECWA), including two stages: the preceding vehicle confirmation, traffic risk computation and assessment. The preceding vehicle confirmation part focus on finding out the preceding vehicle for a pre-defined vehicle, with utilization of all traffic data collected by vehicles and RSUs collaboratively. Traffic risk computation and assessment part mainly work on computing the real-time traffic risk of the pre-defined vehicle, and compared with $Thresh(V)$ to make decision whether to remind the relevant drivers.

When considers the preceding vehicle confirmation, it not easily rely on the minimum distance between the pre-defined car and other cars. Taking *Car* 1 in Fig. 1 as an example, it is obvious that *Car* 2 is the preceding vehicle rather than *Car* 3 which has the nearest distance to *Car* 1. Therefore, when confirm the preceding vehicle, all the vehicles moving in the same lane should be identified first, and then confirm the vehicle with the nearest distance with the pre-defined vehicle as the preceding vehicle. The whole work has been presented in Fig. 2 [11].

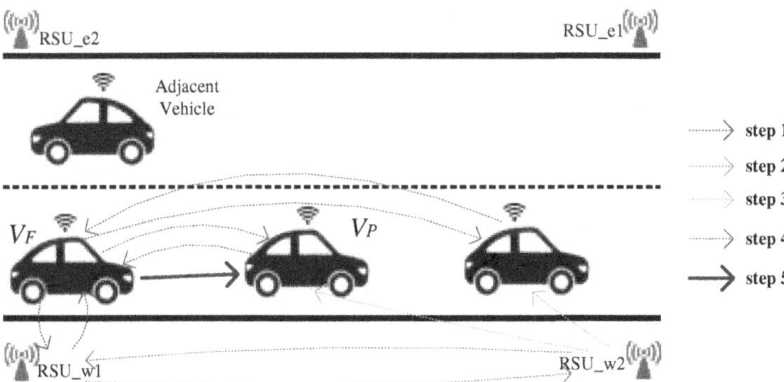

Fig. 2. The preceding vehicle confirmation (Color figure online)

At first, we should confirm all the vehicles in the same road with vehicle V_F. As blue lines shown in Fig. 2, when V_F enters into the road, it should communicate with the nearby roadside unit as RSU_w1 to inform its presence.

After receiving the inform message, RSU_w1 would communicate with RSU_w2 in green lines, so that the two responsible RSUs all know V_F. And then, the two RSUs collaborate to inform the vehicles in this same road the entry of V_F in orange lines. After informed V_F, all the other vehicles in front communicate with V_F in purple lines. The vehicle in the same road V_F with minimum distance should be treated as the preceding vehicle after comparison by V_F in red lines of Fig. 2.

Furthermore, traffic risk of V_F should be computed and assessed and defined as $TR(V_F)$. Let's assume a traffic scenario, vehicles V_P and V_F are moving with traffic speed $vlc(V_P)$ and $vlc(V_F)$ respectively. After a duration T, V_F has moved a distance defined as $s(V_F)$ with acceleration rate $a(V_F)$, and V_P has moved a distance defined as $s(V_P)$ with acceleration rate $a(V_P)$. Hence, $Thresh(V_F, V_P)$ should be greater than the different value between $s(V_F)$ and $s(V_P)$ as presented in Eq. 2. Perception reaction time, defined as $PRT(V)$, should be taken into consideration, which of different drivers may vary from 0.5 s to 2.5 s [12,13]. Therefore, the traffic risk of V_F, as $TR(V_F)$, can be calculated in Eq. 3.

$$\begin{aligned} Thresh(V_F, V_P) &\geq s(V_F) - s(V_P) \\ &= (vlc(V_F) - vlc(V_P)) \times (T + PRT(V_F)) \\ &\quad + \frac{1}{2}(a(V_F) - a(V_P)) \times (T + PRT(V_F))^2 \end{aligned} \tag{2}$$

$$TR(V_F) = \frac{Dst(V_F, V_P)}{Thresh(V_F, V_P)} \tag{3}$$

4 Performance Evaluation

We conduct simulations using a public database NGSIM to evaluate the performance of CORECWA, and compared with a well-acknowledged algorithm named as *HONDA* [6]. The traffic data of NGSIM used, including speed, location, acceleration, and so forth, are from Peachtree Street in Atlanta, Georgia, during 4:00 p.m. to 4:10 p.m. of November 8, 2006.

The dynamic changing of acceleration rate of the two vehicles are presented in Figs. 3 and 4. From the observation, we are able to find out that the acceleration rate of the following vehicle have influence from the preceding vehicle. The performance of HONDA algorithm is shown in Fig. 3. From the figure, we can find that in some part, *HONDA* algorithm is able to make correct decision in the some critical time. However, *HONDA* did not detect some important cases so that it can not send reminder message in these circumstances.

The performance of CORECWA is depicted in Fig. 4. From the figure, we can observe that CORECWA can detect more valuable and necessary moments than *HONDA*, especially when the preceding vehicle is in deceleration. When the preceding vehicle is in acceleration, CORECWA as well detects more cases than *HONDA*. That means our CORECWA can assess the traffic risk more correctly and precisely.

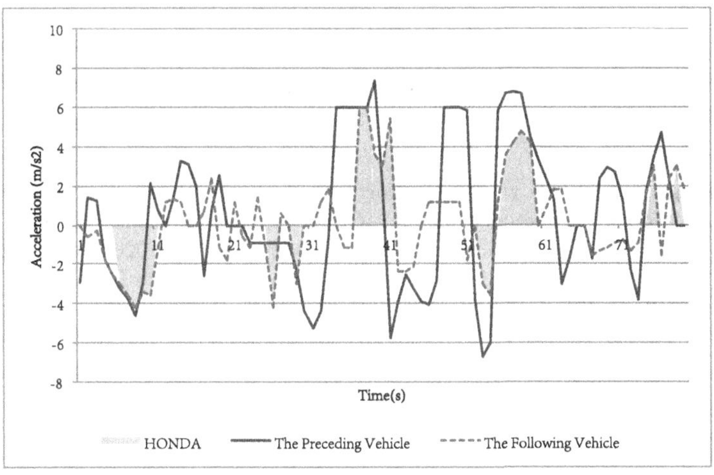

Fig. 3. Performance of *HONDA* algorithm

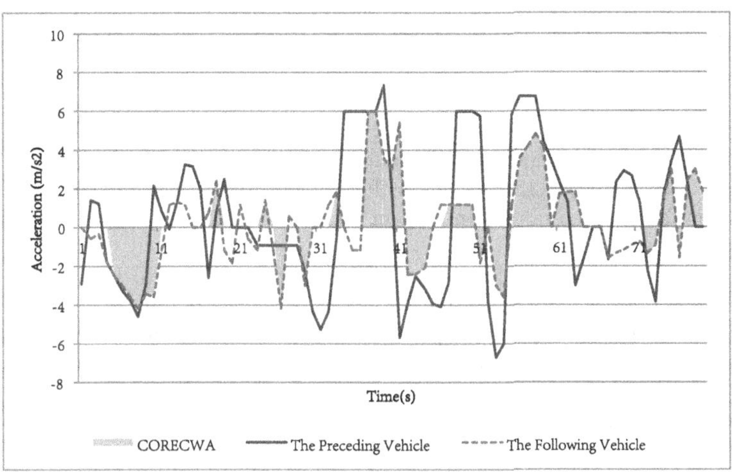

Fig. 4. Performance of CORECWA algorithm

5 Conclusion

Rear-end traffic collision warning problem has attracted more and more researchers' attention. We have developed a collaborative rear-end collision warning algorithm named as CORECWA, to inform drivers reminder message in the critical moment, when the vehicle may bump against the preceding vehicle. Vehicles and RSUs would communicate with each other collaboratively, through V2V, V2I and I2I communication, to help the pre-defined following vehicle to identify the preceding vehicle, and calculate the distance between them, with the utilization of vehicles' velocity, position and so on. Some experiments have been carried out. CORECWA has been evaluated its performance with comparison with *HONDA* algorithm, and the results depict that our algorithm outperform *HONDA*.

Acknowledgments. This work is supported partially by Research Fund of the Education Department of Zhejiang, China (Grant No. Y201534553), Zhejiang Provincial Natural Science Foundation of China (Grant No. LY14F020008, LQ12D01004, LZ15F020001), and Public Welfare Technology Applied Research Program of Zhejiang Province (Grant No. 2014C33108).

References

1. Li, L., Lu, G., Wang, Y., Tian, D.: A rear-end collision avoidance system of connected vehicles. In: 2014 IEEE 17th International Conference on Intelligent Transportation Systems (ITSC), Qingdao, China (2014)
2. Wang, J., et al.: An adaptive longitudinal driving assistance system based on driver characteristics. IEEE Trans. Intell. Transp. Syst. **14**, 1–12 (2013)
3. Chang, B.R., Tsai, H.F., Young, C.P.: Intelligent data fusion system for predicting vehicle collision warning using vision/GPS sensing. Expert Syst. Appl. **37**(1), 2439–2450 (2009)
4. Wei, Z., Xiang, S., Xuan, D., Xu, L.: An adaptive vehicle rear-end collision warning algorithm based on neural network. In: Zhu, M. (ed.) ICCIC 2011, Part VI. CCIS, vol. 236, pp. 305–314. Springer, Heidelberg (2011)
5. Chang, T.H., Chou, C.J.: Rear-end collision warning system on account of a rear-end monitoring camera. In: Intelligent Vehicles Symposium, pp. 913–917. IEEE (2009)
6. Fujita, Y., Akuzawa, K., Sato, M.: Radar brake system. In: Proceedings of the 1995 Annual Meeting of ITS America, vol. 1, pp. 95–101 (1995)
7. Saccomanno, F., Cunto, F.: Comparing safety at signalized intersections and roundabouts using simulated rear-end conflicts. Transp. Res. Rec. J. Transp. Res. Board **2078**(1), 90–95 (2008)
8. Oh, C., Oh, J., Min, J.: Real-time detection of hazardous traffic events on freeways. Transp. Res. Rec. J. Transp. Res. Board **2129**(1), 35–44 (2009)
9. Yang, H., Ozbay, K., Bartin, B.: Application of simulation-based traffic conflict analysis for highway safety evaluation. In: 12th WCTR, Lisbon, Portugal (2010)
10. Sharizli, A.A., Rahizar, R., Karim, M.R., Saifizul, A.A.: New Method for Distance-based Close Following Safety Indicator. In: Traffic Injury Prevention, vol. 16, no. 1, pp. 190–195(2014)
11. Lv, H., Zhou, B., Chen, H., Ren, T., Chen, Y.A.: VANET-based real-time rear-end collision warning algorithm, Technical report (2015)
12. Yi, Z.Z., Erik, K.A., Karl, G.: A new threat assessment measure for collision avoidance systems. In: IEEE Intelligent Transportation Systems Conference, Toronto (2006)
13. Layton, R., Dixon, K.: Stopping sight distance. Kiewit Center for Infrastructure and Transportation, Oregon Department of Transportation (2012)

Analysis of Signaling Overhead and Performance Evaluation in Cellular Networks of WeChat Software

Yuan Gao[1,2,3](✉), Hong Ao[1], Jian Chu[1], Zhou Bo[1], Weigui Zhou[1], and Yi Li[2,4](✉)

[1] Xi Chang Satellite Launch Center, Xichang, China
yuangao08@tsinghua.edu.cn

[2] State Key Laboratory on Microwave and Digital Communications, National Laboratory for Information Science and Technology, Tsinghua University, Beijing, China
liyi@rdfz.cn

[3] China Defense Science and Technology Information Center, Beijing, China

[4] The High School Affiliated to Renmin University of China, Beijing, China

Abstract. The instant communication software such as WeChat, QQ and Fetion becomes popular with the rapid development of mobile terminals and wireless personal communication technology. To refresh the online or offline status of such software, signaling message must be sent every given intervals. However, the signaling message raised by huge number of users will cause severe overhead of mobile networks, which will affect the outage performance of network. In this work, we analyze the signaling overhead caused by such software and evaluate the influence using the system level simulation platform. Results indicate that, the signaling overhead will affect the outage performance when the density of users is great. Practical solution is also raised at the end of our paper.

Keywords: WeChat · Signaling · Overhead · Heartbeat · Wireless network

1 Introduction

The rapid development of wireless communication system has brought varieties of software utilizations, especially when ability of the mobile terminals becomes strong. The network applications could provide flexible functions to users. The instant communication software installed on mobile terminals such as WeChat, QQ and Fetion is a special kind, for such software will send indication message to tag online or offline status through mobile network, which may bring sever traffic load when colony of users are huge.[1]

The indication message of such instant communication software will take up the bandwidth and power resources. When the colony of users is huge, the influence to

[1] We have applied the patent of this work, the application number of Chinese patent is: 201510596158.4.

S. Guo et al. (Eds.): CollaborateCom 2015, LNICST 163, pp. 323–328, 2016.
DOI: 10.1007/978-3-319-28910-6_31

network load could not be omitted. The behavior of the signal is like the paging signaling of network management protocol, but the paging signaling is working using the broadcasting channel and the heartbeat signal from such software will take up the traditional data resource.

Researches about traffic load in wireless networks become popular with the rapid development of wireless personal communications. In [1], the author present the scheduling method used in wireless networks, however, the scheduling method do not mention heartbeat signal such as WeChat. In [2] and [3], signaling overhead has been mentioned in wireless networks but no solution has been raised. In [4] and [5], analysis of signaling overhead in such instant message software has been discussed but evaluation of the performance is still blank. In [6], the discussion using such data optimization technology has been discussed.

In this paper, we mainly focus on the discussion and solution to the traffic load using such instant message software. The rest of this paper is organized as follows: in Sect. 2, we discuss the signaling overhead of the heartbeat signal and a comparison has been discussed; in Sect. 3, the performance evaluation under our system level simulation platform has been given; in Sect. 4, conclusion is also given in this part.

2 Signaling Overhead

To evaluate the signaling overhead of the application layer, the process must be discussed. Traditional signaling information to indicate online or offline status of cell phone is called paging signal, which will occupy specified physical channel. In such channels, the message will not take up the bandwidth of data transmission but collide the public resource.

Take WCDMA system as example. When the system want to confirm the online or offline status of a phone, paging signaling will be sent to detect the status.

In Fig. 1, we illustrate the two possible condition of paging request in WCDMA system. The Radio Network Controller (RNC) will decide the online or offline status every 180 s at least, so the downlink status request will be sent to NodeB immediately. The NodeB will then broadcast a paging request to users located at its range. If the cell phone is online, it will reply to NodeB with an acknowledgement to indicate the fact that' I have received your request and I am still alive'. So the NodeB will tag the status and report to RNC. When the cell phone is offline, there are two possible conditions: when the cell phone is out of service, it will not reply to the paging request[2] and a time out status will be indicated when the request exceed the maximum times, then the system will decide the offline status of given cell phone and tag inactive status in system register; the other condition is that the user report the offline status by itself[3], and the NodeB will report this event to controller.

[2] This condition appear when the signal is weak, e.g. when the user is moving into an area without wireless coverage.

[3] This condition appear when the user will shut down without any outer command.

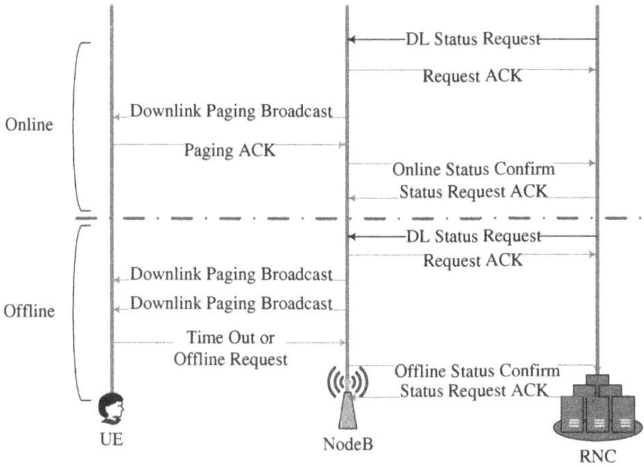

Fig. 1. Process of paging signaling with two possible status.

The paging signaling will not occupy system private resources but only public channel, so the influence has been taken into account and will not affect the system capacity when the amount of user increase under a controllable state. However, heartbeat signal from software is quite different and will affect system performance if the behavior is not controlled.

In Fig. 2, we illustrate the control of online or offline status of the system. It is clear that the application layer is a virtual layer and do not have the entity, so we use the dashed line to express the function layer of WeChat software. In this scenario, the status request is sent by Tencent server, which is a data traffic in wireless networks, so the data with status request information is a heartbeat signal, generally speaking, this information is usually 4bit or less, but it will cost a whole frame to deal with it. When the user receive the information from the target NodeB, reply information to indicate the online status of the application layer is sent using the uplink directly to Tencent server. If the software is offline, the process is quite different from the paging signaling. The downlink data will be sent from NodeB to user under the condition that the user is online in wireless systems, if the software is off, it will not reply to the downlink data in application layer, unless the positive offline request is sent when the application is on. In application layer, the unexpected time out will be detected at the side of Tencent server and then the status of the terminal is marked offline in given application layer.

To conclude, the difference between paging and heartbeat signal generated by application is the resources occupied by signal. The paging signal will take up the dedicated channel and do not affect the data transmission, on the contrary, the heartbeat signal is included in data traffic and worked in application layer, so the lower layer will only consider the heartbeat signal as a common short data traffic. When the number of users increase, the influence to data transmission will become heavy significantly, which may cause the increasing of outage probability.

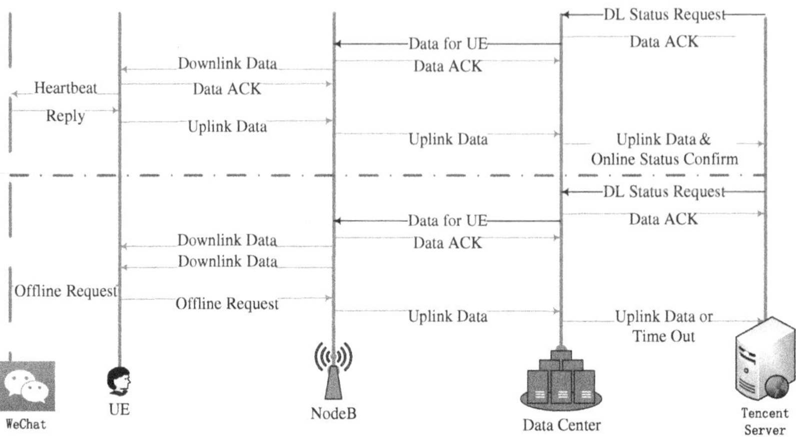

Fig. 2. Process of software on-off with two possible conditions.

3 Performance Evaluation

In this part, a performance evaluation under the system level simulation platform has been given. The system level simulation is close to the real scenario of wireless networks with the support of channel, movement, transmission, scheduling, HARQ, system level to link level mapping and graphic UI model. Simulation parameters and assumptions are given in the following table (Table 1).

Table 1. Simulation parameters and assumptions [7]

Name	Parameter
Cell layout	7 Cell/21 Sector
Radius of cell	100 m
Transmission bandwidth	20 MHz
BS Antenna (DL TX)	4
BS Tx power	6.3 w
Max re-transmission time	4
Carrier frequency	2.1 GHz
Channel model	SCME Dense Urban
Pathloss	L = 128.1 + 20.4log10 (R)
Shadowing Std	4 dB
Noise power	-107 dBm
Simulation TTIs	2000
User number	10 per cell and 100 per cell
Target BLER	0.1

We take the 7 cell scenario as an example. Each cell has three 120° sectors and the radius of the cell is 100 m. In LTE related systems, the small cell has been considered as the future base station with lower transmission power and smaller coverage. So the 20 MHz bandwidth resource and 4 downlink transmission antennas have been taken into account. The maximum transmission power is 6.3 w (38 dBm) for small cell or pico cell according to [8].

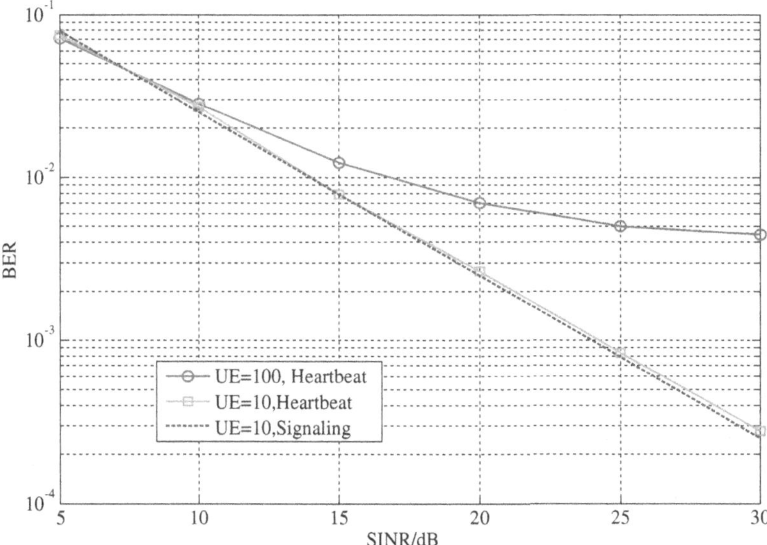

Fig. 3. SINR performance of paging and heartbeat signal with different users (Color figure online)

Figure 3 is the result of SINR versus BER for different kinds of signals. The x-axis means the SINR in dB and the y-axis means the bit error rate calculated using the simulation platform. The green curve is the SINR-BER performance of heartbeat signal with the average user number 10 per cell, the blue dashed line is the performance of paging signaling. It is clear that the performance is similar when the number of users is small, that is because the heartbeat signal will occupy the data resource. If the number of users is small, it will not affect the system performance significantly, that is why the green curve is a little bit higher than the blue one. But when the number of users is huge as is shown in the red curve, the performance will be affected greatly. Even when the SINR increase, the BER is decreasing slowly and levelled off, it is because the huge number of users will occupy the bandwidth resource used for data transmission, which will affect the common transmission because the resource for transmission will be insufficient. This result demonstrate that, the utilization of instant communication software will affect the system performance when the number of users increase, this effect is clear in resident area or working area when users are requiring such service [9].

4 Conclusion

To conclude, in this paper, we discuss the fact that the heartbeat signal from instant communication software will affect the system performance. The contribution of this paper could be summarized as follows:

1. We analyze the process of physical paging using dedicated channel and heartbeat signal using data frame, both advantage and dis-advantage have been discussed through the theoretical analysis;

2. We evaluate the system performance under the LTE system level simulation platform. Result indicates that, when the number of users is small, the influence is not clear and when it grows, the heartbeat signal will greatly affect the system performance;

There is also problem for further discussion, e.g. the complete process of cross layer sharing and the mathematical discussion of such problems, we will make further discussion in related journals.

Acknowledgement. This work is funded by China's 973 project under grant of 2012CB316002 and China's 863 project under grant of 2013AA013603, 2012AA011402, National Natural Science Foundation of China (61201192).

References

1. Taniguchi, Y.: De synchronization-based weighted scheduling adaptive to traffic load for wireless networks. In: 2014 International Conference on Computer, Communications, and Control Technology (I4CT), pp. 130–134, 2-4 September 2014 (2014)
2. Radio, N., Zhang, Y., Tatipamula, M., Madisetti, V.K.: Next-generation applications on cellular networks: trends, challenges, and solutions. Proc. IEEE **100**(4), 841–854 (2012)
3. Dini, P., Miozzo, M., Bui, N., Baldo, N.: A model to analyze the energy savings of base station sleep mode in LTE HetNets. In: IEEE International Conference on Green Computing and Communications (GreenCom) and IEEE Cyber, Physical and Social Computing, 2013 IEEE and Internet of Things (iThings/CPSCom), pp. 1375–1380, 20-23 August 2013 (2013)
4. Zhang, S., Wu, Y., Cai, X.: WeChat traffic profile and impact on mobile networks. In: 2014 IEEE/CIC International Conference on Communications in China (ICCC), pp. 334 – 338, 13-15 October 2014 (2014)
5. Han, B., Liu, X., Wang, J., Liu, C., Wagner, R.M.: Extending an instant messaging system with data services and mashups thereof. In: 2014 IEEE International Conference on Services Computing (SCC), pp. 848–849, 27 June 2014-2 July 2014 (2014)
6. Han, Y., Zhao, M., Zhou, W.: Optimization of OTT small data services: network capacity and cost analysis. In: 2014 Sixth International Conference on Wireless Communications and Signal Processing (WCSP), pp. 1–6, 23-25 October 2014 (2014)
7. Gao, Y., Li, Y., Yu, H., Wang, X., Gao, S., Xue, P.: Energy efficient cooperative sleep control using small cell for wireless networks. Int. J. Distrib. Sensor Netw. **2015**, 10 (2015). doi:10.1155/2015/903853
8. Bajaj, H., Jindal, R.: Thinking beyond WhatsApp. In: 2015 2nd International Conference on Computing for Sustainable Global Development (INDIACom), pp. 1443–1447, 11-13 March 2015 (2015)
9. Wei, W., Yong, Q.: Information potential fields navigation in wireless Ad-Hoc sensor networks. Sensors **11**(5), 4794–4807 (2011)

Exploration of Applying Crowdsourcing in Geosciences: A Case Study of Qinghai-Tibetan Lake Extraction

Jianghua Zhao(✉), Xuezhi Wang, Qinghui Lin, and Jianhui Li

Computer Network Information Center, Chinese Academy of Sciences,
No. 4 Zhongguancun South Street, Haidian District, Beijing, China
{zjh, wxz, lqh, lijh}@cnic.cn

Abstract. With the emerging of vast quantities of geospatial data, large temporal and spatial scale of data are used in geosciences research nowadays. As a lot of data processing tasks such as image interpretation are hard to be processed automatically, and the data process workload is huge, crowdsourcing is studied as a supplement tool of cloud computing technology and advanced algorithms. This paper outlines the procedure and methodology of applying crowdsourcing in geoscientific data process. And based on the GSCloud platform, a case study of Qinghai-Tibetan Lake Extraction task has been carried out to explore the feasibility of the application of crowdsourcing in geosciences. By analyzing the case, the paper summarizes the problems and characteristics, and advantages and challenges are also presented at last.

Keywords: Crowdsourcing · Geoscientific data process · GSCloud · Qinghai-Tibetan lake extraction

1 Introduction

Vast quantities of data are becoming available at an ever-accelerating rate and remote sensing technology is transforming geosciences today. When investigating global-scale environmental phenomena, the temporal and spatial scale of remote sensing data used in research is so large that it is beyond which scientists have previously encountered [1]. In order to process large data set in reasonable amounts of time, major innovations have been made in parallel computing, programming framework, distributed computer systems, and cloud computing. And all these powerful techniques have been widely used in geoscience data process now. However, some complex tasks which account for a huge part of the application of remote sensing data in geosciences, such as accurate image geometric correction and image interpretation are still very challenging for computers, and it is hard to be automatically processed [2, 3]. So it is time to find a supplement way for massive geoscientific data process.

As each and every human brain has the capacity to process data and anyone can be a problem solver [4], the way of using the distributed thinking resources is an imaginative answer to the problems described above. Crowdsourcing is such a distributed model where an organization or a firm outsourcing a problem or task to an undefined

S. Guo et al. (Eds.): CollaborateCom 2015, LNICST 163, pp. 329–334, 2016.
DOI: 10.1007/978-3-319-28910-6_32

external group (a crowd) [5]. Unlike outsourcing, crowdsourcing allocates work to a collection of individuals, so it is able to access globally distributed qualified talent, and the workforce is flexible. Moreover, it has lower total costs of recruitment, training, supervision and turnover. So crowdsourcing has gained much popularity in numerous fields.

In this paper, an exploration is made to apply crowdsourcing in geoscientific data process tasks. The rest of the paper is organized as follows. In Sect. 2, some studies for crowdsourcing and its application in geosciences are briefly presented. Section 3 describes the process and methodology of applying expert-based crowdsourcing in geoscientific data process. A case study is presented in Sect. 4. Finally, conclusions are made and the future work is discussed in Sect. 5.

2 Related Work

Recently, a lot of academic and industrial organizations have started researching and developing technologies and infrastructures to apply crowdsourcing in geosciences. In the academic area, a lot of platforms have been built. Geo-Wiki is a web-based geospatial portal with open access to Google Earth. Experts or the public can use the high resolution satellite imagery from Google Earth to train and cross check the calibration and validation of land cover products such as GLC-2000, MODIS, and GlobCover on the web [6]. Virtual Disaster Viewer, a social networking tool, uses crowdsourced analysis of remote sensing imagery for earthquake impact and damage assessment [7]. A lot of IT factory also put great effort to the study of crowdsourcing and many crowdsourcing platforms are emerging, such as Elance, CloudCrowd, freelancer, crowdcontent, CrowdFlower and so on. Among the numerous crowdsourcing marketplaces, Amanzon's mechanical turk (MTurk) is the most widely used. MTurk provides a platform for performing tasks that are self-contained, simple, repetitive, and short ones. The tasks requires little specialized skills and the public are motivated by money [8]. Though these platforms gained great popularity, there are some practical limitations. On the one hand, most crowdsourcing platforms assume that complex work can be divided into relatively small and independent ones. However, as science becomes more open, it is possible that some work may not be easily decomposed into units small enough. On the other hand, the online community of these platforms usually are not evaluated or pre-qualified and may offer sub-optimal solutions. Tasks that require higher skills or expertise cannot be easily solved.

Geosciences is a subject that is not only data-driven, but also need a crowd with specific knowledge to solve most data process problems. As Malone and Neis et al. have observed a long-tail mode, that is major contribution always comes from the top few contributors, in crowdsourcing activities, expertsourcing, which crowdsourcing tasks to "crowd" that is comprised of experts or research scientists is proposed [9, 10]. Zhai et al. consider the most important elements in expertsourcing is high reliability and trustworthiness. So the major contribution should come from expert citizens [11]. Tran-Thanh et al. proposes several challenges existing in expertsourcing, including data quality, monetary reward, and so on [12]. Woolley et al. studied how the composition of a community, such as whether it includes randomly selected members or experts, affects results [13]. Dionisio et al. explored expert-based crowdsourcing and try to overcome some deficiencies of crowdsourcing [14].

From the research listed above, it is obvious that expert-based sourcing has great potential in geosciences. Having been in service by providing massive remote sensing data for the public for almost 8 years, Geospatial Data Cloud (GSCloud), a cloud-based platform has more than 95 thousand users who all work or study in fields related with Geoscience. They form an expert community in which members have knowledge or expertise relevant to geosciences, so much more complex tasks can be solved. With this advantage, an exploration of applying expert-based crowdsourcing in geoscientific data processing work is carried out.

3 Methodology

The expert-based crowdsourcing activity GSCloud launched includes the following steps: task definition and division, recruitment and talents selection, task execution and time control, quality control and result aggregation. Each step is described in detail below.

3.1 Task Definition and Division

A massive data analysis task should be divided into small, manageable microtasks. When dividing a huge task, several points should be noticed:

Firstly, choose tasks that are huge, and should be done with human computation. Those tasks that can be process automatically should take advantage of advanced computing algorithm and technology. Secondly, the size of small tasks should be carefully considered. It should be small so that an individual user can generate accurate result within prescribed time period, but also should large enough so that users feel they are making meaningful contributions to the project. So task division demands high human intelligence and skill level. Thirdly, estimate the workload, and guarantee that the workload is proportional to the money reward we pay for it.

3.2 Recruitment and Talents Selection

When crowdsourcing a task, the most important thing is to attract a meaningful number of users, and thus research scientists who are interested in the tasks and are capable of doing it can be easily located. After the task has been published, those users who are interested in the tasks are asked to fill out the registration form, in which his or her related experiences are required. And the implementation plan for this task should be written in detail, which facilitate the GSCloud staff to select appropriate person for this task. Some tasks require users to upload partial preliminary data processing results to evaluate the user's capability of implementing this task directly. Then the applicants will be interviewed and as to those suitable person, an agreement about intellectual property, and quality assurance is signed.

In order to encourage tasking people to produce accurate results and to avoid situations that someone accepts the task but does not accomplish it in time, each task is assigned to two or more person to process independently. The reward is paid in accordance with the quality of the results. Only those whose results are good enough can get the entire monetary reward. The rest may only get part of the total reward.

3.3 Task Execution and Time Control

As geoscience has the characteristics of massive data, GSCloud have to share the data required in the tasks with the task performers. Nowadays, ftp is used to share the massive data required in the task.

After the task has been allocated, the next important thing is to control the time. As those users who obtain the task are part-time, the length of time to implement the task should be long enough to ensure the completion of the task. In order to avoid procrastination, which in turn will affect the quality, timely and effective communication between GSCloud staff and the tasking people is necessary.

3.4 Quality Control and Result Aggregation

During the task execution time period, several procedures were undertaken to validate the accuracy of results including a detailed quality self-evaluation report which covers all the error-prone aspects, a thorough internal review by different quality inspection staff to identify errors and problems, and comparison with high resolution data results, for example, image interpretation results can be assessed using Google Earth. After all these quality control work, there is a time period for tasking people to modify and improve their results. Then the quality of the results are assessed again until the data results are qualified. When all the small tasks are completed, all the partial results of various users are combined into a final, reliable and complete result.

4 Case Study

To study the potential of expert-based crowdsourcing in geoscientific data process, a task of extracting four period of Qinghai-Tibetan lakes from Landsat images during 1995 to 2010 is carried out in this paper. As Qinghai-Tibetan Plateau covers a vast area, and the study period is long, so the lake extraction is a heavy workload. Moreover, as the area is mountainous, and has intricate physiognomic types, plus the influence of heavy cloud and hill shade, it is really difficult to extract lakes automatically. So this is definitely a human computation problem-solving task.

Qinghai-Tibetan Plateau covers an area of nearly 2.6 million square kilometers, which needs more than 150 Landsat images to cover. The images from September to November are used. Each period is divided into 3 small tasks according to the geographical division, and there are total 10 micro tasks, among which the 2005 period task is required a team to execute, so it is not divided. All the task information is published on the website of GSCloud (www.gscloud.cn). And more than 150 users have signed up to apply the tasks. After screening, 18 individuals and two teams are selected. During the task execution process, the professional team of GSCloud supervise all the process, and evaluate the results through different ways, including manual sampling inspection, using high-resolution remote sensing imagery from Google Earth to compare the results, and comparing parallel efforts of the two person executing the same task. Complete results are aggregated for each period, and all the qualified results are obtained in a period of two months. Figure 1 is the map of Qinghai-Tibetan Lake in 2000.

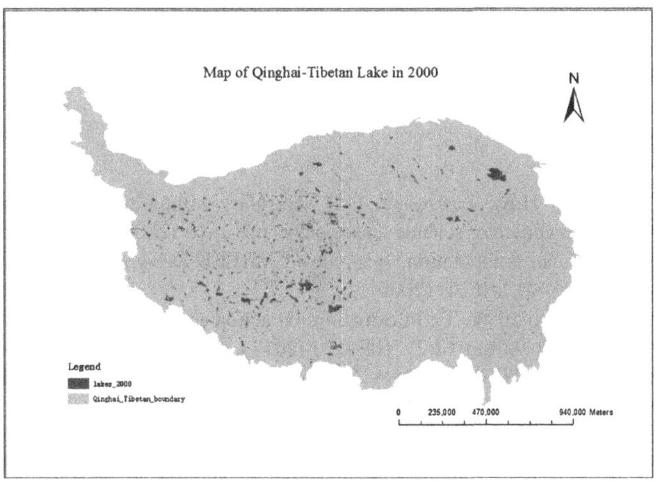

Fig. 1. Map of Qinghai-Tibetan lake in 2000.

In this case, there are some common data quality problems occurred. As the seasonal variations are huge in Qinghai-Tibetan, Landsat images during September to November are normally influenced by cloud and snow, so images of other months will be chosen in the lake extraction task, which will lead to some error. Moreover, as different precipitation on different dates results in different borders of lakes, when the adjacent images are of different time period, it is possible that the lake extraction result in the overlapped area will not be consistent. To ensure the consistency of the lake results in the later data analysis, the larger border of the lakes are kept in the final results. Another problem is the disturbance of snow and ice. So cloud and ice removal work is asked to be done in the data preprocessing. Those areas that are hard to extract lakes, visual interpretation is needed.

5 Conclusion

Applying crowdsourcing, especially expert-based crowdsourcing in geosciences is studied in this paper. The procedure of crowdsourcing in geosciences is described. And by carrying out the Qinghai-Tibetan Lake Extraction task, the advantages and challenges of crowdsourcing can be obtained. By recruiting part-time experts, crowdsourcing does provide data results of good quality in short time and costs little. However, as there is typically little or no prior knowledge about the applicants, how to find appropriate talents or experts for specific tasks remains a challenge. Moreover, the quality requirements of the task should be made clear enough, which demands high professional expertise.

There are a number of directions we are exploring for future work. Most immediately, we are developing a platform, which can be used as collaborative community not only for people to communicate and share knowledge, but also for the public to participate to validate crowdsourced results. Looking further ahead, we are interested in integrating games in the crowdsourcing task to make it more attractive. In addition, more incentive mechanisms will be studied to attract and maintain a pool of experts.

References

1. Bryant, R., Randy, H.K., Lazowska, E.D.: Big-data computing: creating revolutionary breakthroughs in commerce, science and society, pp. 1–15 (2008)
2. Von Ahn, L.: Human computation. In: 46th ACM/IEEE Design Automation Conference, DAC 2009. pp. 418–419. IEEE (2009)
3. Lofi, C., Selke, J., Balke, W.-T.: Information extraction meets crowdsourcing: a promising couple. Datenbank Spektrum **12**(2), 109–120 (2012)
4. Kanefsky, B., Barlow, N.G., Gulick, V.C.: Can distributed volunteers accomplish massive data analysis tasks. In: Lunar and Planetary Science, vol. 1 (2001)
5. Howe, J.: The rise of crowdsourcing. Wired Mag. **14**(6), 1–4 (2006)
6. Fritz, S., et al.: Geo-Wiki: an online platform for improving global land cover. Environ. Modell. Softw. **31**, 110–123 (2012)
7. Barrington, L., et al.: Crowdsourcing earthquake damage assessment using remote sensing imagery. Ann. Geophys. **54**(6), 680–687 (2012)
8. Little, G., et al.: Turkit: tools for iterative tasks on mechanical turk. In: Proceedings of the ACM SIGKDD Workshop on Human Computation. ACM (2009)
9. Malone, T.W., Laubacher, R., Dellarocas, C.: Harnessing crowds: mapping the genome of collective intelligence (2009)
10. Neis, P., Zielstra, D., Zipf, A.: The street network evolution of crowdsourced maps: OpenStreetMap in Germany 2007-2011. Future Internet **4**, 1–21 (2012)
11. Zhai, Z., et al.: Expert-citizen engineering: crowdsourcing skilled citizens. In: 2011 IEEE Ninth International Conference on Dependable, Autonomic and Secure Computing (DASC). IEEE (2011)
12. Tran-Thanh, L., et al.: Efficient crowdsourcing of unknown experts using multi-armed bandits. In: European Conference on Artificial Intelligence (2012)
13. Woolley, J, Madsen, T.L., Sarangee, K.: Crowdsourcing or Expertsourcing: Building and Engaging Online Communities for Innovation? (2015)
14. Dionisio, M., Fraternali, P., Harloff, E., Martinenghi, D., Micheel, I., Novak, J., Zagorac, S.: Building social graphs from images through expert-based crowdsourcing. In: Proceedings of the International Workshop on Social Media for Crowdsourcing and Human Computation, Paris (2013)

Author Index

Printed in the United States
By Bookmasters